☆ *Custom and Reason*

Custom
and
Reason

An Examination
of Modern
Politics

by Joseph Losos 1931-

An Exposition-University Book
Exposition Press, New York

EXPOSITION PRESS INC.

50 Jericho Turnpike   Jericho, New York 11753

FIRST EDITION

LIBRARY OF CONGRESS CATALOGUE CARD NUMBER: 68–24879

EP 46805

To my wife

☆ Preface

From time to time we are warned of the danger of being deluded by the tyranny of labels. Often this warning takes the form of a disapproval of the use of the word "liberal" or "conservative" as merely emotional epithets or vague slogans. Yet these terms persist, and in these troubled times they can be heard with increasing frequency. The critics are wrong; these political concepts may be imprecise, as life is imprecise, but they are vital descriptions of very real differences. Moreover, they have been the enduring stuff of much of the interplay of social thought since the dawn of history, and through these words the nature of politics can best be observed.

That is what this book is about, and to some extent it is an effort to draw a "neutral" picture of political theory. But the insights of the last century should be a reminder of how hard it is to be neutral and how so much description must be tied to a base of value judgment. That judgment is, here, a conservative one. It is not enough to see how things work; it is also important to have some idea of how they should work.

This combination of description and prescription was a part of the thinking of Aristotle, and of Hobbes and Locke and Marx. They would have been as surprised to hear that these elements must be thoroughly separate as most contemporary political scientists would be to find them together. Coolness of spirit has its Alexandrian charm, but it is already breaking down in the marketplace of ideas. The works of Aristotle and Marx were designed for that marketplace, as well as the library, and in its very humble way this book is set in that tradition.

I wish to express my thanks to my many friends who have contributed their thoughts and have given encouragement to me during the creation of this book. In particular, I have greatly profited by the ideas of Dr. Christopher Becker, Dr. Joe Schraibman and Mr. Thomas Weil. Without their excellent advice *Custom and Reason* could not have taken form. I also want to express my appreciation for the assistance and encouragement, both direct and indirect, which my wife, Carolyn, has provided. My thanks, also, to Miss Elizabeth Brislane, Mr. Alvin Extein, Mr. Vernon Hoffman, Mr. Marlin Klein and Mr. William Kohn for their unstinted help. Above all, I owe a vast debt of gratitude to Mr. Gerald Dunne, whose thoughtful support and wise advice have been literally indispensable.

J. L.

☆ *Contents*

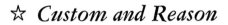 *Custom and Reason*

The Map
of Politics

Throughout history the principal issue of politics has always been the nature and quality of man. There has been a continuing debate between those who believed in the natural goodness of man, and those who assumed that man was basically bad. To others the argument centered over whether humanity had the capacity to create a better life, or whether mankind (or the greater part of mankind) was compelled by natural ignorance or weakness to fail in its struggles for improvement.

This difference of opinion is the basic core of the left/right dichotomy. All of the issues which divide left from right come down to this disagreement about human potentialities. To the reactionary, men are fundamentally bad or helpless, or both. The conservative sees more possibilities, but believes the limitations outweigh the possibilities. The liberal sees mankind as more good than bad, with considerable chance for greatness and virtue; the radical has the highest conception of humanity. Sometimes these contrasting views have been stated bluntly, but usually the reactionary has been afraid of candidly expressing his disdain for his fellow men, while the radical has often feared that his high visions might seem naive. In periods of prosperity and ease the sharpness of the distinction between far left and far right is blurred; in more turbulent ages there is less trouble in observing the differences. The contrast between the philosophy of Blum and Maurras is evident, and, in another manner, so is that between Hobbes and Locke. Hamilton may never have actually said "Your people, sir, is a great beast"; he did write that "the body of the people . . . do not possess the discernment and stability necessary for systematic government. To deny that they are frequently led into the grossest errors by misinformation and passion, would be a flattery." Jefferson almost completely disagreed; Paine dissented completely. At other times the debate has been more subdued. Gladstone and Disraeli, Themistocles and Aristides, held less extreme views of human nature, and therefore of the political struggle, but the context was the same.

The word "political" is a term which can be taken in many senses. Most of these senses are complementary. Whenever people come together to create groups, they face the problems of relations and relationships between the members of the group. These problems come down to questions of the characteristics of these members, or, in a philosophical vein, of the nature of men. The issues of statecraft are therefore the same as the issues of family relations, and so are the great debates of party and union and club. This is merely a paraphrase of Aristotle, with the new varieties of social life illustrating his ideas in a richer setting. As Spiro has put it, "whenever an issue is raised which 'concerns all the citizens,' that issue is as much 'in politics' today as were the issues concerning Athenians two and a half millennia ago." The analyses of Gesell on child-rearing involve the same issues that Rousseau considered. It is not farfetched to compare Amos of Tekoa with Thorstein Veblen, or Theognis of Megara with Nietzsche. The debate over the payment of jurors in Periclean Athens reminds one of the similar debates over the payment of members of Parliament in Victorian England. It is hard to think of even petty political wrangles which do not, in the end, involve the central issue of human nature. A dispute over the coverage of the minimum-wage rules as to inclusion of laundry workers involves a choice between the insistence on a basic wage standard in order to lift the earnings of poor workers and, on the other hand, the lack of capacity of the economy to provide this wage, or the debilitating effects which such a law might cause to spring up among the workers. The argument that a government-imposed support will inevitably reduce the necessary impulses for human advancement presumes the same corruption in humanity that the conservative clerical acceptance of mundane institutions did in the Middle Ages. Galbraith, in advocating high unemployment-compensation payments, argues that men will choose work without the compulsion of need. To a member of the chamber of commerce this is fatuous, as it would have seemed to the author of the third chapter of Genesis (who has been singled out as an exceptional and, in our sense, reactionary thinker) and to Calvin. Karl Marx and John Calhoun might be taken to represent the far extremes on this issue, while the current political dispute narrows to a much finer, but distinctly related difference. The same issues arise in deciding whether to base disarmament on mutual confidence, or on rigorous controls.

So, too, disputes over limitations of management control in industry involve questions of human nature. The farther one is to the left, the more one is likely to believe that each worker is entitled to as much say in the running of the plant as another, and that a democratic organization need not deter either efficiency or orderly conditions. The human interest of the worker comes first, and other considerations must give way. To those on the right, however, the priorities of property rights and effective control by those in charge are much more important, and democracy is irrelevant to the smooth working of an industrial venture. The furthest limits would be slavery, on the right, and absolute anarchy, on the left. In practical political-economic terms, the debate usually centers on the much narrower issues of union participation in management decisions and the existence and extent of grievance procedures.

Of course the day-to-day detail of politics in the usual sense is not always so ideological. Men seek office for the sake of office, and many issues are very enmeshed with personal or geographical disagreements. The issues of right and left may be very confused. The most epic struggles may be complicated as well. The Reformation, for example, involved, as modern scholarship has amply demonstrated, a great number of mixed arguments. On the one hand, the inclination of the Roman Catholic Church to keep worship in Latin and to discourage translations of the Bible was infallibly right-wing. But the princely orientation of Luther and the authoritarianism of Calvin were also rightist. The reformers sought both to spread the Word of God to all men, and to discourage that reliance on human works which gave to human accomplishments a divine scope. More was in some ways radical, in other ways conservative. We see this frequently; it makes the study of political theory more interesting and the conflicts of society less stark. Naturally some men will have no coherent philosophy at all, but this is more rare than it seems, for it takes no schooling to have a systematic opinion of mankind.

It is also possible to start with the same underlying values and reach opposite conclusions on a particular matter. State aid to religious education may seem to one liberal a species of fairness to all children, and to another a support to religious institutions. But it is more likely that the higher one's confidence in human capacities, the less one will feel the need for religious institutions, and consequently the desirability of using tax money to aid their educational facilities. The same issue may range right and left on opposite sides in different periods, as Benton and Bryan, two tribunes of the progressive Midwest, took the opposite stand on gold in the debates of the 1830's and the 1890's. Here again the differences underscore the similarities, for both Benton and Bryan were, at least ostensibly, upholding the underdeveloped people of the West against the entrenched financial power of the East. But the paradox recurs in that the leftward position of Bryan—in favor of man's capacity to change financial patterns against the power of institutions—did not presume a similar desire to champion religious heterodoxy against religious institutions.

But if Bryan was not consistent, or if More was ambiguous, this merely shows how a man can hold varying viewpoints at one time (or at different times; the pattern of moving to the right as one grows older is of course connected with the decline of youthful faith in man) or another. Ideas are important even if men are not always logical in holding them. The most ironic triumph of this premise lies in the need, in Marxist societies whose philosophy is based on materialism, for expert theoreticians, in order to uphold the right ideas.

There are other ideas than those involving human nature, but these others intertwine with the major issue as in a counterpoint. The obvious definition of a progressive—and this word may be used, for simplicity's sake, to cover anyone left of center—is one who believes in progress. The distinction between progressive and non-progressive, or between change and continuity, is clear. In some ways it is too clear. The managers of large enterprises are frequently advocating technological changes opposed by labor unions; to decide then that the former are progressive and the latter unprogressive does violence to the normal usage and creates problems. Many kinds of people want changes, and whoever is in power will naturally not want to be thrown out. In that sense Jefferson in 1801 and Lenin in 1918 were opposed to change. From the point of view of Adams or of Kolchak, the changes which brought Jefferson and Lenin to power were certainly not signs of progress, but the contrary. If progress is carefully defined to mean a particular sort of change, it loses its value as an analytic tool and becomes merely a term of praise.

Insofar as the phrase "a believer in progress" has a neutral meaning, it conforms exactly with the criteria of opinions on human nature which have been presented before. The substance of progress in the minds of more practical radicals like Marx meant a consistent improvement in the human condition, presupposing a vast potential in the human mind and spirit. Progress in politics has a central meaning involving the development of the human environment toward the realization of man's capacity. A conservative will accept such development only with the provisos and limitations which he believes the human condition entails. A reactionary will deny the possibility of any improvement in the state of man. The word reactionary has unfortunate connotations of moving backwards. This may or may not be the case. Plato looked back to a mythical Crete, but he would have changed

Greek society sharply, and in many novel directions. Most observers would say that the Liberty League was certainly not as reactionary as Pobedonostsev, but the program of the League in 1936 required far more backward steps than the Russian leader ever required in the 1880's. But it is true that an underlying distrust of human nature will lead one to refuse to look forward with expectations. The Emersonian phrase that Schlesinger has utilized makes this point. The right are not the party of memory because they have large recollections; if that were so they would all be devotees of Proust and Faulkner. Nor is the party of hope hopeful for some indiscriminate or other worldly good. Both memory and hope pertain to human aspirations, and represent an opinion of the possibilities of the improvement of mankind. In the course of things one who has no high estimate of the potentialities of man may (but certainly not must) take refuge in tradition or memory, tradition's pillar. And thus many reactionaries are indeed Proustians, in a way.

As the continuity/change dichotomy is a variant of our major theme, so is the difference between rich and poor. Surely the latter distinction is the most commonly recognized political dividing line. The tradition of the parties of rich and poor was a cliché in the ancient world and has not declined since then. One trouble is that so many of the leaders of progressive parties, such as Pericles and Franklin Roosevelt, were aristocratic. An even graver objection is that if these were the two groups, the poor would always prevail, as always being the most numerous. But this easy solution is not customary. It is now a truism that most successful protest movements are led and often manned by members of select minorities, often objectively well-off minorities. But the gravest objection is that so many left/right issues are not relevant to wealth or position. Why should the poor espouse freedom of the press more than the rich, or be especially zealous in opposing capital punishment? As in the case of the change/continuity model, the rich/poor division covers only a certain area of questions.

Once again this discussion leads to a broadening of the basic distinction. Other things being equal, a person enjoying wealth or power will not be as disturbed by the gap between existing institutions and the possibilities inherent in man's capacity as a poor person will be. De Tocqueville remarked that "aristocratic nations are naturally too apt to narrow the scope of human perfectibility; democratic nations to expand it beyond compass." There are many destitute men who have a very low estimate of mankind, and they are not apt to be advocates of liberal ideas. But there is an interest for the poor man in believing in the cause of human betterment, for he has much more to gain than the rich man, and of course vice versa. In the everyday swirl of politics the practice goes some way from the theory. To the extent that the matter is just one of self-interest, the theory can become lost, as when a working-class group is anxious for benefits for itself but opposes giving them to an even poorer alien group. The nexus between underlying ideas and the political process can be twisted, or turned around. In the end these motives of self-interest and class position will sort themselves with so many other motives as factors in determining the fundamental question of attitude in regard to human nature and capacity.

A psychological theory of politics always faces the problem of the origin of beliefs. Why are some men lions and others foxes? It is certainly easiest when one can start with an a priori base, like Hobbes or (in a materialist setting) Marx; easiest of all when religion provides that base. Physical differences are helpful, so Calhoun's theories of slavery had a greater appeal than those of Aristotle. It is far harder to start with these foundations today.

However, it is not necessary to explain the underlying causes of opinion. The first step in analysis must be to discover the upper segment of the iceberg, the scope and range of political thought and its application in practice. The lowest depths of the iceberg involve assumptions and faiths which have proved unsuitable for political theory. If toilet training is the key, it should be possible to draw a perfect line from the earliest anal compulsions to the most subtle patterns of any man's thought. If Marxist logic is infallible it is sufficient to find a person's precise economic condition, and all the rest will follow. All the rest never follows, and thinkers who support these beliefs are now generally despised as "vulgar Freudians" or "vulgar Marxists." The great majority of writers on politics today avoid relying altogether on even the most sophisticated variations of these theories.

But of course that does not mean that psychological interpretations are out of favor today. Just the contrary. The probing of the upper part of the iceberg, and the area just below the surface, has proliferated to an unparalleled extent. The institutional emphasis, culminating in the search for sovereignty which permeated nineteenth century thought, has declined, for, to quote Lasswell, "the personal setting of public opinion does matter." The purpose of *The Authoritarian Personality*, and of so many works written since, has been to find out the relationships and preferences which make up that setting, rather than to determine the basic causes of the opinion. An excellent way to do this is to see which sets of beliefs tend to go together, and which ideas involve common premises (rational or irrational) and lead to common programs.

A good place to start is with the group studied in *The Authoritarian Personality*, the reactionaries. Not all reactionaries would fall into their categories, but many of them, especially the more extreme, do fit very well. The strong reliance on and faith in authority, the considerable respect for figures of high status, the great xenophobia, the admiration for force and violent actions which comprise the authoritarian personality are traits which can be seen in people of all backgrounds and positions. Hitler was such a person, both as an impoverished drifter in pre-World War I Vienna and as dictator of the Third Reich. The more extreme such a person is (Hitler is a very good example) the more the violent, blood-minded segments of this personality take priority over the status-minded, respectful portions. Often this depends on the degree of opportunity and power, with respect turning to force as the authoritarian gains authority himself. But often it involves a real difference, one sometimes overlooked in viewing reactionaries. An extreme reactionary will build his ideas around a scarcely or invisibly concealed passion for brute force. On the other hand, a moderate, more conservative reactionary will put his reliance on those forms of authority hallowed by tradition and legitimacy, and often will be fearful of violence, except as a final resort of the historically authorized state. The one common denominator of all reactionaries is their low opinion of human nature. Among extremists this is evidenced by a sometimes almost mad disdain for human life. The Falangist mobs of 1936 shouting "*Viva muerte!*" exemplified this. The old-fashioned authoritarian seeks the supports of a traditional society precisely because he shares so many extremists' assumptions about man's innate wickedness or incapacity, but chooses to find a social pattern capable of preserving civilization rather than to accept the hopelessness of life or the madness of total violence. And of course there are innumerable combinations and permutations of these attitudes.

Very often the students of the authoritarian personality hate it. Most contemporary thinkers in the West are not reactionaries and consider reactionary views from a distasteful distance. But, leaving aside for the moment the distinguished history of reactionary thought, it cannot be said that the average reactionary, the far-right-winger in the street, so to speak, is less able or less intelligent than other people. His beliefs necessarily lead him to reject reason as a standard for humanity, but (like Plato or Pareto) he may reserve it to a minority or to himself. It is impossible to survey political thought without taking reactionary thought seriously, and the reactionaries seriously—although the events of the last thirty years should have made that last clause an unnecessary reminder.

The place of reactionary thought comes out more clearly when its neighbor, conservative thought, is examined. Conservatism, in this sense, is definitely more moderate than reaction, and as a rule more amorphous. The more right-wing conservatives will of course shade into reactionaries, while the more left-wing conservatives naturally resemble liberals at times. The underlying bond is a low view of human nature, but one higher than that held farther right. Therefore authority, although still highly regarded, becomes less important than such values as property and incentive (or opportunity). The achieving personality (to use McClelland's term) is more typical of conservatives than the authoritarian. There is less emphasis on passion and violence, and more on reason, and a reason accessible to a larger number. But it is still a circumscribed reason, and a controlled sense of opportunity. The conservative is most likely to seek to put the rougher instincts of man under wraps, unlike the more extreme reactionaries, who glory in them. And conservatism, in contrast to traditional authoritarianism, will tend to rely more on a congerie of forces, such as a multi-class system or a distribution of power, rather than the stern and imposing might of authority or legitimacy. As conservatism tends leftward it diffuses its concepts of authority and emphasizes the flexible features of opportunity, until a Peter Viereck looks quite like a *ci-devant* liberal. Russell Kirk, on the other hand, may be classed as a very conservative conservative or a reactionary; within the prime definition a natural abundance of views exist. To the extent that everyone right of center can be included together one can say, however, that their low view of human nature tends to lead them to advocate authority, property, and order.

The comparable standards of the left are classic; liberty, equality, and fraternity. The liberal, holding a moderately high view of human nature, is more likely to emphasize liberty as the highest value. Here, too, the range between Schlesinger and Reuther is wide, and encompasses a great breadth of minor differences. Reuther, who might be considered a moderate radical, is certainly more egalitarian than Schlesinger. This marks the radical, whose very high estimate of humanity centers on a strong belief in equality. This is plainly marked in very radical causes like Marxism, where the idea of equality forces liberty to take a very inferior place.

The left and the right are thus mirror images of one another. Liberty and property (or opportunity) are the fundamental beliefs of those near the center, while the more rightist thinker prizes authority and the more leftist chooses equality. Order on the right corresponds to fraternity on the left. These ideas take their place from the underlying estimate of human capacity and nature, and for that reason they have remained since human politics was first recorded. The conflict of liberty and equality has been a cliché since the Girondin/Jacobin divergence during the French Revolution. It can be seen in the differences between the policies of Pericles and Cleon, of Drusus and Marius. Cromwell and the Levellers engaged in the same debate over priorities that concerned the Ebert government and the Spartacists in 1919. Something of the same thing may be seen in the differences between the Pharisees, with their emphasis on the reshaping and development of the law as a more flexible code, and the stark equality-centered faith of the leftist sects.

The disagreement between the adherents of authority and property is less remarked upon, but it is as constant. Perhaps the best example is the distinction between Plato and Aristotle, a distinction which resembled that of Aristides and Cimon. Clarendon and Hobbes, Mounier and de Maistre, show the same contrast. It is not an accident that the clearest examples can be found in the fifth and fourth centuries B.C. in Greece, late Republican Rome, seventeenth-century England, eighteenth-century France, and the present age. What is implicit in any time becomes explicit in a period of turmoil and political probing. But it may be that with close enough attention these categories can be unearthed in almost any place. In their own way Tawney found parallel situations in pre-Elizabethan England and Schlesinger discovered them in the age of Jackson. The work of their critics has been to rearrange the dramatis personae, not to discredit the political theater.

Much of the work of political science in recent years has been directed to showing the consistency of these patterns in various communities. The tendency of the far left in contemporary Japan, for example, to exalt respect for humanity as a value is consistent with a preoccupation with class relationships and with radical attitudes on the everyday issues (such as arms expenditures) of Japanese politics. These opinion surveys almost always confirm the expectations of theory, because the varieties of thought are not, as a rule, random but interrelated in the minds of even those who never consciously think of politics. This works backwards, as well; the liberal who becomes upset over Negro movements is likely to re-examine his views on taxation or labor relations after a while. When Luther recoiled from the revolting peasants his whole world-view (as evidenced by his views on usury and the Jews, as well as his attitude toward princes) moved right.

But even if every boy and every girl born into this world alive is either a little liberal or a little conservative, it hardly follows that they spend their lives puzzling over the implications. In fact, as in *Iolanthe,* they spend much of the time thinking about sex. A truly inbred reactionary (or radical, etc.) need hardly think at all, since his fundamental philosophy would dictate his opinions almost automatically. On the other hand, some people can have sharp discontinuities in their ideas, derived perhaps from having reached settled opinions on different matters at various times in their lives. A harsh foe of progressive education may be a Keynesian, without feeling any inconsistency; if this were not so human beings would be computing machines and not people. But these irrationalities or special variants are likely to cancel out, and a politician running for office in a district populated largely by voters hostile to John Dewey would be very ill advised to go around praising John Keynes. Politics makes strange bedfellows, but not often.

There is more in heaven and earth than can be found in this philosophy. The arts presuppose values quite different, and in some ways surely superior (as artists have reminded politicians and political thinkers for a long time) to those of the political world. There is no oddity in liking Jackson Pollock and von Mises, because radicalism in art involves only the secondary definition of radicalism—a preference for drastic change and novelty. To some extent, it is true, a preference for standing on old ways will lead one toward the traditional in art and the conservative in politics, but the two cannot be subsumed together. There are other issues of the human spirit which are also independent from the debate on human nature, or largely so. Physics and metaphysics, all the regions of science and religion insofar as they do not impinge on questions of society (which, of course, they so often do), are separate. The diversions of life, from sport to sleeping, ought to be completely apart from politics, although as we know there have been (and are) times when they were not.

This does not mean, of course, that all of the arts have no political relevance. On the contrary, the subject matter of most of literature deals with the quality of human nature, and is therefore implicitly connected with politics. The arguments over the position which Melville and Hawthorne held on human goodness are precisely comparable to the similar arguments about Palmerstone and Disraeli (which is clear to the reader of *Billy Budd* or *The Scarlet Letter*). The symbolism of Ahab's search has divided critics in the same way as the American Civil War— if Melville is more complex, this only means that the transformations of art add more hues to the painting. In the works of contemporary critics like Trilling or Wilson the revolt against Calvinism or against Lincoln is a continuum which starts in the books and moves into history; the Marxists disagree with the judgments but see it in the same way. But this should be separated from questions of form. Henry James' appreciation of the vastness of human fallibility naturally placed him on the right, and made his aristocratic world-view a natural part of his thought, but his style did not imply any political viewpoint. Much of the critical confusion of political epochs (like the 1930's) comes from mixing up the political implications of literary thought with the manner in which that thought is expressed. There are limits even to the Moloch of politics.

It should be comparatively easy to divorce baseball from the affairs of government, but as has been suggested, religion is a more complex matter. The course of theology, or of the scientific equivalents of theology, leads into questions of the nature of order in the universe, and from there to the nature of order in this world. Put less abstractly, this is the issue of absolutism and relativism, of natural law and pragmatic concepts of right.

A strong believer in natural law assumes that there is a set of rules which are immutable and which do not depend upon the differing circumstances of time and personality. It is necessary that these rules should be understandable by men, but they are not subject to change at human discretion. Not all laws in any commonwealth are believed to be natural laws; in most systems of natural law there is a chain connecting the most vital, absolutely ordained statute down to the most marginal ordinance. The center of the system in Western thought has usually been God, but this is not necessary, as the history of Stoic thought demonstrates. The heart of the matter is permanence, a quality independent of time and place. The relativist believes in some form of impermanence. To the radical sophists, as to the sociological legal school, the angle of perspective is completely governing; each situation requires, or might be said to require, a new law. This is parallel to Einstein's relativism (in a very simplified sense) just as the laws of Newton resemble the laws of Grotius.

Differences of opinion as to the permanence of law do not imply similar differences on the nature of man. The first involves the non-human or pre-human assumptions of natural phenomena or the preconditions of human laws or systems. A believer in natural law can have any number of views of man—consider Plato, the seventeenth-century Puritan thinkers (for example, Prynne or Rutherford), Jefferson, and Marx. Each can be categorized as a believer in natural law, but the political content is of course very different. Here again a confusion arises if one considers the prime difference between right and left to be one of change and continuity, rather than one of the quality of man. Jefferson's devotion to change, to what seems today even an almost anarchic flux, is well known. Yet his devotion to a system of natural law is well demonstrated by the Declaration of Independence and his proposed laws for Virginia. There was no conflict in Jefferson's mind, nor need there have been; he believed in a constant development in institutions and forms of government to reflect man's capacity for improvement, but not even a violent revolution could change the preconditions of society, the natural law. There are two planes, one involving becoming and the other being. This is just the case in Aristotle's thought, for although the oak is vastly different from the acorn the one is a necessary adjunct of the other.

Marx was also beautifully teleological; it comes easily to an absolutist, and most easily to a radical (in the political sense) absolutist. It is easy to see that many believers in natural law have been left of center. In addition to those named above, Robespierre and William Douglas come to mind. And on the other side of the line, Hobbes and Sumner qualify as relativist rightists. But Plato and Aristotle were both absolutist and right-of-center, in differing degrees, while John Stuart Mill and Veblen were relativist and to the left of center. In short, it is hard to draw any correlation between positions on these two issues.

This question of natural law, insofar as it is concerned with social systems, is clearly not as irrelevant to politics as differing views on painting, or on football. If one accepts the view that the condition of man is the first consideration, the permanence of fundamental standards of law (and here of course law must be used in the same broad sense that politics has been defined) is the second consideration, and much of political theory is the meshing of these two. Even the everyday world of affairs bears the imprint of the debate over natural law, for it is not farfetched to see the Protestant movement, the current of the Enlightenment which culminated in the French Revolution, and the rise of socialism as three absolutist causes which sought to impress their concept of right on a more relativist (and to them, more wicked) society. There can be no doubt that this was true of Christianity and Islam.

It is in this sense that religion too is a branch of politics. Such a statement is naturally a thoroughly distasteful one for any devout believer, but it has probably become a commonplace of today's thought. From Carl Becker to Eric Hoffer the growing acceptance of the ideological nature of religious thought, and the converse acceptance of the religious nature of ideology, has come to maturity. Religion should not be looked on as a unique case. Any issue which involves, in some form, a judgment on social organization will become intermixed with the political argument and become a lesser consideration in our list. And so it does come about that if one faction in Byzantium prefers the Blues and the other the Greens, a purely sporting rivalry will become political. Any difference of opinion may do, or any difference in physiology or condition. The history of race relations is a beautifully unhappy example. Forster recalls that in a school that he attended having a sister became a key factor in one's social standing. To that extent the difference between those who had sisters and those who did not, a distinction which to anyone not involved was supremely trivial, probably became an important issue of school politics. Questions of equality and group cohesion converted a childhood rag into a miniscule replica of adult politics (Forster made the comparison with anti-Semitism). The behavioral theorists have traced the political/social relationships in boys' camps and after-school activities, which will come as no surprise to those who have lived through these experiences.

It is therefore not possible to escape from politics. As intensive study of non-governmental institutions has increased in recent years these fundamental issues have appeared and reappeared in corporations and unions, so that the analyses of governmental structures have come into a universal usage, with in-groups and out-groups, federalist power structures and centralized bureaucratic systems turning up in the strangest places. In one sense, the pluralists have triumphed; every enterprise is something of a sovereign today.

Where so many of the behavioralist political thinkers have been timid is in abdicating the theorist's role of advocacy. The complete political world of Lasswell is similar to the one of Aristotle, but Aristotle would never have considered description to have sufficed. The broader the political arena is pictured the less room there is to be a bystander. By having a mind, we are political. Marx may be called cynical in his rejection of any view of politics not colored by a class orientation (although he and Engels qualified this enough to permit a great deal of free thinking), but it requires too much faith in disinterestedness to assume that one can disregard one's basic thinking or feeling. But, more important, if politics is so important, and if ideas are the key to politics, then to think is to act, and the act of commitment is one of the most natural forms of behavior. And in the end the least political of men, like Jesus or Immanuel Kant, may be the most influential and fundamentally politically important.

☆ *II*

The Globe
of Politics

Since almost any description of politics contains an implicit political judgment, it follows that this very explanation does also. In the first place, this postulate of a basic issue in politics presupposes some absolute in political theory, a differentiation between viewpoints which always exists. This is, in a mathematical sense, a law, and a starting point of the analysis. In the second place, however, the flux of institutions and alignments assumes that the absolute will extend only to bases, and not to results. This law of politics is not a moral law, nor does it assume a right or wrong answer to the questions of statecraft. There is thus no answer provided that gives the solution to the question of human nature, no score card on which the real value of human wisdom can be determined. If one man is a reactionary and another a radical, these tools of study cannot judge which is "righter"; in these terms, the very concept of "right" is irrelevant. This irrelevance, of course, must be rejected by one who, like Leo Strauss, would create political theories on moral foundations. These foundations are amoral.

Yet, in a subtler sense, even this attempt at a relativistic neutrality cannot be wholly valid. The question of human nature and capacity is so important that any work on politics or any description of the political arena is likely to impinge on the fundamental question. The hidden premises of a simple outline may often prove to be laden with value judgments. The history of the law is a good illustration of this, as often the most naive or precedent-following opinions have been dissected into strongly political judgments.

This concept of a constant disagreement between adherents of different views of human nature does contain a political value judgment. To say that this difference will not change is more than an absolutist statement (in the sense of the absolutist/relativist dialogue); it is also a conservative statement. For this is itself a conclusion on human nature—that it will never improve to the point that the superiority of man will be evident to all, as radicals and to some extent liberals would say, nor will the degeneracy of man become a tenet of faith sweeping the field, as reactionaries would assert. The tension of a constant disagreement involves, a priori, an analysis that the extremes are most likely to reject. It is a view that is more congenial to the conservatism skepticism than to a liberal hope.

It is then particularly suitable for a political analysis advocating a brand of conservatism to start with this premise, and that is the intention of this essay. That is not to suggest that men of many other outlooks, extremists of left or right, might not share these premises (if this logic is sound they certainly should), but that the premises go most easily with a set of beliefs a little to the right of center, beliefs which do not expect so very much of mankind but which do not despair of the human condition. Above all, beliefs which never foreclose the value and necessity of the great debates of the human mind are compatible with a liberal brand of conservatism.

The spectrum of political thought takes more form when it is observed, so to speak, from within. The greatest discovery that a conservative can make is a simple one, but an insight which on its face seems riddled with paradox. The most complete difference lies between the most extreme radical, who cherishes human possibilities to the utmost, and the extreme reactionary, who holds the lowest view of them. Yet there are so many examples, especially, but not solely, in this century, of the extremists behaving almost identically and even proposing very similar systems. The customary personal dislike, usually hatred, between the men of the extreme left and right often coexists with a striking parallelism of their designs.

Nazism and communism are standard examples today, and need no belaboring. Schlesinger has marked the pressures of both on the "vital center," and has further demonstrated how radicals of other times, like Mike Walsh in the 1850's, tended to agree with the reactionaries (the Fitzhughs and Dews, for instance) of that decade. Many more illustrations can be used. In ancient Greece the periodic eruption of radical uprisings aimed at leveling property and displacing the rich shows that bolshevism is not a new notion. On the other hand, Sparta, the homeland of the right, also stood for a philosophy of shared wealth and livelihood, at least among the ruling class. Cimon, the aristocratic Athenian, sympathized with a state which rejected, in theory, even minor differences of wealth, and when Agis and Cleomenes, centuries later, sought to enforce what a modern socialist has considered a real form of social equality, they looked to the same credo that Cimon had. Pericles and Aristides, on the other hand, in their several ways tried to develop the values of the middle, and just as Aristides preferred Themistocles, his liberal adversary, to the radical right of his day, so Pericles used the tactics of the welfare-state politician and glorified the liberal values of moderation and compromise. The contract is between debate and violence—a Fascist would say, between talking and acting. The vast difference in principle between Marius and Sulla was clear enough to their contemporaries, but to many of us their use of terror, their contempt or disregard for constitutional government, and their reliance on military power seem very similar. The point of agreement between the most radical reformers like Knox and the most fervent Jesuits such as Mariana on the validity of revolt against monarchs was notorious in the sixteenth century, and was succeeded by the strange accords of left-wing independents and Jacobites in early-eighteenth-century England and reactionaries and Jacobins in early-nineteenth-century France. What Robespierre and Villèle had in common was not much different from what Marius and Sulla shared—a passion for the directed commonwealth and a scorn for constitutional compromises. Neither of them had much use for the *haute bourgeoisie*, or for moderate reformers, nor have their respective successors.

Eyck recalls an incident when a Communist, Kopp, bent a steel ruler to show Baron von Maltzan "that it was simpler to join the ends than two adjacent points, and thus that the Bolsheviks could more easily collaborate with conservative professional diplomats than with their own Social Democratic neighbors." They found the radical right even easier to make treaties with.

And in a like manner, the conservative and liberal have tended to be often alike, despite their fundamental difference on the largest issues. Especially in times of grave social crises, the center, instead of flying apart à la Yeats, hugs together. The shared values of moderation and opposition to violence have usually seemed most important when the forces of left and right have threatened to destroy the groundwork of both conservative stability and liberal progress; the politiques of the 1560's, the doctrinaires of the 1820's and the Third Force of the 1950's mark the continuity in France, where crises are habitual. The confluence of Madison and Hamilton is perhaps another example. The disagreement on human nature becomes a compromise when the alternatives are too stark. A foreign adversary with an extreme philosophy forces a "burgfriede" among the more centrist disputes of a rich community, as Florence in the late fourteenth century, Britain in 1940 and the United States in the 1950's might suggest. But this is not so paradoxical. It is understandable that one a little to the right of the center might be close to one a little to the left and not so close to another much further to the right. It is much harder to understand why the extreme left and the extreme right, holding such diametrically opposite opinions and filled with rancor, should so often coincide.

The most obvious explanation is that both are highly dissatisfied with man, and therefore society, as they customarily are. The gap between human potentialities and the limited, vice-ridden state of actual behavior has always saddened or enraged radicals. In some ages this has led to a rejection of earthly values and an appeal to superhuman powers. Even at its most fatalistic, such a philosophy (or religion) has political overtones, and in the thinking of Joachim of Florus or Tolstoy it is explicitly connected with a disapproval of the existing political order. This shades into an expectation that some force, usually some man, will bring about the regeneration of man and society, in short, messianism. The original idea of the messiah developed during the period when the ideals of some of the Judaic prophets appeared to have been lost in the disappointing turmoil of the political world. From the mid-fifth century B.C. on, the precise expectations of the Second Isaiah seemed increasingly dim, but the vast hopes behind these expectations remained, and were converted into utopian dreams, or later produced the Gnostic rejection of society. Voegelin has compared this to the rise of Marxism, which also developed the message of the French Revolution into a more radical, messianic weapon. Camus' discussion of the revolutionary transformation of human rebellion is another view of this same phenomenon viewed from the liberal sector. Much the same thing happened on the right. Plato's utopia also involved the complete rejection of the forms and methods of the city-state, and paralleled in time the messianism in Judah. Both the Jesuits and the Calvinists were willing to destroy much of the order of the day to build their more exacting order; the aristocratic anti-capitalism of the nineteenth century was a natural successor, and was a source of fascism in turn. The modern comparison between Marxism and the reverse utopias of the right is similar.

The very fact of being extreme may well lend itself to this antinomianism. The conflict between the Papists and the Imperialists in the Middle Ages did not divide on a recognizably left/right pattern, although there were such elements of disagreement at work, perhaps on both sides. But it is significant that the more extreme thinkers, such as, say, Innocent III and the author of the York Tractates, espoused views which would have, if immediately adopted, undercut the whole system of politics and religion. There is a natural fervor which strong opposition to the status quo instills; when this is combined with a sense of political direction it takes drastic forms, and the very rigor of the dissatisfaction unites both far left and far right. At the turn of this century it was commonly remarked how the youth of France and Italy were becoming either violent critics of parliamentary government, or of capitalism. Russia in 1917 and Italy in 1922 showed how much the two spirits had in common, while Sorel had even before then pointed the way in his own thinking. How much more the brilliant fury of the Mussolini of 1922 had in common with the calculating genius of Lenin than either shared with, for instance, Poincaré or Jaures! Cohn has remarked that the difference between a modern totalitarian party and a free trade union is as great as the difference between the Taborites and an artisan's guild. Since we have seen so many contemporary examples of this, the phenomenon of the extremist changeling no longer is very startling. The Mussolinis and Doriots have had numerous counterparts. The switch of Joe McWilliams from ardent support of Trotsky to virulent Nazism in one year is perhaps a record, but it was not surprising that when Whittaker Chambers ceased being a brilliant Communist intellectual he became a brilliant reactionary intellectual.

These examples indicate a reason for extremist solidarity more deep-seated than grave discontent and a zest for action. At most times reactionaries have tended to uphold collectivist social forms, and so have radicals. Liberals and conservatives have been more likely to be individualists. Plato had less room in his Republic for the individual as a political force than Aristotle did, and Marx had less than Keynes. At various times this distinction has been more important than at others; in the early nineteenth century there was a tendency for even advanced radicals to be highly individualistic, while today (or more accurately, twenty-five years ago) even moderate liberals were strongly collectivist. The rise of the modern state has greatly enhanced the popularity of individualism among conservatives. Nevertheless, these patterns have been generally true. The form in which conservative thinking clothes its individualism today is often one of free enterprise, whereas four hundred or two thousand years ago it would very likely have been an aristocratic model, but the toga of Cato the Younger would have fit de Witt (as de Jouvenel observed) or Robert Taft. These men opposed the collectivist Caesarian idea in different ways and with sharply different focus, but the history of aristocratic liberty has brought up the same issues since at least the time of Pesistratus. The conservative argument has been to warn of the dangers inherent in popular leaders who have gained power by taking up the cause of "the people" and have increased the governmental power, or in other words, their own control, through these means. Social upheavals then give way to tyranny, and the only gainer, as Cicero claimed, were the tyrant and his entourage. This analysis has seemed most acute when Napoleon and Stalin were compared to Caesar; when Andrew Jackson and William Gladstone were the targets it became too forced.

Reactionaries have not been fond of ambitious radical leaders either, but the complaint has been one of means, rather than ends. The Platonic idea of the best state is very similar to that of the worst, except that the philosopher-king has absolute power and wields that power in a beneficial manner, while the tyrant has absolute power and abuses it. The vice of the tyrant, in Platonic terms, is that he has the utmost opportunity to do good, and by perverting that opportunity, becomes the worst possible ruler. If he changes his character (Plato's career was after all largely devoted to this very task) he does not become merely a little better, but has potential for greatness. So to many very traditionalist Frenchmen in the first years of the nineteenth century Napoleon became much to be preferred to, say, Mirabeau or the Girondins, and Hugenberg had no trouble in accepting Hitler. At some points it becomes hard to tell whether a leader is very radical or very reactionary—Perón may always be a mystery, and the evolution of Stalinism is a very nice case. It is characteristic of these rulers to exalt the state and statism, and to drop even the pretense of advocating liberty.

Furthermore, both extreme left and extreme right have generally tended to emphasize passion and instinct. This attitude on the right has already been commented on, but it has its equivalent in leftist quarters. The emotional standard—the party of

progress is the party of the heart, to twist Clemenceau's epigram—which throws aside mean calculations of economics or
custom and seeks to find the human answer appeals to radicals.
This is of course allied to the antirational sense of discontent
and violence which many reactionary movements display, and
which has been discussed above. The idea of fine distinctions
is inimical to the far left and to the far right. That willingness
to live with tension and uncertainty disappears as one moves
away from the center. In its place there often appears a deep-
seated cynicism, directed by the right toward men and by the
left to institutions.

Thus we have come, in several senses, full circle. The reactionary and radical think of each other as deadly opposites, but
to the moderate conservative their extremes invariably meet.
The psychological paradox is solved, for the doctrine of abasing
man and that of exalting him must both come to the same, or
very similar tenets. This would not be so if either could carry
the day, but the very conflict in humanity which the moderate
conservative accepts and understands drives the extremes together at an anti-center, where there is no gray but only a black-
and-white contrast. The chiarascuro of moderate liberalism or
conservatism is unendurable to the extreme, often for intensely
personal reasons; whereas the moderate can understand these
extremes while marveling at the paradoxical nature of their
agreement.

This understanding can be compared to the greater comprehension which a man with a globe possesses over a man using
a Mercator map. It is not a matter of madness or cynical nonsense (like Hitler and Stalin in the famous Low cartoon) to
get to the right by traveling left, but almost a commonplace in
the world of global politics. It is the flat Mercator map which
contains the absurdities—the strange cases of radical collectivism
which, from Cabet to Castro, invariably seem to produce authoritarian societies despite their overt hatred of authoritarianism,
are like Greenland on the Mercator map. The impossibly bloated
arctic islands which grow like inexplicable tumors on these maps

are reduced to their normal shape once the proper geographic tools are used. So it is here.

The flatness of the political globe cannot, however, be relegated to the domain of ignorant notions, for it clearly embodies the hopes and disappointments of generations of men. To these the resignation and lack of fervor which the circle manifests must seem a little cynical at the least, and in some ways a preposterous denial of the potentials of human capacities (or incapacities). To the devoted radical especially a theory which equates his ideas with that of the most complete disbeliever in progress involves a sordid disdain for humanity. And it must be remembered that the "true believers" have usually numbered the greatest moral leaders, the enthusiasts of the ages. But there is morality in balanced moderation as well. It was the author of the Eighth Psalm who asked "What is man, that thou art mindful of him?"; but also he wrote "yet he has made him but little lower than the angels." Perhaps in the long run the greatest virtue does rest in the *juste milieu*.

The description of the political spectrum in terms of a circle is not a radical departure. A. Lawrence Lowell suggested a similar design in his study of public opinion fifty years ago. Lowell's divisions into sanguine and non-sanguine correspond to the left/right or progressive/nonprogressive division here, and his separation of the contented and discontented divides the extreme from the center. His sanguine, discontented quadrant is the radical sector, his sanguine, contented the liberal, non-sanguine, contented is conservative, while the non-sanguine, discontented quadrant includes what is here called reactionaries. Since in practice the distinctions operate gradually and often imperceptibly, a circle is more useful than a square or box. For convenience, the liberal-conservative half will be referred to as "lower-circle," and the radical-reactionary half as "upper-circle." There is no reason why the circle should not curl downward rather than upward, but as in so many cases it is better to have a uniform rule than a perfect one.

The preferences noted above now fit into place. For example, the belief in liberty is a salient point with all liberals. As one moves leftward and upwards on the circle liberty is still a slogan, but it tends to become altered or converted into another word for equality. On the other hand, as one moves to the right into conservatism, liberty increasingly becomes a form of particular rights or privileges, until liberty becomes a bundle of liberties. These will generally tend to diminish and particularize as one climbs into the reactionary sector. On the far right liberty is least prized, and there it meets the tendency of the radical to widen liberty and decrease its emphasis until it disappears. The result of the unlimited liberty of revolution becomes, as Dostoevski's Shigalev prophesied, unlimited despotism.

Property has a similar experience. Among conservatives it is of course frequently the major premise of society, and it is usually supported in some form or another (with emphasis normally on its widespread distribution) by liberals. As one goes further left it is more and more disliked until it becomes an abomination. Its fate among reactionaries is less clear-cut, but also unhappy. It is upheld as a traditional value, but increasingly reduced to a status below that of authority. The demands of the legitimate state, the requirements of religion, or the ethos of tradition come first. Finally, the extreme reactionaries consider it as decadent as liberty, in fact a part of the "pluto-democratic" values of the center.

The situations of equality and authority are the same. Equality is presumably most cherished on the far left and least on the right. But as one studies reactionary thinkers one is struck by the growing regard for collective solidarity, sometimes a mystical equality, sometimes an equal society of the elite. At the most reactionary, as in Sparta or Nazi Germany, equality is accepted as a central doctrine. "One nation, one people, one leader" was the National Socialist reply to Liberty, Equality, Fraternity. Property or opportunity were not mentioned. The radical attitude to authority is very similar. Of course it is not an approved part of progressive doctrine, but in the struggle to expedite man's rush forward it is very frequently a necessity. The dictatorship of the proletariat, the cult of leadership, the rule of the saints, were all to be temporary, but unavoidable. Even the tender-minded radicals, when faced with the gap between what must be done and the inconveniences of humanity, opt for a decision based on authority. Edward Bellamy and Sir Stafford Cripps had the highest regard for humanity and the possibilities of voluntary cooperation, but each (and Bellamy foresaw this without living through it) called for forced labor of sorts.

The concepts of fraternity and order present the same story. The radical naturally thinks of all men as brothers, and their peaceful living together as an ideal closely allied with equality. Fraternity becomes more specialized as one goes down the circle, becoming more and more a form of voluntary friendship. To the conservative I am not my brother's keeper, cant aside, and the best guarantee of living together amicably lies in abiding by rules. These rules, the outward form of order, become more rigid as one moves into the reactionary sector. The precision of order on the far right is usually military, and in sharp contrast to the pervasive fraternal beliefs of the far left. But both involve a search for complete unity.

Thus the emphasis on the collective is a frequent mark of distinction between the upper-circle and lower-circle outlook. Plato's rejection of the definition of justice which rendered to each man his due, and his substitution of a total pattern of social classes, is a classic example of this collectivist viewpoint. The evolution of macroeconomics is a similar development, as was the propagation of Gierke's theory of *genossenschaft*. But the differences between the experiences of these various collectivist theories are very informative. The Platonic idea of justice has always been considered immensely brilliant, and was almost completely irrelevant even in its time. Gierke has had some little success, largely due to the work of Maitland and Figgis, but it has so far been only an intellectual victory. However, the economic triumph of macroeconomics, in one form or another, has been outstanding. The concepts of the latter have fit in with and encouraged the often-considered movement in this century of the entire left, liberal as well as radical, to some form of collective thought. The other ideas were not so strategically well-placed. At different times the climate of individualism will be paramount and will permeate almost all of the circle. The sixth century B.C. may be so classed; the eighteenth and much of the nineteenth century were unquestionably such periods. Other ages—and our own century is an obvious example—are predominately collectivist. At some times the left will swing to one philosophy (such as collectivism today, or individualism in 1800), so that it will seem that the distinction on this count between moderate and extreme is invalid. But the distinctions remain, and Marx is still more of a planner than Keynes.

There are exceptions to this rule. Anarchists, of course, are almost always strongly optimistic about human nature and very idealistic about human wisdom, but their individualism surely exceeds that of the timid liberal or the more timid conservative. To the anarchist there is absolutely no conflict between the maximum of liberty and complete equality. It is significant that anarchism has never succeeded and that anarchy, despite generations of idealists, remains a word of scorn. In practice the philosophy of anarchism, when it has been effective, as in many Mediterranean countries in the years 1880-1914, has degenerated into an opportunity for violence, or an excuse for brands of nihilism. The concept of the anarchist movement, especially of the non-violent anarchists, was in effect a call for uncurling the circle, but its libertarianism gives way to a dog-eat-dog individualism which seldom lasts long, while the idealism proves ineffective.

The Social Darwinism of the right is a natural analogy. It is remarkable how these ideologies which, like those of Bakunin or Nietzche, present extreme doctrines of human nature in individualist forms, deteriorate in the hands of followers into mass movements which retain the passion but lose the freedom. This is then followed by a congealing of the emotion, leaving the residue of a doctrine of the all-powerful state. The pressure of the circular truth in politics creates these awful paradoxes, linking Spencer with Rosenberg, and Mazzini with Stalin. It is frightening to think of the future course of Paul Goodman's philosophy.

That is not to say that there are not entirely sincere people who hold beliefs which are practically impossible. The most noble men often do insist that liberty, equality, and fraternity are inseparable, and their beliefs are entirely rational. But their sincere beliefs do not refute the constant tendency of the political spectrum to become a circle. The tendency of a class of predominately small-town, old-fashioned, usually *petit bourgeois*, and highly individualistic people to support parties of the far right has caused similar confusion. Poujade and the Social Credit party in Quebec were very good rallying points for these groups. The Nationalist Party in South Africa is largely of this type, and Nazism flourished among them before its rise to power. Yet this is a philosophy of small-town, small-power vision. It is very individualist. It is in some ways a derivation of typical conservatism; in its opportunity-minded individualism, it is very close to liberal conservatism. Lipset took this to prove the fallacy of the left-right continuum implicit in this analysis.

But these are merely anarchists of the right. There is nothing inherently inconsistent about a love of provincialism and a deep if eccentric respect for each individual on one hand, and a belief in anti-Semitism or in the banning of labor unions on the other. The trouble lies in the fact that these Poujadistes, if one may so class them, are extremists. Their habitual distrust of all kinds of social progress is usually built on a nagging distrust of their neighbor, not to mention the stranger beyond the village gate. Like the anarchist they see no trouble in combining their extreme belief with the individualism of the lower-center and with a part of the moderate's program. The Poujadiste may be a fanatical anti-truster, but this derives from a blind distrust of change and not a commitment to competition. That alone makes neither of them lower centrists. These reactionary fears, like the anarchist's hopes, stand in the way of a free exercise of individual opportunities. For in the realm of active affairs, the Poujadistes break down as the anarchists, and their society in practice turns out collectivist, as the Vorster government attests. The Frenchmen who voted for Poujade usually later voted for De Gaulle, and if they are now unhappy, it is more likely to be over the price of wine than over the freedom of the press. When Hitler reduced individualism to nothing in Germany the Thuringian libertarians did not revolt. The solution of the petty enterpriser to big business is often more cartels and not more competition.

In the end, therefore, the pockets of incompatibility turn out to be exceptions which prove the rule. The closer politicians come to office, or thinkers to a unified system of thought, the closer they come to conforming to the circle. Particular issues, such as the value of anti-trust legislation or the desirability of prohibition, may attract diverse elements pro and con. The broad political arguments are seldom so fragmented, and if they are, the inexorable pressure of life tends to reset them in the classic pattern. And usually even the smallest political disagreement will fit into the circle.

To test this proposition, it is not necessary to look very far. The issue of treatment of criminals is a good example. Of course the farther left you go the more humane the philosophy of penology becomes, for the question of the goodness or badness of men is palpable in this matter. The dividing line between conservative and liberal might reasonably be drawn on the question of capital punishment, although of course there is no set line. The farther right one goes the more one hears arguments for the need for draconian regulations and for "going back to fundamental laws." Strict punishment and revenge are considered adequate explanations for criminal laws on the right, while usually only deterrence is acceptable on the left, and at times on the far left nothing is acceptable.

So the criminal law should almost disappear in radical societies, and most radical revolutions have this as a goal (expedited in the first instance by the disappearance of lawyers). But somehow even the death penalty comes back, with a vengeance, literally and figuratively. It does no more good, it would seem, to abolish the idea of crime than it did to try to abolish crime by multiplying criminal offenses.

Time does not eliminate these conflicts, nor does it matter whether their discussion takes the form of political theory, legislation, or penology. This is also true of much theology. The dispute between "low church" and "high church" was not an obscure invention of Anglican divines, but has been around since the New Kingdom in Egypt. The argument of high churchmen is that ceremony and stateliness provide the material indicia of religion required by fallible men to cement their spiritual yearnings. They hold that every man in each generation is not capable, without the aid of a sanctified tradition, of maintaining the religious spirit. If some few are, they should not rob the masses of their traditional supports. Transplanted to politics, it does not require a T. S. Eliot to show how political authority and religious tradition are inseparable, for the term "throne and altar" had a dignified tradition before it became a catcall for rebels. The ardent low churchmen often are prominent among those attacking the "unholy alliances" of prelates and princes, and the Bunyanesque faith of the free man among his devout comrades, scornful of liturgy and popish dogma, was among the roots of the revolutions of the modern age. The heirs of Bunyan, however, have sometimes strayed into Marxist dogmas or have let mysticism replace ceremony. The rational faith of equal religionists faces the same problems of elitism or new dogma which the analagous political democracies have faced; in fact, the disillusionment of the religious radical was an old story when the anguish of the circle had not yet troubled many political thinkers. So many men have found that new presbyter is but old priest writ large.

So even religion is not sacred. And in the domain of the profane, the perennial battle over sexual freedom is much the same. The reaction of the far left against liberty frequently takes a drastically sexual form, as Robespierre and Mao Tse-tung demonstrate. But that does not mean that at most times and places the various arguments for more sexual freedom—against censorship, for more education and public discussion, and so forth— are not circular goals pursued by progressives. There are puritans on the left, and quite mild, un-Jacobin puritans among them, but the usual position of the liberal (if not always the radical) is one of support of these freedoms, even against personal inclination. And of course many rightists believe in holding the lid down on sexual matters even if they have no personal reasons for condemning them. The perhaps hypocritical separation between social policy and individual behavior, the door between the public and the private, bespeaks the classic conservative mind. After all, as J. P. Morgan allegedly remarked, that is what doors are for. The extreme reactionary tends to break down the door and make everyone conform to the public standards of morality, as does the far left.

But it would be a mistake to pay too much attention to the meeting of the extremes. Just as day-to-day travel does not require the use of a globe, so the small and innumerable details of politics can be found on the smaller road maps of theory. The questions of whether to broaden the role of parole facilities, of how much Latin (or Hebrew or Sumerian) there should be in the liturgy, or of whether to permit books containing improper four-letter words in the public libraries, are, as has been indicated, as much basic political issues as a tax bill. In everyday terms, it is enough to think of right and left as opposed camps. The question of unemployment compensation presents, as suggested before, a clear left/right matter, and so does the compensation of executives, or of army officers. When the fluoridation issue first arose it amazed many people, who thought that the import of politics into such an issue was pure idiocy. And so it may be, but if you believe that men are a very sorry lot, it is not much of a surprise if you refuse to permit them to make experiments with the water supply, even if (perhaps, especially if) their aims are noble. However, the conduct of foreign affairs will always reflect circular opinions of the diplomatic process. The radical naturally relies on the unchecked direction of the popular will or of the chosen tribunes of the people; even a liberal like Wilson distrusted the scheming of diplomats. But conservatives usually prize the arts of diplomacy, and man the diplomatic corps. The reactionaries should be expected to admire the most elitist principles of diplomatic procedure, but as one proceeds up the circle on each side the emphasis is more on the leader and less on the staff. Lloyd George and Hitler both saw fit to ignore the "striped pants" fogies who epitomized the nineteenth-century balance of power and of classes. The differences of historical periods are less important than the circular verities.

At times, as on the matter of conservation, it seems that the principle of preserving goods at the expense of the enjoyment of the living, a fine conservative idea, has become a liberal slogan. But on closer analysis this paradox is resolved. The principal liberal concern is for present enjoyment—camping, hunting, wildlife observation—as opposed to the more commercial values of farming or sheep-raising. When conservation is used in its literal sense, as in replenishing timberland, the greatest advocates are just those forces one might expect—large corporations which can take the long view, wealthy holders of land, or ascetic lovers of wilderness. The small lumber-cutter and the parks enthusiast are in a way for the same thing, the present use of the land for the greatest current pleasure. When liberals do support long-range programs which must sacrifice present good for future betterment, they abandon liberalism to that extent. Theodore Roosevelt was never a thoroughgoing liberal, as the Bull Moosers discovered in 1916. In fact, once a liberal begins to think of his cherished ideas in terms of the use of future generations, he is likely to change those ideas, in substance if not in form. This, in effect, is the story of Edmund Burke.

One cannot ignore immediate self-interest; the eager lumberman may support the most reactionary candidate but cut down every tree in sight. But it is a mistake to miss the forest for the trees. The field of economics is not an exception to these rules which apply in all the social sciences. In the long run the rich and the powerful will usually behave conservatively and at times in a reactionary fashion (but seldom in an extremely reactionary fashion) because their long-term self-interest naturally places them there. In the longer run self-interest may give way to other ideas, which may contradict financial interest. Interest is a murky term. Some values may be much more involuted than pecuniary gain, but deeper in intensity. But if they conform to a pattern of values, they will invariably fit into the circle. This can be seen most readily with those to whom free speech is a paramount value; Oswald Villard was no less selfishly consistent than Henry

Villard because he valued money less and talk more; of course the man who has two standards, one for himself and one for everyone else, is harder to place, but such unalloyed selfishness is not a problem—usually that man will have such a low view of everyone else's nature that his politics will be easily categorized as reactionary. There are many quirks, but the consistent patterns are usually very near the surface. Economists have long gone beyond the narrower equations of the hedonist calculus. There is a place for Engels, and perhaps Cyrus Eaton, certainly for the Buddha, but our rapacious lumberman is only an ideological sport.

Ideas are the crucial factor, and financial interest will usually affect them. Interests which have no ideological base are of secondary importance in politics, and in economics. The very study of economics divides into the same left/right categories that we have outlined. The spectrum of economic thought may be separated by a line between those who emphasize supply considerations, and those who put the greatest weight on demand factors. This makes political sense, for demand involves the enjoyment and use of goods and services, while supply is concerned with the creation and development of these things. The higher the view of human capabilities, the more right it seems to use the wealth and the institutions of today to serve the interests of humanity today. This explains why Burke and Theodore Roosevelt were not progressives, and it explains why economists who stress the problems of supply rather than demand are right of center.

This has obvious practical importance. On the question of wage policy, the left urges wage increases in order to increase demand, while the right points out how such increases will raise the cost of the goods produced and thus restrict supply. The left urges tax laws which will provide the maximum buying power; the right advocates taxation which most encourages production.

The dichotomy also takes more subtle forms. In the elementary economic equation, Money times Velocity equals Price times Transactions, or as usually summarized, $MV=PT$. The left side of the equation is the left side of politics. Those economists who have centered their study on money have been, as a rule, left of center, as the history of the Cambridge School illustrates. Vienna and Chicago have paid more attention to price. Naturally, a philosophy centering on money lends itself to a judgment which places great emphasis on income policy and the dangers of unemployment. As price becomes more significant the dangers of inflation come to the fore. The value judgment which starts with placing a high estimate on man's abilities and rights tends easily to prefer demand considerations to supply, and therefore money factors to price factors. To the right, the emphasis on money seems naive or unhealthy, as Schumpeter's criticism of Irving Fisher's monetary theories shows—at worst, the zest for a money policy seems an escape from natural laws. Conservative monetary theorists such as Milton Friedman have a tendency to propose surprisingly radical programs. The modern fiscal and monetary theories share a common reliance on the value of the flow of money in the economic system; they differ largely on the degree to which they would manipulate that flow. Naturally the most liberal Keynesians urge the most manipulation.

Velocity has not played such a large role in leftist economics, although its impact on heretical faiths has been seminal. The more radical the economist, the more he is apt to be velocity-minded. What is Marx's surplus value but an artificial impediment to the free velocity of money? The same may be said, to some extent, of Keynes' marginal propensity to save. On the other hand, transaction-minded economics is in some ways the oldest but also the least developed branch, for every authoritarian ruler has emphasized the necessity for more transactions. The mercantilists were first of all transaction-oriented.

The affinity of Keynes to mercantilism, and of the socialist state to a production-consciousness worthy of Colbert, demonstrates anew the circle. Once again, this does not indicate that the socialists are insincere or that they have abandoned their principles. In the extreme case where everything is subordinated to production, such as Stalin's Russia, this is true, as the supply factors take pre-eminence and the radical theories turn into reactionary facts. But in contemporary India or Bolivia the need for production is kept subordinate by the left to a clear effort to expand effective demand. Money, in every sense, is the key, and monetary problems are the preoccupation of every progressive underdeveloped country which is trying to raise its standard of living. A rich nation is likely to be a creditor nation and more concerned with stable price levels.

This brings up the greatest paradox of modern political theory, a difficulty which has puzzled thinkers and confused politics for at least seventy-five years. Classical economics has been chiefly a study of prices and price relationships, from Ricardo to Stigler. The everyday supporters of free enterprise have certainly been considered conservatives since at least 1880. Yet the theory of classical economics, of laissez faire, to use the popular tag, has always been avowedly liberal and even progressive. From Herbert Spencer to Frederick Hayek the classical liberals have strenuously denied that they were conservatives; Hayek has a chapter in his *Constitution of Liberty* entitled "Why I Am Not a Conservative." But nevertheless they are, in our scheme, conservatives.

The everyday sense is correct because it gets to the heart of the matter. The classical liberal, or his younger cousin, the Lucite permanent revolutionary, does believe that men are capable of great things, but only after a time. The poorest he that is in England will enjoy as much as the richest he enjoys today, but the poorest he will have to wait until the economy produces the wherewithal. Each man must have the broadest economic freedom, but that freedom does not guarantee the better life. And it is inevitable that economic freedom, in the classical sense, must lead primarily to property, for property in some form is the great reward of classical economics. It does not do to say that liberty and property are inseparable, for one involves an individual act and the other a social function. The property theorists have usually accepted the given society as the best to be hoped for; in the midst of economic problems both Cicero and Hoover argued that things would work out, and the fact that Hoover held to the faith of free enterprise did not convert his policy into one which emphasized human capacities. For if man is easily perfectible and highly able, why accept any of the limitations of free market capitalism; why allow any unemployment?

This always proves a severe stumbling block to the truly liberal free enterprisers. There have been idealistic men of the left who have thought of the free market as a species of utopia. They have expected the economic liberty of Adam Smith to provide for the city of Rousseau. But this is to expect property to accomplish what it cannot ever do. The usual result is that, like Spencer, they retain the logic of a radical doctrine but lose the substance. Otherwise they pursue hopeful programs which invariably become lost. Henry George is an ideological cousin to the anarchists; libertarian individualist radicalism, despite the earnest intelligence of its advocates, is purely an anomaly. Andrew Carnegie may have been more ridiculous in his enunciations of glowing faith in human rights delivered from Skibo Castle, but free enterprise makes more sense in *Triumphant Capitalism*, despite its longeurs, than it does in *Progress and Poverty*.

Businessmen do have a natural desire to please the consumers, but this is not the same thing as a mission of mass improvement. It is not realistic to say that "Golden Rule" Jones was more typical of the business community than Carnegie, or Ivar Kreuger.

But Adam Smith, as many historians and economists have pointed out, was a liberal. In the context of the late eighteenth century, the individualist protest against economic restrictions and preference for private action was frequently liberal. In the Soviet Union today a movement to break down the power of the state might be liberal, even if it emphasized property. When the pendulum of power swings one way the spirit of opposition will swing the other. It is wise to remember that Smith was not very liberal, nor for that matter is Hayek very conservative. Pure free enterprise, like pure free speech, involves values very close to the meeting place of liberal and conservative, to the low point of the circle. At different times the spirit of ideas may place them in different categories. In 1776 Smith's mildly liberal theory of property freedom had a pro-labor and anti-merchant bias, but the development of business and the maturing of classical economics made this anachronistic very early.

The very success of an idea attaches it to some social pattern and to the men who have prospered under that pattern. The fervor of the early promises becomes ossified, in the nature of things. The Revolution of 1688 had liberal characteristics, but when Burke appealed to the Old Whigs, he was deliberately appealing to the adherents of the action, not to the proponents of the idea behind the action; Price and Priestley represented the latter. The spirit may give life, but the letter does not kill; it subtly invents a new spirit.

III

The History
of Politics

History is often the despair of the partisans of hope, for they see their hopes become memories. Men have sought the secrets of good government and the good life from the time of the Sumerians, but as the Babylonians discovered, some prizes cannot be won. Just when it would appear that the problems of statecraft were on the way to being solved new variables appear to destroy the very assumptions of the old order. The battle over freedom of the press persisted through the seventeenth and eighteenth centuries, but by the nineteenth the forces of freedom seemed to have won, surely and securely, in most of the civilized world, and the rest would, it was widely believed, soon follow. But somehow the golden age of liberty did not result; scoundrels, on having freedom, printed not only the worthiest of books but less edifying tracts, even what is now called hardcore pornography, so that the heirs of Milton were faced with the task of checking lewd pamphlets. And the twentieth century saw even the purest accomplishments of the eighteenth and nineteenth cast into doubt, so that by 1944 we were back to 1644. Gibbon thought the fears of civilization had at last been laid to rest, but he lived to see how wrong he was. The expectations of Saint-Just and Condorcet went much further, but it seemed to many of their heirs that by 1830, or 1848, nothing fundamentally had changed.

To the Marxist, as to the Spencerian, no disillusionment is called for. The setbacks are part of the dialectic of history, and a natural part of progress. This has always appealed to Americans. So far this faith in progress has always been wisely tempered with enough caution to avoid the dejection which has so often come after the hope. To a certain extent, however, these disappointments have occurred regularly in American history, as a liberal period has given way to a conservative age, and vice versa. The same is of course true of all other countries, and of other epochs. There seem to be currents of political opinions which surge up the banks of thought, and consolidate or remake the work of the previous wave. Thus the years 1896-1902 were marked by conservatism or reaction throughout the world. Mc-Kinley in the United States, Salisbury in Britain, the anti-Dreyfusards in France, and Pelloux in Italy were all part of a spirit that exalted imperialism and seemed to make the specter of socialism a false alarm. But it was not, and the seeds of new ideas were being planted by Freud and Veblen even as the ground seemed least hospitable. The next period disappointed Lord Milner, and pleased Lord Haldane, but then the First World War disappointed the liberals. Our recent past has witnessed a time of conservatism which began roughly in 1947 and continued in some ways until at least 1956, or perhaps 1959, or possibly is still going on. These waves are comparable to the economic cycles described by Kitchin and Juglar; there is no exact measure of their length or depth, but they alter the thinking of theorists, the programs of politicians, and often (witness the decline in divorce rates after 1946) even the morals of the people.

These tidal movements do not prove the impossibility of progress, just as the Kitchin cycle does not disprove the existence of Kondratieff cycles or long-term economic growth. If each new period of liberalism or radicalism marked a clear advance over the last preceding one, or even over the general range of earlier such periods, one would say that the spirals moved upward, that the tide came in further. In a common-sense form this is the prevalent view of liberals today.

Yet the very assumptions which we have made as to the

unchanging nature of the political debate casts doubt on the beliefs of progress. Men certainly eat better now than 2500 years ago, they drive automobiles rather than oxen, perhaps they are more comfortable, it is even arguable that they are happier— although the burden of proof of that must be undertaken by the progressives. But the state of man, in a metaphysical or political sense, has not changed, and his social strivings remain the same. Just as the highest optimism traces its way around the circle to the lowest pessimism, so the accomplishments of each generation must be re-enacted in another form. If the work of politics were like the successes of mathematics, each new colloquy would be built on the completed structure of the previous one. But the issues of social science are never resolved; they reappear in a new guise. And since the new conflict is the same as the old, but differently put, the old can be reflected on, but not incorporated. The French Revolution of 1789 involved one of the greatest struggles over inequality of status and wealth in the world's history. But in 1848, 1871, and 1936, these questions came forward again. It was not possible to say "The matter was disposed of on 10 September 1792, or on some day in 1794." The politicians who did talk this way found themselves anachronisms even in France, or laughingstocks even in Germany. Not that the problems of 1848, or 1936, were new, but that their very antiquity required a new way of considering them, taking in mind the changes of circumstance. The author of Ecclesiastes well summarized this when he commented that "of what can it be said 'see, this is new'? It has been done already, in former times. There is no remembrance of former times." We can never really remember former times because the act of involvement with the living turbulence of these perpetual problems makes us modern. A man who could really think about the question of equality as Marat did (if such a man could exist today) would be hopelessly out of touch with Marat's ideological successors.

It follows from this gap between the ages that each generation must rewrite the history of the past. The great themes appear in new forms, while the lesser ones come and go as we review the past. As Malraux has remarked, "We revalue past ages by present standards, in history as in art. . . . We interpret the past in the light of what we understand. . . . Thus from the time when history set up as a mental discipline (not to say an obsession) until 1919, inflation was a relatively rare phenomenon. Then it became frequent, and modern historians see in it a cause of the decline of the Roman Empire. Similarly, since 1789 history has had a new perspective, revolution being a successful revolt, and revolt a revolution that failed. Thus a new or rediscovered fact may give its bias to history. It is not research work that has led to the understanding of El Greco; it is modern art." Toynbee has observed that Iknaton has been reappraised by each generation of Egyptologists. The greatest thing which happened to the reputation of that pharaoh was not an archaeological discovery, but Freud. Of course the inhabitants of the New Kingdom did not debate the Oedipus complex, but that does not mean that it is not more profitable to see them in a Freudian light than to confine oneself to the language of the fourteenth century B.C. It is not research work that has revived the reputation of Charles Sumner and Thaddeus Stevens; it is the civil rights movement. When Robert Browning was asked in his later years if a proposed interpretation of an earlier poem was the right explanation, he is said to have replied that he had not meant that when he wrote the poem, but he meant it now.

The most literal beliefs of a Rankean may be the soundest view of history qua narrative, and still leave room for a relative view of history as a theoretical ordering of experience. Facts may be comparatively clear, yet different interpretations will make them seem vastly different in the works of warring historians. This especially applies to motivation, and to the intrinsic political situation, which seems so different at different times. Kripfing pointed out that this was very true in nineteenth-century German histories of the ancient world. The contemporaries of Ranke were more divided in their interpretations than were the colleagues of Gibbon. Niebuhr looked on Philip of Macedon as Napoleon, but Droysen pictured Macedonia as a fourth century B.C. Prussia— fifty years of nineteenth-century history altered the case, one suspects. Mommsen's Caesar was notoriously convenient for the National Liberals, but in fairness Caesar has proved convenient for many causes from at least the time of Shakespeare. The vicissitudes of Caesar in European historiography have almost been equally matched in a mere one hundred fifty years of writing about Jefferson in the United States. Pasquale Villari remarked that "Society changes from age to age, and as fast as it turns to us another of its thousand facets we are obliged to remake history under a new aspect. This is the reason why, even when it was written by men of the highest ability, we have to reconstruct it afresh."

It is clearly admissible here to look on these differing historical visions as part of human progress, as Engels did, but it is also possible to believe that they can be categorized as manifestations of cultures which rise and fall, as Spengler maintained. Engels thought that man was going somewhere—steadily upward—and Spengler thought that man was doomed to repeat his experiences in a methodical order, without basic improvement. Considering that both started with the same assumption—that history exists as a by-product of the historian, and behind him, of the social order that produced him—Spengler has the better of the argument, for Engels assumes that the dictatorship of the proletariat will usher in an age exempt from the contradictions and class judgments of all other ages. Engels requires the coming of the Messianic Age; Spengler presumably expects eternal repetitions. But Spengler, like many other reactionary thinkers, will not let well enough alone, for his repeated emphasis on decline and his obvious preference for some forms of thought over others interferes with the symmetry of his design. We may think that some concepts of human nature are much superior to others, and that the ideas which spring from some are also greatly to be preferred, but as long as we accept the idea of a basically unchanging set of ideas on human nature, we preclude a historical system that will destroy the existing differences. And if we say that the dispute over human possibilities resolves itself into a circle, then "history" will not be a method for altering the basic scheme of things.

We are back where we started, which is always the case when

the premises are given. Since the great arguments have always involved the same issues, we have not progressed. Historical writing is not a way of solving these issues, but is the result of the argument. In other words, the important thing is to ask the right questions, not to expect right answers. And just as neither extreme of the political spectrum is going anywhere—i.e., establishing their directional schema of human nature as the necessary pattern—but end one with the other, so "history" is not a progression or retrogression but a working-out of the same themes.

To many historians this has been the basis for a cyclical interpretation. The alternation of liberal and conservative periods suggested above is such a system. Beyond that, the circular view may or may not be cyclical. The United States has had a republican form of government for over 175 years, but France has had five republics in that period, not to mention kingdoms and empires, and other countries have had more changes. The Roman society lasted very long, but Hitler's thousand years continued for merely twelve. The only cycles which a theory of ideas on human nature can postulate are cycles of belief of human nature, and even these may be short or long. The important point is that we start by assuming that this difference on human potentialities is the key difference, that we continue by postulating its constant basic nature, and we conclude by finding that the extreme beliefs of the most differing camps lead not to a new realm of politics, but close in on each other. The historical picture thus becomes the negative, so to speak, of the theoretical snapshot.

But to hold this vision of the circle one must be part of the circle; there is no escaping that. It is a viewpoint congenial to one who has a somewhat narrow expectation of humanity's ability to improve itself, yet a dislike of the more sordid and degrading conceptions of human nature. Moreover, this idea does not divide men into rigid classes or groups, some of whom must be cherished at the expense of the rest. In short, it is an analysis which fits in most well with a moderately conservative view.

It might be said that this rejection of the idea of progress is distinctly reactionary. That is not so. In the first place, we are considering only the fundamentals of politics, not standards of

living or of behavior. Perhaps politics itself is comparatively unimportant, as a Buddhist would think. In the second place, there
is no denying that men's capacities may be rising, that even a
greater degree of goodness is spreading throughout the world;
these presuppositions require only that such changes be ones of
degree, and not of kind. For all we know, man may be participating in a 50,000-year upward cycle. Finally, and most important, the constant debate assumes an eternal conversation between all men at all times toward social happiness, a conversation
without a triumphant conclusion, but also without a complete
failure. No generation, class, or race is too unworthy to partici-
pate, and the signs of betterment are not to be despised because
they will not remove the spectacle of human fallibility.

Plus ça change, plus c'est la même chose. The circular analysis of politics, as we have seen, is inseparable from a historical
concept, because each age of the past is as valuable, in its own
way, as a paradigm of the great conversation as the present (and
of course the "present" is a fictional moment). Most reactionary
analyses are anti-historical, since they often assume that man
must be rescued from the misery of his ineptitudes. Plato's Republic is a case in point. The social order in the Republic is
perfect, not perfectible, and therefore nothing can ever be an
improvement. The system of education of the rulers is the pivot
of the commonwealth, and its nature is set. The program is
determined for all times as to the pace of the student, the material to be studied, and the effect of the studies on the government of the Republic. There is no suggestion that the number
of those eligible to go the course will increase, or that the system, once operating, would require any changes derived from
experience or disagreement over premises.

The fundamental concepts of modern Western civilization
were built on very different foundations. Plato's rejection of
history—disregard would be too mild a word—is closely allied
to his authoritarianism. The development of constitutionalism was
the great motif of the early modern world, and it was accompanied by the growing subjective awareness of history. Malraux,
as we have seen, evidently placed "the time when history set up

as a mental discipline" in those days of a stable price level which marked the triumph and result of the constitutional state—i.e., the nineteenth century. Moreover, to study politics from a circular point of view requires an examination of history.

The story of the tradition of constitutionalism and natural law is familiar; McIlwain and Corwin have traced the concepts up to, roughly, the French Revolution. The natural-law beliefs of Aristotle were similar to those of the *Minos,* and Cicero drew on these ideas along with the Stoic philosophy. During the Middle Ages it was perhaps the more primitive ideas of the "givenness" of law which prevailed, but which reinforced the much more sophisticated legacy of Aristotle and Cicero. But by the time of Grotius and Bacon, or perhaps even earlier, the classical tradition of natural law had clearly reappeared. And of course the Christian belief in natural law, especially as developed by Aquinas and his followers, also carried on the Aristotelian mode of thinking. Whether one traces the thread through the Christian labyrinth or that of the secular thinkers, the connection between Aristotle and John Adams can be discerned.

Adams, one of the founders of moderate conservatism in the United States, found his place on the circle in much the same spot that Aristotle had occupied. It might seem to be a naive joke to say that Aristotle would have voted for Adams, but one value of the circle is that it makes the joke into a serious conclusion. For that matter, the *Politics* was primarily a detailed political essay of its time, not so different from the writings of, say, Hugh Cecil or Peter Viereck. Cicero was an eminently practical Roman politician, *inter alia,* and his predecessor Polybius— the like thinking of the historian and the philosopher-statesman is significant—was an advocate for the program of Scipio.

Of course this was not a coincidence. The defense of social classes, of a mixed constitution with fundamental laws and safeguards against too-hasty change, and the glorification of the middle class were ideas which fit beautifully into a niche a little to the right of center. Some of Aristotle's legacy could be, and was, used by those farther to the right. His defense of slavery was a great boon to the southern thinkers of the pre-Civil War days,

but this involved a racial bias and a disbelief in human opportunity too far right to be very consistent with the teachings of
Aristotle. The traditional emphasis and the strong sense of order
in the philosopher perhaps had a more right-wing influence in
the age of scholasticism than it had in fourth century B.C. Greece.

On the other hand, these ideas could be put to more liberal
uses. Coke and Otis, and of course Adams too, pre-1783, used
the ideas of constitutionalism and natural law for less traditional
ends. The sources of these beliefs were not found only in the
Politics, as Hayek has pointed out in his sketch of the history
of the concept of *isonomea.* Locke, for one, took Polybius and
converted the mixed constitution of aristocratically republican
Rome and used it to justify a revolution. But the revolution was
one which resulted in another sort of aristocratic republic, and
the same can be said of the plans of Washington and Adams.
Coke and Locke, it is pretty much agreed today, were very conservative liberals.

Conservative liberalism was the hallmark of Whig ideology,
the predominant political belief of the age which Locke and
Newton influenced. Any characterization of a period must be
somewhat cavalier, for of course there are always those underlying differences of opinion which make up the circle of political
thought. But the years from 1685 to 1787 do form a rather coherent time, to which the term "Whig" may be affixed.

The term "Whig" arose out of the rough scurrilousness of
seventeenth-century English politics, but its characteristics were
very different—an urbane regard for form mixed with a deep concern for civil liberties. With all its hypocrisies, the Whig ideology
is the closest political equivalent to the rationalist philosophy of
the Enlightenment, its protector and disciple.

The constituent elements of this body of thought have been
frequently described. The mixed constitution, with checks and
balances, an independent judiciary and a free legislature, and a
system of at least partly-free elections were customary parts of
the platform. The rights of property (and this increasingly
meant commercial property) were stressed, and the autonomy
of property rights as against the power of the state was a cardinal

principle. Above all, the individual liberties of speech, the press, and especially religion, were increasingly advocated as parts of a wider system of liberty. With these the rights of free movement, both geographically and occupationally, and greater opportunity, especially for members of the middle class, were joined with the older and more political guarantees. It was in respect to all these liberties of man against the state or against what often was felt as hopeless remnants of the feudal past that the Whig tradition became most liberal, but this was at most a guarded form of protest, and even comparatively radical Whigs like the Duke of Richmond drew the line at any steps interfering with private property.

This is, of course, a cliché of intellectual history. The course of eighteenth-century intellectual development has been described so well by Hazard, Brogan, Cassirer, Laski, Manuel and many others that it would be of no value to outline further the road from the English Bill of Rights to the American one. The eighteenth century was not a time of only one idea or of only one or two thinkers, and of course the term "Whig" is not perfectly appropriate when considering Diderot, or Catherine the Great.

But Diderot and the enlightened (or perhaps not enlightened) despots were very much part of this current. The activism of the Encyclopaedists and the efficiency of Frederick the Great and Pombal were not so very different from the quietism of Namierian England. In all cases there was at least lip service paid to the almost holy propositions of individual freedom and the separation of private rights from public authority. The former was grounded on natural law; and here the great difference from the ancient ideas came in making those natural laws apply most, as Constant was to observe, not to the citizen as citizen but to the man as an individual. The state was to have limited powers, but here there was no such unanimity, and while the English Whigs, representing the truest advocates of the Whig spirit, complained that the power of the Crown "has increased, was increasing, and ought to be diminished" their confreres across the Channel were likely to be augmenting that power to destroy feudalism or eliminate the Jesuits. The difference, as the case of Joseph II illustrated, was in method rather than objective, for if the power of the government was strengthened, it was (at least in theory) to amplify the liberty of the individual. The model of Beccaria and Verri was England, however, where it was not paradoxically necessary to strengthen state power to increase the freedom of the individual.

But, as always, behind this paradox lie deeper ones, which increasingly came to light during the eighteenth century. The great and growing wealth of the countries of Western Europe made possible a polish and urbanity perhaps never before seen, a grandeur of manner and a civility of style influencing not only the courts and cathedrals, but whole segments of society. Elegance was probably the characteristic quality of much of eighteenth-century living, and an elegance not merely restricted to ceremonial or pageantry but suffusing the whole culture. At the least it gave inspiration to the rococo, which for all its insipidities did produce Watteau and Pope. At the best the rococo was truly classical, as in music. When one hears the symphonies Haydn composed for Les Concerts de la Loge Olympique it is possible to understand Talleyrand's famous comment that no one who had not lived before the Revolution could know how fine life could be.

But not for everyone. The price of this concentration on elegance and beauty was a disdain or, at least, unconcern, for the inelegant and ugly, which encompassed most of the population. Nef has shown how the emphasis on quality and form tended to cut off the bottom sectors of society from the well-being and even the thinking of the age. War was exceptionally civilized, and the officer class behaved with unusual decorum and gentility, but the lot of the common soldier was quite hard, and wars were as frequent as ever. If you were an officer, you were part of the community of arms which possessed an almost Stoic virtue; if you were a private, that was your choice (usually) and your misfortune. This was true of too many other parts of society; Dickens was right when he remarked that it was the best of times and the worst of times.

In many ways this was marvelously Aristotelian, but it was not consistent with the more liberal side of Whiggism. Locke and Voltaire despite all their conservatism held liberal conclusions which inspired ideas which went beyond the limitations of the old Whigs. There were ideas implicit in the social contract of Locke's *Second Treatise* and in the description of republican virtue in Montesquieu's *Spirit of the Laws* which were definitely left of center. In France these suggestions of radicalism had an uncertain history dating from the sixteenth century; in England the legacy of the Civil Wars was a stream of left-wing ideology which never vanished. The belief that the poorest he that lived in England had a life to live as the richest he was implicit in much of the thinking of 1689, even if it required 1789 to make it explicit.

The rise of democracy is a trite tale, and much of the discussion revolves around the beginnings. Laski wrote Holmes that he fixed the start with the *Vindiciae Contra Tyrannos*, whereas Morley allegedly replied that it began with the rise of Joseph Chamberlain. Cleon might be an equally respectable candidate. But in terms of the history of modern political thought Laski's choice was a fine one. The freethinkers of the late sixteenth century—Hotman, Ponet, the author of the *Vindiciae* (if he be a different man) in some ways led to the Whig version of the social contract, but in other ways they led to the Rousseauan social contract, to democracy. As this movement developed during the eighteenth century it resulted in a much more radical consideration of the original contract, making universal suffrage a permanent part of the system of government, not a commencing feature to be abandoned, and questioned the historical institutions which the Whigs had calmly accepted, kings, aristocrats, churches, even property. History, it is now increasingly agreed, was by no means a stranger to the philosophy of much of the eighteenth century; Voltaire was a firm adherent of the historical view and Montesquieu's thinking was suffused with concern for historical patterns. For the great change came when the utopias became more utopian, less timebound. The change from Montesquieu to Rousseau was the converse of that from Plato to Aristotle—the move away from history and from balance, the transformation of the center of thought from the lower circle to the upper circle.

Rousseau's radicalism was intermittent and not always consistent, but Rousseau was not alone. Talmon has sketched the rise of totalitarian democracy in the works of Mably and Morelly, the precursors of Jacobinism and of Babeuf. Condorcet, who was no Jacobin, was certainly also not a Whig, and his conception of consistent progress conceived of history in a sharply different sense than, say, Gibbon. As this suggests, these differences were not necessarily ones of chronology, although certainly the pace of radical thought increased after mid-century. The left/right disagreements, as always, divided men of the same time, and the men who in England were content with the settlement of 1689 or who in France or Austria sought for a constitutional state on the English model found (especially after 1750) that the argument was not merely with the Jesuits and Jacobites but with the forerunners of Jacobins.

As in so many situations where new political configurations shift the patterns of thought, this made for new ironies. The Whig world-view reflected a beautiful lower-center ideology, which started with aggressively liberal premises to reach frequently quite conservative conclusions. In calling this thought Aristotelian an inevitable comparison is made with the political, and other, philosophy of the later Middle Ages. McIlwain has pointed out the roots of the constitutional thinking of the American Constitution in some of the limited-government assumptions of Fortescue and the Counciliarists. The absolute prohibitions on the power of kings and other rulers in the Middle Ages probably derived principally from the logic of the feudal system, but it also bore the imprint of Aristotelian moderation. McIlwain commented that the medieval idea of constitutionalism was one of limited government, whereas the moderns have added the concept of controlled government—of government by the people as well as for them. The Whig idea is somewhat in between. Like the medieval political thinkers, Locke desired a government whose principal attribute was in its limitations. But there was an important difference. In the earlier scheme of things the power of the ruler was absolute in its sphere (witness the development of the prerogative), but each level of society had its separate rights and privileges which limited the nature of that above and below. The Inquisition in thirteenth-century France was bloody by any standards, but the power of the Church, or of the kings in or out of Parliament to tax could only go so far. Egidius Romanus' hierarchy of dominions assigned various far-reaching powers to the several authorities, but beyond the powers no one could stray, no matter how important they were, without changing their rightful authority into a species of tyranny, a lawless power.

The construction of the Constitution at Philadelphia in 1787 —that gem of Whig thinking—also had a scale of powers, divided between the federal government and the state governments. But all powers not allocated to the governments were reserved in the Bill of Rights to the people. And the ten amendments which were adopted so quickly as to become almost an intrinsic part of the Constitution, spelled out the hard-won eighteenth-century individual guarantees—right of trial by jury, right to bear arms, right against self-incrimination, protection against unlawful search and seizure, and the more general guarantees of freedom of speech, press, religion, and assembly. The rights secured by the Magna Charta, with a few famous exceptions, were privileges usually reserved to specific groups. But the Bill of Rights determined on broader rights, protecting everyone. At the same time, the state was stronger, and in essence it could act without regard for traditional restrictions or overlapping jurisdictions. Above all, it was rooted in a proclamation of universal significance—the Declaration of Independence—and established by a rational decision. The Whig limitations were flexible, not rigid, designed to distinguish public from private power, not to freeze the various forms of power into a set system.

But it was this very rationalism which undercut the dichotomy between the liberalism of the premises and the conservatism of the results. Universal suffrage came quickly in America; perhaps it had always been there, in effect if not in form. The American

Revolution was not very revolutionary, but its successors were. Somehow the Declaration itself—pure Locke mixed with a sedate recital of breaches of customary law by a despot—created a democratic force which went very far beyond Locke. The natural law of Pufendorf or John Adams was flexible in the Aristotelian tradition; in Germany, significantly, it was frequently flexible to the point of insipidity. Montesquieu was very much a relativist, but much of the lower-center thinking of his age paid a weak lip service to the fundamental laws. The democratic thinkers took the mild adherence to the rights of men, to virtue, republican or otherwise, and put life into them, until Burke awoke to discover that much of his intellectual heritage had been transfigured. It was as if a man had ridden a horse every morning for years in a calm fashion, trotting gracefully down the block. One morning he discovered a frenzied jockey using his thoroughbred animal as a racing horse, hurtling walls which he had often halfheartedly talked of jumping and even trying to scale walls which he had considered unassailable. Robespierre was much more of an absolutist than Turgot, although in theory they had much in common. The heavenly city of the eighteenth-century philosophers came to resemble Augustine's city more, and Aquinas' less. Above all, it owed something to Wat Tyler as well.

In a subtler way Adam Smith was as subversive as Condorcet. The rise of economics as a separate branch of thought was quite independent of the industrial revolution, but they coincided in effect as well as in time. It is now a stale joke that the bourgeoisie had been rising since the twelfth century, but somehow they had never arisen. One very important reason for this was that the descendants of the successful merchant would become landowners and soon established noblemen. It is instructive to note that the ancestors of Lord Melbourne and of the Princes Torlonia were, not very far back, solicitors and merchants. This, obviously, did not cease in the eighteenth century, but it was no longer so inevitable. The upshot of the work of Smith and Hume was a different outlook on the world, a heightened consideration of the place of the business class. This was no revolution, and the earlier apostles of profit were not critical of, or outwardly dangerous to, the Whig idea. Mercantilism fit into the system of Colbert and of de Witt, and even de Mandeville could be considered a very clever propagandist for the world of the Duke of Newcastle. But the calculating view of the economist imposed a rationalism which inspired more radical interpretations, and the very issue of national wealth and social distribution encouraged the forces on the left side of the Whig system.

If Smith and the Physiocrats were unsettling, the steam engine and the cotton jenny were more so. A period of accelerating innovations is most hospitable to the adherents of uppercircle ideas, and especially (in times following conservative entrenchment) to radicals. By the end of the eighteenth century the troubling changes, especially the demographic upheavals, concerned many men, and not only conservatives, as Jefferson's fears indicate. The industrial revolution was of course one of the seminal developments in human history; it is remarkable, however, how little immediate effect it had on politics and political thought. The landed aristocracy continued to supply the great majority of English leaders long after Watt and Arkwright were dead, and what was true of Britain was much more true in the less developed lands of the Continent. The poets of significance were romantics, not the bizarre idolators of the locomotive, and neither Blake nor Ingres took much interest in cotton mills.

But indirectly the economic and technological changes certainly did influence, or at least affect, the thinking and culture of the West. The first statesmen to be influenced by the new currents were rightist—Pitt the Younger and Hamilton. The pressure of financial calculation and the industrial milieu affected first the men of efficiency in politics, who tended to be then as now conservative. But the early thinkers of the new age were not so uniformly sound. Some, like Ricardo, were conservative in their pessimism but in some ways distinctly radical (especially in regard to their attitude toward landed property). Others, such as Saint-Simon and his disciples, fused the optimism of Condorcet with the new techniques of industry to devise political and economic philosophies of increasingly subversive nature.

Perhaps Bentham and the Benthamites were the most significant of this group.

Jeremy Bentham began his career as a prudent penal reformer, and he never allied himself with truly radical groups, but by the time of his death in 1832 the imprint of utilitarianism had erased a large part of the Whig spirit. The hedonistic calculus measured all institutions and customs with a strictness which, although it lacked the animus of the French revolutionary zeal, accomplished more lasting results. The results were leftward, for the very idea of the greatest good of the greatest number tended to instill a popular bias to utilitarian beliefs. The famous controversy between James Mill, Bentham's chief follower, and Macaulay, the perfect Nineteenth-century Whig, over universal suffrage was a case in point. The fiercely scientific and democratic utilitarian won, and Macaulay ended his career worrying over the government and spirit of the United States, that very utilitarian nation, which possessed, he thought, too much rudder and too little ballast. The future of the mid-century seemed to be securely in the hands of the rising liberal intellectuals like Mill's brilliant son.

Between the young Bentham and Mill the Younger the French Revolution had taken place. The Revolution was one of the great watersheds of Western history which, however, has always signified more than it produced. In one sense all political thought since 1789 has been very different from that which went before; the very slogan of liberty, equality, and fraternity arose from the Revolution. Revolution itself, as Malraux observed, became a legitimate part of politics, converting the mild theory of social contract into a dangerous dynamic of social organization. The feudal way of thinking was effectively doomed in, if not a few months in 1789, at least a few years. The Revolution began with the cahiers and Mirabeau, but it rapidly graduated to Saint-Just and Robespierre, and then made Babeuf possible, and, in another sense, brought forward the Whig Toryism of Burke and the pure reaction of de Maistre and DeBonald. Julien Sorel was very much different from Figaro, and the debates in Parliament on expanding the suffrage in the 1830's were much more "modern" than the debates on the same subject in the 1780's or even the 1790's. An assurance had come to the masses of the people, and had been drained from the upper class. The four principles of popular control of government, of widespread state-administered education, of economic and social opportunity for everyone, and of the elimination of all legal class distinctions were the legacy of the French Revolution. They were not successful in 1815, nor even by 1850, but in each decade they became less revolutionary and more accepted, until by the end of the century their merits became the assurances of conservatives rather than the watchwords of liberals. Democracy changed from an exciting and radical motto to a cliché of all respectable countries, and 1789 (but not of course 1793) became a date revered by everyone, at least by everyone in Protestant or secular lands. All this happened first and most thoroughly in America, and last and least in Russia.

And yet this remarkable triumph of democracy, springing forth from the embers of the fires of the French Revolution, burnt down so very little of the Whig edifice. The great upsurge of the bourgoisie did not overturn the values of the eighteenth century, but placed a new class alongside the old. The demise of the old merchant aristocracies may have followed the path of Buddenbrooks, but the new ones, more aggressive and numerous, settled down to a system little different. The Revolution brought forth Stendahl, but also Balzac, and the July Monarchy was a splendid case of resurgent Whiggery. Guizot and Webster lost out to Napoleon III and Jackson, but if the parties of democracy or Bonapartism talked a different game, their net differences were not really very great. Even the far left, as Brogan observed, was much more concerned with priests than with bankers.

The Victorian age was a time for bankers, and the political qualities which had developed in the eighteenth century were basically the same ones which suited the nineteenth. The protection of individuals against government power, the protection of property rights, and the establishment of representative legislatures were pursued at least as vigilantly as before. The individualist bias of the eighteenth century was intensified by the nineteenth. In short, the dominant motif of the lower circle, which had emerged sometime around 1700, remained the chief theme of the times. As Franklin Ford has commented, "it has seemed increasingly difficult to take very seriously any departure from the basic premises bequeathed by the giants Hazard treats until, at the turn of our own century, Einstein repudiated Newton, while Locke's ideas were assaulted on the political front by Vilfredo Pareto and Nikolai Lenin, allies in nothing else, and on the psychological, by Sigmund Freud."

Was, then, the French Revolution really not important? Ford goes on in his analysis to deny that interpretation, considering in the main the democratic and calculating tendencies already referred to. The upheavals of the end of the eighteenth century created these divergent strains; but the great accomplishment of the nineteenth century was to synthesize them. To most thinking people in the Victorian age the legacy of Locke and the legacy of Rousseau were combined to become a rich and undisturbed inheritance.

The most conservative features of this intellectual heritage were perhaps the easiest to absorb. The eighteenth century had, as we have seen, treasured property rights and historic privileges. The medieval dominium became a private right, jealously preserved from the imperium of state power. Even revolutionaries were solicitous of private property. During the American Revolution there was great care taken to acquire in Pennsylvania only those properties owned by the Penn family in their capacity as proprietors, and to leave undisturbed any holdings possessed in a private capacity. Even the French revolutionaries displayed this concern; the chateau of Chenonceaux was not confiscated because it was discovered that the mansion had clearly been private property in the sixteenth century! The *enragés* have seemed especially important to Marxist historians in our times, but the normal liberal thrust of the eighteenth century was, as Salvemini remarked, one directed toward the protection of private rights, including property rights, against the power of the state or the Church.

This became the watchword of the century which started in 1815, but with a difference. The vast economic opportunities and the formally egalitarian (equal as to opportunity, of course) ethos served to make the idea of private property a much more aggressive and popular belief. Guizot's famous advice—enrich yourself—was the program of Carnegie and the religion of Samuel Smiles. Hurst has shown how, in the United States at least (and this was to a lesser degree true in almost all of Europe) the emphasis on free enterprise was not due to a belief in laissez faire, but was caused by a very different conviction that individual energies, supported by the tacit backing of the state, was the best way to achieve the good life. To de Tocqueville this rugged individualism was the wave of the future, and he commented on the consistency between the weakness of the traditional institutions of centralized coercion and the plethora of voluntary groups. Equality was not forgotten, but even on the far left it often served as a support for liberty.

It is a cliché now that perhaps the most important liberty which developed was a liberty with quite conservative overtones, the liberty of contract. The greatest contribution of classical economics, after it had reached the stature of being classical, was this strong advocacy of freedom of contract. The British systematically brought this idea to India, the Germans incorporated much of it into their philosophy of the legal state, the Austrians refined it into one of the bases of neoclassical economics, and the Americans systematically incorporated it into the Constitution, enveloping corporations and freedmen equally under its wing. Even the Communards of 1871 were timid in transgressing this vital freedom.

Myriads of leftist commentators have poured scorn on this fervent faith in such a commercial liberty, a faith which increasingly, as the nineteenth century neared its close, was used by creators of large business aggregations. But this liberty was intellectually allied with other liberties, and with a Whig environment of individual choice as part of a broad individualistic movement. The abolition of serfdom in Russia and of slavery in the United States and Brazil were also by-products of the belief in freedom of contract. It is now noted with regret that the freedom of movement throughout the world reached its apogee in the eighteenth and nineteenth centuries, culminating in an almost complete abolition of passports and visas. The distinction between the forms which this freedom took in the two centuries is instructive. The grand tour was perhaps easiest in the days of Sterne, but for the masses of travelers, and even more for the greater masses of immigrants and emigrants, the latter half of the nineteenth century was the time of maximum opportunity. But toward 1914 greater restrictions on immigration began to arise just as the technological facilities improved greatly, thus foreshadowing our century.

Something of the same tendency can be seen in military relations. In the years before the French Revolution wars were, as has been noted, rather frequent but usually gentlemanly. But the goal of the nineteenth century was not merely a convention to assuage the rigors of war, but a comity in which wars would not take place. This was not achieved, of course, and one must remember that the 1860's, that most Victorian decade, was marked by two German wars, Italian internal and external violence, the bloody American Civil War and the (comparatively) even bloodier war which almost wiped out the population of Paraguay. It is significant that most of these were in one form or another civil wars; the violence of internal friction erupted beneath the increasing acceptance of the value of international peace. But the years after 1870 were remarkable for the prevalence of peace. It must be remembered that these were great years of capitalist development; the road from Cobden to Angell was one which emphasized the connection between the profit mentality of Manchester and the hatred (or better, unprofitability) of war. Perpetual peace was not a dream, but a possibility for social action, just as the whole area of foreign policy was no longer reserved for the attention of rulers and a small diplomatic class but increasingly became a subject for parliamentary debate and popular agitation. The Diplomatic Revolution of 1756 was a jewel of elegant intrigue and management, quite contemporary in spirit if not in result with the libretto of *Cosi Fan Tutte.* The peace of Europe may have been preserved in 1863 by the Rothschilds, but there is no doubt that the Midlothian stump speeches of Gladstone altered the balance of power in 1880. The middle-class gravity of the Victorians was probably implicit in the individualism of the age of Mozart, but no one would mistake Isolde for Tamina. And so when war came it was fiercer and less conventional than it had been before Valmy.

This is an explanation for the spread of conscription in the nineteenth century. This practice, which had been introduced in modern times by Frederick William I of Prussia and utilized on a large scale by the French revolutionaries, became a common feature on the Continent in the late nineteenth century. At first blush there was a striking inconsistency between conscription and the prevailing libertarianism, and this did serve to keep the draft out of England and the United States. But on the European continent every self-respecting country considered conscription necessary. Since the protection of national liberty was the responsibility of the whole people the freedom of the individual gave way to the greater national freedom.

The surge of nationalism was thus closely related to the entrepreneurial achievements of the time. Private rights and individual freedom were means, and were cherished not for themselves but for the wealth and power they produced. Perhaps this was an inevitable result of the widening of the ideals of the Whig tradition; as they became more all-inclusive and more concrete, as they were changed from ideals into facts, they were compromised. In some degree the compromise took the form of reducing the idea of liberty to a rather doctrinaire opposition to any government action in the field of economics. Above all, the legacy of Aristotelian respect for the state became a basis for nationalist faiths rather than Whig accomodations. In some ways this took an ironical form. The anarchist tradition of the French revolutionary times, the spirit of Godwin was transmitted through Hodgskin to Spencer, who started as a radical land reformer and ended as a high priest of capitalism. On the other hand, the depth of regard for human freedom which impelled

Mazzini led to a cult of national freedom, in which the adjective "national" threatened to become more important than the noun "freedom."

The nineteenth century experience of monopolies or nationalist movements did not shatter these forms of individualist optimism; this was largely left to a later age. But the images of a *juste milieu* were altered long before the problems of our century came to the fore. Most of the thinkers of the nineteenth century prized reason as much as the men of the preceding period, but their regard was subtly (and sometimes not so subtly) different. The brilliant analysis of Maine treating the development of civilization as a progress from status to contract was a triumphant vindication of the Whig emphasis on the rational determination of living human beings rather than the irrational cake of custom. But it is indicative that the Lockeans had concerned themselves with the social contract, whereas Maine was interested in the state almost solely as an arbiter of private contracts, perhaps divorcing the state from reason. And, in considering Spencer and Maine, it is impossible to ignore Darwin. There was little human reason in Darwin, but a great deal of the reason of history. There was something impersonal in the rationality of the Newtonian universe, too, but that cosmos could be understood by the intelligent man and used as a guide to the *recta ratio* that measured all activity. There was always a somewhat upper-class tinge to this. The Darwinian principles compelled everyone, even in spite of themselves, to be a part of history. The expansion of interest in history in the nineteenth century was explosive, and in the writings of Hegel and of Bancroft it took on an almost divine quality. But the circular paradox was implicit in this development, for as reason became incorporated into history the aggrandizement of reason became a search for a mystical perfection, with the danger of denuding reason of the human rational element and of using history to find messianic solutions. Both Marx and the German National Liberals accepted the premises of human reason and historical progress, but Marx evolved a theory of determinism leading

to a perfect society, and the National Liberals cheerfully subordinated their liberalism to the Bismarckian system of a strong
state and government interference with the economy.

The Germans, of course, had never really been very ardent
for individualism in politics. But it was not merely in Germany
that something changed after 1870. The great wave of individualism, which had seemed to increase in strength and universal
appeal from generation to generation, met new opposition everywhere, and an increasing opposition. The instrumental character
of the Victorian beliefs in individual action required that this
action be successful; if not, there were no scruples for changing
the formula. The utilitarians were, as a rule, very much believers
in private action, because this was the most efficient way of
improving mankind. Their intellectual children, the pragmatists,
were not so individualistic, because by 1900, as Keynes suggested,
the government was a much more honest and reliable tool of
social action. It was all a question, in William James' terms, of
which paid the most. It was not merely that the utilitarians and
pragmatists were relativists, although this was certainly true.
Montesquieu had been pretty much of a relativist, but his conservatism and his eighteenth-century sense of the possible restricted his willingness to experiment.

In 1850 even radicals frequently believed that the less state
action took place, the better chance there was for a better society.
But, somehow, by 1870 even many liberals were growing to
doubt this. Perhaps the very fact that the years after 1850
marked the first time that the technological changes of the industrial revolution paid unmistakable dividends in a higher standard
of living for the working class of Western Europe and America
whetted the appetite of the left. At any rate, the leftist intellectuals, having accepted individualism as a tool for progress (and
this meant increasingly material progress) tended to opt for
speeding the process up. Marx was, of course, the seminal figure
in this change, but by the seventies many much timider souls
were supporting various forms of collectivist public policy. The
successors of Francis Place were soon amazed at the meagerness
of his vision.

This had been implicit in Place and his cohorts, however. Dicey's famous demonstration of the erosion of individualism after 1870 has been shown to have been incomplete. Parris has pointed out that Benthamism had a collectivistic as well as an individualistic side, and that Dicey himself had observed the measures passed under utilitarian aegis or administration which enhanced the power of the central government. In a way Chadwick and the factory inspectors were the heirs of Bentham, the Bentham whom Parris called "the archetype of British collectivism." In the United States the vigor of local governments in supporting and regulating economic endeavors had not, as Hartz and Handlin have revealed, ever been frustrated by laissez-faire ideology.

But this was usually the doing of Whigs, not democrats. Bentham himself, however much a collectivist he may paradoxically be termed, did advocate an elimination of the usury laws. In many respects the attitude toward these laws was a barometer of the spirit of the times, for it was the work of reformers like Bentham that had secured the repeal or curtailment of these statutes, as a part of the large program of terminating the ancient and outworn restrictions on freedom of choice. But no sooner had the laws been repealed when opinion on the left moved once again to press for their re-enactment or revitalization. It was not the Marxists who had the greatest effect on thinking in the late nineteenth century, but the more moderate liberals— the Socialists of the Chair in Germany, the Fabians in England, Ely and Ward in the United States. They did not choose a thoroughgoing collectivist policy, but they were troubled by the outcome of that movement which Nelson has defined—from tribal brotherhood to universal otherhood. It was not the expectations or premises of the Victorian individualists that, in the main, they rejected, but only the methods by which these were reached. To Bentham and to Henry Clay the material well-being of the great majority was the final criterion while Spencer had pushed this to the point of becoming almost an anarchist utopian. The next generation of liberals (and some conservatives) retained the faith in democracy and in material progress (while the aging

Spencer correspondingly despaired), but increasingly the promise of American life, of all life, was believed to subsist in forms of social action, above all in state action.

Conservatives were already deploring this in the 1860's. By 1914 anyone speaking persistently of the dangers of big government was clearly marked as a rightist. To be sure, the stalwart opponents of state intervention in economic affairs still classed themselves as "liberals," but the designation always required inverted commas. Liberalism, in our sense, denoted advocacy of more government intervention, and the cause of radicalism boiled down to the one cause of socialism. The British Liberal party, heir of the Whigs and the very model of the Victorian liberal spirit, traveled along this road with a beautiful simplicity. By the end of his career Gladstone was talking about having the state create the conditions which would make equality of opportunity really equal. That was a long way from his earlier program of eliminating the income tax; by the time of the Lloyd George Budget and Winston Churchill's social-security measures the party of Palmerstone was almost unrecognizable. The very first measure of the Campbell-Bannerman government was the act to relieve trade unions of many legal liabilities, a move which Dicey—and almost all conservatives—considered the pure negation of the rule of law.

This different attitude toward the rule of law involved a new view of the law itself. As has been remarked, there was a distinctly relativist leaning in utilitarianism and in the economic thinking of the contractual thinkers. This too was largely retained by the post-1870 liberals, and extended. The traditional certainties (such as the Bible) were no longer certain, and to these the nineteenth-century certainties were added. Sumner rejected the traditional beliefs of religious orthodoxy; his pupil Veblen added to this rejection the whole apparatus of capitalist thinking. This relativism took many forms. In the Anglo-American legal domain the thinking of Holmes, who was not a liberal, was extremely powerful in overthrowing much of the body of natural-law thinking; on the Continent armies of legal positivists did their best to equal the accomplishment. The beneficiary of

Holmesian thought was not tough-minded conservatism, but two generations of liberals. The revolt against formalism, to use White's term, broke down the forms which, to so many, preserved a reactionary and unthinking privileged class.

The vocabulary of the revolt was electrifying, the results were not, before 1914, up to Veblen's hopes or Halsbury's fears. For one thing, the prosperity and peace of the years before 1914 prevented the shift in opinion from turning from a revolt to a revolution. In considering the liberalism of the early years of the century it is necessary to keep it in perspective. This was also the heyday of imperialism—it is wise to remember that modern imperialism is not some old vestige, but a phenomenon which dates from the 1870's and reached its peak in this century. The decade of the Asquith reforms and the Square Deal was the Edwardian decade. The wealth and elegance of that time was strikingly reminiscent of the 1780's. Once again great wealth and culture seemed to make upper-class life a form of earthly paradise, and once again this took place at the very time that intellectual currents were moving turbulently leftwards. To a surface observer the world of the Webbs was much harder to find than the world described in the novels of Sackville-West and painted by Sargent.

And of course on the surface the world of the Webbs was not so novel. Had Francis Place lived in 1900 he would surely have been a Fabian. The change from Whig to utilitarian was much greater, in some ways, than the change from utilitarian to Fabian. Thus the great accomplishment in Britain of the Whigs in the area of free speech was perhaps the Fox Libel Act of 1792, completing a century of agitation against the power of judicial control. Nothing quite comparable was secured in the next century; perhaps the closest thing was the substantial reduction in taxes enacted by the mid-century liberals, which greatly expanded the opportunity for the dissemination of news and opinions. Both acts were in the direction of reducing governmental interference with free expression, but the first was a formal protection, revising the power and especially the locus of state control. The second was economic and/or social, and in a subtle way the weight shifted from a guarantee of individual rights under law to an encouragement of individual opportunties. The liberals of 1900 were also concerned with the potential of enhancing these opportunities, but through, and not despite, the state. Increased education and anti-monopoly measures were more to the new way of thinking than battles against censorship, although of course the latter were still fought (and in many places lost). A sea change was taking place, but very gradually.

What was true in Britain or the United States was, *a fortiori*, true in Germany or Russia. The state had never been much deprecated in Germany, so it was natural for liberalism to become increasingly a collectivist faith. And of course in Russia most of the period of bourgois liberalism had been skipped, to the embarrassment of Marxist theoreticians and to the inconvenience of Kadet politicians. Even in France the authoritarian and collectivist influence of Comte, although it had been overcome by the predominant influences of the time, had been much more persuasive than it, or its copies, could ever be in the common-law countries. Once the tide began to flow the other way, the forces of continental collectivism—the ideal of solidarity, the cult of the state, innumerable varieties of socialism—gained ground rapidly from Iberia to Siberia. Settembrini, the symbol of the waning older liberalism, predicted to Castorp the coming of the Portuguese revolution of 1910, but even that, so reminiscent of 1830 or 1848, had social overtones as congenial to Naptha as to Settembrini. Mann, in the early 1920's, awarded the prize in the battle for the mind of the coming generation to the Jesuit, and the next quarter-century would certainly vindicate his decision. The changes in thought went much deeper than the slow movement of everyday politics.

The political disputation in *The Magic Mountain* is especially fine because it casts in the role of the twentieth-century fanatic not a radical lover of humanity, but a splendidly complex figure of the upper circle, part radical and part reactionary. Before 1914, and to a large degree even afterwards, it sometimes seemed as if the forces of change would benefit the far left almost exclusively. This was not so, and the development of right-wing thought, often overlooked when the political processes seemed to constantly veer toward liberalism or beyond, was very striking in the decades after 1880. The updated royalism of Maurras and the renovated cyclical thinking of Leontiev were of a familiar sort, although imbued with a new vigor. But Paretian elitism or the various racist beliefs were newer and more potent. Within the reformist milieu of the prewar years a new spirit, newer even than that of 1870, was coming about.

It is of interest that Freud and Spengler were Germanic. Spengler, who conceived the idea of *The Decline of the West* in 1911, had been preceded by the British archaeologist Flinders Petrie, whose *Revolutions of Civilizations* contained most of Spengler's basic ideas. Petrie loosely interpreted his cycles as patterns of historic behavior, but his German successor elaborated upon these tendencies so as to create an inflexible rule of life which absolutely forbade meaningful human progress. The latent conservatism of late Victorian England was changed into a powerful reactionary ideology which not merely explained the problems of the Seleucids, but also voted against the German Social Democratic party.

The case of Freud is more complex and perhaps more important, but essentially very similar. In the late nineteenth century Frazer had laid the groundwork for much of modern cultural anthropology, and in so doing had defined a world very different from that of most of his contemporaries. To Frazer the most important event in human history was the seasonal death of vegetation and fertility, and its rebirth. The reaction of primitive men throughout the world to this supremely vital annual crisis took the form of magic and religion; it was invariably an irrational reaction. The step from the ritual murder of the old king to the Oedipal murder of the father was a natural one, but it went much farther. The sea of unreasoning, frequently evil impulses broke through into the historical periods not dimly, as in Frazer, but powerfully, and affected everyone in their subconscious. The facts of sex were paramount, and gravely disturbing. There have been many liberal Freudians, but the liberation they preach is always ambiguous, and the work of the master persistently shows signs of the fears of human nature which he always held. The vile potentialities of the hidden urges of Freudian man are as frightening as an H. G. Wells horror fantasy (also the work of an ambivalent pre-1914 thinker, a Fabian with a mad imagination) and as upsetting as the conjectures of Frazer. The tribal order of Maine—that status-bound archaic community—was the subject of *The Golden Bough*, but Freud found its psychology in every man, and Jung found its irrational memories everywhere, unforgettable and wild. While socialists were assaulting the rational contractual society, the new psychologists were undermining the foundations. Whereas most of the left complained capitalism was not rational enough (there were exceptions even here, such as Veblen with his instincts), the attack on the right against reason itself was probably even deadlier.

This is the combination which Ford, as quoted before, considered a new crisis of the European conscience. It was a crisis which disrupted the arts at least as savagely as it had the political arena. It is a commonplace reflection today that almost all of the arts were altered almost beyond recognition between 1890 and 1914. One can barely visualize Frank Lloyd Wright in the 1880's, or T. S. Eliot, but Kandinsky or Stravinsky are impossible to imagine. Abstract painting and sculpture were the most perfect expression of anti-rationalism one could conceive. The innumerable busts of the eighteenth century were succeeded, as in the Rodin Museum, by bodies without heads. By 1914 the rising painting had pictures without heads, bodies, or anything else one could identify; soon Klee and Mondrian would paint pictures which even the most enthusiastic backer of Whistler or Monet, in the 1880's, would have very likely refused to call art.

This revolution in art was not political, and cannot be placed upon the political circle. However, there were striking parallels between the artistic and political developments. Abstract or representational, the painting of the West after 1910 had a starkness which contrasted to the innocence of the previous years. Just as the nineteenth century system of international capitalism seems today a kind of utopianism, so both the romanticism of

Ingres and the impressionism of Manet and Renoir appear intensely innocent today. It is not that the painting reflected a faith in capitalism or progress—Courbet and Degas are evidence to the contrary—but that there is a parallel in the disparate fields which can be traced despite the most different circumstances.

Such a parallel can be discerned in the history of reason in Western political thought and the use of light in Western art. Light has traditionally represented the spirit of human goodness and sanity, as in Zoroastrianism. But its role in medieval painting was circumscribed; in Byzantine and pre-fourteenth-century works the golden halos served as a kind of distilled light, the physical equivalent of human reason, the inferior replica of the bounteous divine light. This was quite similar to the role of human reason in Aquinas and other scholastics; reason had its place in medieval philosophy, an important place, but it was always firmly limited and controlled by divine law as known through faith. The artistic revolution of the Renaissance—beginning in the fourteenth century—brought light and reason into their own, as prime forces. It was not entirely a coincidence that Pico and Botticelli were contemporaries, or that the century and habitat of Van Eyck was that of Flemish capitalism. The rationalism of Erasmus and Reuchlin expanded the humanist world in much the same way as Piero's light—always that of the noonday sun—and Carpaccio's Venetian warmth marked a new vision. The gloom of Bosch and El Greco was, like that of the Spanish monarchs, ominous, but time was on the side of the Dutch. The parallel between the amazing victory of the bourgeois, commercial, thoroughly reasoning civilization of seventeenth-century Holland and the light of Vermeer is edifying. As the constant, reassuring beams of the sun pour into the middle-class homes of Delft to brighten the lives of burghers' wives and their efficient servants, the shift from status to contract can be seen as the procession from Ravenna to the Low Countries.

In more absolutist lands the seventeenth-century light is more furtive (as with Caravaggio or LaTour) but perhaps more piercing; this is true of Rembrandt also, whose light only half-shares the rationalism of his age. The next century carries on from Vermeer and Descartes, not from Rembrandt and Hobbes. The culmination in 1787 and 1789 has been traced; in painting light triumphs equally with Fragonard and Tiepolo. Perhaps no painter ever so apotheosized light as Tiepolo did, and his late-eighteenth-century visions of perfection were almost like illustrations of the inner soul of Becker's heavenly city of the philosophers. The nineteenth century did not renounce light, as it did not decry reason; both the pre-Raphaelites and the plein-air schools sought to extend its use. But this extension of light, like the similar expansion of the domain of reason, perhaps lost in purity what it gained in practicality. After 1860 the impressionists subordinated light to color. By the end of the century the rays of the sun, and its visual effects, were conveyed in painting largely by blobs of color, by concentrations of images which showed the result much more than the appearance of light. In philosophy Cartesian rationalism was retreating under the attacks of experimental beliefs—pragmatism and behaviorism, for example—which studied the results of human choice instead of commencing with the idea of reason itself. The very idea of a fixed reason, of *recta ratio*, became very old-fashioned by 1900.

With the coming of abstract art light almost disappears. Picasso had many periods, but none of them could be called "light periods." Even in fashionable portraits the backdrop became gray or even, as with Sutherland, menacing—the ambiance of even millionaires or debutantes excluded the sun. There are exceptions, of course, but it is very little exaggeration to state that since 1914 light has had almost no place in world painting (for Western painting has, through some syncretism and more conquest, become international); the triumph of color is complete.

This is more of an exaggeration in respect to human reason, but it is a nice question as to how much. The years from 1914 to 1947 witnessed one of the great ordeals of civilization. There have been so many books and articles written to describe and analyze the multitudinous breakdowns of this period that a summary would be egregious. The two wars were so beyond the scope of what had been thought conceivable in 1913, and so much greater in intensity than anything in three hundred years—or, in another way, in human history—that in looking back one sometimes wonders how anything is left of European life. All the dangerous implications of nineteenth-century nationalism and industrialism came out from under the shell of progressive humanitarianism. The First World War was a shock to the whole body of liberal capitalism and to the spirit of moderate socialism. Five years after the Armistice Lenin was secure in Moscow and Mussolini was premier in Rome, Nietzsche had overthrown Kant and the sexual mores of youth had changed as much since 1914 as they had in the previous fifty years. The late twenties were a time of consolidation; Locarno, the New Economic Policy and the Wall Street upsurge seemed to indicate a return to prewar standards. But the decade after 1929 was much more revolutionary than the early twenties had been, culminating in the supreme horror of the Second World War. By 1945 there were Communist troops in Berlin and Keynesian professors at Oxford.

From the vantage point of many conservatives these events were a mad succession of catastrophes, the needless and perhaps manipulated destruction of a beautiful order. From the political point of view, the years from 1914 to 1947 were marked by two dominant tendencies—the ascendancy of the upper circle over the lower circle, and the success of relativism vis-à-vis absolutism.

The success of the upper circle is indisputable. For the first time since at the latest, 1700, the lower-circle ideas were definitely losing ground; the tendencies of the 1870-1914 period became strong trends. The American New Deal was the most moderate of the collectivist movements which took command. For a time the philosophies of extreme radicalism/reaction, Nazism and Stalinist communism seemed invincible, and it was not only Max Lerner who almost despaired of the liberal values and conservative traditions in the time of horrors between August 1939 and December 1941. And everywhere the power of the state was so increased that the almost sacred distinctions between public and private, individual and collective, of the eighteenth and nineteenth centuries were terminated, and terminated in favor of the government. Within the government the central power grew everywhere at the expense of local and regional authorities. The most successful adversaries of these trends were not free men, but powerful groups. Even before World War I some thinkers, liberals and conservatives, had developed pluralist theories as an antidote to the growing power of the state, and while pluralism as a political credo was rather unsuccessful and whereas the strength of unions and corporations did decline in proportion to state power, there was a certain increase in their absolute size and social importance.

Unfortunately, this growth was at the expense of the individual. The plight of the solitary human being in this collectivist and technological age has been portrayed so often as to turn his image into a sort of folk myth; everyone from Charlie Chaplin to Ayn Rand has had a stab at this. But it seemed to some the greatest problem was that in a time when no standards seemed secure or permanent there could be no abiding values. The relativist implications of the intellectual revolution of 1890-1914 had borne fruit, so that the fears of Shakespeare's Ulysses seemed to be fulfilled, force was right, or rather, right and wrong, and even the name of justice seemed lost.

If this were only a question of intellectual processes very few critics would be greatly disturbed. The success of the Cambridge Platonists provided ample academic excitement at Oxford, no doubt, but the movements of Stafford or Cromwell were what really concerned the times. Nietzsche's suggestions as to the origins of Greek drama were very suggestive, but they were not the subjects of popular denunciation. Perhaps even his celebrated comment that God was dead might have become an epigram reminiscent of the ancient Cynics. But Nietzsche's philosophy of the superior ethics of the superman came to have connotations in politics which demonstrated to many, especially to many conservatives, that the transvaluation of values meant no values at all or, worse yet, very evil values.

A sign of this occurred at the time of the Dreyfus case. The argument of Maurras was splendidly relativistic. He admitted, after it became impossible to deny, that Esterhazy's evidence was a forgery and that therefore it had no conventional merit as proof of Dreyfus' guilt. But, he argued, when one considers the villainy of the Jews, the danger of Germany, and the precarious but precious state of the French nation, Esterhazy's act of forgery was a public service and true, in a deeper sense than the surface truth of the Dreyfusards. In a twisted way, this was a canny application of William James' pragmatic philosophy. The concept of truth became, as it were, an operational term, a word to be used rather than cherished, a means to an end. The cause of Esterhazy was supported by many rightists to whom relativism was a wicked word, but they often accepted the logic nonetheless. When it was the turn of the left, in considering the Soviet Union, the same standards appeared on the other side. But then again, many who were clear-sighted in deriding the timeserving nature of Marxist apologetics found good in Nazi reasoning, at least at first. In retrospect the road to Auschwitz appears as the highway of moral relativism, the main thoroughfare in a maze of streets leading to the Kinsey Report and to the schools of John Dewey and the latest Webster's.

It is no defense to this argument to maintain that James and Dewey were very upright men; it is in the nature of politics that rectitude and wrong seem to intertwine, among the other paradoxes of thought. The optimistic creations of the nineteenth century so often seemed to have given birth to the strangest progeny. This can be seen in the successes of the historical spirit. The rapt attention given to history in the last hundred years, accompanied as it has been by the development of a large and industrious academic discipline, has influenced political thought profoundly; it is hard to think of any part of political thought where the historical relationship is not felt. A thoroughly historical approach lends itself to a relativism, for each time has its values, and as one understands all it is much easier to forgive all. Spengler, to whom all of culture was historical, was completely relativist; if one sees, in the German phrase, the world as history, it is much harder to see the world as morality.

This would have been unacceptable to Lord Acton, as it was to his spiritual successors. But there were fewer and fewer such successors in the twentieth century, as the force of relativism spread. Charles Beard, who became famous as the result of a striking progressive re-evaluation of American history, proceeded to doubt all standards, including the progressive ones. Those who maintained absolutist views of history were frequently believers in a totalitarian faith. The Marxists in the 1930's were often the only remaining believers in a historical faith in Western intellectual circles; they and the Fascists shared a sense of absolute direction while the lower circle sometimes seemed paralyzed by a failure of nerve.

In short, the Whig ideology, deriving from Aristotle and the Stoics, had not only lost ground in the voting booths and in the streets, but had also lost its intellectual cohesion. That historical preoccupation which Malraux observed had come full circle to Plato, whose totalitarian descendants used history to escape from history. The Marxist eschatology was at the same time an extension of the progressivism of Buckle, and its negation. The other followers of Buckle seemed to have forsaken progress without finding a philosophy to replace it.

IV

The Climate
of Our Time

So much of the political analysis of the last twenty years in the United States and Western Europe ends at this point with a pessimistic wail or an existentialist shrug. The phrase "the decline of the West" has become a cliché, and in light of the hydrogen bomb, even an understatement. Mankind has invented an explosive almost capable of destroying life on earth, and may now be carefully completing the task so as to remove the "almost." To Nef and Weaver, and to many liberals as well, thermonuclear armaments seem a fitting climax to the madness of the last fifty to one hundred years—liberals tend to say fifty, conservatives one hundred, and reactionaries usually choose two hundred years.

But the world has gone on since Hiroshima. That is not exactly a correct way of stating the fact. It has, despite the ferocity of a cold war which sometimes threatens to break into atomic war, thrived immensely. The standard of living has risen almost everywhere since the late forties, and is well above 1939 standards in most lands. The great majority of people are not in a state of despondency; on the contrary, one of the growing problems of the time is the population explosion. There may be occasional families who can see no future to life on this planet, but the vast majority of people everywhere seem to be propagating ever faster, while the accomplishments of medical science reduce the death rate. While philosophers are dejected or seek answers to ever more trivial problems, the bulk of the population grows richer and fatter. The churches are enjoying a boom and the colleges are of course more numerous and more full than ever before in history, but the crises of the theologians and the concerns of the professors are not effectively communicated. Once again we live in the best of times and the worst of times, although the balance may be upside-down the eighteenth-century condition.

The majority opinion of the world of thought is usually ahead of popular opinion, and usually right (if only because it makes events correspond to its predictions). But many of the reviews of contemporary thought have overlooked a number of important developments of our time, developments which change the picture usually drawn. The canvass of thought, as we have observed, usually brings the history of intellectual thinking, or art, up to 1945 or 1947. But since then, very clearly since 1947, a new period seems to have come. This is especially clear in politics, both theoretical and practical, but it is also true in the arts and perhaps even in other fields. This period was clearly one of consolidation, of conservatism.

In politics this development is often considered, especially by those left of center, to be merely a reaction to communism. It is true that the events of the years 1947-1950 brought a realization to liberals that communism presented dangers as great, in most respects, as Nazism had. The various shocks of the Prague seizure, the Berlin blockade, Alger Hiss and Klaus Fuchs were supplemented by a great intellectual realization of the implications of Stalinism. But it is very shortsighted to think that this merely meant that McCarthy (or Adenauer) became politically possible, that liberals were willing to have enemies on the left or that conservatives were able to capitalize on past fraternizations or invent present ones among the leftward groups. The assumptions of liberal superiority were shattered much more thoroughly, so that intelligent people could admit to being conservative. There had always been those who objected to the trip to Finland Station, or who decided to get off; now there were many who were eager to study new routes, or who even suggested that entirely new means of transportation were now appropriate. The 1920's had revealed that the choice was not merely between different leftist visions of the future, for fascism provided a right-ist vision to consider. Now the center, and especially the conservative center revived. Socialism reached its peak shortly after the Second World War in Europe, and the power of the labor unions has declined almost everywhere since 1946. In the United States the unions vowed to repeal the Taft-Hartley Act; now they do not even mention a drive to eliminate the Landrum-Griffin Act. The pattern of free capital markets, of large-scale investment through private savings, and the use of higher interest rates to check inflation and to guide the economy seemed dead in Western Europe in 1946 (the last seemed very dead in the United States at that time). The return of this pattern was in some cases (such as West Germany) so swift and so effective that the socialist critics were still assuming the impossibility of systems that had recovered completely. The sharp repudiation of theories of racial superiority in our time shows that some intellectual currents are reversible; in this surely we are happily back to the views of the eighteenth century.

This did not mean a return in economics or in politics to 1900, or to 1925. Stravinsky's neo-classicism did not usher in the harmony of the rococo, and the revival of interest in the cultural heritage in every field did not cause modern writers or painters to work in the manner of their forebears. The result was something different from the past, quite different from the "classics," but much more compatible with the older standards than the works of the post-World War I generation had been. Keynes was not discarded, but his teachings were absorbed into economics without eliminating the neo-classical economists.

This conservatism is new, in the sense that it has considered the disputes of the past age, and has incorporated them in its heritage. Each new generation—and we can start our generation with 1947—argues the same problems, for the fundamental problems are the same, in a new fashion. But this newness comes from supplementing the old, not starting afresh. Marx is still important, and of course there are hideous factories and sweated child-laborers in the world. But the plight of these children, and the answers to their problems found in *Das Kapital,* look different in the new environment of thought and technology. As the "modern" adherents said to the "ancients," we see farther than our predecessors because we can stand on their shoulders. Our greater vision is around the same old circle, but it grows more acute. Some sights will be lost, of course, as certain issues and various thinkers become forgotten or neglected. But the main sign of change will be the recasting of the same material in new forms, the seeing of the old problems through the eyes of a generation that has accepted the experiences of the last one as completed, done, and seeks to use that experience to go further or intends to throw out parts of it as irrelevant.

Examples of this can be seen in the recent past. The Russian thaw, for instance, produced a move away from the upper circle that changed the nature of the Soviet system, while in no way rejecting Marx or Lenin. Thus the stabilization of the Russian standards of law and economic power produced an easing of internal and external tension which pleased most Western critics as it increasingly infuriated the Chinese Marxists. It is not useful to class a whole society as being in one quadrant of the circle—there are always some varieties in a social system—but Stalinist Russia conformed fairly closely to a position of extreme reactionary thinking, with of course strong extreme radical components. After Stalin the lower-circle tendencies expanded. Some—the growth of a middle class, the use of economic rewards rather than controls in many areas, the new Libermanian attention to profits—are somewhat conservative. Others—the extension of some personal liberties, the increase of welfare benefits (*Fortune* has aptly referred to the Khrushchevian welfare state) are liberal. The same thing has happened in Spain since 1959, where a fiscal and monetary policy designed on free market models has liberalized the economy (and amazingly has been quite generally referred to as a "liberal" policy, showing the strong roots of the Old Liberalism) and somewhat modified the government. The news from Madrid is perhaps reminiscent of the liberal period of the Second Empire in France, but who would have dared predict in 1945 that capitalist economics could have been widely greeted as an integral part of a liberal improvement? The options of the future are thus not confined to the *dirigiste* choices; if at times it seems as if the state is an irresistible juggernaut, this can be an oversimplification.

The 1960's have perhaps marked a new shift to the left—certainly a "new left"—yet the tendencies of the 1950's have often prevailed. The impact of Castro and Mao must be matched with the startling counter-revolutionary successes in Brazil and Indonesia. But from a theoretical standpoint the impasse of Chinese Marxism is even more important. The concepts of permanent revolution seem to have been pushed to the extreme, and that extreme seems like a *reductio ad absurdum*. The reliance of Mao and his orthodox followers on a combination of hieratic devotion and a youthful brutalism as a guarantee of the future of pure radicalism makes that radicalism seem impossible as a viable system. It may be that the age which began in Paris in 1789 ended in 1965 or 1966 in Peking. But it is not enough to be against something; the experience of the new left itself shows that a theory cannot survive merely as a collection of rejections.

This is obviously most called-for if one proposes to advance a conservative political theory. The changes of our time have called out for a development of new conservative theories, but at the same time they have required these new theories to take into account the changes. One must face both ways, uncomfortable as that position is. So much of the "new conservatism" has been right of center, without doubt, but in all fairness the thinking of Russell Kirk, for example, should be designated as reactionary. To be conservative in this relativist age one must leave the traditional Kirks without abandoning all their virtues.

In practical terms this must mean different things to different conservatives. There is obviously no conservative party line, nor is there one line of thought which is solely conservative, and which excludes the not-completely-acceptable deviators. There is no uniformly-accepted dividing line between the reactionary and the conservative, or between left and right conservatives. There is a zone of difference, and one's view of this zone will frequently be influenced by a sense of what is worth debating today, and what is not. So much of right-wing argumentation since 1947 has been devoted to the evils of communism and the dangers of socialist or semi-socialist programs. Alger Hiss and appeasement policies made excellent targets for criticism, and in the main this is quite right, but in the late 1960's this is increasingly irrelevant. In the late seventeenth century Lord Halifax asked if the militant Protestants were "still to smell the match that was to blow up the King and both houses in the Gunpowder Treason?"; some memories are too much for even the party of memory. Some of the criticisms against Stalin are no longer valid as against contemporary Russia, and others are not worth the trouble discussing in the West. For example, the freedom of the Soviet legal system from bourgeois ideas has resulted in a theory of the legal process which permits the state to dominate all relationships in a way very inimical to freedom and, as events have amply proved, to human dignity. But the monstrosities of "law" perpetrated in 1937 or 1952 are not the issue today, and as for the basic idea, it is stale and unprofitable to come to the defense, once again, of the adversary system or the concept of the rule of law. What is much more profitable now is whether the evolution of a milder Soviet legal system will result in a body of law more subtly, and perhaps therefore more dangerously, slanted toward the objectives of the ruling circles of the state or, under different circumstances, toward the tyranny of the majority. To take another example, everyone (who cares, at any rate) now knows that the elimination of the death penalty by the Bolsheviks was a delusion, and a bloody delusion at that. Facts such as these are the background of a modern conservative theory, but they are not the stuff to construct a new philosophy. It is of more interest today, from our point of view, that the most savage penalties frequently inflicted in Russia today are for "economic crimes," for behavior which is guiltless or meritorious in the West. A new conservative theory must show not only that Stalinism was a vicious system—even the Communists half admit that—or that the events of 1917–1918 were lamentable—that will always be worth saying, but not so worth repeating—but that the Marxist states of the 1960's even in their more benevolent form are not models of the good, or even a somewhat better, society. Liberals have denounced the Castro who established a police state; conservatives must go farther and dispute the Castro who provides free telephone service.

This is even more true in discussing the welfare state. The most discouraging aspect of so many right-of-center journals is the repetitions of the same arguments, *ad nauseam*. The problems of the massive state, imposing taxes unthought of fifty years ago and controlling or owning much of the property of the country, has attracted conservative opposition for a long time. But the 1947 conservative counter-revolution has changed the liberal cause as well. Socialism is not the prime cause of many socialist parties in the advanced nations any more, and the dangers of big government are now clear to the left. In the less advanced countries the rise of socialism has presented new situations, to which the refutations of the neo-classical liberals have only partial relevance. It is not that conservative thought has stood still. What has stood still is the transmission of this thought to its needed role as a source of programs in new areas of politics.

What is now relevant and what is old hat is of course a matter of opinion, and there should be no stigma to an idea just because it is old. The joke that Barry Goldwater would be a fine actor for Eighteenth Century-Fox is witty, but not so crushing; if Hitler and Stalin are the producers for the cinema of our century, we can do without attending the later film. There is, however, a futility about a program designed to abolish public power in all forms or to slash welfare legislation sharply; one cannot help but wonder what good a theory is which relies on planks which seem so foreign to the majority opinion everywhere. And if this program bases its arguments on replies to socialistic theories which have been abandoned or highly refined by the present adherents of public power or the welfare state, the futility grows. It is not a duty to combat one's opponents' most advanced ideas with equally advanced ideas of your own, it is a necessity. To ignore that necessity is to risk having your ideas become fossils.

In this respect political discussion is like war. The French generals have been notorious for a century for always fighting the last war, learning their lessons well, but always too late. The French lacked vigor in 1870 in advancing into South Germany, but they made up for this in 1914, when it was wrong. In 1939 they had learned that lesson well, so the French army shrewdly manned the Maginot Line. There are parallels in other fields. Carr comments that the lessons of 1814–1815 were carefully studied in Paris in 1919, even down to the trivia; just as the pitfalls of Versailles were avoided after World War II. In each case real errors were wisely avoided, yet each peace has seemed more badly managed than its predecessor. Joffre was not an ignoramus, nor was Clemenceau, and by 1946 the nuances of history were scrupulously studied, but each age made new mistakes nonetheless. The lessons of one generation are learned by the next, but it is fitting that each generation is entitled to its own errors. This is, in a way, implicit in our circular view, for each new set of problems will result in a new realignment, in the eternal circular pattern, and no great issue is ever permanently settled, or its puzzles finally answered.

But that is all the more reason to ask the right questions. The old frames of reference become outdated, and opinions with reference to them become pointless or twisted. Thus the greatest problem of the Victorian creed has usually been that it sought to pose the problem of economics in a form that became outworn. The liberalism of Herbert Hoover was so unlikely that the merits of his conservatism were lost. There is nothing wrong in fashioning a theory of conservatism out of the ideas of a previous liberalism; that is a staple, and a very good staple, of moderate conservatism since Aristotle. But to think of this conservatism as the latest bit of liberalism, or as a species of radicalism, is worse than a crime, it is a blunder. The Radical Socialists in France and the Liberals in Italy lost most of their influence in this way, and the Republicans in the United States have often been in the same danger.

This happens to liberals, too. The optimistic theologians had their premises and their mode of thinking so eroded in the years after 1918 that, in the absence of effective intellectual champions, their replies to the neo-Orthodox onslaught became derisory. Today the ideology of the labor-union movement throughout much of the world is in danger of being reduced to a similar position. Once again, this observation is not a judgment on some ideas as wrong and on others as right; Norman Peale and Walter Reuther are not submitting their beliefs to a theorists' examining board. Every idea has its place in the history of thought, but nothing is so forlorn as an idea that has missed its time. In retrospect, the fate of the advisors of the would-be Henry V was sadder than that of Marshal Bazaine. One of the lessons of history is not to study too mechanically; a political theory that looks backward (and of course all must, to some degree) looks at its risk. The men at Versailles were intelligent and studious, but how much more successful the Marshall Plan has been than the war-guilt clause! Once again, we must conclude that the use of history is essential, and highly dangerous.

It is necessary then to determine what assumptions are no longer worth debating, and which ideas merit new investigation. In so doing it must be emphasized that these are not matters of right or wrong, and that there is no one liberal conservative ideology, as the following will clearly show.

The best place to start is at the conclusion of so much of twentieth-century thought; the disappearance of certainty. The triumph of the uncertainty principle in physics is now assured, and there are no Newtonian counter-revolutionaries. In the political world there is too much lamenting, especially in the lower circle, over past order. It is all very well to say that the horrors of totalitarianism prove the need for a natural law to curb the new leviathans, but their existence and various successes cannot be waved away. The famous comment of St. Augustine—what is a state without justice but a gang of robbers—has been much quoted, but such states have existed and do exist. And what is justice? The question is much like Pilate's, and without much doubt most intelligent men and women today share Pilate's uncertainty. It is tempting to say, unequivocally, "We are against the sort of government of the Hitlers and Stalins," but this proves unhelpful. Where does this put Brezhnev, or Salazar, or Voerster, or Pattakos? The gradations are many, and at each step clearly well-meaning, "reasonable" men uphold repulsive regimes. Who is to say that anything is impermissible; the case for any system can, and has, been maintained. If suppression of free speech is opposed to justice, then those who seek that goal may be dismissed from consideration. But if dismissed, why should they be permitted to proselytize? If they succeed, they will subvert the right order. Where this argument leads is obvious; it is a sort of application of Zeno's paradox. If we execute those convicted of murder—Eichmann or a random thug—is justice then the *lex talionis?* The effort to find an absolute today starts from no absolute standard, such as the Bible or a divinely-ordained institution, and so it is extremely hard to say *"non licet,"* and make that judgment stick. As recent events have shown, even the Communists have this problem. So we accept much more that would have seemed out of bounds a short time back. The atomic bomb is a clear case of this; so is the use of listening devices which would have seemed macabre invasions of privacy a generation ago. The army of the Fourth French Republic unquestionably used torture against Algerians in the 1950's; who would have thought that a republic in France (governed during part of this time by a socialist) would have done such a thing? The due process of the United States Supreme Court of the 1920's is largely dead, and we have a new one, advocated as an almost immutable law by the intellectual heirs of the men who discredited the old philosophy; this is not very surprising, historically, but not very convincing as a permanent embedding of an absolute law.

What is absolute today? Since very few people believe that the Ten Commandments are truly God-given, in a meaningful sense, we must consider their message *de novo,* and the absolute sanction is not undeniable. The commandment "Thou shalt not kill," surely the most ethically powerful one, is not so compelling when one no longer can assume that some forms of taking life are, by definition, not killing. Of course the pacifists can start with a clean record here, but what does one then decide about automobile traffic, or even skyscraper construction? If human life is absolutely sacred, and one knows that the chances are strong that the construction of a bridge will result in a few deaths (as is so often the case), how can any bridge construction be justified? And if one accepts the argument of the pacifists, the fault must then lie with any system that uses arms—i.e., the Dutch in 1940 and the Hungarians in 1956, as well as their oppressors. There are thus almost no just societies (surviving, at any rate), and most natural-law advocates are offending against natural law.

If that is not the very most vital article, what is? Incest may seem one of the most hated practices imaginable, but we must remember that the Egyptian rulers, and their Greek successors, practiced it frequently. Homosexuality was considered a virtue in Sparta because it aroused a manly courage and fear of shame. The anthropologists have done much to make us see that there is a great deal of truth to the French maxim, other times, other ways. What seems essential may often be merely habitual. And one must consider that incest and homosexuality are practices which involve, by and large, willing parties. It often seems today that the greater danger lies in those who would use community power to intrude into the freedom of the individual, that natural law subsists in the freedom of the governed, not in the regulations of the government.

After surveying Nazism and communism, this is a very understandable conclusion, especially for moderate conservatives. Natural-law supporters such as Hayek and Fuller have used this as their principal argument; it is a good one. The trouble comes in defining it. Which liberties are absolutely sacrosanct? The liberties of the First Amendment of the United States Constitution seem sturdy, but they are more porous when one looks at them closely. Freedom of speech is desirable, and Justice Black would apply this to strike down all defamation laws. But even he admits that picketing may involve coercion as well as persuasion, and it is harder to judge the harangue which is part advocacy, part threat, and part incitement to immediate breach of the law. And what of falsely crying fire in a crowded theater?

The other freedoms are even more knotty, when one reaches for absolutes. Holmes, in commenting on the Kantian principle that man should be used as an end, and not as a means—a beautiful expression of the concept of politics and ethics as a tool for individual human betterment—observed that this was just not done in the world. Military conscription—more prevalent today than ever before—and the technological sacrifices mentioned above are good examples of this, taken from societies which pride themselves on humane values. The respect for human dignity is admirable, and perhaps a special virtue of modern American technology, as Margaret Mead has suggested, but that virtue is too connected with a dispensable wealth and assurance to be considered a permanent fixture.

This is true, *a fortiori*, of the smaller details of politics and economics. The supporter of the capitalist system, circa 1900, often said to his critics on the left (especially his younger critics), "I sympathize with your idealism, but your plans won't work." But all sorts of things turn out to work. A nation can unbalance its budget indefinitely, a people can reorient its whole mode of living. The Russians could never build a great industrial plant under Marxism, but they did; the Egyptians surely could never operate the Suez Canal, but it turned out to be not so very difficult after all. So many more things are possible than were dreamt of in the philosophies of the comfortable Victorian Horatios!

And in the course of proving all these wonders our very dreams have turned to nightmares. Lincoln Steffens looked into the future, and saw that it worked, and in a way he was right, as the Soviet space probes indicate. But what was the price? The accomplishments of Hjalmar Schacht in autarchic finance were impressive refutations of a century of financial theory, but it is a reasonable conclusion that we were better off when we thought in more limited terms. That most incredible result of relativist physics, the harnessing of atomic energy, is a jinni which it would have been far better never to have released. As more and more becomes attainable, we see clearly how many more problems each accomplishment involves. Schumpeter commented that, with perhaps the exception of agriculture, there is no intrinsic reason why all the means of production and distribution cannot be nationalized. But this does not eliminate the problems of distribution, it merely rearranges them. The price tag is still there, but it is calculated differently; differently than the socialists intended, in many cases. The problems, the circular issues, are the absolutes.

Often this doubt as to the reality of improvements leads to a deep cynicism, a reactionary disbelief in all human betterment. Theorists like the author of Ecclesiastes or Pareto have deduced from the mutability of human accomplishments a contempt for popular institutions. But why are democracies more fallible than other systems? It is so much easier to deride the adversary's faith than to accept the implications for your own. Great relativists like Veblen or Spengler manage to avoid analyzing the society they prefer with the same trenchant acuteness they use on everything else. The more thoroughgoing relativists are led to a complete absurdism, so that any sort of personal feeling determines one's opinions.

Some of the conceits of sociological jurisprudence and of vulgar Freudianism have caused a revulsion from these complete rejections of standards. This revulsion has often taken the form of an appeal for values. But this is an unsatisfactory plea, for whose values will do? Hitler had values, a very complete set. To paraphrase the epigram on men's clothes, if you have to look for "values," they are not worth finding. It is far better to end one's journey with a Camusian acceptance of the absurd, than to insist on an answer. This is another way of saying that there is nothing more than to find one's values in the working out of one's own intellectual journey, in life. There are so many kinds of existentialism today, but a common denominator of all of them is a rejection of everything outside of the achieved meaning. Values are made, and not found. There are parallels in many unrelated fields. It is now generally accepted, for example, (although this is still subject to dispute) that a fiscal policy of borrowing instead of taxing does not shift the burden to later generations. The burden is shifted from one group to another.

So one can no longer accept, much as one might revere Burke, that our generation owes to those before, or after, a debt. The debt, in the New Deal phrase, is owed to ourselves. We cannot be sure what our descendants will want, or require of us, just as we do not accept the claims of our ancestors as binding. This is evident in the discussions over language. This is not a rebellious generation, in terms of overthrowing the old tongues or systematically revitalizing them (the Chinese are perhaps an exception). But it is hard to find a point where one can say that because words had a given meaning before, or that because some words had no standing in the language, this must be so today. So the relativism of the contemporary dictionary-makers operates in a void. Or rather, it operates as a function of life, as a reporter rather than as a Bible. But, in that case, why have dictionaries at all, as many critics of the Webster *Fourth International* have asked. If anything a noted writer writes is good English, the way to command of the language is success, rather than the other way around.

Another parallel between art and politics comes to mind. Byzantine and medieval art were thoroughly religious and functional, as was art in primitive societies. Paintings and statuary had no place outside their position within the religious structure, as Malraux observes, and they were admired as symbols, or representations, or talismans, but not as objects of art. With the Renaissance painting and sculpture emerged as works in their own right, but the connection between the subject matter and the art object remained strong. But as time went on it grew weaker. Family portraits, which replaced religious portraits, were viewed in the galleries of other people, and after the eighteenth century, in museums. The Medicean museum, like the Hohenzollern conscription, was an invention which the French Revolution transformed into a vast innovation. With the nineteenth century art criticism and the spirit of art for art's sake increased the autonomy of art; the eradication of the subject matter and the arrival of the museum without walls in our century completes the separation, a victory for art similar to but surpassing the Greek experience.

With a very few changes of words this might be a description of the development of relativist ideas in politics and the law. Politics, like art, has become, little by little, liberated (one can use that term with or without a smirk) from religion and a fixed moral law. The road from Bentham to Dewey, or from Savigny to Kelsen, was paralleled by that from Corot to Braque. In both cases autonomy, in the sense of an emancipation of art and politics from their place within a hierarchy of rules and traditions, led after a while to a thorough victory for subjectivity, or perhaps a new set of standards. Some critics have seen the beginnings of this relativism in the art of the baroque, or even the Renaissance; art foreshadowing life.

Of course there are discrepancies. In politics there will never be the degree of unanimity that often prevails in art—although one must remember that abstraction and surrealism do not encompass all of painting, and there has been room in this century for Prokofiev as well as Piston. The absolutist/relativist disagreement is a warmer issue today than the question of art qua art vs. art as a tool, and perhaps it is more possible to look for a revival of a natural-law consensus than of a tradition-oriented art. The elaboration of relativistic thinking in the ancient world, among the Sophists and Cynics, in some ways exceeded that of the moderns, but this gave way to the absolutism of the Stoics and later of the Christian thinkers, reinforced, of course, by the influence of Plato and Aristotle. The transition from Hellenistic and Roman art (if these were ever separate) to the absolutist Christian art was less sharp, because art had never reached that subjective state that it has today.

The parallel is nevertheless instructive in several ways. The progression of art toward a very subjective form of creation has raised the same cries of alarm and despair that we have remarked in politics, and much of the same analyses. There is a common argument in both areas which is impressive, but which has failed to have much, if any, influence. In the realm of politics, it can be summarized as follows: The modern generations do subsist on the capital of their elders, and squander it. This can be true in economics, as when a society fails to replace its depreciating facilities, and it has happened in the area of morals. Here the facilities consist of the stock of moral ideas, inherited from the religious efforts of past generations. Many of the relativist thinkers were men of the highest moral rectitude, whose own standards of morality were as high as the most pious churchmen, but this was the result of inheritance. Their ideas, working through time, were debits on the books of ethics, which would lead to a lawless and perilously subjective world. One example was Justice Holmes. The Hobbesian implications of his relativism were checked by his inbred New England morality and by his fine sense of public concern. But his ideas have served, so the argument runs, to weaken these very qualities. His followers carried on this destructive logic, pushing it ever further. Holmes provided the Supreme Court with a certain minimum of control over the federal legislature and over the states, but Learned Hand would almost have completely eliminated that control. Charles Curtis extended the Holmesian belief in legal subjectivity to a point which almost entirely destroyed the sense of legal standards as something different from the whims of judges. And the final indication is the career of Alger Hiss, one of Holmes' last law clerks. Perhaps worse is to come, as the virus reaches a third generation.

Bernard Berenson's comments on modern painting are much the same. Picasso, he observed, was a fine draftsman and a skilled painter, but he deliberately hid these abilities and provided a very bad example for less capable men to follow. African art, of interest in its milieu, becomes a part of our current art world in a fashion that does an injustice to the merits of its indigenous culture and our own. The imitators of Picasso fall prey to the shoddiest tricksters in a culture without standards; at best they work for themselves and fail to convey a sense of beauty to their audience. With both arguments, the final conclusion is that we live in an ugly world, and that the forces of ugliness were set into motion by men who appreciated beauty, but who robbed their posterity of it.

The greatest difficulty with this argument is its very pessimism, for it presents a pattern of degeneration far more forcefully than any program of revitalization. But it is apparent, to almost everyone, that the revolution in all the arts which has taken place since 1910 cannot be repealed. All of art looks at the world, and at itself, in a manner which is there, which has permeated even the smallest details. But, once having accepted this, one can see various developments today which show signs of creating new order out of what has so often seemed chaos. The accomplishments of modern architecture, for example, perhaps the most splendid of the works of modern art, and the influence of architecture on painting and sculpture have been a potent factor in developing a neo-classical element in the international style, a style which has increasingly imparted a spirit of order despite (or perhaps because of) its non-representational form. The road from surrealism to pop art may be leading back toward a very old kind of painting in a radically new style. We do not live in a world bereft of beauty, it is just that we must find our beauty in more complex constructions.

The direct political implications are encouraging for conservatives. The efforts of the Nazis to destroy modern art were futile, and the anti-formalism of the Soviets, of the Mexican radicals, and of the 1930's American liberals were and are all very unsuccessful. This is in part precisely because conservatism does not require a new message, a final meaning for life. So much of modern culture accepts MacLeish's dictum that a poem should not mean, but be. This slogan is less disturbing to conservatives than to their opponents. These conservatives who would write off modern art as a disaster are ignoring the welcome reminder that art provides, a reminder of the individuality and complexity of life. Khrushchev accused the young Soviet abstract painters of homosexuality partly because he was, in some ways, extremely conservative and opposed to new ideas. But it also was because he was afraid of the implications of this private and formal culture on the new Soviet man. The ingenuity of these new men may produce the classics of the future. The incongruities of the *fauves* now seem to provide a net addition to our awareness of life, even of beauty.

As in politics everything is now possible in art—sledge

hammers as musical instruments or toilet seats as *trompe l'oeil* decoration. But that does not mean that one must accept them all equally; surely by 2000 many of the more bizarre media or instruments or styles will have been discarded. The atonalists have not swept the field. This might indeed have been the case if their only competition had been with doctrinaire followers of Brahms, but on the contrary much of modern music has been developed by men like Stravinsky or Prokofiev who have used the new in the spirit of the old. This is at least as important in the area of political theory.

Holmes himself is a good example. In the later years of his life, he was amazingly often regarded as a liberal; today the most tough-minded parts of his thinking are frequently stressed in order to describe him as a reactionary. This is not altogether unfair. There was a quality of permissiveness in his thinking which led him to accept the will of the majority and the power of force. But to stop there is to look at Holmes and at much of modern thought through one eye. Holmes did not believe that the judiciary had no function in preserving constitutional rights—witness not only his free-speech opinion in *U. S.* v. *Abrams* but also his opinion upholding property rights in the *Mahon* case—but he prized many things as worth fighting for. To doubt is not to lack faith. It may be that the best faith can come only through that doubt in the absolute certainties that are often so intolerant; a faith, to quote Holmes' magnificent Harvard Law School Association speech of 1913, "in a universe not measured by our fears." This meant in Holmesian language that a natural right was one which was felt deeply enough. In a German town raising the price of beer would produce a revolt, so at that place at that time the given price of beer was a natural right. We cannot rely on an overlaw to engrave our rights so firmly that we need but read the tablet to discover them; we must constantly weigh them and redefine them. It is well to remember that Francis Biddle, as well as Alger Hiss, served as a clerk of Holmes. Weighing and balancing of rights is what the liberal justices on the United States Supreme Court have so disliked in recent years. The relativism of Frankfurter, Holmes' disciple, has become an integral part of American jurisprudential conservatism, a conservatism which accepts neither property rights nor personal liberties as absolutes, but seeks to devise methods of reconciling these and other interests, with regard to upholding the basic constitutional traditions. It is possible to disagree with some of these compromises, without dissenting from the validity of the task of balancing.

For this balancing has become the life of the law. Perhaps the most important legacy of the great revolution which Holmes did so much to forward in the law—the demolition of absolutes and the acceptance of judicial lawmaking (to an extent)—has been the thorough conquest of the idea of law, in the common-law countries, at least, as a conscious tool of judges as well as legislators in their task to create a public order and to at least approximate a just society.

Even if one concedes that natural-law theories cannot maintain their wonted vigor, it does not follow that all theory of value is obsolete. There is no inconsistency in understanding that all segments of political thought derive from supportable views of human nature, and yet in upholding one view as the most desirable—perhaps not desirable without all doubt, but desirable as we see it. The sharp contrast between a world of unquestionable right and wrong and a world of unlimited license is unsound. It is just that lower circle which so cherishes individual liberties which can most appreciate the gradations between an individual preference and the law of nature.

A. L. Hart has expressed this in a somewhat different way, in discussing the distinction between law and morality. In his debate with Lon Fuller he upheld the Holmesian thesis that law and morality were quite separate. But this does not, Hart asserted, imply that law is immoral or amoral. The law, which merely means the sum total of commands and permissions customarily obeyed in a community, is neutral in a moral sense; the fact that it calls for a certain course of action or code of conduct does not affect the basic rightness of that conduct. In some matters (in one corner of a square, as Charles Curtis conceptualized it) are rules which have no relation to any formula of right or wrong—laws prescribing probate practice, for example. In other matters law is dealing with questions which also directly concern ethical problems, and a student of the law, or anyone (and of course we are all such students at some point in our life), will naturally hope that the law's injunctions coincide with his own ethical principles. That is comparatively easy in dealing with the clearest ethical questions, although we have seen that even murder and other heinous crimes are sometimes easier to condemn than to define. But each of us has our own definition, no less important for being personal. And in most questions, in law and *a fortiori* in politics, the issues are not "moral," but no less strongly held for that. There is no certain way of determining whether taxes should be levied in one way or another, bearing on one interest or class or on another, but that does not mean that argument on the subject is fruitless. It may be that in the last analysis everything comes down to incomparable tastes or visceral feelings, but one can judge the result of one feeling as against another, and the consistency of the various faiths. That is the value of any theory, and the purpose of the argument for liberal conservatism presented here.

But there is one more thing to be said in respect to relativism. Murder may not be easy to define under all circumstances, and property may, if you look at it one way, be theft. But the vast majority of the time one can define murder, and within the Soviet Union stealing property (of the state, for the most part, but not common property any more than Rockefeller's) is punished. There are basic ideals which may not be immutable, and which may involve opinion, but whose abridgement will almost surely present very grave dangers. Once again we speak of paying a price, not invoking an absolute prohibition, but then some prices may be prohibitive. If all thought is looked on as a circle (this is not the same circle that we have been talking of), all differences are matters of degree. There is nothing outside of this circle, so differences in kind, absolute distinctions, are impossible. But the greatest differences on the circle, 180 degrees apart, are as sharply separate as one can imagine. They approach in significance differences of kind, even if strictly speaking they remain differences of degree.

So it is with political thought. The most valued concepts of our scheme of things may be class-oriented, time-bound and if viewed *sub specie aeternitatis,* purely subjective, but if they serve to make for the best government and to subserve the necessary standards of civilization, we must defend and assert them as if they were absolutes. These "as ifs" are vital as a bridge between the broadest comprehension and a much narrower resolution, without which we run the risk of becoming either fanatical or despairing, or of leaving power to those who are. This sounds much like a counsel of compromise, but that is not so. This "as if" can be an advantage. The problem of much of natural-law conservatism—Lippmann's, for instance—is that it uses a system of unbending principles to defend a program of objectives which puts a high premium on choice and personal freedom. Freedom itself then becomes an absolute, which raises the question of what one does with reprobates who query the absolute itself. Shall you give freedom to those who would deny it to you? This is not merely a practical issue of government, important as it is in that context, but also a theoretical issue of political philosophy. If freedom is incontestable, those who would oppose it are clearly wrong, and their freedom to contest ours is not valuable, but merely an ideological convenience. In times of stress one makes exceptions in applying principles when the need is great and the loss is small, and what can be less important than preventing the growth of clearly erroneous doctrines? We should be willing to see the value in any belief, but not let that discourage our pressing our view of the good life one whit.

This requires a measure of realism as well as toleration. The example of the Suez Canal again comes to mind. Many of those who insisted that the ships would shortly collide in mid-passage were letting their hopes dictate their predictions. A disdain for the Egyptians was translated into a judgment on nautical skill when the real judgment should have been made on political theory. Eden's fears about a vital waterway in the control of a dictator whose political needs would impel him to press constantly against the civilized systems of law and economic order were not unreasonable. The international legal safeguards of the late nineteenth century were by no means ideal, but to erase rather than to improve them is a backward step, with even more disagreeable implications ahead in the coming age of atomic proliferation. But to say that the Egyptians could not enlist or train capable navigators was not a shorthand way of saying this, but a way of discrediting the whole argument.

A classic case of this misapplication of judgment was the argument over whether the trains in Italy ran on time during the 1930's. The factual basis of the statement was much canvassed (Gilbert Seldes had statistics on late arrivals in the cities of Lombardy and Tuscany), and the theories of order much more discussed. On the other hand, many liberals were outraged at the assertion, claiming that it was totally irrelevant whether every train arrived on the second. But the most important question—and it was rare that the contestants were willing to grapple on this issue—was whether, if one assumed that the trains did run on time, this sign of good order and efficiency informed the whole society in a fashion that led to a better system. It seems rather clear now, in reading Moravia or Silone, that the very quality which the trains should have represented was absent, and that a corrupt disregard for human convenience grew rather than receded under the Fascists. This is a value judgment, but it is not devoid of factual content. The last, but most important and most difficult, matter then remains: what qualities are most important in identifying the right kind of efficiency, and what is more important than even the most efficient system? But even this is not a question which is absolutely separate from experience; as our discussion of modern art has suggested, there are ways of making tentative conclusions even about the incomparable. As regards the trains, one examination might be as follows: First, did the trains really run on time? Second, if so, did this really signify a boon to the Italians—did this alter their notorious habit of being late, and if so, was that a good thing? Third, if that is so, what effect did this change have on the whole way of life and the political system of Italy? To be specific, was too much spontaneity in private life and freedom in public life lost? If the engineer were shot, or if his family went without food as a punishment for late trips, perhaps the whole thing was not worth the effort; more realistically, if many other tasks were neglected and if a coarse petty tyranny was instituted, was the price too great? Lastly, did even the finest accomplishments encourage a regime whose other actions were so gross and, in the end, so destructive of life and locomotives that the loss far outweighed the gain?

The last question is the most important one, and the one most subject to different opinions. But, as has been suggested, the differences of opinion are not unbridgeable or uniform. There is no way to prove that the life of an engineer is worth more than the punctual adherence to a timetable, but there are few who would maintain the opposite. We have here not only the force of human compassion, which should not be rejected out of hand, but also (and to a conservative this is worth more in the long view of history) the developed standards of civilized life. When the feelings of compassion have been refracted through the glass of time, and especially of those times whose principles of conduct and social cohesion seem most conducive to peace and tranquility, the resulting rules gain in force. They are never proved true, in the absolute sense, but their truth approaches the 180-degree point much more nearly than any other.

This, perhaps, is another way of describing Holmes' "can't helps." Of course this is not literally true, for we can help not to do almost anything. In his last years it is possible that Stalin let his access to power drive him into a kind of bestial madness, so that even the least offending men were unsafe. The Soviet Union did not disintegrate between 1950 and 1953; in fact the growth of industrial production continued and (in the short run) the opposition to the purposes of the state contracted. But if Stalin had not died (and of course perhaps he did not just die) the bands of pressure might have snapped altogether. Even if they had not, what was lost in human spirit might have seared a generation beyond repair. Khrushchev's famous speech at the

Party Congress in 1956 represents a sort of "can't help" in a symbolic form; when the men who serve in responsible positions under a society find that its essence is indefensible, the price of beer (to return to Holmes' example) is marked as too high.

How does an outsider, an ordinary citizen, discover this? This is where the natural-law advocates reach for their laws, their public philosophies. There is a grandeur and a power in many of these, but as with the Ten Commandments, we can respect them but not altogether bend the knee before them. It is very difficult to believe that God commanded Moses to rework the Babylonian and Caananitic heritage of laws into the Pentateuchal codes; even the Decalogue seems a bit strange for such an author. But the most elevated sections seem to come closest to a godly message when they are seen in the light of three millennia of human behavior. We judge even the Exodus of our ideals, but once we see what is most valuable, there is no need to be ashamed of insisting on it as if it were divine. This is a rational act, and so it is natural that it should begin with the preservation of those very capacities which make rational analysis possible. This is the upshot of the case for liberal conservatism today, and it is not a theoretical case only. The experiences which point to conservatism are the same ones which present a standard to which we can repair—the integrity of the minima of human decency, and the social systems which nurture it.

This is a challenge to modern conservatism, and to the other political theories as well. Since it is so easy to move, it is all the more important to know where we are moving. The allegory in *Through the Looking-Glass* is a liberal favorite (Woodrow Wilson used it with great force) and a profound observation. One must run fast to stay in the same place. It is necessary to run fast, and it probably always has been; but it is also good to stay in the same place.

V

Four Arguments
for Conservatism

This brief for conservatism is based, as befits a dissertation written in our time, on a highly ambivalent view of man and the world. The constant permutations and disappointments of historical change disappoint every messianic hope. These disappointments are inevitable, given the underlying truth that men will always differ in their view of human nature, and therefore of the possibility of social betterment. This historical awareness gives rise, as Niebuhr has argued, to a world of irony and paradox. This irony has permeated the literature of the century, so that any reading man must see the universe as something like Mann's magic mountain, a turret of reviving health and deepseated illness, whose cures are never complete and whose philosophies are hopelessly paradoxical. But, as in Mann's parable, this presumes a potentiality for goodness and a free will which is to man's credit. The ambivalence has, as it must, two sides—we refuse to see the future as transcending history, à la Marx, but we also refuse to escape history into an ersatz past, à la Plato. Humanity, with all its difficulties, is not an inert or beaten mass, but a race worth being ambivalent about.

A much older myth comes to mind. The story of man's fall, in the third chapter of Genesis, has been a political fable for at least two thousand years. Adam and Eve, by eating the fruit of the tree of good and evil, bring upon themselves and all mankind the suffering and travail which has beset us since. But had they not eaten that fruit we would presumably have been ignorant, blissfully ignorant, but incapable of creating anything. The fall has seemed the greatest conceivable misfortune to centuries of right-wing theologians, but to many people today it seems much less so. The pain of existence is almost, in the modern economic sense, a social cost of human knowledge. The idea of the happy fall has taken a new form; it is happy now, not because it led to redemption, but because man, through this knowledge, can, if not redeem himself, design his own world. This is not redemption, and perhaps a poor substitute, but it is our own. It is the task of liberal conservatism to accept the implications of the fall, as we see them, but also not to ignore the possibilities of the gains made by eating the fruit. Of course we see this wisdom as dearly bought, or else this would be liberalism; it is finding just how dearly bought that much of contemporary political theory is about.

One could come to this conclusion in a library, or in judging one's own feelings about people. Perhaps, in the last analysis, everyone makes his visceral decisions about his fellow man first, and thinks later. But successful beliefs must be thought and communicated, not merely felt. The success of conservatism since 1947 has been due to a shared viewpoint, which arose out of the events of our time. There were many sources of these beliefs, but we can single out four as being especially influential.

The first, and the most moving, was the impact of totalitarianism. At first the totalitarian regimes produced dismay only among their avowed foes—i.e., the Communists were hated by the right, and Fascists by the left. In the 1930's it was common for liberals to say that of course the methods of Stalin were coarse and the one-party system was bad, but their goals were just and, anyway, look at the educational system (or child nurseries, or the hydroelectric projects). As for the right, one needs but remember those to whom Hitler was better than Blum. By 1950 it was accepted by Henry Wallace that the salient feature of communism was not child nurseries, and Blum's death in that year called forth a consensus of regret which was never reached in the days of the Third Republic.

At the outset it would seem that this consensus should benefit the left, for what could be more abhorrent to human dignity than the concentration camps? The behavior of both Nazism and fascism were case examples of the fantastic evils of a policy which degrades human life and holds very little store for human goodness. This attitude was prevalent during and just after World War II. It was often said then that the clear lesson of those years was that one must never permit a regime which despised humanity to gain ground, that above all the ideals of liberty, equality, and fraternity must be cherished. Communism's one merit, even to some conservatives, was its intrinsic idealism. But, as the cold war progressed, the dangers of that very idealism became more and more perceived. It became more and more appreciated that the perils of a brutal totalitarianism are nurtured by an unrealistic idealism as well as by a too-realistic pessimism. The believers in a serene human dignity had created the institutions which, in the hands of men of a lesser dignity (or skill), were viciously abused. Many men could talk of high human aspirations—the Nazis spoke of these, for the Germans, repeatedly—but if these aspirations were not realistic, the efforts to achieve the goals became satanic.

All this became most important with regard to the state. This was, par excellence, the institution relied upon by Fascists and Communists alike, and by so many liberals, to bring about a better age. The Marxist dialectic provided for the withering away of the state, of course, once the system of communism was accomplished. Lenin explicitly reiterated this prediction in his writing; in his action he contented himself with creating the most totally powerful state in modern (or perhaps all) history. On the right this zest for governmental power was not confined to the wildest Nazis. Mussolini declared, in 1931 (in other words, during the milder years of the Fascist rule) that "my formula is clear. Everything within the state, nothing outside the state, nothing against the state." At that time the left could observe that Mussolini's state was a guardian of capitalist interests, that Mussolini was a tryant. But as time went on it became clear that the tyranny of Stalin far surpassed Mussolini's, while every ambitious dictator enhanced the power of the state at the expense of the private sectors of society. Among the most prominent in those sectors were, of course, the property-owners, whose profit in Mussolini turned out to be scant indeed. In the process of helping Italian industry the Fascists socialized much of it and, through cartelization, destroyed the energy of most of the rest. And at the end, in his wretched Salo days, Mussolini's last laments were his failure to destroy capitalism, along with the Church, the monarchy, and any other conservative institution he could think of.

How disastrous the violence and collectivism of the far right proved to the stability of all responsible conservative beliefs and values! But at the same time the collectivism of the far left cut equally into the validity of liberal ideals. All of the Marxist paradises involved a denial of the civil liberties so laboriously developed by generations of liberal thinkers and statesmen. The unions and the liberal organizations were destroyed as effectively by the Communists as by the Nazis. But the liberal revulsion was at a disadvantage, so to speak, as compared to the conservative. For the weight of the vast bulk of liberal thinking since around 1870 had been, as we have noted, toward using increased state power to benefit the people, and this is basically true of liberalism today.

It is not that opposition to the government, per se, is the antithesis of totalitarianism; if that were the case, anarchism would be the truest cause. Almost everyone accepts the state in one form or another today, and the reality of coercive power in society. But the principal question in this regard is how to control that power, reducing it in some cases and diffusing it in others, so that its results may be most unlike totalitarian society. Phrased thusly, we see that liberalism has other goals which are opposed to this, while liberal conservatism has the least other desiderata. And this is logical, for it is a belief which does not forsake human hopes, but is somewhat critical about their success, is most clearly a belief to combat the messianic one-mindedness of totalitarianism. The strength of the totalitarian faiths arises largely from their wild expectations; significantly even the most thoroughly anti-human specimen was styled National Socialism. The roots of the totalitarian movements were on the left, and their early beginnings were almost always in working-class milieus; the clearest opposition in the long run rests with the conservatives who least share these aspirations, but who also do not share the far-right contempt for mankind.

The everyday politics of this conservative opposition have been presented frequently; Hayek's warning of the Road to Serfdom is perhaps the most famous. But it would be a mistake to consider this as only a current difference, dependent upon the contemporary positions of conservatism and state power. The moderate conservative claim to be the surest foe of the total state derives from the nature of the position, not only from a dislike of the modern state. Cato the Younger was not concerned with the economic issues which have so colored modern conservatism, but his distrust of Caesarian power and his attachment to the mixed constitution and the settled institutions proved to be the most principled opposition to Caesar. De Tocqueville, writing as a conservative in a time when liberalism was usually (especially in the United States) very individualistic, foresaw the dangers of a democratic uniformity and a popularly-supported state far better than most of his cohorts. De Tocqueville's conservatism has a consistency which Mill's liberalism lacked just because this suspicion of the uses of power, of reliance on the state (even while accepting and supporting many forms of state action) was so natural to a liberal conservatism. This tradition is not necessarily economic or social, and does not rest on the self-interest of the rich. It can sometimes be profitable for any group to support a very strong central power, and when the wealthy most fear for their property they will swing farther right. The surest antipathy to totalitarianism comes from the exponents of a belief; a set of principles which opposes both the unrestrained power derived from a limitless view of human nature, of radicalism and of the unrestrained power justified by a thorough contempt for humanity.

This conservatism has exercised a dual restraint. The concern with the absolute power of the state is not new—Cato's opposition to Caesarian land legislation was an early example of this, in a perhaps excessive degree—and it is the heart of all opposition to the centralization of totalitarianism. But in addition all movements of total state power involve a realignment of authority within the state, and a change in the intellectual spirit of society. The primary opposition to tyrants has always come from a belief, probably in the beginning a feeling, that the top job in a community should not be seized by a strong man. Kingship derived its authority from a traditional right, but was nonetheless deeply suspect in all the most politically advanced ancient societies. For a new man, a parvenu, to appropriate to himself this power was abhorrent to the thinking of both right and left. The objection to Peisistratus was not that he misruled Athens, but that his very suzerainty was misrule. Plato saw this differently; in his view the good absolute ruler was no tyrant, but a sort of king, and the tyrant was an immoral despot. Left-wing Roman political thought took a parallel form after 100 B.C., for Marius and his supporters and successors rejected the value of the division of power and authority in the senatorial Republic in favor of a popular dictator. The familiar agreement of the upper circle— Sulla, for example, reinforcing the work of Marius as he fought him—in attacking the ideas of a mixed constitution, a check on concentration of power within government, and a concern for legal principles, was very familiar in Greece and Rome. The best defenders of these lower-circle ideals were usually men like Cato the Younger and Demosthenes, to whom the principle of absolute rule was obnoxious for reasons of custom as well as liberty.

What we have called the Whig idea very much reflected this Catonian spirit. The United States Constitution is an excellent example. Hamilton commented, in *The Federalist* papers, that "it is impossible to read the history of the petty republics of

Greece and Italy without feeling sensations of horror and disgust at the distractions with which they were continually agitated, and at the rapid succession of revolutions by which they were kept in a state of perpetual vibration between the extremes of tyranny and anarchy." The debates at Philadelphia evidence a steady attention to the lessons of the ancient world, and those lessons were thought to have been best taught by the Catos, who fought tryanny without supporting anarchy. It is significant that the dangers of agrarian laws were often stressed in 1787, and that Hamilton was disturbed by the prospect of revolutions before 1789.

The nature of the 1787 system has been presented so often that there is very little one can say that is not hackneyed. So many of the details were framed after a sharp and at times heated sectional or group disagreement that it is not entirely accurate to say that the fine balances were the result of a devotion to principle. But it is remarkable that the compromises, often so factional (in the pejorative eighteenth-century sense) produced a constitution so well devised to manage faction. The end result was not one to kindle progressive hearts. The Bill of Rights was added partly to do that, but many anti-Federalists dissented to the last for idealistic reasons. The petty or fine-spun compromises were part of the grander compromise so brilliantly upheld in Madison's Letter No. 10, and less wholeheartedly supported by Hamilton in No. 9 and elsewhere. In *The Federalist* papers both Madison and Hamilton spoke as liberal conservatives; both were alarmed by faction and by the dangers of democracy and of power-lust, but they thought a system which offered opportunities for the best in human self-government would discourage the limitless drives which might appeal to the worst. The French alternatives in the ensuing years pointed out the reality of the Hamiltonian revolutionary extremes.

These antitheses often seemed old-fashioned in the nineteenth century. Advocates of increased government power or of increased efficiency in government usually denied that there was any correlation between their goals and an authoritarian society. This was especially true of liberal optimists; Bentham, as we have seen, advocated, at the same time, more powerful and effective state action and a very high form of individualism. But the dangers of this pragmatic liberalism were never lost sight of; the old Whigs predicted that democracy would ruin liberty throughout the century. Thus a Whig M.P. named Marsh, in arguing against the extension of the suffrage in 1860, remarked that "democracies might be anything, but they were never liberal." But, ironically, it was often the efficiency of the old absolutisms that best proved the point. When the ancient (generally thought to be moribund) Senate of Austrian Cracow fomented a revolution in Galicia in 1846, the Austrian monarchy repressed the revolt and the Senate, and thoroughly weakened the power of the Galician aristocracy. Napoleon III and Bismarck introduced universal suffrage to secure a popular base for an authoritarian state; the Whigs were dished and Caesarism took a new form, with the tools of the left used to justify the power of the right. The cross-fertilization of the right and left in the service of nationalism was greatly enhanced by the collectivism of the post-1870 years, and by the conversion of most of the right to nationalism. By 1914 even England was familiar with the neo-Hegelianism of T. H. Green and Lindsay, which ascribed to the state a purity and worth which selfish individuals, especially businessmen, could not begin to emulate. In Germany this sense of awe before the idol of the state, always a German tradition, inured to the benefit of the state of the King and Emperor, a traditional monarchy halfway to becoming a hierarchical welfare state.

But there was not much traditional about the absolutisms of the twentieth century. To some critics, such as Arendt and Friederich, the rise of totalitarianism was a novelty, a new thing under the sun. The total state, the eradication of areas of privacy and separate values which existed even in earlier despotisms, seem to them a difference in kind. This is a twin to the radical argument of the new society which will usher in the golden age; it is only fitting that the messianism of Marxism should, with its immense disillusionments, bring forward an apocalyptic anti-messianism. To one who accepts the circle, both seem very unlikely. Such a discontinuity in human experience would convert the present age into a time of revelation, perhaps of final human degradation.

One wonders how new any of the totalitarian systems are. Sauer has commented on the "interpretation that has emerged since the war [which] defines Nazism as but a modern variant of classical tyranny." The Platonic city surely was as severely centralized as anything in modern practice or theory. Even Mao Tse-tung does not advocate holding wives in common. Herodotus remarked how the Persians, whose empire was the most efficient but not one of the most despotic in the ancient Near East up to his time, had all the mail transmitted on the royal roads inspected. The economic life of Ptolemaic Egypt or the religious life of Habsburg Spain was surely as regimented as was true in Nazi Germany. Egypt could have given Germany lessons in the idea of *Führer-Prinzip,* and Spain in *limpieza.* Toynbee has even categorized all Christian Europe from 400 to 1700 as a totalitarian society. Contemporary China demonstrates both the lengths to which a modern state may go in the effort to destroy diversity, and the difficulties which these efforts involve. Perhaps it is harder to establish a total centralization now than in the days of Justinian. Of course Stalinist Russia makes the despotism of Alexander II seem panty-waist, but Stalin's evident regard for Ivan the Terrible should suggest a worthier parallel. Of course technology improves the power of the state, but in fairness to human ingenuity one must consider what the automobile, or, for that matter, the printing press have done to limit the effectiveness of governmental fiat. The Han book-burning and the Christian anti-pagan campaigns were not perfectly successful, but the same (at the least) can be said of modern examples.

But perhaps the most serious successes of the modern totalitarian states have been in more subtle things. Arendt has remarked that the appearance, after the First World War, of a new class of stateless people was an encouragement to, and a symptom of, the Kafkaesque potential of the state to reduce all relationships to a macabre rubble. The disintegration of the customary patterns meant, so the argument goes, that the old responsibilities of the government to the people, and vice versa, were eliminated. In the Austrian Empire the state may have been remote and often unrepresentative, but the traditional sense of law and order discouraged demagogues and afforded everyone some role in society. Hitler was a Lueger in a system where the state, in its old form, disappeared, and was replaced by a party (the Madisonian faction) masquerading as the government. The party became the state, destroying the rightful governing institutions and restraints, and the state swallowed up the normal forms of party activity, even (as in Russia) the forms of a totalitarian party. The result was a theory of vast national unity and the fact of very parochial dominance by one man or a cabal. How different was the Madisonian balancing of factions, preserving the limited state by diffusing the party antagonisms!

One trouble with this is that it proves too much. One can say that whereas in 1900 a man was a citizen (in a republic) now he is a national—or stateless. But in Central Europe in 1900 he was a subject, and the history of subjects shows that they were not always treated as sharers in the community of the state. As for outlawing parts of society, it can hardly be said that killing and expropriating Jews, or mistreating Poles, is a twentieth-century invention. It is true that the medieval Jew was a member of a separate communal group, and that he had the option of conversion. Hitler in this respect resembled the more bloodthirsty of Assyrian kings. The Ramesid Egyptians and Ptolemies, and Stalin and Franco, were less virulent and more successful, in the long run. Diocletian was no less energetic than Caligula, but he imposed his absolutism (which was in some ways more rigorous than Tito's) in an ordered way.

For the most inexorable extension of state power, or power by a party elite, can grow by stages and subtly reach full mastery. One man cannot exercise an absolute sway, subverting all forms of authority, but he can create a new authority—if his moves are too revolutionary, like Julius Caesar's, his heir is likely to be the legitimate beneficiary of his changes. From the days of the French revolutionary terror it has been apparent that a radical movement could be as tyrannical as any despot, and more irresistible. And, after all, it was the democratic society of Athens which fiercely maintained the distinction between citizens and metics, those stateless inhabitants whose status so appealed to Maurras and other precursors of modern fascism. All the features of modern totalitarianism have been present before, and present in recognizable form. Totalitarianism is a recent way of putting, and looking at, the combination of extreme collectivism and revolutionary activism of the upper circle. The wild mixture of hieratic form and inner formlessness does not mark the coming of a new bankruptcy, but an old condition, familiar to the inhabitants of the Hellenistic age, that time which so resembles our own.

For, to quote an observer of that period, do not ask why the former days were better, for it is ignorant to address such a question. It is a pitfall of conservatism to ask that question, thinking that things have indeed degenerated, but this, in the strictest sense of the word, is reactionary thinking. And it is the danger of liberalism to believe that, even if very slowly, the world is steadily improving. The most effective counter to totalitarian systems is not to disbelieve in them, or to lose one's sense of history in opposing them, but to use against them the arguments of limitation.

Which of course brings us back to the philosophy of liberal conservatism. There can be no gainsaying that nationalism and the varying cults of efficiency captivated many on the right, and still do. But it is not hard for the liberal elements in conservatism to dissociate themselves from these causes, because the worship of the state and the covert admiration for the perfectly ordered society have proved too disastrous, even as the mystique of the party and the group has come to seem dangerous. At its least virulent the Fascist state has shown its unfriendliness to the conservative values, as commentators on Salazar's Portugal have remarked. There is probably more in common between the bureaucrats in Lisbon and Moscow than between the former and their *haute bourgeois* partners in Portugal. How much more is this true when one considers the middle class in the Western democracies, whose history has been a story of opposition to the absolute state! Liberalism, certainly the often conservative liberalism of the Fair Deal-New Frontier in the United States and Wilsonian socialism in Great Britain, is also the heir of that tradition. But even that liberalism still retains an inkling of the concept that there is a special virtue in the state, that limited power is probably wrong per se, and that the Whig sense of limitation is outmoded. To be a conservative is to look backwards, at least at times, and to treat the future as an extension of the past; nothing can be more uncongenial to the adherents or apologists for totalitarianism. Almost everyone comes to welcome the power of the government at some time or place, but the conservative quadrant has most come to realize how dangerous it is to convert that acceptance into an unqualified reliance. One may attribute this to cynical self-interest or fear of the universal suffrage state, but it is a handy reflex in our time.

But all this is of little point if one sees little, or nothing, wrong with totalitarianism. To many, and not just Communists, the greatest fault in the world is to be reactionary, in whatever sense it is variously used, and totalitarianism is not so sinful in Dar-es-Salaam, or Pretoria, that it lacks defenders in high places—for limited purposes, of course.

What is wrong with totalitarianism? If to be conservative is but to be stuck with old-fashioned notions, there is no use in opposing them to the new order(s). Hitler remarked that he would have been ridiculous coming in a great carriage, like a be-wigged monarch. His way was modern, so he claimed; to the Marxists their way is the only modern way. To this many people in the West would easily reply that the novelty of totalitarianism was deceptive, and most would say that the virtues were nonexistent. Unfortunately, this does not settle the matter. The persuasive power of communism is still very potent, and especially with many to whom the great disillusionment of 1939 or 1948 are of no interest. The totalitarian Communist answers to the issues of colonialism (and its bastard child, neo-colonialism), was, and poverty must be refuted as if Ribbentrop and Molotov had never conferred, and as if Silone and Mattheisen had never been dismayed.

Fundamentally, there is no refutation—the underlying circular questions of politics always remain open. But the basic assumptions of these new faiths are buttressed by, and ostensibly proved by, factual data. Marxism was erected on certain predictions of social and economic developments, and to the extent that most modern radical movements have also stressed economics, they too, to a very great degree, have raised their edifices on statistical foundations. But to a great extent the majority opinion of Western thought has come to doubt many of the formerly accepted factual beliefs which grew, often from mildly liberal beginnings, to become the data of Marxism and of other radical ideologies. And this re-evaluation has served to reinforce the moderate conservative view of the past, that very view which we have seen as being most opposed to the tendencies of the extremism of the right as well as the left.

In short, the second argument for this lower-circle conservatism is that, in dealing with the history of the last two hundred years, its assumptions have been most useful. This is perhaps the greatest legacy of that thoroughgoing conservative intellectual counter-revolution of the 1947 epoch, which wrested the offensive from the left and the far right, and whose insights, old in some ways but very new in others, deserve much wider recognition. In the 1930's the liberals so often bemoaned an alleged cultural lag which froze the leaders of business and government in outworn attitudes; it is the right's turn to look to the new for guidance.

The economic recoveries of West Germany and Japan are obvious examples of the pragmatic success of economic conservatism. These *wirtschaftwunderkinder* were raised on the outworn diet of classical economics—high degree of saving in the private sector, minimum government interference with, but encouragement of, private investment, and a tax structure weighted toward these ends. The successful development in Japan of even the minutiae of American capitalism may be in part attributed to the marvelous Japanese facility for adaptation, but it is remarkable that the mature American capitalist system seemed so worth copying, or that the results have been so exhilarating.

The extensive foreign private borrowing of Japanese industry followed the lines of American borrowing from Europe in the nineteenth century, and proved more efficacious the more unrestrained it became. The comparison with the largely governmental lending to India has been increasingly embarrassing to the adherents of public-aid programs. The Japanese standard of living, burdened as it is with the rising of foreign-held debt or equity ownership, has far outrun the Indian standard, which has been greatly subsidized by aid grants.

Of course, as is pointed out in reply, all the successful postwar societies have large welfare programs. But it is significant that their success has followed the primary economic success; the accomplishments of the business revival have made possible the great welfare systems. The classical liquidation of the old currency and the Erhard reforms of 1948–49 came first; later the very extensive welfare programs were expanded. The Keynesians had many proposals along the lines of the new orthodoxy for Italian unemployment in the late 1940's; the advent of classical fiscal and monetary policies and the unleashing of the Lombard entrepreneurs in the early 1950's did much more to accomplish the task and provide the basis for other liberal reforms in the south. The world today does not await the coming of welfare systems and plans to eradicate poverty, for the work of the Fabians and the Keynesians has been done everywhere. It is a common mistake to think of Latin America as embedded in a reactionary mire, without any of the benefits of the last hundred years of reform. Quite the contrary is true (at least in the cities); Brazil struggles with a six-hour day and the social-security system of Chile is so elaborate and costly that it is said that even Chilean socialists propose terminating the whole thing and starting over again.

One way to clean the slate is, of course, to eliminate private property, and with it all the tedious compromises and halfmeasures of the liberals. The Soviet example shows that that can be done; the heavens will not fall in, a Communist society is possible and effective. But in judging the triumphs of this society the promises of the Marxist dream, or if that is unfair, of the current Communist leaders, should be weighed by the standards of our time. Let us, for the moment, not consider China, as too new a system. The Russian experiment has lasted a half-century, with over twenty years of peace since World War II. The heavy industry of the Soviet Union has grown very impressively, and there is no unemployment. But the great accomplishments of the current capitalistic economies—consumer industries which have so raised the living standards of the United States, and France, and Finland, and now Mexico, are not paralleled in Russia. In heavy industry the Soviet Union has raced toward equality (not yet reached) with the United States in steel production, only to find that it was, in modern terms, the wrong race. Then the Soviets discovered the vital role of chemicals and aluminum. The Russians are noted for their mathematical aptitude, yet they are still trying to catch up in the computer derby.

All of this does not prove the capitalistic way of life is better; such comparisons never can. It is true that the reading of books, excellence in athletics, and skill at chess have thrived in the Soviet Union, but the maxim that man does not live by bread alone is a peculiar one for Marxist apologists. Bread, we had always been told, was what really counted, and not prayers or theoretical books; but of late the successes of bread production have not been considered a salient Communist accomplishment.

This is not to say that the Communist system can never provide the good things of life, bread as well as tractors, automobiles as well as rockets. An ordered system of production will produce substantial results, even if it is brutal in the process. Hitler did eliminate unemployment in Germany in the 1930's, and millions of apartment rooms are being provided in Russia today. Only disorganized authoritarians like Sukarno fail completely. But that is not the point, or it certainly should not be made the point. The totalitarian faith assumed that one justification for the seamier side—and even to many adherents it was seamy— was the unique answer of the all-powerful state in economic planning. But Erhard has done what the Nazis said could never be done under a pluto-democratic regime, and as for the much-awaited collapse of the American system, poor Varga waited until his dying day for this in vain.

Moreover, this is relevant in considering the politer disagreements of Western economic policy. The arguments of the democratic socialists and of many liberals against capitalism were to a large extent based on the same statist premises, even if far more moderate in conclusions. But many of the details of this view, both historically and from the aspect of analysis of contemporary economics, now seem very dated. For example, the accepted story (developed by the Hammonds and other Fabians) of the ordeal of the British working-class in the years from 1790 to 1850 has undergone drastic revision. The greatest hardships were suffered not by workers in the mills, but older trades, like the weavers, who were bypassed by the industrial revolution. It is now clear that once the Napoleonic Wars were over the English working class enjoyed a distinct rise in its standard of living. The vast accomplishments of nineteenth-century capitalism have long been admitted by radical thinkers—the famous tribute of Marx is equalled by the almost excessive praise of Laski—but it has also become clear that the social costs they claimed were not so prevalent as they thought. The great price declines of the century, especially in the United States, disguised often spectacular rises in the real wages and living standards of the working class.

The vigor of the "revisionist" schools in business history has similar implications. The re-evaluations of Morgan, Rockefeller, and Insull have recast the place of these men in American economic history; the broader studies of business practice in the Gilded Age and in the early twentieth century have altered many of the commonly-accepted assumptions. Many of these assumptions were based on the politically or socially determined dicta of contemporary observers, men like Henry Lloyd and Gustavus Myers, whose facts were strongly influenced by a socialistic view which put no stock in the mechanics of capital formation and economic developments. Their judgments were often repeated by writers who were not socialists, but men to whom the jeremiads of Veblen were more understandable than the statistics of Mitchell. For example, the concept of watered stock, which so exercised generations of investors and shippers, and has been repeated by so many historians, partly involved a misunderstanding of the difference between book value and market value, and the unimportance of capitalization in questions of product pricing. It is now obvious that this question of watered stock was really significant only in public utilities, such as the railroads, where the rate return was in part determined by government regulation. And here the complexities of replacement cost and original cost have been largely ignored by liberal writers who have overlooked the consequences of price changes, the vast importance of which we have experienced so amply in more recent years.

This work of revision has not been confined to the United States, for the formative influence of the merchants in the early Middle Ages and the pacifying role of big business in the nineteenth century have been increasingly accepted and reaffirmed. The European stereotype of capitalism as a cause of war had roots similar, in many respects, to the American view of the robber barons. This was frequently joined with the allied accusation that capitalism, especially the mature, overripe finance capitalism which had exhausted its home markets, was responsible for imperialism. Both these charges arose out of the accusations of radical thinkers of the late nineteenth century who seized on the recrudescense of militarism and aggressive tendencies as evidence of the link between the greatly-enhanced scope of private wealth and these militant, un-bourgeois developments. The schemes of Zaharoff gave credence to the accusations of socialist journalists, which became solidified into theory by Sombart; the remarkable career of Rhodes provided the liberal Hobson with a thesis which Lenin converted into a part of the Marxist canon.

Not very much is left of these conclusions, and even less of the inevitable theories constructed out of them. The case against financial or industrial causation of war has mounted impressively. Thus the financial pressures exerted in Paris and Berlin on less-developed countries to influence their policies were invariably the result of political decisions imposed on the businessmen, not vice versa. The great international banking houses, such as the Rothschilds, were almost always very pacific, and occasionally influentially so; with good reason, as Polanyi has demonstrated, as the peace of the nineteenth century was especially conducive to the prosperity of the rich, and its warlike sequel has certainly not been easy for the Rothschilds, or their competitors. Of course there were exceptions—the case against the armament manufacturers is an often-cited example. Yet Trebilcock has shown how much even the British government engineered the creation of capacity in the gunpowder industry in the late nineteenth century. Perhaps more research would explode most of the theses of the armament barons. So the facts are not very suitable for the capitalist-war thesis, as the prosperity of the Krupps in the 1950's indicates. Most of the allegations about merchants of death have not held up in the court of historical research. The arch-villains of 1914, men like Von Hötzendorf, Berchtold and Sazonov, were politicians and generals, while the businessmen were much more notable in their efforts for peace—Cassel and Ballin are good examples. As for Rhodes, he has proved to be the exception that proves the rule, for his love of money, advanced as it was, was far outdistanced by his zest for power. Rhodes' behavior in regard to the Jameson raid and his whole philosophy showed that his imperialism grew out of a rejection of moneymaking as an end in itself in favor of an overweening political ambition.

The majority of entrepreneurs were not Rhodeses, and their eagerness for peace was matched by a disinclination for imperialist adventures. Rhodesia did not pay Rhodes for his efforts, in the short run, as a commercial venture, and the great (and greatly wicked) ventures were undertaken by monarchs like Leopold I of the Belgians, who could proceed as a conqueror rather than a businessman. The European ministries and even Theodore Roosevelt (who pushed the Morgan interests into China) did the urging, but except for mining ventures there was not a great deal of enthusiasm on the part of business in the advanced countries. Fieldhouse has investigated the evidence and concluded that the Hobson-Lenin thesis has very little evidence to support it; this confirms the Schumpeterian analysis of imperialism as an atavistic military urge, rather than an advanced capitalist economic one.

What all this adds up to is a general confirmation of the Adam Smith-Cobden view of capitalists and capitalism. Businessmen, *pace* Smith, may be rapacious or devious, and they are often timid (Chamberlain's attitude in 1938 has often been cited as an example of this), but this does not add up to an indictment of the system. In one way, however, these characteristics are revealing. Smith, who as recent commentators have remarked was definitely a liberal, looked toward a freer market system and a reduction of government controls as part of a social system where greater economic opportunity would reduce the advantages of the privileged groups. Cobden's similar position was a small-businessman's ideology, designed in large part as an attack on the aristocratic, landowning ethos. But there is no value in denying that the development of modern capitalism has resulted in a society in which opportunity is not perfectly equal, where, through inheritance and other social arrangements, great wealth and economic power can and often does reside in families for many generations, and where these families basically represent an upper class. And of course even a perfect equality of opportunity is not pure equality, and all the less so in a highly complex and multi-stratified society.

All of which does not denigrate the smooth-working and impressive benefits of capitalism as it has worked in the twentieth century. The remarkable thing about the reassessments of recent years is the manner in which they have confirmed many of the qualities claimed by earlier supporters, but in a more subtle and roundabout fashion. Thus the business community has been largely acquitted (for the time, at least) of warlike tendencies. But far less reliance is now placed on the preservation of peace through the replacement of warlike urges by a universal desire for trade, which will make all men interdependent and therefore pacific. This eighteenth-century expectation, which was so utopian yet thoroughly materialistic, was noble, and an excellent refutation of the idea that business must be mean-spirited in thought and execution. Today, however, we place less trust in a reform of human nature through capitalism, and more trust in those qualities of prudence and fiscal conservatism engendered by the system. Merchants and manufacturers do not, as we know, have an unusual degree of fraternal spirit—there are Cadburys, but also Marches among the roster of tycoons—but in most cases the more timid and selfish instincts of commercial policy will result in a peaceful program. In 1938 this was craven, but that is an atypical example. More to the point, perhaps, is the United States' experience of 1898, where a largely artificial surge of benevolence whipped up a strong fervor against Spain, a feeling held most avidly by Populists and radical journalists. The most unwilling groups were the wealthy mugwumps, magnates like Carnegie, and large portions of the business community; the national leader who was least bellicose was Mark Hanna, the leftists' bête noire. Today almost all liberals are agreed that our policy was too belligerent and to a great degree imperialistic.

There is a parallel with this in the analyses of the workings of the market system by friendly economists. The progression of mathematically-oriented thinking from Bernoulli to Stigler has added many layers of insights and redefinitions to the Benthamite calculus, and it has greatly amended the eighteenth-century assumptions of invariable profit-seeking. The view of today's economic system is therefore far more complex, and interposes innumerable steps between the gain orientations of individuals and the well-being of the world. But the net result is to see in the aggregation of institutions, cross-purposed motivations, and even irrationalities a total picture where, as in de Mandeville, private avarice is public gain. Corporations and other institutions grow in size and market dominance, but (cf., Galbraith) this tends to even out through a balance of countervailing powers. The desiderata of even businessmen are found to be much less simple than Bentham thought, but this has led to viewing all the varied desires as having a price. Utility theory has given way to considerations of indifference curves, and competition in price is now supplemented by competition in quality. And as all the human goals are thought of as now competing in the value systems—leisure against status, as well as saving against spending—everything comes to have a price, to be part of this larger market. As one writer has recently rather sadly observed, even the rites of passage—coming of age, marriage, death, all so tied up with myth and religion in man's history—are now becoming a part of the commercial fabric. As we have retreated from the simpler contract-oriented nineteenth-century world we have built a paradoxically more price-conscious universe. The end result of game theory is to convert even the most autocratic power situations into games where the calculations of gain pervade; Monopoly games in the Kremlin are not just a *Wall Street Journal* conceit, but a symbol of our time. In all this the thrust of contemporary economics owes much more to the neo-classical school than to Veblen or Keynes.

To some conservatives, such as Ropke, this is the dark side to the accomplishments of the free market. But it is possible to come to the opposite conclusion. The considerations of price—considerations of comparative advantage, of gain limited by risk and prudence, of limitation rather than hope—are, as we have noted, basically conservative forces. That is not to say that the immediate content of these new ideas must be conservative—Galbraith clearly is not, and the schemata of Neumann and von Morgenstern can be put to many uses. But how often the upshot is to place the vagaries of the complex mid-twentieth-century capitalist (or even socialist) systems into frameworks which are explicable in conservative terms, and which reinforce the simpler concepts of the past rather than replace them. The utilization of these criteria by Kahn to evolve a civil defense program is a case in point; Kahn accepts the underlying situation and works out rational alternatives of response. Kahn's leftward opposition is torn between denying the rationality of his choices and a refusal to accept the concept of choosing between evils. Without going into the merits of Kahn's case, his thinking is a good specimen of the applicability of these price considerations in non-economic matters; the broader market ideology infuses this non-utopian calculation into quite non-economic political areas. The work of Downs on the economics of voting, the market-relationship analyses of Alchian, and the legal-economic corporate theories of Manne reinforce this view. These markets may be impure or disagreeable, as corrupt voters or manipulating financiers distort the democratic process. The new version of the process is less edifying—voters maximizing their well-being by treating their vote as being of more use to them as a commodity than as a direct political implement of choice, or investors determining the security price structure by selling or buying already issued stock, and thus affecting corporate control through the price level rather than at annual directors' elections or through new stock issues—but highly acceptable to one who considers that everything has its price, and that the function of a good society is to improve the options rather than to reform the system.

All this, as Kahn demonstrates, is not confined to a capitalist market setting. In another setting, Lange has postulated the use of market theory under a purely socialist economy. There is no reason to deny such a possibility, but there is a good chance such an economy would tend to build up the forces of individualist conservatism (with an attendant backward look) that we see in contemporary Poland. Abram Bergson has aptly termed this "creeping capitalism." The tools used in discussing civil defense, or the optimum use of strategic bombing, or of duopoly bargaining, have been of use in analyzing Roman-Armenian relations in the time of the Empire. All of this reinforces the price-conscious ideology of the conservatism of our time. This, however, is not entirely consistent with one of the habits of thought of many conservatives. Many conservatives have adopted the idea of progress as an argument for their brand of change. One of the liberal concepts of the early nineteenth century was a rejection of the past in favor of a new dispensation. Free trade, or the industrial revolution, or the growth of the bourgeoisie, or all of them, were said to have changed the whole course of history. In Spencer this is a sort of twist on Hodgskin, just as the Saint-Simonians made Condorcet a kind of industrial high priest. This view has become a handmaiden of progress, and from there a business interpretation of the progressive faith. The *Fortune* credo of the permanent revolution is a fine example of this view today, and as the future is confidently awaited, the past is rejected or ignored. From the liberal viewpoint this progressivism is often spurious, for as Camus remarked, "progress, paradoxically, can be used to justify conservatism. A draft drawn on confidence in the future, it allows the masters to have a clear conscience." This clear conscience is gained by admitting that in the old days conditions were harsh, but no longer, and the future grows better. In 1850 it was admitted that there had been sharp injustices in the eighteenth century, but prosperity had come to all. By 1900 the miseries of the early days of the Industrial Revolution were lamented, but the triumph of Victorian progress (or American good government, according to Carnegie) had put that behind us. The 1920's had replaced prewar greed by the philosophy of service, but it is remarkable that the Lucites have had to rediscover this all over again, and confess to the sins of the 1920's. In the Soviet Union this process is becoming a feature of state policy.

It is much easier to be frankly a conservative. Revisionism need not justify only a certain period, but has the whole history of our economics, and our politics, to draw on. Freedom of opportunity did not begin with the Chapelier Law or the Industrial Revolution, as a reader of lives of self-made men from 1200 on discovers. One must admit that the rise of wealth has not necessarily spread it more evenly, or less evenly. Some of the liberal capitalist expectations were quite naive. Free trade has not leveled many fortunes, and the early laissez-faire concept of a constantly-dropping interest rate seemed very prescient in the 1930's, but ridiculous today. Vindications of John Quincy Adams and Calhoun are not surprising, and the amazement which greeted Peter Viereck's apology for Metternich has thoroughly subsided. Even kings have their day, and the foreign policy of the American republic in 1945 took cognizance of the stabilizing influence of monarchist institutions. The Democratic administration in Washington—admittedly led by conservatives such as Grew—decided that it was a mistake to dislodge the Hohenzollerns in 1918. The cries of "hang the Kaiser" had made his or his son's retention as ruler of Germany very unlikely; the upshot proved to be a very great change for the worse. So far at least, events seem to have vindicated the decision to permit Hirohito to remain the emperor of Japan. The personality of the Emperor was of course a factor, but there was an awareness of the value, for a liberal as well as a conservative, in preserving the symbols (and of course this invariably goes beyond the external forms into the realities of power) of tradition. There is much more to liberal conservatism than the capitalist system, or the last two hundred years.

So many of the optimistic liberal conclusions have been cast into doubt. That picture of Prussian Junkerdom, a cold authoritarian system which opposed all forms of democratic progress, has surely undergone revision. The worst threat came from a mixed crew of, by and large, déclassé and even proletarian adventurers, most of whom came from the south of Germany. In the end Prussian aristocracy scored as well in the test of human decency as almost any group in Germany. The same was true in Japan and Italy. All three, moreover, were nations with traditions of education and learning. The experiences of Germany and Japan disproved the idea that mass education would be "democratic," if by that one concluded that ideas of equality or constitutionalism, or even any generally accepted political standard of sophistication, would gain ground through the schools. Education, that darling (now and for the last hundred years) of liberal thinking, has been realized by almost all thinking people to be a value worth no more than what one puts into the process. There is a fine bit of irony here; Dewey's progressive educational ideas were a marked triumph in the war against absolutist philosophies of education, but Dewey held, throughout his long, illustrious life, an optimism about the triumph of virtue as fine as Plato's. The world is more intractable; there is no assurance that all men, or all children, if left to their own good judgment, will see and approve virtue. Of course both Plato and Dewey do have means of guidance (Plato far more than Dewey, but both assert the course is that of nature—as do all their critics), which has in turn given rise to the opposed fear, the Pavlovian syndrome which haunts modern thought. Here too, opinion perhaps tends to extremes, for after fifty years of communism the skepticisms and capacities for free thought on the part of Soviet youth are a revelation. Once again, the Friederich-Arendt thesis is liberalism turned inside out, but the capabilities of the state, modern or ancient, to build a "new man" or to eradicate the old one have here too been exaggerated. Hitler, Stalin and Trujillo, perhaps in their various ways three of the cruelest, most malevolent rulers in world history, grew up in pious, conventional surroundings. Who is to say that they were badly educated by their religious mentors, or led astray by the secular, rationalist world in which they made their way? And there is good argument that their legacies were also revocable. The erstwhile schoolchildren of the 1930's, in Dusseldorf and Dneprotrovsk, are, at least so far, not turning out to be the totalitarian mass men that they were educated to be.

There are too many complexities in the world for many of the old political axioms, and the liberal ones are especially vulnerable. Just as education has shown its weaknesses and two-sidedness, so does the twin faith in the people, or the workers, or the "masses." The lessons of mass violence of the last twenty-five years have illustrated the enduring quality of the mob. The American public could be supercilious about those of Bagdad or Bali; Watts and Detroit may have done more than ten Whittaker Chamberses to shake the liberal ideology. As for the Communist states, the examples of perfection which the workers' states provide should have (and largely have) eliminated much of the discussion about the special virtue of the proletariat. In the United States in the 1960's there is developing a sociological literature, largely written by liberals, which assembles evidence showing the political indifference and often the anti-civil-libertarian and xenophobic ideas of lower-income groups. The left-of-center assumptions that anti-Catholicism or anti-Semitism in the past were the work of reactionary and highly affluent groups has been largely disproved. Hofstadter's work has shown the demagogic and prejudiced quality of much of the left-wing thought of the American West in the 1880's and 1890's; his *The Age of Reform* has traced some of these intellectual currents into the Progressive movement. It is hard to deny that much of the Populist feeling was grounded on an ethnocentric hatred for the Rothschilds and the Morgan partners. The predilection for seeing history as governed by conspiracies grew in late-nineteenth-century thought; the upper circle was (and still is) highly influenced by these suspicions of evil networks of Jews, Jesuits, or plutocrats (or a mixture) engaged in devilish work. Schumpeter has commented that there is a close parallel between those who believe that everything has been determined by "a committee of supremely wise and malevolent Jews," and those who think that membership in this committee is open to the top financial magnates of all races. The mass popularity of these various conspiracy theories, which have so damaged all conservative values, cannot be dismissed. The clearest evidence of modern scholarship is that these theories with their simple explanations are usually very wrong (the big business-war thesis is an example of this) and that they can infect large groups of presumably educated people.

Furthermore, it is hard to find a golden age when one could surely count on "the people.'" In that great age of popular revolution—the latter half of the eighteenth century—when enlightenment (with or without a capital E) swept Western Europe, this specter of popular disorder was as dangerous as ever. The anti-Jewish mobs of 1753 and the anti-Catholic mobs of 1780 were far more popularly based than the memberships of the Whig or radical groups that finally established fully equal rights and laid the groundwork for the modern English atmosphere of individual rights and humanitarianism. In fact many of the radicals had second thoughts in 1791 when these same mobs tore down Priestley's home—these ambivalences of the democratic urge have long been known, but recent events have thrown a new light on them. It is no surprise today to be told that the Narodniki were successful with the Russian peasantry only in the area of encouraging anti-Semitism, or that Tom Watson achieved his greatest success when his populism emerged as purely racist.

The spectacle of the ardent "democrat" as a virulent xenophobe has been a standard of twentieth-century history from Hiram Johnson to Sukarno, with Germany again the prize example. The weight of the evidence seems to confirm the suspicion that this demagogery was usually quite popular, in both senses; literally, a flattering of the people. Sociological studies within the last twenty years have often disclosed that the lower-income groups may be to the left economically, as a matter of self-interest, but that their general political views may be very far to the right. The authoritarian personality, far from being only the ideal type of a Fascist general, is frequently found in the working-class parent.

This is, of course, another way of phrasing the axiom of the meeting of extremes which forms part of the base of the circular theory. It is not insignificant that Schlesinger has accepted this, in a limited form, in his thinking, and it follows that from this he goes on to propose a Niebuhrian (and therefore rather conservative) analysis of human nature. Schlesinger has also stated that after the experience of totalitarianism, George Babbitt does not seem so bad after all. Other progressives have used other examples, as even Francis Bacon has been drafted into the left wing, but the message is clear: The left's old villains do not seem so bad after all.

This, of course, dovetails with the first point—the impact of what the mass, absolute state can produce has driven many men of good will back to a greater appreciation of the values which were so easily attacked before. This is not a one-way street, for the comprehension by conservatives of the liberal spirit is an equal part of this process. But the fading of the Victorian age damaged conservatism some time ago and the optimism of the left is now most vulnerable. As between the partners—conservative liberalism and liberal conservatism—it is the belief with the fewest illusions about mankind and the most regard for accepted institutions which can make the greatest claims to vindication.

A third argument in favor of our conservatism is the lack of success in improving the human race which has become manifest in our time. Progress, that great god of our forefathers, has palpably suffered in reputation since 1914—that is such a cliché that one is ashamed to say it. As we have seen, progress per se is not of necessity a left-right issue, for Rousseau was probably no less to the left because he believed that perfection was the original state, and that man declined thereafter. But construing history as a downhill path is not likely to enhance one's confidence in human capabilities, which perhaps accounts for even Rousseau's willingness to espouse some rather conservative proposals for man as he now exists. The vast, idealistic optimism in man's potentialities which the late eighteenth century inspired took—Condorcet and Godwin are the clearest, but of course not the only examples—the form of projecting great and steady improvements in the state of man. Marxism was the true child of this enthusiasm, and is the most progressive belief in world history, since it postulates a man-made heaven on earth coming as the climax of human development.

Perhaps it is too easy to scoff at this today, and many thinkers, by no means all Marxists, have turned to science to vindicate the reality of much of the progressive idea. The standard of living —the value of goods and services consumed per capita—is at a record high throughout most of the world. The marvels of very rapid transportation and almost instantaneous communication surpass the hopes of the great optimists of a hundred years ago. The very details of Condorcet's vision as to mass education and popular government have to a great degree been carried out. The affluent society of college-educated workingmen, attending concerts or listening to fine music on their hi-fi sets, traveling to all parts of the world during their extended and ever-increasing vacations, and choosing their governors in free and reasonably frequent elections, conforms quite well to the optimistic dream. Yet the Idea of Progress is in bad repute. This might seem unfair or paradoxical.

There certainly are good reasons for this unpopularity—Buchenwald and Vortruka are the most well-known explanations. Yet the savage viciousness which has been exhibited in our time has not been unprecedented; the armies of Genghis Khan or of Sargon could be as ruthless and sadistic, and the burnings, torture, and various forms of execution inflicted in the Europe of Erasmus and Montaigne show that inhumanity in an age of learning did not begin recently. In the eighteenth century the famous affair of Calas, from which Voltaire earned his most noble fame, demonstrates how cruelty and bigotry have persisted at all times. But that is the point, for the vindication of Calas was supposed to be a milestone in the freeing of man from these bestial instincts and beliefs. It is no longer possible to assume this, and the very triumphs of technology have given these instincts more opportunity to be effective. There have been all too many "final solutions" in the past—the Assyrians were quite thorough—but it took longer, as a rule, and was less completely coordinated.

Technology and political science have gone different ways for one simple reason. Man is capable of learning more and more of the universe, and of using the materials of the universe for his desires. But there is no indication that his goodness, or his capacity for judgment and for social organization is improvable. There is a straight line in one field, but a circle in the other. The mathematicians are successfully solving Hilbert's problems, even if it is a slow job, but Zeno's paradoxes remain paradoxical. It would be possible to deduce from this the need to check or turn back the growth of scientific knowledge, but that is quite evidently out of the question. What is called for is a philosophy which can deal with this fickleness of progress, so as to determine which technological advances require a change in the political apparatus, and which scientific advances are, from the view of politics, retrogressions. Of course this is no science, for one man's gains are another man's loss—one reason why the idea of scientific progress has been so ill-fated. The greatest questions of scientific application involve these issues of judgment and choice, questions which cannot be determined scientifically themselves—such as the value which one gives to the encouragement of automotive development—and which depend on one's underlying views.

But in drawing this dichotomy between scientific progress and non-scientific inertia there is a perhaps too-great gulf described.

Man may be the same old Adam, but his institutions, like his machines, have had a long time to grow. In the battle of the ancients and the moderns the latter claimed that they had the advantage of standing on the shoulders of their predecessors, of being the legatees of cumulative wisdom. For what does that count in political theory? Once again, the history of painting may be relevant. In the first place, each great artist is nonpareil; the high-school student of today may know more physics than Archimedes, but he cannot paint better than Botticelli. But there are constantly details of perspective and the nature of paint which do accumulate to the benefit of the artist. And there are more important linear developments—each generation acquires, in addition to the specific information accumulated before, the chance of seeing the work of more predecessors. Some are lost and forgotten, but there is a longer line. And this has generally tended toward that universalism of art, that liberation of art from servant to master, which we have noted before. This process may have come to one conclusion in the Graeco-Roman world, to begin the process from scratch again in the early Middle Ages, but that could (and to some extent, did) happen with the sciences. The potentialities of painting as a form of expression, as an independent field of human endeavor, even as a religion, have, as Malraux has shown, grown steadily.

But this expansion is not necessarily an improvement. To most Western art-lovers it has been, in the twentieth century especially, an often frustrating process; art was more easily popular in the sixteenth century than today, and more popular in the ancient world than in the Renaissance, according to Spengler. But if popularity is inversely correlated with true value, one of the assumptions of human progress is cast in doubt. This paradox of the poverty of the spirit in the midst of intellectual plenty is a familiar one. In no age has the scope of human knowledge seemed so vast. In almost every field we know so much more of the remote past, and of the emerging present. Twelfth-century music is no longer a forgotten art, but it thrives alongside the revolutionary products of the present. The interest in the minutiae of the past grows at the same time that the present is so fruitful. In the law the multiplying reports of recent years jostle the also-growing researches on long-past decisions. But we pay less attention to *stare decisis* than we used to, and Coke and Blackstone are less quoted—there may be more year-books in print, but far fewer citations in the court opinions. The body of scholarship on the ancient world has expanded magnificently, aided by the great work of the assiduous archae-ologists, but the impact of the ancient world—including the Bible —on life has never been less. The knowledge of human and animal pre-history has multiplied unbelievably in the last hun-dred years, so that as we reach out toward the Milky Way and beyond we reach back into the time of Rhodesian Man and far behind. But this is misleading, because as the knowledge of man's origins or of ancient Greece becomes larger, it becomes more specialized, and of less interest or accessibility to the great majority. Five hundred years ago the world was thought to begin with Adam, whose history and significance were universally known in Europe. Now we believe we have far more exact and extensive knowledge of innumerable periods predating 4004 B.C. —the facts and import of which are little known. Moreover, even the very story of Adam, which has also produced a whole new literature of higher criticism, has increased as the public knowl-edge of or concern with the book of Genesis has faded. Theodore Roosevelt stood at Armageddon and battled for the Lord; we now have far more detailed information about how many armies stood at Meggido and battled for their lords, but that "we" is, by and large, not us, the non-specialists in ancient Near Eastern history, so that more information is less understanding (or ap-parent understanding).

But this understanding may have been a mistake—why should we want to think the world was created two hundred generations ago, when two billion years is more likely? Unfortunately know-ing more, or thinking one knows more, is no *vade mecum* to a better world. The trouble with too much knowledge has been that it becomes fragmented, the province of specialists who become increasingly immersed in details. What is gained in one sense is lost in another. This then becomes an issue of judgment, of comparative values. For example, it has been suggested by Platt that the answer to the fantastic proliferation of books, new books and rediscovered old books, is the remarkable new inventions in miniaturization and microminiaturization of written material. It is not ridiculous to imagine machinery which can store everything printed in a small space, and reproduce what is desired at a moment's notice. This would solve the space problem, and perhaps the accessibility problem which now so troubles us. But this would make the chief problem worse, for it would greatly ease the task of those who are writing to gain a wider attention for ever more specialized studies. As the capacity grew, the range of books would grow to fill it, making the problem of choosing between them, and ordering their plentitude of knowledge and opinion even more difficult. The tempting answer of censoring or prearranging, which might be made technologically far more simple, might seem very plausible. More might well mean less.

Total destruction is always an answer to the proliferation of a too-expensive society. As a generation sees its past become a burden it may develop a subsconscious desire to burn the artifacts that weigh it down—and this may not always be subconscious—for when lovers of the past object to tearing down old buildings they run the risk of encouraging a desire to sweep the whole of history away. There can be too much of a good thing. This may be true of humans as well as books; the tools of modern war may be the most natural instruments of Malthusian thinning in a world whose population is growing as fast as ours is.

Technology is not an enemy, but each step forward has such varying possibilities that progress in science can turn out to be movement in many directions—up, down, or sideways—in the areas on which it impinges. To return to painting, consider how the developments of the last hundred years have affected the history of that art. In 1840 one might have predicted that the museum and the growth of art-for-art's sake would lead to more and greater Ingreses and Delacroixs; this was the opinion of the men who were respected. As these painters were better known, and as their great forerunners were more understood, their impact would grow. The invention of photography, by making the dissemination of good art much easier, and by clarifying the picture of the real world, would presumably accelerate that trend. Nothing was farther from the case. Many painters recoiled from painting what the camera could capture, while others sought to catch the forms which the camera suggested, rather than the realistic picture which it portrayed. The great new technological age of our day is contemporaneous with a time when all art has turned back to the past. Almost every style of art preceding Masaccio or transcending Europe has interested modern painters, just at the time when scientific discoveries and new techniques had so changed daily living that it has been said that life had altered more from 1870 to 1960 than it had changed in several thousand years before. This turning toward the past has been true of all the arts. In literature the influence of Eliot and Pound in going back beyond the seventeenth century followed the French symbolist movement, which had so carefully cut the cord connecting the art of the early and late nineteenth century (paralleling the Impressionist Revolt). In music it has been said that much of modern music is closer to Guillaume de Machault than to anything in the eighteenth or nineteenth century. There seems to be more in common between even the Play of Daniel and the theater of the absurd than there is between either and the "realist" drama of the year 1550 (or 1700, depending where one places the change).

The relevance to political history is obvious. The years of rationalism, of middle-class liberalism, were the years of realistic art and harmonic music, and like these art forms, what seemed to the nineteenth century to be the height of progress, the last or latest stage in an upward climb, was merely one phase. Maine's progression from status to contract progressed backward, or, in Tawney's terms, to function. The underlying facts of Maine's analysis have not been disproved, just as Spencer's projection of greater and greater differentiation and specialization have been confirmed. But Maine and Spencer lived to see the social consequences of their ideas take strange forms; Justice Holmes and

Beatrice Webb proved to be strange followers, not to mention their disciples. Maine's work was an inspiration to all who came after him, but what he thought of as the one avenue of progress became a two-way street. An American legal scholar, Nathan Isaacs, has traced the rise and fall of Maine's three periods of legal change—those of fiction, equity, and legislation—through several cycles in English history. What started as a one-way process in history became at least as meaningful when considered as part of a cyclical pattern. The plight of a world which has turned from contract to imposed relationships has been the fear of several generations of individualist conservatives since the time of Maine, but despite the dangerous inroads into contract since 1861, here too cyclical patterns have taken place. Forced labor now is much rarer than twenty years or even ten years ago, and it is worth remarking how badly the closed shop is faring in many parts of the Western world.

Trees do not grow to the sky. It is of interest how many irresistible tendencies are successfully resisted. At some time the chief worry is that technology will leave large parts of the population without work, or reduced to make work. Automation is the current name for this alleged menace, which has certainly been a question in many places (and times, as Ibsen's *Pillar of Society* suggests). But at other times and places the fear arises that education or various economic or military demands will inexorably leave too few people to do the necessary work (either too degrading or too demanding). Most economies seem to fluctuate between the two problems; a given developed nation is almost never without one problem, and sometimes has both. The steady pressure of urbanization was going to coop everyone up in monstrous jungles of great buildings and crowded streets until it was realized that the centrifugal push to the suburbs was creating a new problem of empty city centers and soulless developments, with (as Jacobs has persuasively argued) too few people in the streets. Here again both conditions can be and have been serious problems, but neither is inevitable or a straight road to disaster. The terms of trade for countries and for continents have shifted back and forth in a striking manner since 1700. But when the pendulum moves one way the losers tend to talk as if they suffered from a novel and inexorable burden of the market economy.

Liberal conservatism, with no bias toward perfection or ruin, can accept the defeat of the loftier hopes and the gloomier fears. The often-cited failure of the democratic form of government (meaning in most cases governments elected by universal suffrage bound by some constitutional guarantees) to triumph everywhere has been a leading source of chagrin for all lower-circle people since 1914. So much of the "American dream" is tied up with this goal that the disappointments of fifty years of dictators have at times wounded even the vaunted American optimism. Often more reactionary thinkers will deduce from the collapse of a democratic government the unworthiness of lesser breeds. But as the complexities of world policy have been brought home, and at the same time the difficulties of other countries become more our business, it is becoming more popular (on the lower-circle left as well) to see universal suffrage as one value among others in a process of flux. Ayub Khan seems preferable to Mrs. Bandaranaike; it is not enough to say of a dark-complexioned foreigner that he is undemocratic to damn him forever, nor is it always tragic that the one-way road to democracy is not so easy. The realization of the mistake in opposing the German monarchy in 1918 was a sign of this new belief, a belief which is capable of taking a dimmer view of progress without denigrating all human experience.

This middle view, weighted toward the cautious side, is probably easier now than it was fifty years ago. Then so much of the Victorian milieu seemed the crowning accomplishment of man, and the comfortable faiths of slow progress—sometimes Darwinian, sometimes a watery piety—appealed to even many conservatives as inseparable from civilization itself. The breakup of the old order upset both the lower-circle worlds of liberalism and conservatism, but it is the latter's opportunity. Here the prevalent relativism is most clearly of use, for if different attitudes and conceptions produce different systems, it is up to conservatism to think in different forms, or to make the old forms more flexible.

The change in sexual mores is a case in point. The Victorian ideal of puritanical propriety was clearly, as seen from our vantage point, an unusually high tide in the ebb and flow of morality. To the Victorians however (Lecky, for example) the "high standards" of the nineteenth century seemed a great advance in the climb away from barbarism. But what this meant in practice was that when the political and economic temper of the times was very libertarian, by and large the legal restraints in the area of sex and sexual literature became remarkably severe. This may be another evidence of the rules of the circle, for as liberty expanded in some areas it contracted in others, distributing the pressures differently but perhaps not changing the total drive. At any rate the ethos of the mid-century, persisting until the First World War in large part, accompanied the high tide of contract, but in many ways contradicted the free spirit of contract-orientation. Both have now lost ground, but the sexual restrictions have suffered the most. It is common for conservatives —often very visceral conservatives—to treat this decline as the foulest blot of our century. But, in the first place, since we understand that much of change is not necessarily for the better, or certainly directed in one way, why be surprised that morality reminiscent of the late seventeenth century, or of first- and second-century Rome, has recurred? That sexual liberty (or license) was the cause of the fall of Rome is highly doubtful, for the spread of easy divorce and the loosening of traditional morals was followed by many years of prosperity and power; a much better causal relation can be found, as Gibbon claimed, between the rise of Oriental religions—often very ascetic—and the fall of the Empire. Restoration England did not mark the end of English greatness. The puritanism of Robespierre and Mao Tse-tung is a warning of the implications of this asceticism. In short, what seemed the finest accomplishments of human progress in one generation may seem much more debatable to the next one.

It is also sometimes true that a development will produce

both good and bad results, or that a value will be both encouraged and discouraged by a change in thinking and in technology. Aries, in his *Centuries of Childhood*, suggests a novel approach to the question of privacy and the family. It is customary to think of contemporary society as one which has reduced the scope and power of the family and produced a spirit of rootlessness (or freedom, to give the same thing another name). But Aries maintained the opposite. "The history of the family in the nineteenth and twentieth centuries was supposed to be that of a decadence. The frequency of divorce and the weakening of marital and paternal authority were seen as so many signs of its decline. It seemed to me (and qualified observers have come to share my conclusions) that on the contrary the family occupied a tremendous place in our industrial societies, and that it had perhaps never before exercised so much influence over the human condition." Aries reasoned that the developing idea of childhood as a time of life, separate from infancy but not yet adulthood, has led to the emphasis on the family, the institution responsible in the main for guiding the child. It used to be that most children perished before they grew up, so that too much feeling could not be lavished on them; today, medical science has made acceptable the involvement which so intensifies the feelings of familial unity. This in turn has encouraged the family way of life, and the increase of home living has contributed. Private bedrooms, the diminution of that random coming and going which characterized other social systems, have built up the family. This family is the immediate group, quite contrasting to the amorphous gens which older cultures thought of as the family. And this *petite famille* is accustomed to this high degree of privacy—privacy as against the world, against distant relations, against other members of the family (as the right to one's own bed and bedroom indicates). Thus the modern age, so belabored for destroying privacy, has also abetted it.

All this, as Aries pictures it, is a linear development superimposed on cyclical changes—changes in the treatment of boys and in the attitude toward education and sex. One example is especially suggestive. Aries discusses at length the uncouthness and wildness of much of the educational process of the late medieval and post-medieval periods. He comments on the slow advance of more grave and orderly systems of pedagogy and the intermittent process of taming the boys. He observed that "in fact, the campaign for greater seriousness would triumph only in the nineteenth century, in spite of the contrary evolution of child welfare and more liberal, realistic pedagogics. L. Wylie, who spent his sabbatical year 1950–51 in a village in the south of France, was astonished by the seriousness with which the masters at the primary school treated their pupils, and the parents, who were peasants, their children. The contrast with the American attitude struck him as enormous: 'Every step in the child's development seems to depend on the development of what people call its *raison*.' This *raison*, this self-control and this seriousness, which are required of the French child at any early age while he is working for his certificates of study, and which are no longer known in the United States, are the final result of the campaign launched at the end of the sixteenth century by monks and moralists. It should be added that this state of mind is beginning to disappear from the French town; it remains only in the country." Once again, we see two phenomena of the straight-line development and the great cycle of reason and contract, rising from 1600 to 1850 or 1900, and now falling, and the little cycles interweaving. We have not progress, but various progressions and retrogressions, some steady and others engaged in occurrences and recurrences. The keys to these puzzles surely do not rest in the pockets of either those who think man incapable of advancing, or invulnerable to declines.

Progress can thus be very disappointing, as human nature finds a way to return to its normal customs. Whether technology is good or bad, its cataclysmic effect is often exaggerated. The automobile, the movies, any number of modern inventions were expected to result in a twisting and disruption of family life beyond repair; however, it seems that the television set and the barbecue pit (hardly a product of the electronic age) have more than put things right. Inequality and privacy will come back, if in different forms, even after the most concerted efforts to discourage them. Revolutions may demolish all institutions, but somehow the outcome is familiar—even while rebellions go on the thread of familiar experiences keeps the tenor of life balanced. Pasternak has caught this in *Doctor Zhivago,* in his vignette of the duck dinner in the midst of the misery of the Russian civil war. Perhaps even the very delays which are so paradoxical amidst the speed of modern transportation, and the publicity which so mars the ease of instant communication, are subtle forms of this tendency for life to resume its customary patterns.

As one change comes to alter the condition of life, another will restore a balance. In other ages labor was thought of as degrading and work was strictly a means to an end. Now work has become the principal focus of existence, so much of our thought is devoted to considering what to substitute for work as a goal. In the age of mass education the depth of ignorance leaves its imprint; de Jouvenel has complained that Montesquieu would have fewer readers today than in his time, and Irving Howe would probably agree. The differences between the ages are not so great that the problems are incommensurable; rather, as one aspect of the matter is cleared up another becomes urgent. Cancer and heart diseases are so serious today because the ills which formerly killed us have been overcome.

We are told, however, that political conditions change much more rapidly today than in former times. This is not so. The peace of Vienna took one year, all told, to be consummated, but we still await the final conclusion of World War II. The problems of 1948—Berlin, the balance of power in the Middle East, disarmament, are still with us, and in many of the same forms. Galbraith has commented on the lengthening of the time necessary to develop industrial products. To be sure, when things do change sharply they change quickly, but that has always been true. What transformations can compare with those of France from 1789 to 1794, or Rome from 52 to 42 B.C.? And in the end even those changes were less cataclysmic than they seemed at the time. In two centuries the difference between a culture possessing the radio and one possessed by television may seem vastly less momentous than it does to McLuhan.

This is the principal reason why so much of the faith in progress, or in any kind of human accomplishment, has become so much a matter of science and technology. As the other hopes have receded the glories of the scientific marvels have grown in splendor. To some this is almost a substitute for humanity; Marianetti's futurism appealed to the early Fascists.

Much of progress is a myth, and at times a dangerous myth. "We want to glorify war—and contempt for women," the futurist manifesto read, and they thought of the swirling, anarchic world of automobiles, dynamos, and airplanes as just the world for these ideas. All the reactionary measures of Stalin were justified by the need for more heavy industrial production, as well as for ideological reasons. Progress, if it is measured by tons of steel produced or the increase of rail or air facilities, is in some ways a substitute for human values. The upper-circle reactionary/radical meeting place is populated by fervent believers in this kind of progress, for if man can do nothing else, he can create these massive demonstrations of human splendor. They do not require the support of consumer preferences, and they (like the pyramids of the Old Kingdom) are perfect symbols of state power. The connection between these accomplishments and arms production is very close, both in terms of economic support and in terms of national pride. Guns rather than butter was a rather crude bit of Nazi theorizing; the proof of Soviet merit claimed for the sputnik is much more subtle, but not so different.

The accomplishments of science are remarkable, and they do show the glory of man in that realm where progress is most real. We have seen how this progress does not imply progress in the human spirit or the future of politics. It is ironical that we seem to be in the midst of an almost unparalleled age of technical and scientific advance (although the time of the dawn of history, circa 4000 B.C., can rival our age) when so little remains of the other sorts of progressive confidences. This irony may be a very tragic one if we destroy ourselves, so there is all the more reason to prefer a political theory which will neither embrace technology as the last surviving god of the progressive pantheon, or ignore it. As with the phenomenon of totalitarianism, industrialism and its limitations have provided the background for the success of a mildly conservative philosophy.

The last source of modern conservative beliefs is the most ambivalent, but also the most sensitively powerful. The decline which the idea of human reason has experienced in our century has had very large consequences for political theory. This decline has cut many ways, but no political system has been immune from its blows. Although liberal conservatism has been as much a victim as any, this tendency has presented opportunities as well as problems.

The mere defining of reason is a difficult matter. Plato had a very high regard for reason, but not the same kind of reason which Jefferson admired. Plato confined the attributes of reason to a small elite, especially trained for its use. Moreover, to him reason was not reasoning, the free consideration of a problem from every viewpoint, but logic. Mathematics, as the *Meno* illustrates, was the perfectly rational science. From a historical point of view, this was a poor definition of reason. The Sophists, for instance, reveled (as Plato complained) in the cacophony of opposing beliefs, upheld in the market place as well as in the schools. Reason, as Milton aptly put it, is but choosing, which is not what one does in solving a geometry problem.

The more to the left one is, the more this reason seems a birthright of all men, to be used to the maximum. Jefferson was more spacious in his beliefs than Milton, and the Fabian socialists more thoroughgoing still. The simple old-fashioned progressive political scheme features a dichotomy between the rational left and an anti-rational or irrational right, with the Fascists carrying on the obscurantist cause where the orthodox faithful and the Burkeans have left off. There is some truth in this, for to the extent that human reason is a prime attribute of goodness and capacity, it is among the basic values of the left. The visions of the good life which all radicals have maintained depend at least to some extent on a confidence in the superior rational abilities of the masses of men; if the state withers away these qualities of thought must shoulder an immense burden of responsibility, so that those who espouse that idea must believe in human capacity to think out these responsibilities in a successful manner, free from tradition or restraint.

However, the idea of reason used by many progressives is not the same thing as the reason of Milton and Jefferson, despite its common origin or sentimental similarity. A reason which embodies a collective choice aimed at achieving a common goal through intelligent consideration is a different thing than the thoughtful decision of a rational individual. We can term the former as mass reason, as contrasted to individual reason. In the movement by the left toward collectivist beliefs it is the former, mass reason, which has come to be prized as the sort of reason worth preserving, even while the rhetoric of politics which they use continues to employ the older, more individualist terms. At the same time the progress of relativist ideas has differentiated individual reason, so that the distinction, which Rousseau would have scorned and Jefferson doubted, has become a central part of modern politics.

This development can be seen most clearly in the area of economics. Neo-classical economic theory has delineated the role of individual decision to the point where the comparability of utility schedules has been denied—each man is thought to have unique standards of value, incapable of being balanced against that of any other person. Translated into more general terms, this means that the working of each man's reason is *sui generis,* and that rationality is a subjective matter. A policy which aims to maximize individual reason, the reason of all men together, must provide the utmost chance for each person to do what he thinks best. The philosophy of Adam Smith is justified by making his "hidden hand" the hand of an uncommitted nature, permitting anything so long as it is supported by some efficacious interest. It is difficult to distinguish this reason from emotion or vagaries, since all we have to go on is the end result, the human choices which cannot (like a jury's motivation) be inspected. But, as with a jury, the rational nature of choice is abstracted from the total process as a sort of residuum, the portion of the choosing act which can be seen to arise rationally or which later seems to have fit into a rational picture. At best this is sketchy, and psychologists who have sought to determine exactly how the reasoning process works can only report that it is a difficult mixture of motivations, influenced, for example, by tendencies to reinforce decisions once made or to systematize perhaps irrational judgments.

Mass reason in economics, on the other hand, is quite perceptible. It involves the establishment of group decisions and their systematic procurement. If a society desires a given result, say full employment, then it is rational, we are told, to have an economic order which will provide this. The vagaries of an unregulated economic system are, from this vantage point, a reliance on chance—a fine joke on the earnest Benthamite individualists. Planning is in this view more rational than its alternatives, almost by definition, since from the mass rational viewpoint the act of thinking (which takes place in separate minds) is equated with the choice of a state or society. Or, to put it differently, if it is wise or noble for one person to think out his economic course, buying cheap and selling dear, it is all the more rational for many persons to think out the course of an economy, fusing the interests of all concerned.

Since almost no one truly believes in an absolutely unregulated economy all of individual reason contains at least a bit of mass reason in it. But the conservative premise of our century has come to include, as a crucially important base, a refusal to carry this very far. And this distrust has, as has been noted, been reinforced by the tendency of modern economic scholarship to doubt the efficacy of interpersonal comparisons, which is another way of saying that the modern doubt about universal values has undermined the assumptions of a mass reason which can include and transcend the reason of individuals. If our society considers the elimination of unemployment its first order of business, this is an understandable decision, but it is not necessarily rational— it may be the result of political considerations arising out of the structure of the voting process, or it may derive from a confused choice made by voters once in four years. But, it is said, the free market is irrational, in that private good is not public good, and the calculations of individuals do not lead to the public results which are desirable. But if this means that there is a separate good in the public realm, it is an espousal of a reason in conflict with individual choice. If it means that the individuals would choose rationally what they cannot perform by themselves, it can only establish a sort of remote exercise of reason. Thus if I reason that my spending may produce unfortunate economic ups and downs, and that I can do nothing to alter this acting alone, I may support counter-cyclical spending by the state to achieve a broader result than could be achieved through voluntary action. This is a mixed form of reason, as indeed any form of conduct carried on through association and not individual action tends to be. But if the state decides that I must serve in the army the only kind of reason which can be discerned is one found in a social policy, about which my personal mental processes have no relevance. The same is true of a five-year plan or a tax law. If ten men assemble, and six of them decide that the rational course for the group is for everyone to work longer, while the other four prize leisure above all else, all that can be said is that three-fifths of the participants had a (not "the") rational view of the desiderata of the group. This is, for them, perhaps rational, just as it is rational for a Platonic philosopher to propose that the leaden masses have no share in the government.

But it is important to be candid about this evaluation of mass reason. It is not only Marx or Plato whose reason is being impugned, or Rousseau who is being attacked, but the premises of much of the Stoic tradition as well. *Recta ratio* was another way of proposing the same sort of super-reason, a body of values separate from and above the decisions of individuals. The reason of the Thomists clearly qualified as a sort of mass reason, or perhaps as a sacred reason. In Reismanian terms, the inner-directed value is opposed not only to the other-directed, but to the now-sometimes-forgotten tradition-directed value as well. And this was a deliberate result of much of the individualist revolt of the eighteenth and nineteenth centuries. The theater of Racine has been called rational, but in the sense that it conformed to a model of logic and symmetry. Ibsen's plays, on the other hand, are rational in that they bring the motivations and circumstances of real people directly into focus, in that they are "realistic." Ibsen's characters think out their problems as flesh-and-blood men and women—and thought is a vital part of all of his works—whereas in Racine the overall reason, like that of a beautifully-planned formal garden, is paramount. Dewey was also an apostle of reason in his efforts to overthrow the older, but also rational systems of education. The older rationality was the reason of discipline, the life of conformity to rules which were established as emanations of thought-out systems. But Dewey insisted that the reasoning process is an ongoing one in each child, so that it is more rational (and of course more valuable, so he maintained) that a child learn to work something out by himself than to learn the workings of an arithmetic system. The mathematic term "elegance" is an accolade to those to whom logic is the handmaiden of reason, whereas to the Progressive educationalist it is irrelevant. Dewey, of course, thought his relativism would produce democratic values, just as his predecessor Mill somehow hoped to get certainties out of doubts if only one could trust men far enough. Without this trust (and, in fairness, neither Mill nor Dewey were by any means doctrinaire believers) one must accept individual reason as perhaps selfish or limited, but as an entity to be judged for itself and not as a part of a cosmic theory of justice.

The blows struck against the validity of universal theories of reason may be considered, then, arguments in support of a liberal conservative point of view. But does this not raise more problems than it solves? Much of the history of conservatism, from Aristotle and Cicero on, is a history of reliance on some cosmic conception of reason. This, however, is a testimony, strange perhaps to one who thinks of political theory as one-dimensional, of the permutations within the circle. There are many conservatives who believe as strongly as ever in natural law today as in the past. But today this law is not confused with human reason; the order of the universe is set apart from the mechanism of the human brain even by those who would believe that the latter does receive emanations from the former. An example of this can be seen in the acceptance of the fact that judges do make law—the independence of human faculties is not inconsistent with a belief in a higher law, but it requires a division between the influence of natural justice and its reception in the human mind. Reason is a quality which cannot be expanded beyond its individual setting; it is subjective and not objective.

Politically, the experience of those who have thought otherwise is a lesson for conservatives. The Robespierrian idea of reason was not, for example, an odd notion, but the objectivizing of some of the Whig ideas of rationality into a collectivist credo. The spirit of the Enlightenment was ambiguous, but it contained a large degree of rather conservative individualism. Reason meant freedom from the tyranny of superstition and (Voltaire is an example) of fixed ideas. Reason, as Candide discovered, was not a discovery of what must be, but of what was; Montesquieu's Persian travelers came to much the same conclusion. This was not what Rousseau thought, nor Talmon's other totalitarian democrats. The latter, by denying the reality of human disagreement, undermined the freedom of the will which underlay the Whig idea of reason. From there it was logical, to quote Talmon, to go to "this democratic perfectionism [which] was in fact inverted totalitarianism—the outcome of an expectation that the fruit of democratic sovereignty stretched to its limit would be but a single will." This was the upshot of Robespierre's religion of reason, the substitution of an idea of absolute faith in reason for the distinctions of individualist reason. This Reason, this bloody goddess, had no connection with astute choices in the market place or careful analyses of party loyalty, but was superior to such things—and therefore fatally inferior.

In our time we have seen too many examples of this to be condescending to the naiveté of the 1790's. The upper circle has either denounced reason or tried to convert it into a Goddess, whose pronouncements are rational per se and mightier than any human reasoning. Thus to Marx the process of dialectical materialism was the embodiment of Reason, since it worked on absolutely necessary rational grounds. But the individual, by Marxist reasoning, had no real choice but to follow his objective class interest—or if he did escape, his action was *ipso facto* irrational (unless he were a noble Marx and foresaw the greater rationality of history). There is some validity to the connection which Hayek has perceived between this and the demand for planning. Many of those who laud planners are by no means fanatic devotees of an inflexible determinism, but they do tend to look on the wisdom of the process as being superior to the choices of the participants. The rub often comes here when the superior wisdom comes down to the choice of the planner set against the other choices, and when, in the absence of some proof of intrinsic superiority of the former (because in fact these are invariably circle-oriented decisions) it is necessary to use force. Stalin's agricultural policy may have been, from one point of view, an elegant bit of the dialectic; to us it looks like a notorious example of brutal force used to benefit the Soviet industrial system (and therefore, of course, the Soviet ruling class) at the expense of the Russian peasants. This sort of reason leads one to prefer irrationality.

Perhaps then it is not so strange that this is also the century of irrationality. Frazer and his successors, Freud and Jung, detected the underworld of feeling beneath the Victorian urbanity of hypocrisy. Freud was not a radical, for instance, but on the contrary it is probable that his stay in Paris persuaded him—as it did Le Bon at that time—of the evils of human nature. Freud did not admire these depths, nor did he advocate the elimination of the rational checks on the deep-seated instincts. Frazer had not advocated a return to the sacrifice of the old king, and Freud did not propose killing the father who resembled the priest-king, writ small. But by emphasizing these primordial instincts they did alter the tone of thought. Freud and Jung both emphasized the importance of dreams as an emanation of the subconscious. The dream is, par excellence, the manifestation of the irrational, and when an age pays a great deal of attention to dreams—as was the case in the late years of the Roman Empire—there is an almost automatic devaluation of reason, that surface sentiment. Freud, in his exposure of these subterranean urges, did, to a degree, make them acceptable, or at least comprehensible. Moreover, he (like Marx) denied the potential of free thought, individual reason, as a counterforce to these urges. Hypocrisy is a miserable vice, but it is to be preferred to a bold cynicism. The latter, proclaimed by men to whom Freud, if not Jung, was anathema, nonetheless took advantage of that frank consideration of human oddity and depravity to do things unthought-of in a more straitlaced age. Thus also the German expressionist painters of the 1920's opposed, as a rule, Nazism and all that it stood for, but their biting caricatures of the human appearance and of natural forms presaged, in a disturbing manner, the malign cruelty of the Nazis. When the worst can be imagined, it is not surprising that the capacity for shock is reduced. The mid-Victorian age was not merely prudish, but also reticent in matters of political morality as well. The court ladies in Berlin were horrified at the thought that the German artillery might actually shell Paris in 1870. Gladstone succeeded in arousing British public opinion to great indignation, and perhaps won the election of 1880, by recounting the atrocities of the Turks in Bulgaria. The Turkish conduct in the Balkans was not notably humanitarian, but it is safe to say that it would be considered small potatoes as cruelty goes these days, just as bombardments now would make Moltke seem quite milksop by comparison.

This loss of respect for reason works in many ways. The attributes of human reason seem less important, so the terror of the concentration camp or of organized mass coercion seem less pernicious, or a normal part of an unthinking world. At the same time, political movements become more irrational themselves, as the mania of mass emotions finds it easier to sweep all before them. Cohn showed how the irrational choice of the Nazis (whose concentration camps reduced the supply of men and matériel just when these were most needed) was similar to the frenzy of German mobs in the Middle Ages. The Whig emphasis on reason seems at times, like the art it accompanied, a historical sport. The age of Klee, of pop art, of Jackson Pollock and John Cage, seems to have no room for the articulations of thought.

It is sometimes said that this is a theory applicable only in extreme cases or in a metaphorical sense. The success of

Joseph McCarthy is a reminder that the challenge to reason can take other forms than hysteria or totalitarianism, however, as does the recrudescence of the milder forms of mystique such as Gaullism. But there are other signs of the retreat from reason. There has been a change, for example, in legal theories of insanity in the United States which suggests interesting problems. The mounting disapproval of the early Victorian formulation of legal insanity in the McNaughten rule is very likely to sweep that rule away. There is an almost complete rejection of the test of knowledge of right and wrong as a determination of mental control. This may be quite sound and desirable. But the danger of an alternative test of self-control—the determination of whether there was an irresistible impulse—is that impulses will be profitable (as drinking is in Japan) as they are unchecked and, presumably, uncheckable. Many impulses are irresistible in the short run, but capable of control in the long run. The premium is thus on the man who will not train himself to control himself, who does not use his reason. The danger arises that a climate of opinion which doubts human reason may assume that we are all so impotent, and any heinous crime must be the work of a diseased mind. And who is to cast the first stone; are we not all disturbed?

So the rational standards dissolve. But since there must be controls, instead of the standards built on reason, new ones, often more arbitrary, and inevitably based on collectivist standards, emerge. This implication in civil law—in tort and to some extent in contract law—has been noted. Holmes remarked that perhaps no criminal could help himself, in which case the condemned should think of himself, as he goes to his death, as a soldier dying for his country. The metaphors of the battlefield are more fitting for an irrational age than those of the market place, but the admonitions against living by the sword may have relevance to a body of thought as well as to the physical body.

So too the growing emphasis on seniority as a rule for promotion, and the insistence on fixed retirement ages as a standard for demotion inculcate a contempt for intelligence and choice. These tendencies have reasonable causes, and represent thoughtful efforts to avoid arbitrary unfairness in an era of mass institutions, but the remedy serves to bureaucratize the mass and therefore make it more unwieldy and unthinking. Where rigid rules of seniority exist (and it is noteworthy that it is the right which currently defends seniority in the Congress; expediency can easily betray principle) skill and care avail nothing against longevity, while at age sixty-five even the best must leave. This will often mean, in practice, that timeservers will occupy the best positions and be quickly replaced by others of their type; its indirect effect in reducing the value of astuteness or intellect is more important. Above all, the acceptance of some of these unthinking rules tends to depreciate the effectiveness of thought in other areas.

This is the nexus between the dull erosion of reason and the fierce dragons of anti-reason. The disappearance of thinking is not to be feared, and the harder the world the more successful the thinking man must be. But this thought may be classed as either subversive, like profit-minded calculation in Russia, and driven underground, or tied to bureaucratic rules so that it is forced into official forms. Much of the horror of Kafka's dream world lies in the juxtaposition of an irrational horror with the housebroken scrupulousness of the rational people, helpless in a Boschlike madness. In good times thought will suffer from the condescension or boredom of a people to whom reason is a distant good, and in bad times the needs of reason may then be swamped by the fires of passion.

Robinson Jeffers, in his individualistic reactionary fervor, has caught this:

> The deep instincts, fear, envy, loyalty, pride of kind
>   and the killer's passion
> Are past your power. They are terribly in earnest,
> And the other mere speculation. No wonder they are
>   earnest; for ages
> Beyond reckoning those who retain them have killed or
> Enslaved those who renounce them.

Mere speculation is the individual reason; when it is thought of as "mere" it can be audacious or resourceful, but it will lack the fine assurance which comes from a belief in reason as both an attribute of individual excellence and a prime value in the state.

It is worth remembering that the social systems which rely on reason are substitutes for the wilder instincts, and that if reason is abandoned something else must take its place. The denigration of free will in criminal law is an example of this. Knowing the limitations of reason, many penologists think that malefactors should be treated, not punished. But these idealistic concerns—and they usually are just that—impose an incapacity which may well be more burdensome than punishment. If the questions are matters of illness, why should we worry about the procedural safeguards built to protect the accused from unjust punishment? Treatment without trial is kindness to the sick, and if, as some who deal with abnormal psychology believe, we are all sick, the only question is who the doctor should be. The surface constructions of rational jurisprudence seem stupid and ineffectual in dealing with such things as anal compulsions and Oedipal urges. This suggests the specter of brainwashing. But we need not consider the extremes, which are often exaggerated. One of the gravest problems is the impatience with the protocol of law and rationality. For example, the adversary system is a product of the Anglo-Saxon spirit of individualism and free play which has served as a key ingredient of the Whig recipe. There have been many attacks on this system on the grounds that it would be better to help the accused by understanding him—just as the psychiatrist knows better than the patient what the latter really wants. This understanding approaches condescension; in a world of reason it is better to take the muddled thinking of men rather than the superior knowledge of a higher wisdom.

The reaction against a firm trust in fixed rules is not altogether foolish. It arose after the rigidity of Calvinist or Victorian ideas came to seem too narrow-minded. The seventeenth-century Puritan dislike of flexibility in the criminal law was related to the nineteenth-century dislike of permissiveness in the area of sex; in both cases high principles came to seem like, and often were, fronts for a narrowness and hypocrisy which made the cause of reason a gray, imprisoning force. The nineteenth-century romanticism was in part a fight against these very forces; our century has far outdistanced the Gothic revival in reviving barbaric qualities. The noticeable decline in the vaunted English good manners, the evidently uncaused rowdiness in Sweden and the United States, and the general problems of delinquency in the most affluent societies seems to many to be a blight on our age. Its existence, and ubiquity, is connected with the fact that the Whig ideas have lost much of their power.

But this is where the liberal-conservative ideology should gain strength, even considering its affinity to those very Whig ideas. On the one hand, the fears and beliefs that produced the Whig or Calvinist beliefs—such as the flexibility of the Star Chamber or the recklessness of the absolutist courts—are highly relevant in this time. But the excess of purity, the substitution of a rigid law for the belief in reason, was mistaken, and a philosophy which may have been relevant in 1665 or 1865 need not be so now. The best constructions of conservative thought— such as the United States Constitution or the British Civil Service—have never been tied to a closed system of particular laws, but have succeeded because they were built on a combination of faith and distrust in humanity. Individual reason is a value which does not involve an acceptance of either mass regeneration or an overlaw, but it does require an encouragement to human effort and diversity. With all their faults, the developments of the last twenty years in vastly expanded college and pre-college education, and the proliferation of activities for which scientifically trained men can be engaged, are indications that reason is not passé. There is no reason to give up to Jeffers' wild passions; in 1940 reason seemed bankrupt, yet Churchill outlived both Hitler and Stalin in fact and in spirit. There are many promising signs for the cause of reason today: the improvement in the quality of secondary education, the spread of paperback books (proving that modern technology can be an ally of the solitary thinker), the mobility of the intellectual markets for both the scholars and their work, and even the availability of computers and other devices to make highly complex decisions more manageable. In many ways the sophistication of our age is a tribute to the depths which thinking can now reach, a vindication of Holmes' judgment that the greatest of ancient thinkers might seem shallow now. On the level of the average citizen, this is manifested by the incredible amount of choice which one is offered in every aspect of life, from food to music.

The opportunity is also the danger, in that this choice and potential can, like the computers themselves, displace us from the act of reasoning and the belief in individual reason. Thus Freud's sophistication undercut its own base, and a faith in psychoanalysis may deprive the world of more rational inquiry than all of the Freudian corpus of analysis. Reason is something separate from the storing-up of knowledge; where reason becomes an impediment to a fashionable sense of knowledge, where the zest for capturing all of reality (as with the Marxists or the other lovers of conspiracy theories) takes precedence over dealing with events in a rational manner, not all the paraphernalia of the scientific method can rescue the stature of reason. Mary McCarthy has caught this problem in her excellent novel of mass reason, *The Group;* only through escape from the clichés and the masterful theories, such as psychoanalysis, can her few heroes make their way through a jungle of self-deceit. The woods are thickest where the confidence is greatest, for when men will imagine that there are sure answers to the tougher rigors of thinking, and the harsh problems which come with it, thought will seem to be a needless burden. The radical left often thinks it can do without individual reason—grading in school, for instance, may seem like a form of wanton cruelty to less capable students—and will try to replace it with more gentle values. A devotion to reason implies a dissatisfaction with those who cannot think, and a premium on intelligence as against goodness. Kingsley's credo— "be good, and let him who will be clever"—is more heartwarming than the icy formulas of pure thought. This, more than the irrationalism of the reactionary right, is the chief danger to the cause of reason today. Reason is a noble word; the attributes of the reasoning mind, and the conditions of a system of rationality, are much less inviting.

In the last analysis, it is not easy or painless to be rational. Even with the current emphasis on cognitive skills there remains a popular prejudice against the "brainy grind," immured in books or theories. And it is even harder to trust a government or a society to the interplay of men's minds. The risk that the thin margin of reason may be overcome by the underworld of passion seems often so great as to make reliance on reason unsound; the potentials of passion may make it seem selfish. Even the battlers for reason, the progressive believers, often tend to betray their trust. We have seen countless revolutions which began by setting loose a torrent of political activity and sectarian excitement, so that each small eddy of opinion had a party and a band of spokesmen, but which ended (often very shortly) with one absolute party and no free discussion whatsoever. The attractiveness of the mass rational ideas comes from the satisfaction which we find in escaping the inconvenience of debate. Even Marcus Aurelius and Thomas Jefferson were willing to silence unfriendly groups rather than to engage in an unceasing dialogue; while Saint-Just mouthed the rhetoric of terror he was appealing to a phantom of Reason.

That is why a philosophy which expects only a modicum, but which is very intent on that little, is a good defender of the rational cause. "Cogito, ergo sum," is not a grandiose phrase, for it guarantees no glory and no status. To be may indeed be synonymous with making mistakes, for rationality may provide very poor answers at times. But it is the mark of human accomplishment, the quality which makes us superior to beasts.

The most startling part of Freud's message was the depth of wildness in the subconscious of the most proper people. Just as Piranesi's eminently rational-looking structures often become, on close examination, dungeons of the most incalculable hopelessness, so the irrationalism of our time is coeval with, and at times a product of, the rational wizardry of our age. It is not only a matter of Snow's two cultures, it is the paradox of a time when physicists accomplish works of incredible genius but at the same time evolve theories of uncertainty which increasingly make all of physics metaphysical. Spengler has remarked on the significance of irrational numbers in the history of thought; the tendencies which he noted have increased in recent years. But, Spengler to the contrary, this is not an either/or proposition. It is just because we know the irrationality implicit in even the most rational matters, and the madness involved in some of the gentlest passions, that we must try to encourage the better side. The dark side of Vienna, circa 1900, was dark indeed, but Lueger led to Hitler only in one sense; Hitler came to power in Germany first of all. The bureaucratic tradition led to Eichmann, but also to the workers' housing of inter-war Vienna, and the neo-classical economists. It is the task of liberal conservatism to bring out the best in these complex situations, a task made easier by the disillusionments and discoveries of the past generation.

☆ *VI*

Bases of
a Conservative Theory

These four arguments are of course interrelated. The lessons of totalitarianism, the new approaches of contemporary thought, the dissatisfactions with industrialism and progress, and the awareness of non-rational factors, are different facets of the recoil from optimism which we are experiencing. The enthusiasm of the left which gained ground in the late nineteenth century and which so influenced the first part of this century is much subdued. The questions of the next years will be focused on the problems relating to the new unity of the globe, and this promises to be the new arena of the political struggle. Liberal conservatism is a logical beneficiary of these lessons of the past; if the conservative momentum is not to be lost they must be applied to the issues of the coming years.

No one can presume to speak for the whole sector of political thought which we have described as liberal conservative, and there are real differences of principle among the various thinkers and active politicians who hold to this position. Furthermore, in different parts of the world this point of view will appear in various forms; Djilas will naturally take different positions than Popper. But there are a few prominent strands which can be discerned, strands which present a choice of policy.

In considering these, it is valuable to start with the common denominator of the liberal-conservative ideology. By definition, those a little to the right of center hold a view of human nature which is somewhat pessimistic, but mixed with a fair amount of optimism. Since there is a strong suspicion of any belief which promises redemption, there is a sturdy distrust of programs which promise vast improvements or certain betterment, but there is also an analogous disbelief in apocalyptic disasters or in programs designed to save humanity from itself. This appreciation of man as a mixed being leads, as has been noted, to an individualistic philosophy. This is especially true today as a badge of distinction from the moderate liberal, whose individualism has been mixed with group ideas for the last hundred years. And, more concretely, this conservatism has reached a position of distrust of the modern state, especially insofar as the state has become a symbol of mass emotion and potentially limitless power.

But from this point there are serious differences of opinion. One line of thought derives from the individualist liberalism of the late eighteenth and early nineteenth centuries, and is very much opposed to the state and devoted to the idea of the free market as a political-economic concept. The other seeks to integrate the more traditional idea of the state, and of other conservative institutions, such as the church and aristocracy, into a contemporary individualist setting. This latter viewpoint tends to find its roots farther back in history, in the Whig tradition of the seventeenth and eighteenth centuries. The first group, which shall be called for the sake of convenience the free-market school, usually prefers to be called liberal and often indignantly denies that it is conservative at all; the second group, which shall be referred to here as the traditional school, is more concerned with using the state for conservative ends. It must be remembered that this group is traditional only in comparison to the free-market conservatives or the left-of-center thinkers; by comparison with more right-wing conservatives or reactionaries these traditional conservatives are not traditional at all.

This is a thumbnail sketch; the details are much more complicated. The traditionalists, heirs to the Whig tradition, are Tories or proto-Tories in some senses, and even the free-market anti-statists often have an ambivalent attitude toward different forms of state power. And naturally any given individual—and this is especially true of active politicians—will sometimes take something of one strand, and something of the other. But the two lines of thought can be differentiated, and the differences have served to separate and at times disrupt the moderate conservative forces. In the main, however, these differences have been much less significant than their historical antecedents would suggest, and it is our intention to see to what degree a theory of conservatism can be constructed from both sources. But first it is important to examine the two viewpoints more thoroughly.

The free-market view is a direct descendant, a very direct replica, of the Manchester school of the early nineteenth century. This school accepted the idea of progress, but sublimated it to the freedom of the market place. In so doing, it naturally evolved a philosophy which centered on economic questions. But even as the materialists of the left have ended by paying more attention to politics than to economics, so the free-market conservatives have utilized the market as a paradigm of the good society. The negative orientation of their concern with the state has been allied to their positive conception of the society built on free-market principles.

In many respects this view is much more positive, more hopeful, than that of the traditional conservatives. The Manchester ideology arose out of the early-nineteenth-century current of political radicalism, and its early proponents, such as Cobden and Bright, were to the left of the Whigs. It was not accidental that they were Little Englanders and supporters of democracy, as well as foes of economic intervention by the state. In their mind the market was part of a program which would bring the good life, a highly individualist but thoroughly anti-aristocratic world of free spirits. The theorists of the Jacksonian party, in their search for an egalitarian individualism, also advocated a free-market society. The state they envisioned—and one can see the connection with the Benthamites—could be very strong in its sphere (as in the nullification crises) and extremely weak in all else. The sharp disdain for the past and its archaic injustices can still be seen in the criticism which Hayek and Ashton levy against the pre-economic-revolution societies. Henry George, Henry Simons (whose 100 per cent deposit reserve would be extremely radical, and very much an extension of governmental power) and even Milton Friedman at times showed the potential of a free-market radicalism even after 1870.

But as the fruits of the market have proved generally conservative, the advocates have by and large been conservatives. In this respect they have suffered the same fate as the anticlericals and the nationalists of the nineteenth century. The free-market school has aged better because its ardent individualism has proved more valuable, but it has shifted from a philosophy allied to a liberal democratic ferment to a defense of a conservative socio-economic system. Often this has proved hard to uphold, as the advocates have thought to have the best of both worlds. But the emphasis on free choice as mirrored in the market place must serve to support the results of the private property system, unless the underlying institutions of that system are changed. Many of the early free-market supporters, such as Hodgskin, and later ones like George, thought in terms of such a change. As an effective social philosophy or even a political slogan this has been largely impractical. This is an old irony, but it is worth mentioning once more—a theory which was evolved as the basis for liberal revolution, grounded on experience and utility, is now generally classed as very right-wing and out of touch with reality. The renascence of free-market thinking since 1947 has enhanced the appeal of many of the features of the pure free-market thought, and even led to political popularity for men like Erhard, but the credo of a Goldwater still remains reactionary.

But the pure doctrine of Manchester has never been the sole argument for capitalism, and it has had fewer true devotees since 1914 than before. In the United States the protectionists have customarily held a strong place in political-economic thought, and various reservations to laissez faire have been fitted in. Hurst has remarked that the triumph of free-enterprise ideology in the United States, and especially in the Midwest, was a victory for opportunity, not for anarchy. He suggests a "release of energy" theory; that is, the function of government was to release the bountiful energy of the people in order to improve the standards of living and increase the general wealth. As a rule this could be done best, the mid-nineteenth-century American opinion went, if the role of government was sharply curtailed, but not always, by any view. Tariffs, railroad subsidies, the local contribution of equity capital, and judicial supervision of various kinds were accepted for the same reason as the customary Jeffersonian policies (which were often applied only to the national government). What was important was the upsurge of prosperity and wealth, the standard by which the policies were judged.

The relationship of this with the Benthamite emphasis on results is striking. The modern successor to these beliefs is the concept of capitalism as a producer of wealth, the rising-standard-of-living thesis. The theory of permanent revolution presented by *Fortune* magazine is a good specimen. Borrowing a thoroughly radical concept from a thoroughgoing radical, Trotsky, *Fortune* argues that in fact this revolution is our constant lot, the experience of rising affluence under dynamic capitalism. The justification for inequality is, as Schumpeter and Hayek also suggest, the bonus which this gives to those who will improve everyone's lot shortly. *Fortune* is far more sophisticated than the everyday defender of capitalism, but the basic thesis is as American as apple pie—the pie will grow in size, so even the smaller portions will be superior to the larger cuts of a stagnant or declining non-capitalist dessert. Beyond this, the spirit of improvement, the chances for ascending the ladder, are enhanced by a system of opportunity which ensures common improvement by maximizing the improvement of the able.

These utilitarian beliefs have come out of the economic and political atmosphere of 1750–1850, and have customarily relied on many of the same assumptions about economic values. To be sure, arguments over tariffs or subsidies have caused harsh disagreements between the true free-market camp and its protectionist cousin, but this is in the nature of an intramural dispute. The former has sought to base its social goals on a foundation less pragmatic than the expansion of wealth, but its ideology is often equally economic in origin and business-oriented in practice. The unwelcome potentials of governmental activism are more apparent to Hamilton's heirs than they were in 1791, but as with the Jeffersonians, so today it is difficult to keep a socio-economic philosophy from depending in large part on material results for its persuasiveness.

At this point a gap arises between the free-market conservatives and the traditional conservatives. These latter trace the best principles of good government to the ideology of Coke and Montesquieu, the seventeenth- and eighteenth-century libertarian ideal spirit.

Among their varied beliefs, the following can be summarized as typical:

1. The constitutional form of government is especially valuable, because this is the finest solution to the ancient problem of preserving liberty. Constitutions, of course, are not only sheets of paper subscribed to by a gathering of powerful men; they are, or should be, the settled work of a viable nation, securing the rights of the people through a system of limited government. The idea of constitutionalism had a left-wing ring in the Burkean scheme, because it suggested an attempt to devise a systematic answer to a fluid problem, strait-jacketing the historical process into a rigidly doctrinaire form. The socialist schemata of our time have aroused the same protests from Burke's successors, but they are as a rule careful to distinguish between constitutions planned for a given purpose, or framed as a deliberate façade (such as the Russian constitution of 1936), and the legitimate successors of the American Constitution, which fit into and expanded a scheme of ordered liberty. Much of the distinction is substantive; a constitution which limits and divides governmental power is the kind of constitution which the traditional conservatives desire, and the fact that it may be the work of a given moment is not so disturbing, if in fact it provides guarantees of protection. For example, the entrenched clauses set into the South African constitution of 1910 were precise and artificial, but they spelled out what in other circumstances the

Privy Council might have been expected to uphold through judicial oversight, or what a provincial governor might have imposed on the legislative system. The constitution thus has become a means and a symbol of that rule of law which is a central part of the traditional conservative philosophy.

2. In this respect the Hayekian respect for natural law is a link to much of the traditional viewpoint. The historic emphasis on right reason in developing the social-contract theory and the principles of liberal government (especially on the Continent) led many of the Whig thinkers to oppose to brute authority the spirit of reason and natural law. The doctrinaires, poor politicians but admirable specimens of this liberal conservatism, were firm believers in the need to rally to the principles of right against force, and the experience of modern totalitarian power, surpassing even that of Napoleon, has deepened this belief. But this often leads to a respect, on the part of conservatives of the traditional school, for traditional elites. The Whigs of the eighteenth century were frankly pro-aristocratic when the fledgling free-marketers were often crudely radical. The great Whig families of England have been compared to the Venetian aristocracy; their *haute bourgeois* successors have often carried on this spirit of *noblesse oblige* and (sometimes) hauteur. This implies very different standards than the market. The men of breeding and taste who preserve the libertarian values of Whig ideology are often competitively ineffective. They are often small minorities in the world of affairs. Thus in Britain today the qualities of individualist culture can be appreciated far more through the BBC than in the brash milieu of the commercial television systems, and many of the Tory moderates who comprise the core of liberal conservatism in Britain flout free-market principles in their support of the advantages sought by the BBC. The whole issue of the "liberal establishment" focuses on this, and it is not a new battle. The "great tradition" in the Anglo-Saxon world owes very much to the civil-service, anti-corruption, anti-violence concern for minorities and proprieties which the Russells and the Trevelyans, the Adamses and the Storeys did so much to create. But the assumptions of virtue which mug-

wumpery brings to mind had demerits, as the recent inspection of Trevelyan's behavior in the Irish famine of 1846 illustrates.

The Irish have learned to hate this gentility, but they are now developing this same tradition in their independent and now secure republic. Traditional conservatism tends to build up the respect for these elites, and in turn the slow accretion of a comfortable but intellectual class will make traditional conservatism more viable. This connection between social stability and a flexible conservatism will tend to moor that ideology to a theory of natural law, as a means of connecting the fluidity of intellectual uncertainty with the stasis of form. Lippmann, who at various times in his life has expounded the traditional conservative position with skill, has presented modified forms of this natural-law belief, most recently in his call for a public philosophy. This implies a fixed consensus, but without pinning down more than a few rules and a broader area of general discipline.

3. The mention of Lippmann suggests a third hallmark of this area of thought which is most distinct from that of the free-market conservatives. Lippmann, in *The Good Society*, carefully insisted, in upholding the free-market idea, that it was not laissez faire or an unregulated economy that he was defending. The free market worked, Lippmann argued, because its system of free choice and maximum opportunity was not that of a jungle, but was given life and scope by the system of law, especially as defined by an independent and decision-bound judiciary. Free enterprise is not the condition *sine qua non*, but might indeed be an enemy, as the history of the fellow-servant doctrine disclosed. Lippmann sought to isolate the extremes of Manchester dialectic, the relativist legacy of Bentham and the rigidities and extreme positions of Spencer from the great Whig tradition, while still using that tradition to uphold the free market as a feature of the good society.

Peter Viereck has gone further than Lippmann. He is unabashedly conservative, and in the role of a moderate conservative he has sought to incorporate the moderate Toryism—all of the conservative, as against reactionary thought—of Disraeli and even Metternich, into a common moderate theory incorporating the best of the conservatism of the last two hundred years. Viereck ostentatiously prefers Disraeli to Gladstone, and lauds Keynes over the classical school, but his defense of government as a limited tool designed to preserve law and order within the limits of a developing society places him in the same camp as the Lippmann of the 1930's (and *a fortiori,* of the Lippmann of the 1960's) and of Robert Taft (who insisted he was a liberal). But there is a meaningful question here—Viereck seems to many conservatives a bedfellow of Schlesinger, Jr., with whom he does share many positions, and his Keynesianism and willingness to endorse liberal proposals in the everyday political world are significant. The uncompromising positions of free-market conservatism derive from its "liberal" nature, and the liberal quality which they uphold is precisely the philosophy which the traditional conservatives often reject, or at least distrust as being too dogmatic or reactionary. The boast of the British Conservatives that they have always accepted much of the leftist innovations and incorporated them into their ideology, is a model of traditional conservatism.

But with any genuine conservative—and there are some rather liberal intellectuals who now (irony of ironies) call themselves conservatives but are not—this is an acceptance of contemporary society, and not an enthusiasm. The so-called "me too" principle of the Rockefellers and Rab Butlers is not a radical philosophy. In fact, radicals often consider it the most dangerous form of conservatism, because of its compromising allure. Stuart Hughes, for example, has denounced sophisticated conservatism, surely another way of describing traditional conservatism in our sense, as a major threat. The emphasis on efficiency and reliance on the state which he detected in this group were especially dangerous because they disguised a capitalism as hardboiled (he thought) as the more unabashed sort, but with a pseudo-socialism which took in some who would have rejected the real article.

It may seem strange to equate traditionalism with sophistication, but this is often the case today. The fervor of the Manchester school seems outdated today, and it is exactly that combination of state power and individual freedom which typified the eighteenth century that presents the most modern aspect today. Peel was in the great conservative tradition in the 1840's by espousing more and more of the Mancusian ideas, but it is just the opposite now, or so it seems. This can be seen in particular cases. The traditionalist has less need than the free-market advocate to pay lip service to the ideas of equality or progress, so that he need not be limited by the assumptions that individualism or the capitalist system must serve those ends. Thus as given measures arise he can be more flexible, and support even radical measures as political tools (while perhaps distrusting the economics) as means for long-run social stability. Taft's proposals in the areas of housing and education laws were examples of this; the same might be said of even Bismarck and Witte. He is less likely to fit political institutions into social or economic straitjackets; the reactions to the Bricker Amendment in the United States and to Poujadism in France are cases in point. These were cases where distrust of the state and of strong executive power—good individualist conservative beliefs—took forms which were likely to weaken the institutions of authority and national responsibility which are, in the long run, very important parts of liberal conservatism. Traditional conservatism—and it is necessary to emphasize the use here of "traditional" in a particular sense—comes close very often to Rossiter's category of liberal conservatives, men whose day-to-day political allegiances are often far afield from the right-wing political doctrines of the time.

4. There is a more right-wing characteristic of this traditionalism, however, a tendency which comes from the same source as the comparatively pro-liberal politics mentioned above. Just as the traditional conservative sees no need to support all the ideas of the Benthamite revolution, so he often supports, or half supports, classes or principles of a very eighteenth-century ring. Viereck's defense of legitimacy and the aristocratic way of life is a good example, as is Arendt's appreciation of the beneficial value of the traditional Central European state. The popularity of de Tocqueville, Burckhardt, and John Quincy Adams is significant, for these men were critical of the liberals of their time for

their extreme individualism and self-regarding politics (now the conservative position) but also, and more importantly, for the failure of the left to look at the whole sweep of history and the need to evaluate present policies in a long-run sense. Any such Burkean historical approach affirms a real conviction that in the long run we—and this "we" is civilization—may not, and hopefully will not be dead. Schumpeter, echoing MacDuff, observed that Keynes had no children; even very liberal Whig conservatives look to the effects of current affairs on a broader gamut of affairs than any liberal. For example, the question of judicial review is so precious to the traditional conservative not only because it is usually likely to be a good protection for individual rights, but also because its symbolic and undemocratic nature is valuable in preserving that sense of historical decorum which is the finest long-run guarantee of the liberties. This involves values which are far more venerable than those of Manchester, for instance, the qualities of beauty and morality which Nef has set against utility and efficiency. Ropke, who in general is a member of the free-market school, has dissented with some of the utilitarian connotations of that philosophy in order to defend more conservative values. Ropke commented that "the vital things are those beyond supply and demand and the world of property" and objected that "everything paradoxically in a welfare state is commercialized, everything is an object of calculation." Ropke's disagreement with Hayek on the subject of the industrial revolution is significant—he even suggests that the Hammonds may have had a point in their emphasis on the misery of that time. But whereas the Hammonds and Tawney meant to condemn the selfishness of capitalism and its cold harshness, Ropke and Nef condemn it for disrupting a more beautiful and aristocratic world. Hayek points to these latter arguments to equate the Fabian position with that of the aristocracy, just as English free-market conservatives have warned of the regression into feudalism or mercantilism since the 1860's, but this is not enough today. Conservatism in the guise of liberalism has worn thin, and one must consider moderates who do wish to re-examine the values of even industrialism or democracy.

This can lead far to the right. Ropke is not very moderate in some of his strictures on the contemporary world; the danger always exists that these aspects of traditionalism can become truly very traditional. But the same can be said for defenses of capitalism which end up wholehearted apologia of the status quo. There is a possibility that ardent eulogies of Disraeli lead one down the primrose path to Toryism, pure and simple; the same thing is true of arguments in favor of General Electric. But we are considering liberal conservatism, so it is important to make clear what is not in that category. The free-market theory is not a defense of business per se, and certainly not of big business per se. This involves opposition to monopoly, of course, although defining that is most of the problem. It is not an automatic pro-management, anti-labor-union philosophy, and even if it is conservative, it still retains a degree of free-market suspicion of landed property and of non-market sources of property rights (such as patents and royalties). And it is legitimate to say that theoreticians, such as von Mises, who reduce everything to a starkly mechanical pattern of the market may be classed as somewhat farther to the right than the term "liberal" would include.

As for traditional conservatism, as used here this excludes the very traditional positions—the medievalism of Kirk or of T. S. Eliot, and the theocratic ideas of some Roman Catholic thinkers. It certainly is different from the various authoritarian doctrines—Gaullism or its many imitations and near equivalents which have now come to supplant the semi-Fascist doctrines of the thirties and forties. And, more debatably, the sternly classical and anti-democratic viewpoint of Ortega and Babbitt, and their successors (such as Jaspers and perhaps Ropke) is perhaps too pessimistic, too doubtful of human nature to merit the term "liberal conservative," although their analysis certainly has been a strong influence. In short, what we here call traditional is a mild sort of tradition, consistent with a considerable degree of faith in human nature and a strong willingness to accept and even support many of the democratic features of contemporary life.

These categories also exclude other segments of right-wing thought. In the nineteenth century there was a large element, especially on the continent of Europe, of anti-clerical doctrinaire liberalism. This was a philosophy which considered the Catholic Church the principal threat to freedom, and often combined a very strong individualist ideology with a narrow antipathy to Rome, and often to "aristocrats" as well. This offshoot of eighteenth-century radicalism evolved into a set of beliefs at once still very radical and (especially on questions affecting the bourgeoisie) quite conservative; its greatest growth occurred in France. But the days of Combes are dead, and the free-market conservative camp has almost completely dissociated itself from this view, especially as the anti-clericals often advocated as great an extension of state power as the socialists.

In the last place, liberal conservativism emphatically does not encompass ideas of militarism covered with a libertarian veneer, theories of politics which involve great concentrations of governmental authority while at the same time repeating arguments for less government. It is quite opposed to mystical or conspiratorial theses, and the other loosely upper-circle doctrines which the fall of Hitler or the death of Stalin have unfortunately not eradicated. And above all, it does not include racist doctrines or other reactionary forms of ethnocentric or nationalist belief—but that should be self-evident.

With all this excluded we still must face the differences between the two groups of liberal conservatives. Much of this gap has been remarked on above, but one more distinction deserves further attention. The free-market idea is not a business philosophy, pure and simple, but it cannot help being a theory which is attractive to businessmen, and which in turn presents them at the center of the stage. To be sure, Adam Smith did not have an especially high regard for grasping merchants, but by and large his successors did, and their respect has remained a central fact in market politics since the time of Ricardo. After all, it is merchants who make up the personnel of a market, not laborers or soldiers. The value of a free market may redound to all classes and groups, but it is customary for the commercial community to see it first. The market concept is not so congenial to the traditional wing, nor has it usually been so. Aristotle had much less use for merchants, and his view of usury is a significant contrast to that of Bentham's. The idea of the rule of law is common to both, but there is a difference between the Ciceronian and the Sumnerian idea of that law. Both Sumner's "forgotten man" and the middle class of Aristotle's *Politics* inhabit the middle rank of political life, but what a difference their status is! To Aristotle that rank is an opportunity to govern the state, to Sumner it is a temptation to be milked by the state. Aristotle's middle class is composed of solid farmers and men of learning, but evidently not by men of commerce. The latter are the chiefest of the forgotten men, or were until Franklin Roosevelt came along. Aristotle did not glorify the bourgeoisie, and even Cicero constructed his politics of concord with the senatorial class as much as or more in mind than the equites. Daniel Webster's politics of concord was set in Boston, and his Atticus was a hero as well as a correspondent.

There is an unwelcome tendency in some of the traditional conservatives to try to turn back this evolution. Viereck, as we noted, has sought to glorify Disraeli, the founder of modern British imperialism, over Gladstone, the champion of the morality of the private sector. His efforts to justify this on grounds of labor paternalism demonstrate how weak that strand of conservatism is; the history of nineteenth-century English politics, as Roberts has shown, disproves the thesis of Tory benevolence and Whig selfishness. When Viereck and Lippmann (in his most recent phase) attempt to make liberal conservatism bear a largely collectivist ideology, they run the Theodore Rooseveltian risk of encouraging the forces which contribute to the upper circle. Tory socialism is a distant cousin of national socialism in its idea of the potent state as a superior patron of the poor; the road from the liberal Toryism of Peel and Gladstone is more consistent with the lower-circle values than the avenue of Disraeli and Milner. This does involve a glorification of the bourgeoisie, but no apologies need be made for that, especially in light of the performance of other ruling classes in totalitarian states in our century.

But the term "bourgeois" has so much less value today than it had a century ago; in many respects we live in a post-bourgeois epoch. The principal shareholders of the large industrial and commercial corporations are in trade, but they are also the socially prominent class. At the other end of the scale the skilled workman who lives in a house in a comfortable suburb, whose children attend college, and whose real income is greater than that of many *haute bourgeois* of the seventeenth century, can scarcely be classed as a proletarian, if one wants that word to mean anything sociologically. In the United States lower-circle political thinking (and as Hartz has remarked, that includes almost all the prevailing ideologies) has always denied the fixed-class nature of politics, even when it most clearly seemed to fit the situation. The depression seemed to change that, but our affluence, and the affluence of Europe, has given conservatives an opportunity to erase some of the "bourgeois" characteristics of free-market thought, while they adapt others to the traditional heritage, in order to develop a theory which can take advantage of the conservatism of our time so as to persuade the next generation.

Where does one start with such a theory? The very best place is with the "can't helps" mentioned above, the most vital portions of our concepts of civilization. Surely the dignity of man is an appropriate starting point for an individualist proposal.

Human dignity is an elusive thing at best in this world, but the deliberate degradation and humiliation of one's fellow man is the very most wicked action of all. It is precisely because the human condition is uncertain and subject to infinite vagaries that intentional cruelty is exceptionally wrong, for it robs a man of the very most precious core of his identity in an absurd universe. All the world's hopes may be fictitious, so that the sanctity of the lowest common denominator—the human body and soul itself—is at times the only thing a man can be sure of. To put this into specific terms, the inflicting of cruel and unusual punishment is an act that strikes at the root of humanity, and which is therefore the most inhuman conduct in the world. The promises of wealth and power are infinitely problematical compared to the suffering of one man put to torture.

It would be satisfying to conclude that a government which used or uses torture to maintain order or to punish offenders is totally bad. This cannot be said, for Elizabethan England, the state championed by Shakespeare and lauded for its dynamic verve, made use of torture. There have been examples of torture used by rulers and countries which have otherwise upheld valuable principles of good government—the Persian Empire of the Achaeneids is an example—but which have used ingenious forms of cruel punishment. But to the extent that this was so they forfeited the right of being considered decent. There may be justifications for torture at some time or place, but the burden of proof is on the proponents to show where or when; prima facie, a government which degrades the human body strikes at the reason for government itself—the securing of the minimum human happiness—and so forfeits its very reason for being.

Physical torture has taken many forms; it is not only the unbelievable cruelties of the totalitarian police which qualify. Putting lighted matches under the victim's fingernails may not be worse than death, nor is the savage beating equal to decapitation, but they partake of the brutal savagery of the most noxious forms. The more difficult problems arise with the largely psychological cruelties. The clearest fact about cruel physical punishment is that it arouses the worst impulses in the punisher, and that no one (except perhaps the most extraordinary masochists) would choose to be the victim. On the other hand, torture imposed on the mind has much more varying effects on different people. It may be assumed, for instance, that almost everyone would be severely harrowed by the experience of being placed repeatedly before a firing squad, only to be spared again and again at the last moment. But to one man the experience of being placarded as a worthless rogue before his fellows would be abysmal misery, to another it might be no punishment at all. To strike at a man's status before his peers shares with physical torture the quality of humiliation; it serves to destroy his inner worth and makes him incapable, insofar as it succeeds, in dealing with other human beings on an equal level. But this is psychic, and may have no effect at all on a thoroughly courageous or inner-directed person. Much of humiliation is culturally determined. Thus various forms of mutilation in Byzantine times was so excruciatingly cruel because it deprived the victim of his status for all time. These psychological cruelties vary, therefore, in brutality; at their worst they may equal the physical cruelties in viciousness. The worst cruelties are those which strike at a common condition of man, even if they are mental; as the torture is more particular the standard grows more subjective.

Of course one cannot lump all the uses of torture together; the occasional brutality of country sheriffs is less iniquitous than the mass cruelty of a totalitarian regime. This is not because the individual actions are less bad, but because they reflect an intermittent and at least partly surreptitious behavior. It certainly makes a difference if our sheriff's action reflects a deep-seated policy, and whether it is at least somewhat checked by the top officials of the pertinent government. The savage policeman is all too frequent a phenomenon, but when he becomes the much more powerful head of state the focus changes; the state then becomes committed to torture as the official policy. Concerted military use of torture, such as that of the French in Algeria or the Americans in the Philippines at the turn of this century, are somewhere in the middle. The use of torture by Nazi Germany was an indictment of the state per se, because this torture was a deliberate system of the government. The French and American governing systems did not stress torture in this way, but their claim to decency was compromised in a manner that police brutality in Marseilles or Birmingham could not equal. These differences of degree are perhaps not moral distinctions, but political ones, inasmuch as it is better for society to have occasional vicious sadists than a rule of government that calls for widespread enforcement of lesser cruelty. Yet to the extent that any torture is used it will degrade a nation as well as a man.

At this point the question of what torture is comes to the

fore again. It is fair to say that a given punishment imposed by
an impassive policeman may be preferable to one inflicted by
an avowed sadist, or even that an identical punishment imposed
by the member of one's own class, race, or group may be more
acceptable than that imposed by an outsider. The simplest,
harshest tortures are least divisible in this way; as one moves
down the scale the distinctions proliferate. But, as we have remarked in the more theoretical discussions of relativism, this does
not imply that judgments are impossible. The more complex the
issue becomes, the more important it then becomes to determine
priorities of value. It is especially a problem for conservatives
to accept limitations on police power, because of their fears for
the safety of society when dangerous men are left to go about
without the check of strong restraint. But it is equally the concern
of the conservative, at least the liberal conservative, that the
brute power of human depravity be checked in the positions of
authority as well as elsewhere; more so, as that is where the
greatest damage can be done. To an idealistic radical this
problem might be easier, for to such a thinker the question of
torture would be equally as clear-cut in its starkness, but with
fewer problems on the fringes. If all police roughness is inadmis-
sible, the matter takes care of itself, especially if one conceives
of human nature as fundamentally very good. But since conservatives think of that nature as quite fallible, and therefore insist
on the strictest limitations of the most savage exercise of that
nature, they must determine where the evil becomes a necessary
part of governing fallible men, and where it transcends it.

Few rules have ever been devised that are very helpful here.
Different legal systems have established the maximum number
of floggings which could be exacted, and in some modern jurisdictions the length of interrogations (which start as a reasonable
fact-finding procedure and end as a form of subtle but possibly
excruciating cruelty) are carefully metered. The West German
law, evolved out of bitter history, banning police arrests during
the night is a good example of a protection against a marginal,
but relevant, form of inhumanity, since arrest, a normal police
measure, can become almost torture when it takes on the menace

of nighttime suddenness. This may or may not be the case; the historic experience of Germany may very well make it more true in that country than in some other lands.

This example is relevant to a sister consideration. The ban against the use of torture is closely related to the protections of the criminal law which are often subsumed in much of the law of procedural due process. This too is a flexible concept, but it can be approached from the points where its subject matter borders on torture. These fundamental rights go to the basic well-being of the individual only a little less directly than physical torture, and perhaps as directly as psychological torture. In fact, they are often concerned with many of the same practices, or more often the same ambience, as the mental cruelty of the torturer. Night arrests are one example, as they involve a form of deliberate humiliation and terror designed to deprive the victim of his power to resist. It is not surprising that their most flagrant use is often found in conjunction with other kinds of disregard of basic due process.

Among these other kinds the following examples are well-known. Arbitrary arrest and punishment, punishment without regard to any rules of law, or rules which treat similar offenses differently, alleged legal trial which, because of the basic prejudice of the judge or jury, the surroundings in which the trial takes place, or the unfair rules of evidence or procedural law, is really no trial but a semblance of one, and trial in which the accused is not permitted (because of his lack of a lawyer or because of the rules) to make an adequate defense. Similar to these situations are those involving more subtle deprivations: trials following long periods where the defendant has been unable to see any member of his family or any friend or advisor, or where the prosecution has taken advantage of a vital defect (such as deafness or drug-imposed sleepiness) to rob the defendant of control of his wits, or any other situation in which browbeating has reduced the defendant or others to a state of impotence.

But there are other trials, in a different sense of the word, which test the minimum worth of a society. If a man is denied the use of the courts for civil actions, or the protection of the police, his security may be endangered more than if he were directly mistreated or discriminated against. If he is outlawed, if it is made unlawful to employ, house, feed, or otherwise deal with him he is denied due process as surely as the man imprisoned arbitrarily. If the vital successes of life were severely restricted to those who passed an examination at the age of eleven (this is not so wild an exaggeration), a brusque and arbitrary deprivation of the right to take that examination or a rigging of the test would also be in the category of deprival of due procedural process.

The utmost of these arbitrary penalties is genocide—the murder of a number of people because of their origin. Genocide is such a heinous crime precisely because of its arbitrary quality, the vile separation of guilt from responsibility precludes the victim, once having been born, from doing anything to avoid his fate. To kill a man for something which he cannot control is similar to torture in that it totally debases the role of reason. In the Nazi dream world nothing anyone did could compare to the status determined by birth; genocide was the vicious culmination of a system committed to arbitrariness.

What we are describing as procedural due process, or rather as the most fundamental guarantees of procedural due process, are those rules of society which prohibit the treatment of one person so differently from another that he is robbed of his ability to cope with the requirements of that society, or which treat all persons without regard to standards of fair play which would permit them a chance to defend themselves from overwhelming collective power. A number of points must be made about this concept. Firstly, these are the most basic rights. It is no reflection on the desirability of the rule against self-incrimination, or of the rule against double jeopardy, to say that one can include them in a lesser category, an area of procedural due process involving less vital considerations of personal rights. What is an absolutely fundamental right and what is not is naturally a matter for different opinions, but if one lumps all rights together there is a grave danger of either throwing a fierce burden on the law to respect every archaic gloss superimposed on jurisprudence by history; or on the other hand, it may lead to a flouting of all guarantees. It has been said that in the sixteenth century all sins were thought mortal, and that today all are considered venial; neither state is conducive to a measured form of legal protection of human rights.

Procedure is a nebulous word, but like many nebulous terms it is highly strategic in its value. There has been a tendency, deriving from the revolt against formalism which so eroded the traditional distinctions around the turn of the century, to minimize or ignore this distinction. After all, it is argued, where does procedure stop and substance begin? Is the statute of limitations procedural or substantive? Is any rule which seriously affects the outcome of a case, or involves a man's liberty, only procedural? The weakness of this argument is in the word "only," for procedure is of great importance, just as the argument against "technicalities" in the law is often misguided, since it is just these little things—what can be smaller than the habeas corpus writ, which only requires a form of judicial action, and guarantees no man's freedom—that make up the warp and woof of the fundamental legal safeguards. It is unfortunate that Frankfurter, who in the main was a keen defender of the gradations of constitutional theory, adumbrated (in the case of *Guaranty Trust Company* v. *York*) a philosophy in American constitutional law opposed to the separate value of procedure. The spirit of procedure is a spirit of measure, just as the balancing of various rights proposed in the preceding paragraph; it implies a devotion to fair play, irrespective of consequences, which can be subtly destroyed by a mixing of substantive considerations. Wechsler's principle of neutrality is a definition of this quality, in a way; the good judge will look to a general rule even if it involves the triumph of a bad cause or a bad man in the particular case. This does not ensure the preservation of sound laws or permanent rights, for in the last analysis only substantive rules can do that. But just because procedure is separate from substance there is a superior permanence to these procedural forms and so the idea of neutrality is an acceptable substitute for the conception of

natural law, a relativist replica of the more elaborate but indefensible broader patterns. This replica cannot serve to frame a
system of good government, but it can provide a minimum barrier against the worst evils. It is precisely because the merits of
any procedural safeguard are so limited that they are so important. It is the same consideration as that of personal dignity; a
warning to any state that some things are too much.

However, because these are procedural limitations, their scope
is fairly narrow. A third and last point should be considered here
—the basic guarantees of the citizen in society are negative and
do not make possible the good life. These rights are not, in a
meaningful sense, even rights to liberty. For after all, even
habeas corpus will not prevent a government from imprisoning
or executing anyone for doing anything; it only grants him the
right to have this done in a civilized manner. Let us suppose
that a law were passed making the sale or use of neckties a felony.
This would not be arbitrary or unequal in its application, since
it might provide for ample notice and would affect everyone. All
prosecutions under the law might be conducted with scrupulous
fairness, and with the historical precedents of sumptuary laws
there would undoubtedly be learned and vigorous precedents
brought forth. Yet the end result would be to make a totally
self-regarding act illegal. This example seems forced or peculiar,
because such a law would be improbable, even in Communist
countries (although it may be the rule in China, to judge by
appearances). Other laws affecting perhaps equally self-regarding
behavior exist throughout the world. There is no defense against
the proliferation of such statutes in the sphere of procedural due
process, and it is well to remember that.

For these minimum guarantees are just that—minimum. They
can be found under political systems we might abhor. In 1796
Bishop Horsley commented in the House of Lords that the
British people should be satisfied with these minimum guarantees
which, he stated, placed them at a great advantage over the
poor Turks, and not agitate for dangerous liberties. Even at that
time and place this dictum was greeted with considerable denunciation. Yet there is this to be said for the Bishop, that in limiting

ourselves to this minimum we should establish a solid base of agreement, excluding only the farther reaches of upper-circle thought (and even they will usually not come out forthrightly against these principles). To that extent something has been gained, for we are familiar enough with governments which have violated the most basic rules of procedural due process in innumerable ways; once the due process has disappeared the liberties vanish as well.

There is the further value that this agreement helps to elucidate the analysis of other, more substantive rights. Much of the discussion about the rights of political extremists has been confused by the tendency to lump together freedom of speech and assembly, and the right to counsel or to cross-examine freely. Since these are separable issues, an agreement on the procedural terms of reference and on their content frees the discussion of the other rights to deal with more far-reaching matters. Of course, there may still be disagreements on the former, in such areas as right to counsel and right to examine documents. But it is significant that the British have established the most respected protections in the area of due process, and as a rule have less trouble in delineating the procedural protections than anyone else. The British do not always have the most libertarian system, but they do have the most secure procedural rights.

The British experience demonstrates that this does not avoid serious disagreements. For instance, the dispute over capital punishment has been especially intense within the last decade. This involves questions very similar to those raised by the issue of torture. Obviously, executing a man is a serious affront to his dignity, at the least. But it is not so clear that it reaches to the same degree of cruelty as torture. Every man must die; while intense suffering can be avoided. If it is accepted that the base inclinations can so dominate a person that he is a permanent threat to everyone else—and this is a conclusion which anyone who does not have a thorough faith in humanity usually draws at some time or another—then society (and perhaps he himself) is better off dead than alive. Cruel punishment cannot be so defended. There are, for the liberal conservative, two conflicting

values here. On the one hand, the faults of human nature are
real and abiding, and in some people and at some times they lead
to acts which are so revolting and dangerous that, as an example
and in order to satisfy feelings of revenge (there is no point in
ignoring these feelings, which do and must exist), the death
penalty is suitable. On the other hand, there is a degradation
involved in its use and, since the judge and jury, as well as the
criminal, are not infallible, the chance of an error is always present. The considerations of basic dignity, of the individual and
of society, are competing against the suspicious demands of that
society. Both these considerations go to the root of what is meant
by the fundamental values, and accepting the premises set forth,
a compromise is a logical result. In fact, capital punishment has
been largely abolished, but its use has almost nowhere been
entirely eliminated for a long period. The example of Eichmann
and the Israelis is a case in point—where the inducements to
capital punishment are sufficiently strong, general principles of
abolition are waived.

But because the taking of human life is such a severe measure,
its incidence will always involve special questions of principle.
To make the punishment fit the crime is in general merely a
cliché, but in matters of capital punishment it does suggest a
fundamental rule. The death sentence for petty theft now seems
one of the worst blots of the eighteenth century; even more so
the cruelty of William III almost justifies Lord Acton's judgment
on Glencoe. Acton's history may suggest a hanging judge in our
time, but that is what fundamentals are for. Just as capital punishment may be justified in extreme cases, so historians are right
in using moral denunciation against those who abuse it in less
extreme ones. Where executions are a form of enforcing laws
beyond the zone of normally criminal action (in the area of
thought control, as in 1692 or much of the twentieth century)
the laws become evil. It is one thing to say that men will differ
on the rules for a society, and to extend this tolerance even to
the most severe upper-circle laws; it is another to enforce the
latter by death, so as to remove the chance for debate. But even
here we must decide what is beyond the zone of normal criminal

action, and opinions will differ—what of treason, for instance? It was wise not to execute Davis and Lee in 1865 and the Russians now seem to appreciate this wisdom. But was it wrong to execute Beria, or Goering? It is no fault in the idea of fundamentals to be increasingly troubled with the penumbra.

We have already moved, therefore, from the very most basic *non licets* to areas of compromise, and from here on this essay will be a journal of more and more compromises. But before setting forth it may be worthwhile to re-examine the bases, to see why the values of minimum rights and dignities are so important. In an absurd and relative world, why should anything be really valuable? Once again, we must say that there is no final answer to that question. But we have come through a half-century of horror and terror which will equal that of any time, and just as it may suggest that nothing is truly permanent, it also suggests that some things should be. The brutal knock on the door at night is a paradigm of this vision; the Kakfaesque wandering in a sea of arbitrary ruthlessness is another. Some of this has just come about without central planning, some was methodically planned. Some of these planners are better off, to be blunt, dead. There is an enduring need to erect strong theoretical barriers against their conduct, against their cruelties often so much worse than murder, and against the whole climate of that spirit. Most of these men have worked through or for a totalitarian state, and therefore the opposition to that state is the condition *sine qua non* of opposition to its fruits.

The terror of our terrible age is the enemy, but matters are not that simple. There are many cases of violations of procedural due process by less powerful or monolithic regimes. Two recent examples from Africa are significant, both in their setting and in their results. The dismissal of Chief Justice Korsah by the government of Ghana in 1963 was a reminder of the authoritarian examples in Western history; the passage in 1963 of the Sabotage Act, its subsequent enforcement, and the subsequent harassment of all forms of multi-racial opinion, demonstrates the ingenuity of the South Africans.

Neither of these measures is totalitarian; they do not involve a resort to total state power, or a thorough blanketing of all opposition. The action of the Ghana government was reminiscent of the moves taken by the Bourbon kings against the *parlements,* and by the Stuarts against recalcitrant English judges. Admittedly, the cause of due process was not dead throughout those times; the Habeas Corpus Act was passed during the reign of Charles II, almost ten years before the Glorious Revolution. But that revolution accomplished, as one of its first enactments, provision for the permanence of judicial tenure except for abnormal behavior. The English Bill of Rights roughly coincided with the beginning of Hazard's crisis of conscience, and has often been considered as a key measure in the development of that Whig epoch which we have considered. It was not an accident that the security of judges was one of the first, even if not *the* first, steps in the new politics of the time. It was not indispensable and it was not a panacea. Judges must be appointed, and the appointments are always, as Theodore Roosevelt demonstrated in his inspection of Holmes, political in a small or large sense. Many judges (almost all the state and local judges in the United States for example) serve limited terms, and most of them are subject to the same sort of elective ordeal that mayors or senators undergo. Nor are judges perfect even when secure in their office; Bacon is a prime example of the truism that genius and virtue are not inseparable. The value of having judges who cannot be removed by the chief executive—the question of judges removed by popular vote is more complex, although it does raise many of the same questions—is like the advantage of having road signs; one cannot be sure you will find your way with them, and you may without them, but their presence is a mighty assurance of proper guidance. Judges may be wrong-headed or stubborn, but once it becomes clear that their decisions are grounds for dismissal, cowardice becomes the rule and there can never be a sense of confidence in the decisions of any judge on a sensitive issue. At that point all the legal system becomes arbitrary, per se, since the most basic legitimate avenue of protection against any form of government protection, and the symbol of justice, loses its judicial quality.

It has been remarked that Nkrumah executed very few of his adversaries, and that in a state without a written constitution (such as Great Britain) the legislature can wreak more havoc than the most cowed or tyrannical bench. These are valid observations, and indicate the complexity of dealing with the rule of law. This is but a small sector of the political terrain, covering only a few issues. What makes it so important a plot is its centrality. Without independent judges a nation loses a natural check on even an all-powerful legislature, a body which by interpreting the newer laws and by standing by the settled meaning of the older ones, can at least slow down a powerful ruler; the events in Ghana were just such a situation. The environment of an honest court is a potent tool in the arsenal of civilized society, even if this may often be an illusion; once the security of conviction in its honesty is gone it is extremely hard to restore it.

The South African case is, by its novelty, more interesting. Nothing has formally happened to the courts, which are by general opinion carrying on with admirable aplomb and fidelity to due process. But the duly-elected Parliament has undercut them by providing for arbitrary arrests for a renewable period of anyone deemed a danger to the state. It might be possible for a man to be held in confinement for a succession of terms running altogether for many years, without having ever had his day in court and without having had any legal consideration of his case. Parliaments meet, after honest elections (given the franchise), but Mrs. Suzman cannot be sure whether she will sit from one day to the next. Yet this has come about in a country with all the trappings of legal tradition and with almost all of the normal democratic (for whites, at least) institutions. And yet it is apparent how much the First Amendment liberties of speech and press seem a façade when the fundamental rules of due process are disemboweled.

This conception of the rule of law may seem too thin and ethereal to be useful. To many defenders it is a much broader thing than a severely procedural conception. The idea of the rule of law usually involved a belief in a natural law which ruled over the vagaries of men's caprices. McIlwain has traced this to

Sophocles' Antigone defying Creon; the *Vindiciae Contra Tyrannos* anticipated John Adams in stating that "authority pertains to laws against men, not to men against laws." But if we accept that all laws are, sooner or later, man-made and subject to human variability, we cannot be sure of any fundamental assurance. Each measure must be weighed on its own scale. Instead of lessening the worth of the narrow procedural meaning of the rule of law, this enhances it. All other rights take meaning from the steady sense of security in a civilized order which it gives; in South Africa the press may seem free, but it cannot truly remain so, within a state with no protection from arbitrary confinement. As long as the courts remain free and the organizations of the state must conform to their basic patterns, the hope of liberty can evolve from the systems of due process, as the English experience of journalistic and publishing history of the seventeenth century indicates.

In another sense, the primacy of procedural due process needs no defense; it is there. The term "civilization" has been used, perhaps a bit loosely, but not inadvisedly. It can be defined as the sum total of the qualities which experience has disclosed as essential to humane intercourse. The principal merit of starting with due process is that it encompasses areas where disagreement is rare among men whose ideas include any of the lower-circle values, and thus embodies a consensus of opinion about the minima of decent living. Seeing that men can devise such beastly laws, and that the possibilities of state power are so infinitely treacherous, the mode of rational judgment implicit in this narrow definition of law becomes the core of orderly living. There is a parallel here to the modern disillusionment with the logical reason, the *recta ratio* of the Stoics; so too its operation in a code of substantive law is broken. But just as the value of individual rational thinking is thus enhanced as a barrier against unchecked passion, so too the concept of the code of individual legal rights stands as a barrier against a total relativism. In both cases the lesser role of reason may seem timid, but it stands as a charter of the individual verities.

This is nebulous, and in its workings it may seem petty.

H. L. A. Hart has classed the rule of equality before the law, the requirement of equal treatment in equal cases, as an administrative rule. But this is neither nebulous nor petty. Civilization is a big word; administration, despite its plethora of letters, seems to be a small one. But it is just these littler things that make life, absurd as it is in a cosmic or personal sense, less absurd in a social one. Terror enters when the rule of law, in the narrow sense, disappears, and it is more terrifying to be deprived of legal rights than to be starving—the consequences of hunger are at least predictable. Thompson, in his history of the French Revolution, recounts an appealing story. After Thermidor the remaining Jacobins still sought to continue the Terror, and wished only to limit its use. When called to task for this, the defense was stated that justice was fine for the people, but terror had to be retained for the aristocrats. "No," the cry rang out, "justice for everyone" —the demands of law take precedence over class issues. So we have found amidst our much more brazen terrors, where arbitrariness has made all of living a futile or pointless game. To return to Antigone, the chorus chants "When the laws are kept, how proudly the city stands! When the laws are broken, what of the city then?" The rules of ancient Greek burial are of absolutely no importance to anyone today, yet the message abides; what must be done is to secure, in a changed world, the minimum principles which had relevance to fifth century B.C. Athens and to an increasing part (as the Ghanaian example shows) of the world today.

In one sense this is new, in that viewing the idea of the rule of law in such a relativist fashion has limited the greater scope and wider appeal of the Ciceronian dicta. We cannot even be sure that the independence of judges or the right to counsel are sacred to good living; once again it is only fair to note that Elizabethan England lacked both rights. Nor is it possible to state that the time between arrest and arraignment must be one day or one hour, without fail. But this is not an insuperable difficulty, for the values we do maintain are their own reward, the assurance of our sort of world. There is no way of knowing when a Shakespeare will appear, or where, but the cruelties of the

English law of the sixteenth century—and they were greater than those of the fifteenth, or the eighteenth, so that one cannot merely lump "the past" in one disagreeable lump—were inimical to the great development of the rule of law which has truly glorified the English system of government. The theme of culture vs. civilization is hackneyed, but it has its validity; decency endures, whereas Shakespeares are unpredictable. A system beginning with these procedural guarantees and eschewing torture opts for civilization, with all the Appolonian stuffiness and regularity that implies. Shakespeare's contemporary, Thomas Smith, glorified the English commonwealth but overlooked the detail that torture had slipped into the common law; how much better was Voltaire's boast that he wished to be remembered, above all else, for his defense of Calas. In reducing the best of values to little ones, concrete and procedural in the main, the grandiose word "civilization" takes form. It is exactly the problem of the present disorientation in politics which makes this more than ever important. Malraux's religion of art is most pernicious when it combines the prevalent relativism with a culture-ethos which glorifies the mysterious; the current preference of Byzantium over Florence is in itself a part of the disorientation (or better, an over-orientation). We should choose as a beginning a limited area where one can say, "This is the 'can't help' of a worthwhile state." Law may not be, as Cicero declaimed, the highest reason implanted in nature, but is reason enough to fight for.

It is not easy to decide what areas of procedure are fundamental and what are not. Hayek, for instance, considers the non-arbitrariness of law to be one of the very bases of the rule of law. But before admitting this idea into the pantheon of fundamentals it is worth considering the point further. There are actually a number of different considerations wrapped up in this one concept. If the complaint is that the arbitrary law deals unequally, in the sense that if affects equally placed persons in different ways, this does involve the administrative maxim of good government which we have remarked on. A bill of attainder is the clearest such law—a singling-out of an individual or class for no reason, other than the *ipse dixit* of the legislator, for punishment or discriminatory treatment. This is arbitrary in a special sense. The legislature may, for instance, have weighed the matter with great care, as the South African Parliament has in its lengthy considerations which have uniformly led to greater and greater racial discrimination. There may in fact be good reasons, in the everyday sense of the word, for singling out some men for special treatment. The law in the French Third Republic which prohibited members of former princely houses from residing in France, and the similar treatment of Prince Otto of Habsburg by the Austrian Republic today, are not arbitrary in a popular sense. But the reasons are the same sort of reasons that lay behind Hitler's Nuremberg laws—they are conditions of birth and ancestry, and not punishments for actions. Arbitrariness thus means having the use of criteria which we find impermissible beyond the scope of reasonable decisions.

There are other kinds of arbitrariness which are more difficult to classify. A law should be published and open to easy discovery to avoid the stigma of arbitrariness. But what then of the common law? Bentham bitterly complained that we would not treat a dog with the cruelty which humans were undergoing in that no man could know if his behavior was criminal until a judge had ruled on it, which might be much too late. And yet, after a century and a half of Benthamite and civilian codification, it is now generally agreed that throughout the civil-law countries the pendulum is moving toward a more flexible standard even while the common law becomes more codified. No code can be so exact that it will foresee every circumstance or every avenue of litigation. Therefore some decisions will be surprising or, at the least, not wholly predictable. It is at this point where such customary rules as *stare decisis* and *res judicata* place their role, for these traditional legal forms which in particular cases may prove so disagreeable or inexorable, have as their purpose making a very uncertain proposition less so. But certainty is not an overriding virtue. Most penologists have agreed for many years that the flexible parole system is a more suitable way of regulating prison terms than the fixed term, and the Puritan distrust of judicial latitude in setting sentences has almost vanished. In criminal law *res judicata* is applied unevenly; the rule against double jeopardy applies far more strictly in favor of the defendant than for the prosecution.

These ambiguities exist in the executive branch as well. A state that tied the hands of the executive would fail to operate, and executive action can be much more important to any vested right than judicial determination. The United States prides itself as being a nation under law, but no citizen has a chance to review the details of the budget or the military program. Inasmuch as no one of any note on the right or left has suggested that the power of the president in these areas should be eliminated, the only question is how much arbitrary (in the sense of indeterminate and flexible) power there should be.

Certainly the term arbitrary in this sense does not imply a thoroughgoing arbitrariness in the ordinary sense. Modern historical scholarship has debunked much of the simple arbitrariness of history—the despotic Turkish emperors are now granted many rational virtues, and even Abdul Hamid II is allowed a sensible program. Caligula may have been mad (at least until he finds a defender) but Tiberius, Nero, and even Domitian have been upheld. For that matter Hitler was not arbitrary; far from it, no victim (that is, the vast majority of mankind) of his policies should have been surprised by the methodical pace of his designs. Real arbitrariness is a supreme luxury, as Caligula and Emperor Paul of Russia discovered, for it must alienate all but an extremely few supporters. No man can be truly oblivious to all public opinion, even if it be the very selected opinion of his praetorian guard, so he must exercise some caution in his irrationality.

This is especially true today, when even petty tyrants are methodical and great tyrannies are run (as the military jargon has it) by the numbers. That is certainly a very doubtful merit. Because so much of procedural due process does shade into a penumbra does not mean that everything which is not black must be left, willy-nilly, as white. The Supreme Court was faced with such an issue over twenty years ago, in the famous case of *United States* v. *Lovett*. The Congress had singled out certain men as so undesirable that funds would be withheld from government expenditure if they were retained on the payroll. This was not a bill of attainder in the historic sense of a capital punishment; it imposed no punishment, in the formal sense, on anyone. There could be no legal complaint if the President were to summarily fire civil servants without cause—it was done en masse in the nineteenth century, of course, and the practice has been known to exist more recently. But the congressional pressure was rightly held to be in the nature of a bill of attainder. The separation-of-powers doctrine, which in the main serves as a protection for individual rights by setting one branch against another, here has a much more immediate effect. The withholding of a government job is a serious measure—in a Communist country it might be tantamount to a sentence of starvation—and it is important that only the right people have the right to decide this. Not that executive persons are wiser or more judicious than legislative ones, but that is their province. There is the further question of the propriety of even executive firings, when these are accomplished under some kind of judicial hearing. The Court has had occasion at several times to extend some or all of the rules of judicial procedure to these executive tribunals, when the result of the hearing is a public branding which reaches the status of punishment. Arbitrariness can be considered a violation of customary power arrangements.

So far we have discussed procedure in its formal sense, as a rule of court. But this idea of procedural due process has less exact relevance. Many of the political questions with which the other branches of government deal and which are fought over at the polls are, in a broad sense, procedural. We have noted that the doctrine of separation of powers has a distinctly procedural implication, but in a different sense it can be said that the doctrine is itself a procedural tool. If procedure is defined as the manner in which substantive decisions are made and the forms deciding how they are made, then the intra-governmental regulations are procedural. Here, too, there are many good rules which are nevertheless not essential to a free society. Locke and, perhaps to a lesser degree, Montesquieu thought of this doctrine as a part of a free society, but this conception has been a notable victim of history. To whatever degree it was in effect in Great Britain at one time, that time had passed by the Victorian age. It is remarkable how the English, after being for centuries the prize example of the value and need for a two-house legislature, have now almost established a unicameral system, with a vestigial, largely judicial House of Lords reduced to an advisory role.

The lessons of procedure are even harder to decipher when one sees how contradictory they can be. Frequently the right to a speedy trial or hearing conflicts with other procedural rights of notice and investigation. An old regulation may be a guarantee of ancient rights to one person and a flagrant violation of liberty to another—the eighteenth century was full of such arguments. We see this today in the debates over trial by jury in areas like Mississippi, where ancient rights often look like abuses. This, we must remember, is what the British thought in 1774. This is often the point at which procedure and substance intermingle, for behind a rule of procedure there is often a specific interest at stake. These interests very often disguise themselves as procedural advocates but this changes nothing, for even in cases where the issue is purely procedural there can be two equally valid views, between which there is no *prima facie* way of judging (especially if there are precedents on both sides). In applying these principles to the non-governmental sectors the difficulties increase. Many of the limitations on government can be applied to private institutions, which would result in an enlargement of the area of procedural rights, but this would also involve a great increase in the power of the state as a guarantor of rights against non-governmental bodies. It is in the nature of procedure to be time-and-place oriented. Even the idea of a representative parliament itself is not vital. The pure democratic forms—the Athenian assemblies, the Swiss or New England local governing bodies—do have the merit of thoroughly popular rule. Much of the older arguments miss the point. There is no reason why a town meeting cannot be limited in just the same way as a representative body by courts, outside powers, or traditions. It is farfetched to say that a mass meeting must be more reckless than a small group of legislators—it all depends on who is in what body. The Swiss and New Englanders have been notoriously conservative, while the world around the cantons and the townships seethed with change. In Andorra this democratic, or quasi-democratic government is to some extent sovereign, but no less slow. This would hardly work in Bolivia or Iraq. But it seems to make little difference that one country's parliament is more or less popular than another's. The secret of Lebanon's good fortune is not the complex religious balancing, but the spirit which underlies it (as the events of 1958 confirmed); Turkey and Syria had a presidential-prime ministerial representative government, but the results in these neighboring countries have been very different. Even the suggestion of the syndicalists (taken up by the Fascists and now suggested by the Gaullists) that the legislature should represent economic and social, not geographic districts, is not so radical. As long as every group was fairly represented—and that is the catch which has ruined the idea so far—there is no basically anti-constitutional quality in corporatism. The English system, eliminated only in 1950, of giving Oxford and Cambridge universities seats in the House of Commons, served to give the traditional upper-class intellectual (usually religious) community a share in running the country. This may have been right or wrong, depending on one's premises, but it contributed to, rather than detracted from, the viability of the British constitutional system. The argument for one man, one vote, which one would think from listening to Justice Douglas or African nationalists on the road to independence was the sign of true democracy, is as unconvincing as the fear of popular assemblies. No successful government has ever stuck to this theory, and in Africa today the most stable countries (such as the Ivory Coast and Malawi) are building on a very different foundation. If one voted by jobs there would be the problem of housewives—but restricting the vote to men would take care of that—and the unemployed —but they could be disenfranchised, or polled at labor exchanges—and perhaps nothing would change. It is as foolish to imagine that a voter forgets his economic interests in geographical voting as it would be to assume that he would shed his social or geographical allegiances in corporate voting.

But this is perhaps too naive. The vision of men like Sorel— that perfect anti-Whig—implied a compulsion or at least an enthusiasm generated by the corporate system which would make the worker or the manager an adjunct of his work or position; an economic or functional élan. Procedure is important because it channels the legal and political rivers, so that one must look beyond the water level to the direction of flow. Some things do make a difference, even if very indirectly or in a symbolic way.

The example of corporatism is apt. The great value of the geographic representational system, replete as it usually is with customary quirks and historic patterns, is its quality of filtering demands through a strainer which has been proved to be neither too tight nor too loose. Time may make the strainer over-tight by warping the representative quality too much or by causing some branches of the government to keep too great delaying power (as committee chairmen have in the United States Congress today) or it may allow too much loosening (as in executive encroachments in many lands). The former difficulty usually comes from inertia, the latter from too much action; the highest use of procedure is to provide semi-automatic correcting devices. The United States has fared well largely because of the presence of the Supreme Court, intermixed with the amending power of the people and the rule-making authority of the executive and administrative agencies. Probably the greatest fault of the French Third Republic, which the Fourth tried but failed to correct, was the inability of the executive or any other arm of government to check a legislature (usually the Chamber of Deputies, but sometimes also the Senate) which became deadlocked or immobilized by complex disagreements. The problem was usually not substantive—this was by and large a hoax of the far left and right—but procedural. Government went on, but the seemingly excessive power of the legislature resulted in more control by the permanent civil service and an atrophying of the support given to an effective and symbolically functioning state. The idea of government, the procedural mechanism, failed even while the operation of the state continued on its way, and that failure was fatal.

A great merit in this approach is the symbolic value which it stresses, the absence of which has proved so deadly in France. It has been said that the American equivalent of the Crown is the Declaration of Independence and the Constitution; and this is not a mystical Anglo-Saxon or a purely historical phenomenon. Perhaps a crucial factor in overthrowing Mossadegh was his effort to eliminate the Majlis in 1953. The Iranian legislature may not have been a mother of parliaments, and it lacked the ancestral traditions of Achamaeneid grandeur or the dignity of the Peacock Throne, but in its forty-seven-year history it symbolized the success of the Persians (limited though that may have been) in achieving a constitutional state. Nicholson remarked that if government exists for certain purposes such as the preservation of individual rights, it is more important that a state be rightly constituted than that it be independent or democratic, and there is a good deal to be said for that. But the great advantage of independence and democracy is that it attracts that irrational support which converts acceptance to loyalty. To be sure, all procedure is not alike; the Star Chamber was a very proper victim of the English revolution. Those procedures which most tend toward protecting individual rights consistent with a suitably effective government should be encouraged. But it is vital to take this purposeful attitude only in the long run. In the short run Wechsler's rule of neutrality is vitally important. A society with sufficient faith in the rightness of its institutions can afford what may seem stupid impasses or laborious delays. It often seems that a state which will bend its energies before these procedural rules, as the United States has before the Fifth Amendment, is less effective than one which changes the rules to fit the desires of the state, as France has done in its creation of new courts with new regulations to try certain classes of offenders. Of course there was a history of impatience behind this severity in France, a history of procedural impasse which impelled even Aron to say that "the French malady is the paralysis of the state." This proves how even moderate men may forsake the procedures of government, even when history has demonstrated how valuable they tend to be.

It is where the rules rub tightly that the political disputes arise, disputes which quickly involve substantive matters. But it is fair to summarize much of conservative thought of the last few years in this way. There are many ways to run a society, and the relativist doctrine that nothing is inevitable or certainly right is true. But the values of the past, if they subserve the desires of society, must be upheld even if there is no guarantee of their eternal rightness. It is worth starting with little things which may seem to make no difference, such as the minutiae of legislative decorum, before they lead to bigger ones. Thus the high-handed behavior of the Gracchi in treating their fellow tribunes was the first step in the precipitous decline in political standards during the last years of the Republic, and the incivility of socialist deputies in late-nineteenth-century continental Europe set the stage for the vicious anti-parliamentary actions of the twentieth. Each case must be determined on its merits, but we have seen (and this is an example of one of the conservative truths we have examined) that there is a merit in the little, traditional, individualist regulations. Sooner or later they will revive, in a different form, if society continues; but the process of losing and finding them is not worth going through, unless the need is very great.

We hear so much today of a world of rising expectations where demands for food or steel make liberty, much less such pettifogging practices, a dispensable luxury. But this is not to be taken for granted. The attachment to the symbols of a procedurally-bound society which upholds human rights at the cost of efficiency has a lasting appeal, even though Debray may seem to make the greatest impression. In Latin America, for instance, it has seemed that one government has succeeded another without any care for the benefit of the society. But the tradition that the outgoing men are not to be prevented from going to a foreign embassy, or outlawed in other ways, is a valuable and enduring part of Latin-American life, a contribution to civilization. These civilities have done much to reduce the bitterness which the ferment of Latin-American politics might have caused; we can see the results of a clean sweep in Castro's Cuba, where the rules of procedure were the first victim of a movement which soon annihilated all the conservative and most of the liberal values. Procedure is usually in the first line of political dispute, and the first victim of revolution.

This is very often the place where liberals and conservatives come to a parting of the ways. The conservative is apt to consider the limitations on government, or the rules of political process, as the vital portions of the governing system, and to cherish these as the core of the good society. The distinction between private and public is an integral part of this, as is the principle that laws should deal equally with everyone. On the other hand, the reaction of the liberal is to emphasize the idea of democracy, the sovereignty of universal suffrage as the medium through which a general will is formed. This Rousseauian idea, acceptable even where the rest of his doctrine is anathema, was and probably still is part of the American credo; it is as exciting in Rhodesia today as in the Britain of 1848. Even where various sorts of disillusionment have set in, the faith in "democracy" is assured—the word is almost magical, and to be opposed to democracy is to be considered a Fascist, no more or no less.

This presents a nice puzzle for the liberal conservative. The outspoken anti-democrats, such as they are, do invariably tend to be members of the far right, extreme reactionaries and often savage bigots or thoroughgoing believers in totalitarian ideas. If the Afrikaaners speak ill of democratic ideas it seems almost incumbent upon one to laud these beliefs. But, on the other hand, the idea that 50.01 per cent of a given population—Zanzibar's or perhaps the whole world's—must govern and have undisputed sway has always seemed a trifle extreme, and no less now, with our plethora of both sovereignties and global conceits, than in earlier times. It is fine, for example, to denounce the brutalities of communism and remark how their triumphs have come through violence or fraud. But what if they win elections? It is not so unbelievable a trick. The Nazis won a surpassing victory in the League-supervised election in the Saar in 1935, but this was the misfortune of the Saar, and of liberty. Wilson's idea of self-determination had a beautiful sound and much altruism behind it (like the similar credos of Chief Justice Warren today), and its application was finely attempted, by and large, in the work of 1919. Yet now it seems so misguided. The Polish and Czechoslovak boundaries were the result of hard-fought compromises over the relevance of population and natural divisions, yet the old-style decisions of Westphalia and even Vienna worked better —in part because at Westphalia the bitterness of differences were allayed, and at Paris they were stimulated. Once begun, these quarrels tend to end up in Nansen transfers—Cyprus appears to be the next candidate for these inhumane upheavals—far outdoing any of the older methods in undemocratic roughness, just because they tend to a consideration of peoples and not people.

This concept of self-determination may err in deciding boundaries on predetermined ethnic lines. The concept of federation now seems much better from the democratic viewpoint; Yugoslavia and Czechoslovakia seem more of a success in their entireties than the ethnocentric efforts made at defining their limits (which so engrossed the confreres at Paris), and it is now argued openly that the Austro-Hungarian Empire should have been retained. But pure democracy would have let everything be decided by referenda, as indeed the future of parts of Silesia and (in 1935) the Saar was unhappily settled. But why should vital decisions be determined by the vote of one generation, one day, in fact? If the Saarlanders had voted at another time, say, after the Nazi treatment of the Catholic Church had developed further on totalitarian lines, they might have voted differently. Why, Calhoun asked, should a decision made in 1788 by the then American states, rightly decided at that time, bind future generations? And what is the magic in a simple majority? We require two-thirds vote for certain matters, and occasionally three-fourths or three-fifths, for all of which there are precedents. Why not unanimity, especially in respect to establishing a sovereignty? Logically, if the Lockean act of transferring part of one's rights to the state is the fundamental origin of government, surely each citizen should have a right to say "no"; perhaps on reaching the age of twenty-one. Most contracts are interpreted so as not to last too long, and most societies provide for civil divorces of the marriage bond. Yet when we deal with states, even whole provinces cannot secede, as the American Civil War showed. The Britons who applauded the North at that time are often thought of as great liberals, and yet many carried the logic of permanent fusion into their analyses of the Irish question twenty-five years later, to be then classified as arch-conservatives. Since every man cannot choose his laws at all times—which is the perfect exercise of choice, the pure condition of freedom, and completely impossible—one must draw up rules. Just because these rules provide for "democracy" does not lend them virtue, for the determination of the terms in which they operate may color their entire manner. They are all compromises, gaining their sanction much more from custom than from a mass reason.

Even over this hurdle, as we are in this country now, the merits of democracy remain open to discussion. Pure democracy would mean, of course, no limitation whatsoever on the majority will, but even the Athenians went awry with these rules. Let us further assume that the multiple network of minority rights and social and economic gradations are in force, together with all the separations of powers which are present in the United States today. Even then it is reasonable to confine one's democratic enthusiasms to Forster's two cheers. The choices of the majority, or even of two-thirds, may comport with all the requirements of due process and fair play, and still leave a poor aftertaste. If the majority votes for a highway which will cut through my ancestral home, it must, according to civilized rules, indemnify me properly. Properly, that is, according to the standards of the market as refracted through the administrative and judicial processes of the state. These processes may be scrupulously fair and yet the result may be unfortunate. In terms of economics, my loss, my disutility may be much greater than the gains, the benefits perceived by everyone else combined. In the market there is room, as Buchanan and Tullock point out, for this to be taken into account. A man with $5,000 may outbid a man with $100,000,000 in a given auction, if his desires are sufficiently greater. If we permitted the exchange of money in political situations we could perhaps approximate this, but democracy means, it would seem, that no one dare (formally, of course,) sell his vote.

In another context, suppose that the majority supports one candidate and the minority another, and suppose that to the minority the candidate of the majority is a personification of evil —this is a typical case in areas of ethnic bitterness. The leader of the majority need do nothing to rend the social fabric if he takes office; he may attempt to lean over backwards in fair dealing, and yet his very prominence may destroy the commonwealth. This is where compromise has great merit, for through the jockeying and power plays of a complex multi-interest system such men are usually pushed aside, even when they command real majority support. The same is true of measures; there are many bills, of clear constitutionality, whose passage would inflame strong minorities. This is often referred to as the problem of intensities, of the case of mild majorities and fierce minorities. But it is important even in cases of equal intensities, for it is not always worth deferring to a determined majority if the result will be to embitter society.

The Japanese socialists, of all people, seem to interpret this to mean that everyone must agree on any important move. That is going too far in the other direction; the temptation will be, as in the celebrated Polish anecdote, to dispose of the lone dissenter roughly. There comes a time when minorities must give way, and part of their job is to cooperate as the majority cooperates. Thus, the South achieved, with the Missouri Compromise and the Compromise of 1850, a position of minority veto à la Calhoun which met many or most of the criteria of political adjustment. Even in early 1861 many Republicans still accepted the inviolability of slavery in its own habitat as sacrosanct. But in those years the southerners grew more demanding and less willing to accept their position as a minority, which sometimes implies concessions as the price of irreplaceable rights. In other words, one must find a balance between pure democracy and no democracy at all, and one must keep innovating and experimenting so as to keep that balance viable. When liberals, and certainly conservative liberals, speak of democracy they often mean just this, and this is where all moderates can agree completely. There is an exalted quality about this process, tied up as it is with the conversion of a raw state of popular rule into a refined system of modulated control. When the NBC Symphony Orchestra played without a conductor one could sense the feeling of pride and awe that a group of skilled musicians could operate without a master, and yet in keeping with an unspoken system of order, a tacit self-mastery. Toscanini may have produced better results, but politically his absence was refreshing as a tribute not merely to equality, but also to maturity.

The secret of the NBC orchestra was its capacity to abide by the conventions of musical reproduction without external control; so it is with democracies. The patterns of majority rule and the limitations over that rule have been worked on in such detail that "democracy" has come to mean the sum total of these conventions. An American or Greek would be amazed to be told today that democracy required direct participation by every citizen. The comparison of the market place for securities with the political arena is instructive; the complex mechanism of the stock markets provides a valuable, perhaps most important complement to the simpler, Gilbertian techniques of shareholders' control. So the democracy of government needs the complex framework of power channels, even when some of them interpose various bodies between the voter and the government officials. To take an obvious example, the division of the countries into numerous, diverse voting units means that the individual vote may be of much more consequence in determining a local election for a deputy or representative than it would be in a national election. This is the chief reason why democracy is most consistent with voting for men and not for issues. There is a connection between the smallest voter and the largest leader which can be measured and felt, and which in close elections may preserve the sense of importance of the individual without straining the effectiveness of the system. Voting on issues presents a beautiful potential for direct government in theory, but it usually works out that the voter is robbed of effective control. Either the matter must involve qualifications or details too complex to be dealt with in a simple mass vote, and the important implementation or decision is tacitly and undemocratically assigned, or the vote is converted to a plebescite designed to approve the decisions of the ruler. It is paradoxical that the well-organized progressive party, with its devotion to popular control, often ends up with less popular control than most other parties. The British Labour Party, for instance, with its emphasis on issues and constituency voting, has been marked by a sharp split between the elements of party leadership and the more leftist or rightist membership groups; the upshot is usually that the latter are squelched and their representatives forced to vote against their convictions in Parliament. The Tories have less simple democracy but often more opportunity for the individual voter to choose a man who will speak his mind for them in Westminster. Proportional representation and the *scrutin de liste* systems are more elegant, but the old-fashioned single representative system is more amenable to voter control. Under the Weimar Republic, for instance, proportional representation meant that each party organization chose the party lists and the rank of candidates. If some unpopular party figure were placed near the top he could be sure of a seat unless the party suffered a rout; even the rotten borough system gives the voter more say.

So it cannot be said that everything which is good is therefore democratic, or the contrary. For example, the argument of Eugene Rostow that judicial review is somehow democratic is a travesty on the word—we must simply admit that the power of the judges to set aside legislation is not a popular power, but no less (more, in fact) important for all that. If the conventions break down, as in British Guiana or Cyprus today, the forms of order are not likely to be democratic, and when Jagan (or Makarios) pleads for a simple democratic system it is vital to consider what merit democracy has without the conventions to support and enrich it. Until late in the nineteenth century one exception to universal manhood suffrage was admitted: those who were thought to be unable to exercise independent choice, such as those on government relief, were excluded from the ballot. Household servants were the last to gain the franchise during the French Revolution for this reason. Literacy tests are similar. But these matters should not be decided on as a priori basis. There is no certainly simple conservative case for these tests; it may be argued that to place an emphasis on education, even simple education, is a perniciously liberal idea. If literacy is so vital for citizenship perhaps the state should bend more efforts to eradicating it. Yet those who cannot read—perhaps people with mental blocks in just this area—may possess ample political shrewdness or wisdom. At best a literacy test smacks of the simplicist logic, the either/or assumptions which are anathema to moderate conservatism. At worst, as we know, they can be used as tools to bar an unwanted group, or race, from voting. In other contexts they serve to disqualify the outsider who knows only a foreign language, which may or may not be a good thing—certainly not so highly important as Americans or Germans tend to think, as the Swiss example demonstrates.

Thus these questions are matters of degree, and comparatively small degrees at that. It is amusing to think how Macaulay and others labored over the perils of universal suffrage, and how to the democrats of a century ago and more it seemed the finest right worth having. Perhaps the welfare state would have been impossible without it, yet dictatorships are not so far behind in these measures. If the state is the subject of political theory, and the elections of officials the key to rule in the state, and if democracy means that everyone can then vote, of course it is the central issue. But now almost no one—left, right, be-havioralist, institutionalist—accepts all these premises, and the triumph of the unemployed and the women, concluding the democratic surge of the nineteenth century in our more turbulent twentieth, has brought few excitements. The United States Supreme Court now considers the right to vote one of the rights which are entitled, more or less, to equal protection (it is not clear how far this goes to render the limitations so common in

1787 and even 1865 retrospectively unconstitutional), but the franchise cannot be termed a liberty, even so. Women were not deprived of liberty in any meaningful sense before they won the vote; to consider the Britain of 1789 or the Pakistan of today as police states would be ridiculous. There is a vital difference between the exercise of civil liberties, the fulfillment of individual freedom, and the exercise of political suffrage, the use of a shared power to influence, usually very slightly, the running of the state.

That which concerns all should be decided by all, but the degree of concern and the modes of decision are variable, the right subject to the tests of time and precedent. Burke was not wholly wrong with his theory of virtual representation, but there can never be an assumption that one group has permanently sent its proxies in; as with corporate voting, there should be a habitual right of withdrawing these grants and reasserting the right to direct participation. The merit of a literacy test is that, at least in principle, one can read oneself into the franchise; Guizot's advice to the French voters of the 1830's, "enrich yourself," was somewhat more cynical but not inconsistent. It now seems clear that in eighteenth-century New England a minimum of good luck and hard work would permit almost any man enough wealth to gain the vote. It has been said that only a reasonably affluent society can afford universal suffrage; in that sense the social efforts of the whole country are needed for the rise of the non-voting group. In all these cases the vote may most properly be considered a responsibility which is best shared, and can be in most cases, rather than a privilege to be doled out.

It can be shared because this right has become one of the symbols of responsibility in our age; the responsibility of the state to the least citizen, and the responsibility of the citizen to his fellows to share in the public business with maturity and care. Of course much, probably most of this is symbolic, but it is no less important for that. The Pauline boast, *"civis Romanus sum,"* disclosed more than a wise use of available legal tools; it indicated, as if from an obscure document, the emotional strength of the Roman Empire even among Oriental bourgeois. Today the civic spirit involves the vote, the palpable power of citizenship. Many actively political people never taste more than the tiniest fruits of power or never even meet the men whose importance they have helped create, yet their activity lends a richness to their lives and even more to the life of society. The Roman Republic perished when—perhaps not because, but perhaps so—in its final crisis most citizens no longer believed these rights worth holding dear. It is a mistake to require men to vote, as is done in Australia, for such a vote will be ignorant, and a refusal to vote may be a principled protest or a salutary sign of satisfaction. But those who do vote are participating in the commonwealth, even if in a petty way. This can be destructive of other rights if carried too far, as the co-determination idea may tend to make political responsibility the sole domain of power determination, at the expense of private rights. It can be disillusioning, for the fact of open diplomacy secretly arrived at is the best that can be expected in domestic as well as foreign affairs. Too much voting—elections every month, or elections for posts which would better be appointed by a key elected official, are too much of a good thing, turning it into a bad one.

In recent years the left has come to emphasize participation as the true essence of democracy, and thereby to reclaim democracy as a radical slogan. Burnham has demonstrated that the percentage of citizens voting in the United States has declined since 1900 (a wry commentary on the progressive movements of the century) and suggested that this creates a crisis of legitimacy. Lewis has contrasted the sense of participation in Castro's Cuba with the "alienation" of other impoverished peoples. These very examples show how democracy, to the left, means more than choice or consent. It is not enough for the radical that each citizen have the opportunity to share in the governing process; he *must* share. Consent is not enough; support is essential. The leftist goal of participation was to some extent the result of revulsion from the elitism of communism, but it is easy to see how quickly it can turn, as the circular realities enforce their logic, to the credo of compulsory enthusiasm. So it has proved in Cuba.

But withal, democracy in its simple meaning, the sovereignty of the people, is a valuable part of our individualist social order. It arose out of the Whig movement, and it has taken its most successful strides as a part of the systems of capitalist, constitutional nations. The age-old problem of how to reconcile order and liberty, the long-term needs of society and the immediate desires of powerful groups, can be solved more satisfactorily when each citizen has a stake in the government, even if he knows it is not a potent one. Today the four oldest states operating under one form of government are Sweden, Great Britain, Denmark, and the United States; the thousand-year Reich and the never-changing authoritarian monarchies have proved more fragile. And in the course of securing public order the religion of democracy, even if it is nothing more than a golden cloak shrouding the emaciated body of universal suffrage, has become a prized part of that faith which has proved more resistant to the miseries of our century than the cynics have conceded. Like progress, democracy is a nineteenth-century idea which has worn unevenly, but its service to the cause of individual self-awareness should be welcome to those interested in individualism; its alternatives are certainly unwelcome.

☆ *VII*

Reason
and Custom

Much of this comes down to a central question: what values do we wish to emphasize? Any society based at least in part on the preservation of human dignity must give a prominent place to reason, the mainspring of human capacity. But we have seen that reason has lost its clear eighteenth-century meaning and potency. The beautiful simplicity of right reason has been complicated by the fragmentation of ideas and faiths. The two other brands of reason which have been considered are the meaningful choices today: the mass reason and the individualist reason. It is natural, as we have noted, that any conservative philosophy will be likely to choose the latter.

Since this reason is a personal and variable thing, it is not necessary for it to be uniformly expressed to be significant. If I never vote and never take any action to make my desires felt, I may be acting against my rational best interests, or I might be making a lazy decision that sloth means more to me than whatever good I will get out of the game. If I buy anything that strikes my fancy when I have the money, even if I thus fail to end up with a very efficient use of my resources, this may also be due to ignorance, or to a perhaps uneconomic preference for ease or popularity. The economic man is not necessary to neo-classical economic thought, nor the well-informed voter to a moderate democratic philosophy, because value is centered on the individual, and not on a preordained system. Thus we find the role of reason in places where our predecessors saw only irrationality.

This emphasis on the rational qualities of the individual carries a threat of selfishness. To the extent that reason is stripped of some of its grand qualities of cosmic knowledge it runs the risk of becoming another name for cunning or thorough self-interest. No political theory or economic doctrine has ever gone this far, since even de Mandeville or Spencer believed that the process of leaving everything to each man's devices would benefit the whole commonwealth. However, an often-stated objection to elitist ideas of reason, such as Plato's or the neo-Darwinists', is that the benefits derived from the exaltation of reason flow from and are advantageous only to a minority. If the triumph of reason means only that the smarter will oppress the more foolish (as Popper attributes to Platoism and as much of Social Darwinism has seemed to advocate) it hardly qualifies as a sound basis for government. Reason, to be attractive, must transcend such limitations, and be valuable for the whole as well as for some of the parts. Jefferson's famous declaration that "error of opinion may be tolerated where reason is left free to combat it" proclaimed a confidence, not always acted upon by the author, that all men have those qualities of intelligence capable of discerning the right values of society; the natural rights of the Declaration of Independence are persuasive just because of this confidence. Just because reason is confined to individual thought is not cause for despising its importance or its universality. The greatness of the Whig spirit was that, even at its most parochial or hyprocritical moments it paid at least lip service to this faith in man's most godlike attribute, a faith amply justified by the scientific accomplishments achieved since 1776 or 1801.

But of course much else has happened, much less edifying. The case for conservatism shows the need for some other quality to support and reinforce (and, in the nature of things, to water down) reason. The unpopularity of rational religions is a reminder of the weakness of thought unmixed by feeling, a lesson driven home by a generation of neo-Calvinists. Passion and emotion are the enemies of reason, as are violence and mysticism. But there are other qualities which fit into the lower-circle world. The best of these is custom.

Custom is described in the dictionary as a usual habit or an established usage; it suggests a non-rational attachment to the pre-existing or the familiar. It need not be anti-rational however, for what is established may well be quite consonant with reason. Any theory which is constructed on the thesis that man's intellect is sufficient is open to the criticism that this requires too great a faith in the rightness of human judgment. This is especially true when one emphasizes the individual character of reason, and its subjective character. The judgment of time and the patterns of pre-existing society are a pedestrian accompaniment to the soaring capacities of the human mind, but they serve to suggest channels and to direct it. Viereck expressed these advantages well when he wrote that "a virtue to be serviceable, said Samuel Butler, 'must, like gold, be allied with some common but more durable metal.' For 'virtue' substitute 'civil liberties,' the durable metal without which the gold of liberty is unserviceable, is the concreteness of irrational ancient custom."

There was ample talk of liberty in pre-Nazi Germany, perhaps more than elsewhere in Europe, but the customary safeguards of freedom were in truth much weaker. The greatest safeguard to academic freedom has proved to be the sense, so complete in Great Britain and very effective in the United States, that violations of academic tenure are "not done"; the defeat of the court-packing measures in the United States in 1937 is also an example. The illustrations of contrary behavior in countries where Mill or Croce may be highly revered, but not followed, are legion. Reason has a grandeur and a marvelous aura, but reasoning men may come to very strange conclusions. Robespierre's deification of reason was probably thoroughly sincere, and was reached and propagated by means of intensive discussion and brilliant intellectualizing; this in no way reduces the strength of Burke's criticism. In the rich and skilled world today numerous suggestions are reasonable—i.e., not technically impossible or inherently absurd. The Townsend plan came much nearer to passage in the 1930's in a well-regulated democracy than most people now remember. A vast capital levy or a bill to deport a sizable, unpopular minority might do very well—in fact both bills might pass at the same time. Eyck remarks that the German voters—and these were, of course, among the best-educated people in the world—almost passed a bill to expropriate the German princes without compensation at the same time that they elected a semi-senile aristocrat without any political experience president of the republic. It did not take long for the same voters to support first Hitler and then Adenauer. Anyone is entitled to change his mind, and of course there are consistencies which can be found even in modern German voter psychology. But surely there are vagaries, and worse; the worst impulses may be uncontrollable; it is the task of custom to iron out the quirks. Sticking to the middle of the road sometimes seems, in an automotive age, a dangerous practice, but its merits are brought home by the inertia of custom as much as by anything else. The behavior of Eisenhower in the United States of the 1950's and of Godolphin in the England of the 1700's are examples of this; the weight of customary practice (now stigmatized as establishment influences) serves to make the rational decisions of one age into the accepted code of the next, affecting even those who would often be adversaries.

Much of this is fundamental to human nature. Plato may have been the first utopian, but when it came to describing the details of his state he looked as much to contemporary Sparta as to his imagination. Cicero exalted an abstract reason superior to the whims of a passing age, but in his *Laws* the code of the ideal state looked remarkably like a senatorial version of the Roman constitution. For example, a truly new suggestion would be alarming just because it was completely new; a proposal to elect the legislature of a new state by putting out a questionnaire asking everyone to name twenty desirable characteristics and then matching these qualities against a list of these held by leading politicians (as determined by, say, a panel of psychologists) would be novel, and perhaps stimulating. With the use of computers it might be a great new innovation, but the likelihood of sustaining a national consensus would be small. The American Constitution was permeated with a classical and common-law background, which may or may not have been instrumental in the success of the republic. But the case of transition from confederacy to federal republic would certainly not have gone so smoothly—would surely never have come off at all under Hamilton's reactionary program, or under a too-classical oddity such as the Pennsylvania constitution of 1780. Excessive archaism is as wrong as its opposite; choosing leaders by lot might be very antique, but not more likely to succeed than our computer technique.

The cake of custom can be many things; the cake we want, like one produced in a modern factory, is one which has not grown too stale. The gravest difficulty with Burke's thinking was that it tended to categorize everything new as bad, and revered events, such as the Glorious Revolution, which would have been anathema to a 1680-ish Burke. It may be useful to draw a distinction—and of course words are mere conventions, and these distinctions have use only as tools—between custom and tradition. The latter might imply a long continuum of an established rule, which has secured a distinctive principle or system. Custom, on the other hand, is a usage, a state of affairs not necessarily very old or very important. It may at times be old and important, and in vital cases will be, but the salient quality is that of habituation and convenience, not that of age and dignity.

Custom is the junior partner, the dross (in Viereck's terms) of our construction. In ages when reason seemed a bright hope for human regeneration or a guide to a permanent improvement in the human condition, such a partnership as this seemed anomalous, a fusion of an eagle and a sloth. Such opposites could coexist only in a false or irregular system; Hobbes warned against "men . . . grown old, and stubborn, they appeal from custom to reason, and from reason to custom, as it serves their turn."

But the compatibility of reason and custom is a part of our conservative movement; perhaps it is the most important part. We have compared reason to light in its historical development, a comparison which augurs ill for it in the caverns of modern art. Custom has no such historic parallel, but it is not entirely forcing the metaphor to see it as an analogue to form. Like custom, form has always been present, serving to channel and order the freer elements of painting. Its presence has not been equally stressed at all times however; the very term "formal" has often been an insult to those who sought the more dramatic qualities of art. It is not necessarily a prime virtue of contemporary painting either, as many of the abstract expressionists have shown. But it is a virtue today with many painters (and, of course, architects and other artists) and art historians. No longer does light seem a much more impressive attribute; even in painters of the past; Piero della Francesca, for instance, is praised today for a formal exquisiteness much more than for his use of light or perspective. The searcher for truth has found that the lamp of reason does not cast enough light even if he treasures what he does see.

In this analogy custom is not so junior a partner, and the same may be said in politics. In some respects the greatest asset to a state, or to any political organization, is the sense of proportion which custom should inculcate. One of the most impressive attributes of the modern sophistication is the current awareness of the nuances of social and political behavior, but it is not new. Burke, at his less dogmatic, was a great student of the finer qualities of statecraft, qualities which elude exact description. It is not by chance that so many of Burke's epigrams and definitions (such as that of party) have become classic, for these nuances differ in detail over time but not in their underlying nature. But the finest analyst of the intangible elements was probably Bagehot, who had most of Burke's brilliance and lacked almost all of his bitterness. Bagehot caught the little things—the fine distinctions which arise from being in one group, and not in what might seem to an outsider an identically similar one, the peculiarly significant differences between age groups, and the irrational factors of leadership and authority. Bagehot ranks with Maine and Frazer as a precursor of the swirling beliefs of our century, foreshadowed by proper Victorians who little imagined the impact of their ideas' descendants. Weber did much more than Bagehot to popularize the emotional nature of politics, and Weber's successors have itemized it to (and beyond) the point of dullness. But with Bagehot the play of custom and feeling does not lead to a sociological determinism, nor (despite some of the anthropological suggestions which remind one of Freud) to a psychological system. Politics, in Bagehot's books, is just like what goes on in school, with all the interrelations and play of adolescent society. And, as in school, the process of education and reason is at least a backdrop or a contributing element in the political scene. Bagehot is sometimes classed with Pareto or Bergson, but this is to emphasize only one side of him. Lerner pictured him better as a link between the worlds of commercial reason and political feeling.

Bagehot saw the British political structure of his time as one that succeeded well because of this mixture of intellect and fortunate customary forms. It is a tribute to both the British and to Bagehot that so much of his analysis has validity today. The British monarchy was insecure a century ago, and it has been said that many intelligent people doubted that it would much survive Queen Victoria. Much more recently ex-king Farouk was alleged to have said that soon there would be but five kings left in the world—the four in the deck of cards and the King of England. This is usually marked up as a sign of the value of tradition defying rationality, but it is by no means so simple. The English monarchy is not sheer façade, as the passing over of Dalton as foreign minister in 1945 and Butler as prime minister in 1957 demonstrate. The power of the Crown keeps diminishing but it stays remarkably strong. Nor is this a mystery, obviously; anyone on the British left (a rather vigorous intellectual community, it must be said) can follow Laski in seeing it. The throne retains its position because its ambivalent place in a complex system, combining drama, influence, and symbolic grandeur, fits well into a nation where the alliance of custom and reason has worked uncommonly well. James I failed because his reason, which was at least tenacious, took no heed of custom. In this Coke and Selden were more conservative and much wiser. Custom has proved a vital force not just by being there, but by its value as a tool for gradual change. It is significant that among the emerging nations in the 1960's those countries, like Ethiopia or Thailand, which have retained their customary classes and order are generally the most stable and effective. Cambodia is probably the finest and most bizarre example of the value of custom.

Neither reason nor custom are desirable, alone or together, unless the result is desirable. There is no merit in saying of a system that it conforms to reason, unless that conformity produces something worth having. That is why we have begun with the most irreducible values, and not with the qualities which uphold them; the state is made for justice, not vice versa. Societies whose prime values derive from passion or intuition can and have boasted of their accomplishments. It is perhaps fortunate that custom was made a term of reproach in the nineteenth century, and reason has almost become one today, so that it becomes necessary to justify these values in society and in their relation to the state.

The basic rights which were suggested previously fit into the area of custom and reason. Torture and genocide are supreme affronts to reason, in many senses. They serve to deprave the reason of the offender and to destroy the reason of the victim. It is not an accident that states which deliberately engage in these practices are intellectually opposed to reason, or interpret it as a mystical property of historical process. Totalitarianism tends to be unreasonable in the most ordinary meaning of that word, bent on magical deeds which could not be explained in rational terms. The same is true of individuals or other groups which engage in brutality; how often does it seem to people who have been cast up into sadistic actions that, in later thoughts, the whole episode seems like a dream. The underworld of motivation and feeling was the bête noire of the thinkers of the Enlightenment (most of the protagonists of Hazard's epoch of the crisis of the European conscience spent most of the time battling these "medieval" currents of feeling); its revival is linked obliquely—and in Fascist and Nazi thought, not so obliquely—to the revival of this emotional vibration. Of course scrupulous attention to myths and dreams does not imply a hankering for cruelty or mass murder, but it is historically observable that it is most easy to forget the elementary dignities of humanity when one ignores the value of mental analysis in one's own views, and in the heads of other people.

But so many crimes have been committed in the name of reason! This is where custom is of use. Reason can become most extravagant where it is likened to a religious status, as in 1794. Custom tends to hold down these flights and to relate them within the limits of the usual. The most serious problem, from the point of view of elementary human rights, in a society which exalts reason is that reason may become a vast impersonal idea, as in Marxism, before which the petty rights of the individual are swept away. On the other hand custom will prove dangerous only when the customs have become inhuman. A state or group of people in the heat of passionate fervor may see reason as the highest passion, but by the time they have grown customs to suit this mood reason will seem less a cosmic force and more a matter of discreet thoughts. Custom has a way of bringing things down to earth; in the Soviet Union today the myriad of small privileges and smaller habits of conduct (such as poetry readings and private vegetable markets) have reawakened the sense of reason as the sum of intelligent actions. Much of this is manifested in the growth of procedural rules. In the 1920's Marxist legal thinkers classed all past procedural rules as instruments of class exploitation, and it was very easy for the rulers of the state—Lenin less inexorably than Stalin but not without energy too—to use the courts as tools of the state. Nothing is unthinkable, we have discovered, for the most exquisite cruelty to the most offensive kind of judicial treatment. What makes them unthinkable is the slow development of specific laws and rules often, as with habeas corpus, arising from hidden roots. The need for a civilization which prizes custom and reason is exactly the same need as that for one which upholds the basic values of human dignity and the tools of procedure as a minimum standard of human living.

Two objections can validly be raised to this explanation.

First, it may be said that custom and reason can lead to other values. In Chinese history, for instance, there was a beautiful regard for custom, that timeless cement of the family and the state emphasized as in no other culture. And there was always a very great regard paid to reason, a regard which can be seen in the competitive examinations for governmental office and in the glories of Chinese scholarship. Yet these values led to a sterile autocracy, and, moreover, to an autocracy marked by a disregard for the procedural rights of the masses and by a refined and unmistakable cruelty. This objection misses the mark, in that it ascribes to certain qualities responsibility for a whole culture, even for the things which are the result of other causes. The sterility and the heartlessness of late Manchu China are as atypical as the pigtail, which seemed to many Westerners the very symbol of cruel Chinese custom, but was of course a hateful badge of servitude imposed by foreign rulers. Torture has no place in Confucian or Taoist thought, but usually arose in those times of ordeal when the civilizing powers of the Confucian order broke down. The faults of familial piety did not coincide with the excesses of centralized power, and often conflicted with it. The worst tyranny must be ascribed to imperial policies (under the Han or the Chin) neither customary nor rational; the greatest slothfulness arose in the nineteenth century out of customs which, in all fairness, had served to advance the social good for millennia and which seem worth reviving in part today. But this objection is a valuable consideration, for it brings up the important reminder that any society which prizes reason must keep that reason from ossifying or becoming a façade for a rigid system or order. Custom can subserve reason only when reason remains an individual attribute, and when it is kept fresh by re-examination.

The second objection is a similar one, but it takes the problem from the other direction. It has been argued—and this is a standard liberal contention—that values which serve to uphold the status quo and to dissect man and society from a coldly intelligent viewpoint lose the greatest qualities of compassion and understanding. From that aspect the greatest barrier to cruelty and to the summary treatment of the individual is love—the Greek *agape*—and no other consideration can approach it in securing human dignity. The man with a concentration-camp mentality cannot, so the argument goes, be dissuaded by rational means, for he has his own reason which is immune to alteration. His customs are brutal and vicious. But if society exalts the human being, be he stupid or wayward, as a creature to be loved, these calculating ideas must give way. The trouble is that they do not. It is easy to say that all men have been created in God's image and must be loved, but loving one's neighbor as oneself is easier to read about than to practice. The thesis of the circle implies the danger of these arguments that suggest that good will to all men is enough; it breaks down or becomes sour just when the tensions are greatest. It is significant that it is the followers of Mazzini who have come to espouse the most sadistic ideas, and not those of Cavour. Mazzini's humanitarianism was vast and sincere, but his nationalism and encouragement of conspiracy let loose much more desperate forces than the ideas of many baser men.

The humane sympathies of Mazzini are valuable. The moderate quality of liberal conservatism should include a willingness to see the good in man, and to nurture that good. There is a nobility in society, and in the state, in exercising as much compassion as is compatible with the broader principles of good government. That is a phrase which can be read to sound excruciatingly mean-spirited, but it is the rule of every society. When radical revolutionaries take power they invariably discover that their harshness is in the very best interests of the downtrodden, and anyone who suggests more kindness is an infantile leftist, or something of that sort. No government or economic system allocates goods "to each according to his need," and the Red Chinese have not been noted for their constant concern with human dignity or suffering. Compassion starts with the individual, and a universal benevolence which breaks eggs to make the omelet can result in an indigestible cooking technique. But it is not enough to point out that communism has almost always meant millions of deaths and vast suffering; it is equally important to say just where a conservative system will make the avoidance of suffering its principal business. We have started with a complete rejection of intentional physical cruelty, but there are cruelties and hardships much more tangible and much less easy to define.

It is, perhaps ironically, custom which emphasizes these qualities in conservative thought. Since reason is in these terms largely an individual matter, and becomes social only as an extension of the values of the individual, it is necessary to use custom as a means of bringing the compassionate values into politics. Thus the minimum wage does violate the economic rule that a minimum price has no merit in a flexible economy. But on the other hand the maintenance of a minimum standard of living has become a valuable custom. Its value lies partly in its compassionate quality, which thus becomes not an indefinite moral compulsion but a definite guarantee of income, and partly in its use as an antidote to the dangerous forces which may be generated by misery. We shall examine more of these effects at a later point, but one more point is relevant here. The minimum wage has its place because it serves as a customary support to the rational system, not an enemy. Polanyi has traced the rise of the market system to the defeat of the minimum-wage systems of the eighteenth century. The fault in these laws was not their existence, for if that were so the great economic accomplishments of the late eighteenth century would never have taken place. The fault did lie in their increasing unwieldiness, as the subsidy to employers served to depress rather than to raise wages. The modern problem is the opposite; if the minimum is set too high, unemployment results. If we confuse "minimum" with average the whole purpose will be lost. But if these problems are avoided the impact of a minimum-wage law is not inconsistent with the standards of rationality. Compassion has its place as a factor in determining the relationship of custom to reason, and not as a source of a vague beneficence.

There are numerous examples of this function of custom to set limits and bounds of rational economic or political arrangements. In a totally free labor market wage rates would be set by supply and demand, but it is clear that many customary income differentiations persist over the years, despite the ebb and flow of economic conditions. This is clearest in industries dominated by craft unions, such as the construction industry, where restricted entry into the field has served to freeze wage distinctions. But many of the same, often rather arbitrary, distinctions exist in the executive area, despite the absence of middle management unions or the like. Even with the most perfect competition, differentiations based on status and habitual conditions—the customary causal forces—will affect the level of comparative wages and salaries. And, in a broader sense, the vital fulcrums of a market system, such as the expected rate of return on capital, are to a large extent customary factors—the gold standard of the nineteenth century was just such a factor. This is true in non-economic matters as well. Most of law, as Maine pointed out, begins as custom, and gradually sharpens to the point of law. Much of international law is still developing along these lines, evolving from customs into statutes. These customs give reason its necessary setting.

The test comes when custom conflicts with reason. Since reason is of necessity an amorphous term this point is always open to argument. The existence of a custom is perhaps a presumption of its desirability, as Burke assumed, but it is a rebuttable presumption. The advocates of segregation have often appealed to the idea of the worth of social mores, the virtue of upholding what Sumner called folkways. But in a case where the folkways come up against an overriding consideration of reason they must be bent or changed. No such change will remain rational if it is too sudden, but that is another matter. Since the highest value is the aggrandizement of the human condition, the capacity of human reason and its preservation comes first. Nor can one say that reason, because it is individual and not a transcendental quality, has no collective nature. We come back to where we started—the position of the state. As long as a social organism is the product of and under the control of the human reason as tempered by custom, it will most nearly work in fitting our individualist man into the broader social circumstance. It is for this reason that history, the chronicle of past customs, is so necessary to a liberal-conservative theory; it also explains why history must not become, in Popper's terms, historicism, the abdication of judgment to an irresistible mystique. But above all it must be remembered that there is no magic in any quality, and that it is the fundamental musts of a decent society—such as the ban on torture—which give rise to the other values, and not vice versa. This is the lesson of democratic politics; more, it is the justification (as we have seen) for democracy itself.

☆ *VIII*

Order
and Fraternity

The deeper questions are substantive, even where they most impinge on the procedural. In considering the needs of society, order must come at a very early point. The term has a foreboding sound, with Vichy associations and even a flavor of Nazi *Ordnung*. Paskevitch's notorious boast to Nicholas I that order had been restored in Warsaw, which Kadar might have repeated to Khrushchev 125 years later and which has been the first concern of autocrats since the Assyrians, is certainly not a desideratum of any liberal or conservative. But in everyday language almost no one in the free world means this by order. The maintenance of decent safety in normal times, and the preservation of life and property in more perilous ones, is such a basic requirement that the very word is seldom used. It is only when these situations do not exist that any attention is paid to the real horrors of disorder. It is ironic that much has been said of the prodigious power of the state vis-à-vis the individual, and how the opportunities of the fighter with small arms against the vast arms of the tyrant makes the old antithesis unworkable, yet within the last ten years some of the worst miseries have come from malcontents armed with little more than small arms. The mobs in Durban, Cairo, Bagdad, Bogotá and Newark have demonstrated that order is essential to any kind of government, much less a good one. Much of the talk of liberals and free-market conservatives rushes over the fundamental fact that the liberal state needs policemen and the free market requires an imposed order. If a city is in the throes of a raging mob neither life nor property has value; it was easy enough to criticize such a strongly order-minded government as Nuri Said's Iraqi regime, but the complaints looked different when the wild cruelties of Bagdad and, especially, Kirkuk occurred. Even liberals hardly need to be reminded of this in 1968. A simple confidence that the police must be wrong in all cases of civil disturbance requires a vast amount of faith in the good will of all demonstrators, a good will which even the least military government (such as contemporary Venezuela's) cannot maintain. The capacity and will to put down "wars of national liberation" has proved to be the prerequisite of decent government through much of the world.

But does this not doom one to a philosophy of coercion? If order, pure and simple, is the first need of a government this makes all governments right, and the sternest one the most right. Of course this is not a philosophy for liberal conservatives. The first exception to these justifications of order is a technical one. This order to which we have referred is a means, not an end; it is not a desert of motionless tranquility (to paraphrase Tacitus). If the police or the organs of government practice the crimes which their function is to prevent in others, the result may well be worse than the wildest anarchy. The dangers of mob hysteria arise out of the disruption and cruelties of torture, pillage, and murder, which we know can happen anywhere. But if the government is conducting such villainies itself it is almost literally true to say that the state is but a band of thieves. Nazi Germany took the sadistic impulses of an obedient people and charged them with the electric impulses of authorized power. The Communist bullies in the streets of Kirkuk are the same sort that often rule in other lands, and would have ruled in Iraq if the revolt had led to a revolution. Terror in opposition is the cousin of a greater terror in power. It may even be, as in China during 1966–1967, that where the power of the state is greatest the cruelties of disorder may also be most severe. Thus order is not opposed to, but meshes with the fundamental requirements of a good society which have been described, for the point of having order is to secure these rights.

It is not an accident that the Nazis and Communists frequently chose common criminals as the sub-leaders of the concentration camps, for since the very idea of the camps was opposed to order, it made sense to have the disrupters of order serve as petty officials. The greater officials were frequently more criminal, not in some metaphorical sense but very precisely, in that they broke the basic laws which even the cruelest state retains in run-of-the-mill situations. And of course this applies to men who devise laws and regulations which exclude some men from the basic rights granted to the rest; for what difference is there between a mob that wantonly attacks a man without regard for established law, and a judge who condemns a man for doing what is granted or permitted to another?

But even the worst state does these things only on the fringes of its jurisprudence. Just as most of the laws which are obnoxious can be defended on some legitimate ground, so the basic order in even the worst society will usually correspond to a normal police role. It would be easy to think of totalitarian rule as an organized hell, but in the main this evil is, on the surface, banal. It is comparatively easy (for most people, at any rate) to see beyond this banality into the real monstrosity of an Eichmann, but Salazar is more difficult, and the newer African dictators even more so. If order is so fragile, is it not essential to overlook some curtailments of liberty, or property, or equality (this can cut many ways) to uphold it?

This attitude can easily shade into an acceptance of a much deeper sort of order. When most political theorists have talked of order they have meant a greater thing, a value suggesting even the divine. Voegelin has traced this cosmic concern from the civilizations of the Tigris-Euphrates valley; it is a term which is very hard to define but has never been absent from political thought. It fits very well into an absolute monarchial theory; the divine-right theory seems impossibly ridiculous to anyone today, but its mystique of a divine order sounds powerfully convincing in the plays of Shakespeare. Pope Innocent III had rather similar ideas, but with an elected Vicar of Christ rather than a hereditary one. The Byzantine Empire, by combining much of both, held a strong fascination which can still be felt at Ravenna; its bureaucratic rigor was justified by its ceremonial glory, and vice versa. These may be moribund notions, but Chinese history suggests that similar ideas have always come along after a strong dynasty has ruled for a while—they may not be so dead at that. Less hieratic conceptions definitely have a great deal of life and appeal. To some people the needs of a peaceful society presuppose a balance and discipline which are everyday equivalents of the older kinds of order. Some consider almost any strike a dangerous troubling of society; fervent political unrest may seem highly disorderly. Vigorous business competition may seem perilous to others. The lower circle prizes liberty and opportunity, but to the nervous—and the compromising, middle-of-the-road nature of the lower circle can easily lead to nervousness—this must be differentiated from license or privilege or cutthroat competition. But perhaps this also is a very old phenomenon—Isaiah, with all his prophetic radicalism, was concerned that the young were not as respectful for the old as in the past.

When conservatism becomes a theory designed to give reasons for the timeless concerns of the old and the dignified that things aren't what they used to be, it runs the risk of becoming shrill and pathetic. Some young men will be disobedient and rough, and people will always fail to know their place. This attitude was present at the very genesis of the Whig concept. The eighteenth-century Whigs did not wholly disagree with the Tories that there was a great chain of being, an idea which had a great fascination for centuries of thinkers. It is hard to picture a conservative ideology which does not move from a distrust of human nature to some vindication of this belief in respect and obedience. It is present in the thought of many of the contemporary Whigs; the sense of establishment decorum which so enrages the angry young men and provides the ammunition for the Joseph McCarthys and the Rap Browns is to some degree a Whig legacy. But the men of the establishment are often the young radicals of the previous generation, and the bad manners of the young turn into the customs of the old. The chief question is this: does this idea of order serve to preserve the amenities and form a customary base, or does it take a tougher, more authoritarian form?

For example, concern for juvenile cocksureness is understandable, and it can be understood by all parents. The totalitarian device of using the children to ferret secrets out of the parents, undermining the authority of the elders as it encouraged furtiveness among the children, has been a lesson to many conservatives. The Chinese efforts to destroy the family as a basic social unit in a land where it was most strong reminds us of the role of the family as a shield for the individual against the mass power of the state. This shield can be kept strong only by accepting the somewhat hierarchical conceptions of family order. In the same way the sense of responsibility of the old for the young, and the adult for the aged, is natural—that is, we can substitute other organizations, especially the state, but in doing so the closest affections are weakened and the overweening power of a bureaucracy takes the place of the easy workings of a homogeneous organization. Yet even these natural forms of order contain possible dangers. To the far right the state is a vast family; the theories of blood often use the metaphors of the family in the broadest spheres. So too the far left thinks of the state as being *in loco parentis* to all men. Both theories can point to the arguments for familial order as justifying a much wider, and therefore more restrictive kind of authority. Even in the narrower area of family life, there are dangers to defending respect and obedience per se. Should the paterfamilias have the old Roman power of life and death? Or even the Confucian right to unremitting domination over all the members of his familial unit?

It almost seems that there have been more upset elders voicing their protests in the last fifty years about familial decay, juvenile delinquency, and (above all) sexual looseness than at any time before. The storm of these criticisms seemed unparalleled throughout the Western world in the 1920's; now the youths of that decade are complaining all the more about their juniors.

We are reliving the experiences of Turgenev's novels. To all this has been added a great literature on the subject of rootlessness, that prime offense against order which has allegedly deracinated modern man and left him the prey of feverish pressures and strident anxieties.

When the industrial revolution began these fears pressed the Whigs, and their doubts and fears were compounded by the French Revolution to the extent that Whig philosophy was seriously shaken. The main crisis was of course narrowly political, the Burkean concern for the traditional forms of government and property. But part of it was more broadly political—the sense of dismay concerning forms and decorum per se. In this too Burke is a fine example for his constant dismay at the unruly contemptuousness of the revolutionary mobs; the overturning of traditional respect was an important part of his shock. But one can sympathize with his concern and with the current concerns—for certainly there is much to object to in the pornography and the youthful crimes which seem as prevalent in Kiev and Leeds as in Chicago or Marseilles—and yet still find this attitude self-defeating if carried far. If one accepts the thesis that the basic political truths are ever present it is as foolish to talk of retrogression as it is of progress. If there is anything more timeless than the friction between generations and between *honestiores* and *humiliores*, it would be hard to find it. Of course, there are variations in history, but some of the recent fears are all out of proportion. The revolutionary movements of our century have been very radical in some ways, but their tendencies toward the cult of personality indicates that derogation of personal authority has not been an especial feature. To be sure, everyone behind the Iron Curtain is still a comrade, but some are more comradely than others. As for sex, one would sometimes think today that it had been discovered by George Bernard Shaw or Henry Miller. Necklines were lower during the time of the Directory, and morals were lower during the period of the Stuart Restoration. Sexual morality has been subject to cycles of opinion, as we have noted, for a long time, and if the excitement of the mass media is an insult to order of a greater extent than ever before, we must balance against it the reduction in prostitution and the almost complete disappearance of the class of mistresses.

The family, despite all the furor of modern pessimism, is not on the verge of extinction. On the contrary, scholars such as Aries have suggested that it is stronger than ever. In fact it is now complained that the private concerns of the family have weakened the necessary public interest in the state so as to dangerously weaken the base of social cohesion. This criticism, which seems to have originated with de Tocqueville (he used the word "individualism" to describe just this parochialism) has been levied against contemporary American and German life, and may be the staple of discussion in all advanced nations very soon. On the other hand, to be sure, the family to which we refer is not the large, patriarchal gens of antiquity. That does seem to be largely dead, except in very tradition-directed groups. Since this disappearance was a part of the shift from status to contract which Maine analyzed, one can hardly call it a recent phenomenon. The substitution of public leaders for the "natural" family authorities is a normal result of the decline of that old family apparatus. In one sense, the very rise of civilization in the river valleys was the death knell of that family; certainly by 600 B.C. most of the world of which we know had deposed the older figures of authority. The recrudescence of post-medieval kingship may be classed as the last great surge of this kind of order and that is as dead as can be.

There is very decidedly a place for the older forms and spirits of respect; it is part of the customary world to prize much of this, even if it tends toward a preservation of relics. There is no anachronism in simultaneously making use of the most advanced technology and cherishing ancient manners. The most independent and reason-upholding universities, such as Harvard, are often just those institutions which have more than their share of ancient ceremonial and pomp. But when this grandeur becomes an enemy of free thought, or a device to impose the tribal patterns of a closed society, a very different issue arises. These concerns about order can lead to a frantic reactionary mood, a "stop the rot" urge to set one's face against the rabble.

The German right-wing sentiment of the 1920's was marked by this disdain for hoi polloi and morbid fear of disrespect. This seems so odd today; the Germans, of all people, have hardly proved a disobedient lot, whereas the government which replaced the Weimar Republic to the satisfaction of so many of these lovers of order proved so thoroughly destructive of traditional decorum and respect. Yet some of this same gloomy fury is present in the radicalism of the right in the United States, together with many of the same symptoms: a certainty that honor and patriotism (which that old conservative Samuel Johnson called the last refuge of scoundrels) are dead, a grave fear that all the old forms have been lost, and a rage to have them back even if one must destroy all other institutions in the process. In the Soviet Union one can detect the same urges, modified from Stalinist despotism. There the fear of being *nyculturnik,* an obvious concern in the aftermath of a searing revolution, is used to glorify mediocrity and discourage independence of thought or dress or (most of all) economic behavior. In all of these folk who are so anxious to stop the rot there is a violence implicit in their feelings which may erupt, and thus bring much more disorder than impertinent poems or salacious pictures can ever cause.

This is the point at which order tends to become authority, the imposition of a firm direction by a collectivist system. The clearest sign of the reactionary political theories, in contrast to the conservative, is the advocacy of this sort of order. In everyday politics today this frequently takes the form of emphasizing the need for police powers in combating subversion or illicit trade, and in de-emphasizing the conservative plea for less police power over business and licit trade. There was a distinction between Taft and McCarthy, and between Reynaud and De Gaulle, which the unfortunate tactics of partisan politics concealed.

Order, then, is (like everything else) a tricky concept, a good which should be taken in small doses. The natural reaction to these problems on the left is to denounce or ignore the whole idea. As we have remarked, the left answer to order is fraternity.

This is not the invention of the French Revolution, although the term became crystallized at that time. The liberals of the Hellenistic world, perhaps following Alexander himself, sought to make the order of monarchies a popular fraternity. Some commentators have discerned a similar advocacy of imperial fraternalism in Chinese thought, especially in the works of Mo Ti. At present the arguments of both right and left for greater social cohesion rely strongly on the appeal to fraternity. The bold success of the European Common Market is a tribute to the rising feeling that the divisive loyalties and enmities of the past must be forgotten. This is in many ways welcome to conservatives, as so much of the enthusiasm for fraternity has come from an ebbing of egalitarian urges. This is not an accident, as the early leadership of Churchill and the moderate French right shows; much the same is true of the less well-noticed movements toward federation or confederation in Africa and Latin America.

But this might suggest that it is only a Machiavellian scheme of conservatives to support movements which might divide and diminish the ardor of the left. This is definitely not the case. Unification has a value to anyone who prizes the spread of ordered liberty more than the entrenched interest of governments. In this regard the free-market conservatives, with their Cobdenian free-trade heritage, add a valuable element to the conservative viewpoint. The limited, conservative Victorian fraternity had a better effect than the undiluted radical variety. The French Revolution, with all its high-flown oratory about the fraternity of all men, and the wilder manifestations of Anacharsis Klootz and the League of Equals, resulted in a vast increase (not, to be fair, a beginning) of nationalist fervor. Burke's distrust of the loyalty and affection of masses of men was vindicated again; the fine talk about cosmopolitan brotherhood ended up in a narrow enthusiasm about a national state. It was the selfish eighteenth century which was the *weltbürgertum;* the nineteenth century combined romantic worship of a selfless humanitarianism with a fierce love of the *nationalstaat.* This became, especially after 1848, a conservative cause (in this too Burke was a precursor) and nationalism grew to be a rival of humanitarianism.

Here is a challenge for liberal conservatives. As with order, there is no suggestion that fraternity should be rejected. The eighteenth-century cosmopolitanism and the nineteenth-century economic universalism were fraternal in very specific ways, not as part of an elevating program of brotherhood, but for much more limited goals. This was certainly so of the *weltbürgertum;* it was limited by its somewhat aristocratic character, although it benefited anyone who could overcome his upbringing to share in the European culture (and this has always been true in China). As with so much of the Whig tradition, it had its roots in part, but just in part, in the super-national Christian culture of the Middle Ages. The Cobdenite faith was much more progressive, but its progressivism was firmly attached to specific economic methods of fraternity. But we need not accept the other messages of fraternity; Talmon has traced much of the messianism of the forerunners and extremists of the French Revolution. Mably and Morelly preached a gospel of universal virtue which would purify man from his petty selfishness and superstition. This emphasis on virtue parallels the reactionary nationalist emphasis on honor, and is equally reckless in its oversimplification of the human condition. The pitfalls of order lie in despotism, but so do the perils of fraternity. As in so many areas, one of the chief tasks of conservatism is to point out the dangerous circular implications of the fervent applications of the leftist virtue, or virtues.

The potentials of economic and political unification, even world government, should be pressed by conservatives. The urgencies of world unity are not to be ignored, but neither should we forget the totalitarian imperial designs. From Marx's simple faith in a proletarian world the Stalinist and post-Stalinist programs flowed; and it is now familiar that the "idealist" National Socialists looked to a united Europe not so different on the surface from Schumann's or Spaak's. Toynbee has commented, with a chilling equanimity, that "the Mongols in the Thirteenth Century of the Christian Era committed genocide almost on the scale which it has been committed by the Nazis in our day. On the other side of the balance sheet, we must enter to the Mongols' credit the fact that they succeeded in establishing, and in maintaining thereafter for a century, a would-be world state that came nearer to being world-wide than any other that has been established either before or since." To take less frightening examples, the statist compulsions of all the welfare states flow from a conviction that the distinctions between regions or customary groups are as indefensible or old-fashioned as that between classes or income groups. The concern about modern conformity is by no means confined to the right, but the phenomenon of conformity can be traced in large part to the post-1789 conviction that distinctions between men are unjustified, a belief fostered by belief in equality and in fraternity. Tendencies in clothing are an amusing example of this. One would think that with the great advance in textile technology the chance for everyone to dress differently would be greatly increased. As the world shrinks the intermingling of men and women of different cultures should mix in a multicolored fashion show. But even in modern London there is less diversity than was present fifty years ago; the multiple opportunities for variety are more than counterbalanced by the sense of human likeness. The implications of these paradoxes can be studied better after considering the other partners in the progressive pantheon, equality and liberty; it is worth saying here that fraternity becomes a problem just as it becomes an end in itself, rather than a supplement to other qualities.

There is merit in the old conservative distrust of the idea of fraternity, insofar as that idea has served to ignore the real differences of human experience. One of the achievements of modern scholarship has been the discovery of the nuances of minute class-group diversities. Namier was a leader in this, but many of the critiques of the French revolutionary forces have disclosed the great number of subgroups with diverse interests whose identity has been swallowed up in the customary pictures of revolution. Even simple affairs like the revolution of 1830 seem, after studies like that of Pinkney, to have considerable variations. There is some truth in the thesis that Africa can better be studied as a continent of diverse and conflicting tribes and groupings rather than as a sea of oppressed brothers. This is not to deny the oppression, but to accept the fact and the promise of a fantastic diversity. Now that the Italian bloc is coming into its own in Massachusetts politics the Portuguese and French-Canadian groups tend to feel more left out; there are innumerable examples of the rich diversity of social groups throughout the world. It is not prejudice or racism to recognize this; on the contrary, only in a world where fraternity is not pushed too far can the small groups survive in their own way. The history of minorities in the Soviet Union has shown that the embrace of some friends can be more stifling than the persecution of some enemies.

It is clear at this point what the other qualities are, from our viewpoint. As this picture of a desirable civilization is created, most values, important as they are, lead the way to the two most important ones: liberty and property. When order and fraternity conflict with these two cardinal virtues of lower-circle thinking, they usually must give way. This has been implicit in the previous discussions, and it formed an important part of much of seventeenth- and eighteenth-century political theory.

But brotherhood has its place in any lower-circle theory, left or right. To some extent this is once again a matter of compassion, an essential leavening of an often too-somber distrust of human nature. Apartheid is undesirable not only because it is almost surely unworkable (this in fact is not absolutely true; as in so many other cases, if the Afrikaaners or the black nationalists really want to pay the price, which is doubtful, they might well manage a total separation of the races) but because it would isolate a large community from a share in the political and social system of the larger society. If one denies the common humanity —the minima once more—of even the most distant groups, one must surrender a portion of the heritage of social order. Even if a fair separation of races could be thoroughly accomplished, there would still be the problem of permitting free movement and opportunity between groups whose systems were so different. In everyday terms this problem has appeared in South Africa, where the price of separateness is a rigid pass system for black men and an intensifying set of limitations for both races. National assertion in late-nineteenth-century Europe naturally led to the collectivist social order and mutual suspicion which built up after

1870; the individualist values spring most readily out of a milieu in which the minimum social cohesion exists, not an antagonistic world. This is true of men as of nations; the neighborhood where everyone is isolated from his fellow will produce less scope for the free play of private choice, not more. To this extent brotherhood requires no strong faith in humanity, but that minimum confidence tempered with the realization that we are all in the same boat, even if we have different skills. This is where fraternity and equality differ; it is possible to believe that human ability and fitness can be found in any race or ethnic group while still believing that it varies widely within all these groups. It is that variance that is the basis for liberty and property; it is the function of fraternity to make possible the best use of these differences, and not to impose harsher distinctions which will prevent liberty and make all property insecure.

But conflict between fraternity and liberty can arise at the point where fraternity takes on a larger meaning. In American politics today this occurs at the intersection of civil rights and civil liberties. For example, the demands for laws which will forbid discrimination because of race or color in employment or housing have as their laudable purpose the eradication of racial standards, the treatment of a man on racial criteria. But this necessarily limits the free use of property and the freedom of association. To take a notoriously difficult example, owner-occupiers of residences who rent space will be forced under fair-housing laws (many exempt owner-occupiers, to be sure) to either cohabit with people they do not like or sell their property and move. Such a law will reduce the free choice of the owner. The argument for its passage grows in strength when one deals with a group whose general exclusion is a threat to the normal decencies of a society. Thus the public-accommodations laws have more to recommend themselves because their absence can deprive a member of a minority group from the commonest requirements of food and shelter in a strange city; yet even there a small entrepreneur may be forced to associate with those whom he hates. In the case of a large, absentee property owner, presumably the personal, purely libertarian argument vanishes, for he need do nothing himself. Of course the owner can sell his business or building, so that the coercion is always limited by this option. Where the state requires discrimination the much stronger degree of coercion is imposed, and liberty and fraternity yield the same answer. But in the United States, and in many other places, the harder, more complex issues of property, liberty, and fraternity are posed; the answer can be found more easily when custom (as in the long history of public-accommodation requirements) serves to show precedents for the limitations of freedom, but even there custom cannot override the use of judgment; if the values of free choice are paramount, restraints for greater brotherhood should at some point give way. As usual, the clichés of the Whigs do contain the final values of an individualist society.

☆ IX

Liberty

It is part of the irony of modern conservativism that so much of its dialectic should be devoted to defending liberty. The free-market conservatives, such as Hayek and Alain, have written in a way that would cause one to think that liberty is almost the sole prerequisite of the good life. By considering such fundamental rights as a fair trial and immunity to torture separately, we have already lopped off part of what is often called liberty, leaving a perhaps less sacred remainder. Why should this remainder be worth defending at all; what is it in the word that causes hardheaded men to grow lyrical and makes so much of political debate a wrestle for the right of claiming the magic phrase? And, of course, that requires an answer to the primary question, what is liberty?

Isaiah Berlin has recently, in his Oxford lectures published as *Two Kinds of Liberty*, given an excellent answer to the latter question. Berlin distinguished between one kind, which he clearly thought was the genuine article, and the varying notions which he classed in a second group. The first kind of liberty, which Berlin calls "negative liberty," is just that—the right to do what one wants without interference from anyone else. It promises no other rewards, it implies nothing about the merit or intensity of the action. It is freedom from, not to. The second group, in Berlin's opinion, includes many concepts which purported to be libertarian, but were often just the opposite. One of the oldest is the "real liberty" idea; the argument that liberty is not doing what you want to do, but what you should do, or less baldly, what you would want to do if you knew better. This assumes that there is a true good that all men would reach if they were not blinded by some false idea or force. Such a position is ridiculous unless one accepts that premise, a premise which requires a pure devotion to some great belief (Platonic, Pauline or Rousseauian, to take three familiar examples) which can transcend the normal choices. Even in this viewpoint the value can hardly be called liberty, for if there is one man so incorrigible or ignorant as to want something other than his own good it may be a good deed to make him do what he ought, but forcing him to be free is a strange sort of freedom.

This ancient pseudo-freedom has been supplemented by a newer but similar variety; a brand of liberty often called positive liberty. This argument runs as follows: What is liberty but the opportunity to do what one wants? But a poor man, or a culturally (or socially, or politically, etc.) deprived man is denied that chance. He is not really free, since his range of choices is limited; therefore, we must add to the negative freedom of the older school this positive freedom. At this point, it is almost required that Anatole France's celebrated witticism that the law gives both rich and poor the freedom to sleep under bridges be mentioned; this dictum has become almost an intrinsic part of the argument, for it has been used so often that its absence would be as noted as the dog in the Sherlock Holmes story. From there one can demonstrate that a law requiring, say, that no one may work or employ another to work more than forty hours a week without the payment of an overtime bonus is not a limitation of liberty, but an extension. An old-age pension qualifies as an extension of the opportunities of the recipient, even if he has been compelled to pay for the pension dearly through years of tax payments. This is in fact a variation of the forcing-to-be-free theory, the liberty that comes from coercion. Part of the argument lies in a suggestion that the older, stuffier sort of freedom was reserved for the rich or mighty in any case, so that even if their freedom is restricted the benefits afforded the masses more than make up for this loss. Thus in the case of the overtime law it is sometimes conceded that the employer may have lost a freedom of hiring, but the employee gains a greater freedom in that his larger wages give him extra opportunities. He loses no freedom, by this reasoning, because he would have been forced to work longer without a rise in hourly pay were there no statute to liberate him from this domination.

To these upside-down conceptions of liberty (which would end in complete external direction) Berlin has added some different but equally unsuitable ideas. The liberty of the state, that freedom which the ancients probably most thought of as *the* liberty, also can be very misleading. When the Magyars fought for liberty in 1848 and 1849 their cause thrilled the West; when they substantially achieved it the Croats, the Czechs, and the Serbs considered themselves oppressed. Goebbels spoke frequently in the last days of the Third Reich of the German struggle for liberty. To the medieval churchman liberty of the Church meant the right of the Church to govern to a large extent the private life of its members; even Figgis, the twentieth-century pluralist, thought that the maintenance of publicly-supported religious education was a part of religious liberty. It is often very difficult to pin down exactly what liberty means in these contexts, or what it would mean if the speaker could make his own rules. Patrick Henry's brave cry is a notorious example, as Roche has pointed out. Liberty or death is a fearful choice; at the same time it is a fetching slogan. The liberty of which Henry spoke was a carefully limited exemption from British taxes (independence was not the issue); whereas Henry had no intention, then or later, of advocating the freedom of the slaves. Dr. Johnson had a field day with the cant of the American colonists, a criticism which bothered Jefferson, but not to distraction. The grave concern of delegates from Nicaragua or Egypt with liberty is a more modern example.

It is sometimes said that all this is just another case of hypocrisy, perhaps a fine example of the tribute which vice pays to virtue. This is hard on the American revolutionaries and most others—Plutarch might almost have been without heroes if one were to enforce this too harshly. In Berlin's analysis it is a more knotty difficulty, a semantic misunderstanding which arises out of a difference of intent. To the "negative" libertarian, as to the "positive" one, liberty is a great good. But to the latter, it is often merged with all other goods. Plato could propose severe limitations on freedom while talking of liberty because to him liberty was a part of justice; to many modern socialists there cannot be a gulf between liberty and equality. But liberty loses its meaning when it must be a handmaiden to all virtue, the necessary part of any desirable political value. In a way this is the tribute of vice; liberty, that prize desideratum of individualist thinking, is so dear a good that even the surliest tyrant will usually pay lip service to its merits. The philosophers, even if they work from the most authoritarian premises, have been trained by centuries of tradition to fit it into the most unlikely pigeonholes.

This can be seen even in the work of men whose ideology permits a recognition of the limits of liberty. Mortimer Adler, for instance, suggests three definitions of liberty as feasible: 1) "To be free is to be able, under favorable circumstances, to act as one wishes for one's own individual good as one sees it." 2) "To be free is to be able, through acquired virtue or wisdom, to will to live as one ought in conformity to the moral law or an ideal befitting human nature." 3) "To be free is to be able, by a power inherent in human nature, to change one's own character creatively by deciding, for oneself, what one shall do or shall become." To Adler, all three permit one the power to exercise freedom of choice. Yet when one looks at definition no. 2, it is the argument of "real freedom" once more (Adler cites Augustine, Spinoza, and Freud as exemplars, an interesting and revealing trio.) Virtue or wisdom is liberty; the job of the political theorist is to discover who will interpret the moral law, and to this man other men's liberty are consigned. Definition no. 3 is much more complex. It does not suggest that there is a superior law to which the desires of man must be deferred; it suggests that freedom is the internal power to take advantage of the raw materials of liberty. Thus a drunkard or an imbecile may have the opportunities for choice, but it is argued that he is not meaningfully free because he is in no position to exercise those choices. A man who never varies his life, who perpetuates a steady grind day in and day out, is not really free because he has eschewed the range of experiences which can make choice a real thing. If I am convinced that I will die if I walk across the street, I have lost that much of my freedom because, even though there is no law or physical force which in any way deters me from crossing the street, I have cut off my freedom of action by my superstitions.

Adler's third definition presents the most troublesome problem of liberty, a difficulty which must be considered before any defense of liberty can be made. It is easy to reject the concept of liberty which is another name for morality, or equality, or justice; but it is not so easy to disregard a liberty which is man's command of himself. Yet this definition will make political liberty either a barren or a fearfully complex term. For it means that liberty is a by-product of knowledge, a derivation of the right understanding of the problem. Thus this view can be construed in the socialist fashion; freedom might be considered the state of society in which everyone has the maximum economic or social status. Or, and this is a more acceptable contemporary idea, freedom is that state where everyone has the greatest say in affairs, the most participation in the controlling events of the time. To make this participation effective freedom then requires education or political activity. Thus it has been argued that the danger of modern society, a danger greatly contributing to totalitarianism, is the divorce between power and control throughout modern life. This argument was used as a reason for the German co-determination law—Hitler had succeeded because the average German, even if he were well-off and independent in his private life, was at the mercy of forces which could so alter his future so as to make his very personality a puppet of the powers. So too, much less convincingly, it is said that mass men, in the age of mass-media persuasion, lose their creative will and become the playthings of the opinion makers. The task then is to liberate men from these warping influences, to appeal from the drunk to the sober man, in Green's language, by taking away the alcohol of miseducation or ignorance. By this more roundabout way we can come to the lessons of definition no. 2; it turns out that what is wanted is not really what men want. This is not so apparent when the discussion is on the subject of education, but it is in fact the same thing. The argument that an illiterate is unfree sounds much more convincing on first blush than on second; why should knowing more increase a man's freedom? Once again there is a mixture of different goods, a confusion of opportunity for freedom. Thus if I am told that I must build a house or do without, and am given free access to materials which I have no experience or ability in using, I may be thoroughly helpless. I am, therefore, unable to build a house, or one may say that I am powerless to do so. But I am no less free than the trained builder; no one is hindering me from doing the best, or worst that I can. To this one may reply that this is a worthless freedom, and so it may be; all that it proves is that freedom may be of no use to men at some times, or to some men (such as idiots) at any time—a very different matter.

But the concept of definition no. 3 can be even more troublesome. It may be argued that, accepting the objection given above, it shows the fallacy of definition no. 1 (which is more or less the "negative" liberty idea) as well. For, in the last analysis, who can do whatever he wants? The law of gravity is the sternest tyrant in the universe; Berlin starts his little essay by excluding this compulsion from restraints on liberty, but is that not an inconsistency? The phobia against crossing the street may be as compelling to a neurotic as the pressure which keeps any of us from jumping over a house; and for that matter, there is no one so normal that he has no little neuroses or phobias. The ambiance of one's time and place, the influences of one's friends and acquaintances, one's very chromosomes limit "what one shall do or shall become."

It is this objection which is the hardest to answer, but it is possible to say that this too confuses liberty with other values. Political liberty is less than total freedom; no one maintains that the right to murder is a liberty which must be upheld (except for tyrannicides). It is a truism that one man's liberty begins where his neighbor's lets off, but this necessarily implies that liberty is not doing whatever one wants. The implication of this cliché is that liberty is a value only insofar as it maximizes everyone's freedom; the most complete liberty is therefore, in the political sense, a state where everyone does what he wants without interfering with anyone else. But this is, admittedly, an ideal which requires some colder prudence to make real, some Viereckian alloy to temper the golden metal. For the most part this alloy is price, in the broad sense. Thus I am free to do as I please in respect to finding a night's lodgings, and I may follow Anatole France's course of sleeping under a bridge. But if I desire to find more elegant quarters I must pay, and as a rule the better the room, the more must be paid. In one sense this is an abridgment of liberty—just as the laws against murder are—but it is that sort of abridgment which fits into the first Adlerian definition.

To put it another way, there are four different limitations on freedom. One kind is the limitation of non-human forces, and this is not considered a political restraint at all. We cannot run a mile in three minutes. Two hundred years ago we could not manage, by any means, a dozen miles in three minutes, but now this is child's play. The accomplishment of the latter is a triumph of capacity, not freedom, and it is only incapacity which dictates the first inability. A second limitation is the prevalence of laws forbidding action which will injure another. Of course these laws punish certain activities, and therefore inhibit certain forms of behavior. But we do not call liberty the freedom to do anything one wants, so these restraints are not considered deprivations of liberty. The third kind of limitation is the control exercised by the forces of opinion or the circumstances of property. These also keep one from doing whatever one wishes, but since their control is exercised non-coercively they are not deprivations of liberty. The last sort of limitation is control over what is left, a form of coercive regulation which is man-made and not designed to protect the rights of others. We may, if we wish, call the protected rights in the last instance civil liberties, but all that means is that we have reiterated the special quality of these rights.

These distinctions do not always carry beacon lights to help us identify the dividing lines, but they are vital. A system of liberty must permit the second and third types of restraint while making sure that the fourth remains illicit, even though on both ends there is some reduction in complete freedom. The end result should be a maximization of choice in that private coercion is eliminated while the area of free decision is increased. The first part is the civil requirement; the second the basic quality of liberty. As we narrow the term the real opportunities should grow.

The tightest problems come here; for choice comes in all shapes and sizes. We may have a choice to travel by first class or air coach, and either spend more money on comfort or on some other good. That is not a deprivation of liberty. On the other hand the highwayman's choice of one's money or one's life is not that kind of free decision. The question is where to draw the line between these two examples, where to find the limit of liberty.

In one sense, then, all of life is made up of one sort of choice or another. In the terms of Hohfeldian analysis there are many powers, but the cost of a power is a condition of its exercise. If I wish to burn down my neighbor's house, all I need is sufficient wit and the proper materials. I am at liberty to do it, insofar as I can physically manage it; the consequences of my decision (which I may or may not know) will probably be liability for civil damages and criminal punishment. As Holmes remarked, a decision to break a contract is much like a decision to acquire property, in the sense that both mean that a price must be paid for a given act. So too, a calculating murderer can weigh the price for his act.

This relativism, as in so many cases, is valid in its logic but unhelpful in its content. The problem of political liberty is what price is paid, and when. If the price of murder is death or life imprisonment, the liberty of the murderer is not liberty in our sense. The choice of whether to murder or not is outside the range of desired options, which indicates how important it is to set the limits of that range. In order to have the maximum total choice, I must accept the fact that some of my choices will be severely curtailed. Everything that meets even Berlin's standards is not worth defending as a part of the liberty usable in society. The controlling criterion is coercion. The unique feature of the state is its monopoly on coercion, its legitimate right to present its citizens and resident foreigners with these enforced choices. No private monopoly, no matter how extensive, can vote that if its rules are broken, the offender must be sentenced to imprisonment. Only the state can require men to use its facilities—courts and administrative tribunals—and to pay money to it without the consent of the payer. If my freedom coerces you (as it would if I were a highwayman) I am not exercising a liberty, but you are being deprived of yours. It is the task of the state to redress this deprivation of liberty, but to go no farther than this.

Much of the recent liberal attack on the distinction between the state and private organizations is centered on disagreement with this thesis. In the first place, it is said, there are examples of private law-making. When a labor union or a baseball club fines its members or players, this is much like a fine by an organ of the state. This is only half-true, as one can avoid being a ballplayer or a unionist much more easily than being a taxpayer. But that is not completely so, and to that limited extent the power of a union (or a trade association or professional organization) is analogous to state action, and *ipso facto* a violation of liberty. A tax on yachts is not the same as an income tax since one can eschew yachts. Many followers of Veblen extend this to money paid to the electric light company, or even perhaps to the grocery store. The distinction between the government and the grocery store is easiest, for no store has a monopoly on food; there is therefore no coercion involved in the question of where one will obtain food. But suppose the choice is between starvation and accepting a very meager wage—is that not coercion? This also breaks down in any case where there is competition for labor; since no one can compel a man to work or face starvation outside of a totally controlled society (and seldom even there) there is a world of difference. This difference is smallest, in, say, a remote plantation society where mobility is very limited and there are few (or only one) employers.

Hayek makes a valuable distinction between being deliberately coerced and being forced to make unpleasant decisions by a social or economic situation. An impersonal limitation may be disagreeable—unemployment certainly is—but there is not the direct control which bespeaks coercion. The case of the electric utility presents similar questions; to the extent that it has a legal monopoly it does partake of state authority, to a degree, but one can do without electricity. The higher the price of electricity the less will be used; the same is not true of taxation, except in the more indirect sense that private enterprise may be discouraged, or that evasion may increase. In economic terms, demand for electricity is less elastic than that for luxuries but far more than that for the services of the state; in fact there is little elasticity of any kind about the latter. The authority that removes the elasticity from government services is the coercive power which creates the issue of liberty.

But the power of the state is not one-dimensional. It makes a great deal of difference in these terms whether the governmental authority is exercised through physical punishment or fine, or whether it is managed through the criminal law or the civil law. A law saying that given conduct will leave one open to prosecution is more coercive than a law giving private parties a cause of action, because it affects the rights of parties directly. For example, the growth of urban automotive traffic has made the easygoing walking habits of pedestrians in the streets of big cities much more dangerous than before. If it is accepted that there are limits to the freedom which should be permitted or encouraged, two alternatives are clearly presented to the government. The first is to pass an ordinance making it unlawful to cross the street in a disapproved manner or at a disapproved time, the violation of which may lead to fine or even imprisonment. This is clearly coercive; if I choose to jaywalk I am faced with a punishment determined by the government. The second alternative is to treat the question as far as possible as a private dispute between non-sovereigns. This alternative might well call for an ordinance declaring that if a jaywalker is injured by a motorist he may not recover any damages in the courts. Since pedestrians seldom injure motorists, this will be a considerable discouragement to errant walkers. Moreover, this discouragement will leave the walker with much more choice—if he is smart or lucky he will not be injured, and so he now weighs another variable alongside the simple question of whether to jaywalk or not. He may make a private arrangement with a motorist, if the latter wishes, or he may even contract ahead of time with potential motorists as to possible future injuries. In short, the mechanism of judicial determination, even in the area of torts, permits, within the confines of a governmental rule, so much more leeway that the coercive element is much reduced. A *fortiori*, contract law involves much less coercion. Thus I (the prospective jaywalker) can contract with an insurance company to reimburse me for damages even if the motorist will not pay, or I may contract with a hundred other pedestrians to jaywalk together, and pool the risks. As the choices increase the area of liberty expands, even when the framework is coercive.

There is another aspect of the rule of law, sometimes confused with the procedural rule which we have considered above. The supremacy of law here means not a form of adjudication, nor does it mean a complete absence of restraint. Rather, it suggests that disputes over values in a society can best be settled through the media of courts, and between private parties. This distinction is not simply a formal one, although that is important too— the very spirit of the judicial process is a protection against unusual measures. But the chief substantive value of this rule of law is the emphasis this places on individual choice and the volition of private parties. Lippmann, in his free-market phase, put this aptly; "in the liberal order the state exerts social control chiefly through the judicial hearing of individual complaints and the provision of individual remedies—it has a respectful prejudice in favor of the arrangements men arrive at by usage in their transactions with one another, and it permits customary law to grow by using a method of control in which men may, but need not always, invoke the authority of the state." There are three significant points in this quotation. First, contract and even tort law is envisaged as a form of agreement, with the state brought in as a force of last resort. The burden of social arrangements is carried by men whose task is basically that of arbitrator; the coercive power is not the mainspring. Secondly, this rational system—rational in the sense that it is based on the conscious decisions of willing parties—is moored in a customary setting, and this custom (the realm of private law) evolves most readily in this non-coercive atmosphere. Thirdly, the rule of law in some ways implies an individualism which has strong substantive effects. The concerns of private litigation are individual, and the role of law is to convert the disagreements among men into searches for formal judgments. Thus the law of defamation converts the egoism of the conflicting parties into a duel of personalities competing for justice. This form of justice is a set of rules designed to benefit one man and chasten another, and revolves around the immediate parties. It is not accidental that social planners frequently complain of the particularism of lawyers accustomed to private law. In Anglo-Saxon jurisprudence especially, courts exist only to determine the rights of the parties and not to hand down justice—this relativism and individualism is parallel to the spirit of the two-party system and to the Whig idea. The result is a system which tends to convert commands into choices, which emphasizes private action and not public determinations.

This would be most apparent if courts were even more clearly voluntary agencies. To the extent that a court serves as an arbitration board, (and Montesquieu remarked on the antiquity of this concept in early Roman times) deriving its authority from the agreement of the parties, it will look to the immediate body of law and fashion its rulings to fit the instant case. From an individualist's point of view most of state power ought to be, roughly, this. Going farther, the Declaration of Independence pictures the state itself as strikingly similar—an authority deriving its just powers from the consent of the governed. The trouble there is that the consent becomes frozen; but of course an agreement to arbitrate becomes frozen too, once in force, and no arbitration agreement would ever work if one side could retroactively annul its jurisdiction. In other words, Locke's conception of the state is central to this elevated view of liberty and property; a certain freedom is discarded in order to preserve the integrity of the system, but that surrender enhances the value of the remainder. The substitution of contractual agreement for obedience may not be a sure mandate for freedom, but the process has been vital to civil liberty and to the development of constitutional government.

But all these arguments do not answer the central question of the positive libertarians, and their frankly anti-libertarian cohorts: Why should some freedoms be given up, by agreement or otherwise, and others retained as essentials of political liberty? In the last analysis, there is (as always) no final solution which will logically clear the matter beyond dispute. The individualist conservative cherishes the right of each man to make his own bargains, and the duty of the law to spend most of its energies in enforcing them. There are other valid visions of human behavior —obviously, since in the long view this individualism is a minority ideology. Nor can it be driven too far; it is stretching this idea much too much to say that slavery is consistent with liberty, if the slave has voluntarily given up his freedom. The limitation of contracts, in extreme cases, is quite consistent with a high regard for contracts; some freedoms are so basic that they cannot be sold. This subjects the idea of liberty to a relativistic standard, and so it must be; there is no society without coercion, and efforts to find absolutes invariably fail to be thoroughly consistent. Nevertheless, the distinction between the kind of coercion used to enforce agreements and other kinds is very basic, for with it the role of individual action and the resultant scope of private arrangements becomes possible. The freedom lost is much less than the power gained, and the broader area of the power gained, because it is based on consent, encourages a greater exercise of freedom.

The same is true of the other limitations on freedom—the authority of the state to coerce those who interfere with the rights of others is an accepted part of civil liberty. Each man's freedom would interfere with others' in an anarchistic society, so some freedoms must be curtailed in favor of other rights. This presupposes a conservative lack of faith in human perfection, just as there is no reason to deny that all property rights do imply a conservative limitation on untrammeled freedom. If I am physically capable of walking into your house, the legal provisions that you may use to keep me out set my freedom against your property rights, and yet this superiority of property over liberty is consistent with, even essential to, civil liberty. Since only anarchists are for freedom in an absolute sense, all working theories of liberty require the gloss of custom and the experiences of history to make them viable. Liberty must be fused with other values, or even subordinated at times, for the advantages of its fundamental purpose to be realized. This is a limitation but it is also an expansion, for if liberty has no value as a standard without some such limitation, these very limits make it valuable as well as confine it. Above all, in the last two centuries the adhesion of free-market thought to conservatism has stimulated an individualist belief which has predisposed conservatism toward less coercion, toward the individualist emphasis on freedom as against order.

It is therefore not an accident that much of what we consider liberty started as liberties. To the liberal this is a bad place to begin the study, as it is to anyone who looks on liberty as a supreme value, far superior to any other (Hayek, for instance, takes this position; in this he is in the tradition of free-market conservatives). But the disputes of Burgundian Flanders or Stuart England were waged over issues of liberties—or even more archaically, privileges. A liberty or privilege may have been reserved for a specific class or group—academic freedom and the various urban freedoms so began. It customarily involved very specific rights, which had to be exercised in just the right way and extended only to very specific circumstances. The origins of the right against self-incrimination and double jeopardy illustrate this. The circumstances of exercise of liberties often made all the difference—as in the tortuous development of the rights of the press. These examples disclose the durability of the essentially special quality of liberty; we can almost say that in no country is liberty today anything more than a collection of liberties. The recent claim that there is some absolute liberty always comes up against some objection; the example of freedom of the press brings to mind the constant balancing between liberty and the alleged requirements of a fair trial, the right to be protected against defamation and fraud, and the prohibition against incitements to riot or revolution. Even with the most cherished liberties there is no escape from relativism.

Where does this leave liberty; merely a relative value, riddled with exceptions and explicable as a historical throwback, a mélange of customs and privileges? It would be strange to establish a theory on the base of Whig ideas and free-market policies and reach such a result—strange and unworthy. In a world where nothing is sure and where the most important values are limited and in the main time-oriented, there is all the more need for some firm standard, perhaps as uncertain in the last analysis, but worth dying for. Liberty, the collection of those freedoms which make life a humane occupation and not a social task, is indeed the supreme individualist value. Because all standards are impermanent, absolutes must be viewed with suspicion; because this very detachment is impossible in a police state the liberty to be relativistic has become the key "can't help" of a pluralist society. These are not the narrower rights mentioned before—the day in court, the fairness of the institutions of the state—but substantive rights, freedoms to speak, to travel, and above all to retain one's private life free from all but the most needed coercions. The totalitarian horrors have demonstrated that these rights are very much connected with the more basic rights, but they refer to a different set of values. A state may abridge the substantive liberties and not cut at the core of human worth, but it will endanger the beneficent juices which enrich the core. This is especially important to conservatives, for if there is no faith in the millennium of human perfection it is all the more important to treasure the greatness inherent in the accomplishments of individuals. There must be a true support of this liberty, not merely a convenient opposition to the inroads of unfriendly powers, and that requires a consistent philosophy to separate those liberties which are liberty (Berlin's negative liberty is a close approximation in general terms) from those other rights which are not in the sacred circle. Mill's *On Liberty* is the classic effort to do this job, the great definition and defense of liberty as a good worth dying for. *On Liberty* occupies the position on the circle 180 degrees distant from Plato's *Republic;* in some ways it has become almost a bible of Western thought, a holy book which has almost become incorporated into the United States Constitution and the unwritten constitution of Great Britain. Since liberty is our highest value, we are to that extent Millians.

One would think, to judge from the acclaim with which Mill has been received over the century, that his ideas were now hackneyed parts of common life. However, many more people talk this way than confirm the worth of Mill's ideas by their own. *On Liberty* carries liberty farther than most citizens of even the most liberal land would probably go; it is a frequent mistake to assume that it is only upper-circle ideas that are too sharp for popular acceptance.

The heart of Mill's thought lies in his distinction between self-regarding and other-regarding acts. Mill accepts the need for coercion to restrain those acts which are other-regarding, which affect others as well as oneself. In this area the question of liberty does not arise. But in any act which is totally self-regarding, which is not an infringement on the rights of others, there is a very strong presumption that no coercion be applied. This presumption may be overcome in cases where a man, or even a country, is immature or where an act may be very close to the dividing line, but these exceptions are to be granted most sparingly. By and large, anything which concerns only a man's private concerns, or his willing arrangements with other men, should be free from the power of the state and the censure of society.

This is most acceptable in the field of thought and private discussion. In 1859 men were a century closer to the age of religious bitterness, and Mill devotes much of the book to defense of heterodoxy of thought. We have seen how relevant this may be, for today as in the sixteenth century there are powerful forces which will not permit even the most furtive free thinking.

Thought, to be sure, cannot be truly controlled, even today, but on the other hand the examples of pressure and propaganda have led many to believe that it can be twisted. This is, like so much else, no invention of twentieth-century total planners; the intention and theory of the religious purists of the late Middle Ages and sixteenth and seventeenth centuries was also to so isolate and purge society of bad ideas that their efficacy would shrivel. It is not necessary to believe that "thought's a slave to life" to accept the danger that life can at the least hold down the flights of thought's winged fancies. Men may think in the unreachable privacy of their cerebella, but these thoughts have no value unless they can be disseminated. Conversations, speeches, books, letters, and even mass meetings are the clothes which give outward form to thought, and there can be precious little thought without these. There is a distinction between a state that compels its subjects to positive demonstrations of belief, as the Communists are wont to do, and one which is content with preventing any contrary ideas from spreading; but it is a small difference. For that matter requiring public participation is no guaranty that thought will be controlled; one wonders how many of the Romans who shouted "*Duce!*" in the 1930's were all along supporters of Stalin or Sturzo. But that is not enough. It is just because society involves social considerations, because a man is not alone with his God and his thoughts, that freedom to implement these thoughts is so vital. All religions which have lasted more than a few years have bound their believers by acts, and usually by public ones. It is also not enough that a man may read a book in his rooms or talk quietly to friends; free thought can really exercise its place only when it has opportunity to present itself in the broad arena of controversy.

This is where Mill becomes controversial. Only a stern police state will distrust the disclosure of murmurings of dissent and crush them, but even the freest societies will grow restive when these heterodoxies are spread broadcast. In Spain today the government acquiesces in the presence of Protestants and Jews, and even in their worshiping in discreet sanctuaries; but open proselytizing stirs the rage of the orthodox. Almost no one defends this severity in the free world, but the problem of Communist groups (which is the religious issue of our time, as innumerable critics have observed) never seems so easy. There is freedom of the press in the United States, but the author of the book may be indicted for conspiring to advocate the overthrow of the government. Under Mill's terms advocacy is surely self-regarding, an act involving only the expression of opinion; a conspiracy to do so is one step farther from action. The reply that the Communists would behave much more severely to our ideas were they in control suggests that liberty is a good which one can offer only to those who will reciprocate, like a tariff reduction. Liberty then becomes a matter of barter and not of principle, available only to those who usually will not use it very roughly.

A second objection to affording Communists the right to advocate their ideas freely is that even the most personal, and especially the most political, opinions may have subsidiary effects on others, effects which will seriously undermine the entire system of liberty. What if the Communists persuade everyone; is that not an evil which is thoroughly other-regarding in its impact? The second argument is, in fact, very widely accepted. On what other basis can one justify prohibitions of gambling between willing parties, or the ban on prostitution? When a government outlaws prostitution it says, in effect, that this is such a nasty practice, so deleterious to the morals of the participants and others that it will undermine general decency. There is undoubtedly a more general acceptance of these laws now than when Mill wrote, an amusing commentary on the power of his ideas. When the Wolfenden Report bravely suggested that homosexuality was, in the absence of force or the influencing of those too young to have adult minds, a self-regarding act of no concern to the state, one would have thought that a radical new doctrine had been let loose. Justice Denning, a very noted jurist indeed, suggested that this was a dangerous abandonment of moral principles, and Dean Rostow of the Yale Law School applauded the judge in the name of democratic judicial review! The Supreme Court appeared daring when it established, in the Griswold case, hesitantly, that sexual relations within the family were immune from governmental control. Just as we have noted that sexual liberty seems to alternate with political liberty, so one may see that as more battles are fought for the great issues of free speech and assembly, the pettier but often more meaningful intrusions of authority increase, often telling a man how large a house he may build or what sort of games he may play. In socialist countries there may be the most elegant guarantees of freedom, but economic liberty for a dissenter may be contracted to the vanishing point in a thousand little ways. In a capitalist country there may be a profusion of legal remedies for unconstitutional deprivations of freedom, but licensing systems may slowly squeeze out the chance for the odd man.

The underlying cause of this is that Mill has been accepted as the guide for right action by many who have no comprehension or sympathy with his reasons, so that when a crisis comes (and as the cliché goes, that is where the problems always come) they find exceptions. It is not enough to quote the famous maxim that Voltaire may have coined, for when it comes to the test few people do fight for the right of others to champion a cause they detest, especially if the others are bullies and cutthroats in the bargain. It has been frequently remarked that even Milton, in his magnificent *Areopagitica*, admitted disagreeable ideas and their advocates only so far. When Milton wrote that "I deny not, but that it is of the greatest concernment in the church and commonwealth, how books demean themselves as well as men, and thereafter to confine, imprison, and do sharpest justice on them as malefactors" he was doing more than merely distinguishing between what is now called "prior restraint" and subsequent punishment. He meant by this (aside from an effort to appease some of his foes) that an idea which had no justification or was used to establish tyranny (the Catholics were clearly those whom he had in mind) was outside the pale. Liberty was a means to an end, the liberation of men's minds and energies, the key to the widest understanding of God's work. Therefore Milton criticized "a fugitive and cloistered virtue" which could not properly cope with the difficulties of a complex world. If liberty is a way of reaching a desired result—a godly society, or a democratic one, or perhaps just the greatest opportunity for human zest and activity—it is always open to those who wish to limit it to claim that the results are not being achieved. If free speech means that Catholics or Communists can spin a web of deceit, if freedom of press will lead to the triumph of these enemies of freedom, who can support liberty under these circumstances? It is then possible to say "Yes, we think the state should leave men alone in their private concerns, since only by so doing will men achieve the good life and become truly capable"—this is more or less what even Justice Douglas writes. But then it is not farfetched to add "Of course, if we find that the good life is being imperiled by too much liberty, and that the only gainers, politically or culturally, are those who would wipe out freedom or use it for odious ends, then free men will use freedom to its own hurt. This will not do."

But there is another strand in the *Areopagitica*. In a passage much less widely quoted than that mentioned above Milton compares the problem of truth to the Egyptian myth of Osiris, whose body, once hacked into pieces, could never be wholly restored. It is, he concluded, necessary to keep up the search for, like Isis, "we have not yet found them all"; we will never find all of truth until the millennium. It is instructive to match this quotation with the more famous one about the impossibility of truth being "put to the worst in a free and open encounter," which Popper has remarked suggests a ground for assuming that the defeat of truth is a cause for uncovering baleful conspiracies. Others have also read into this a belief that the dominant opinion must be truth, since it has won. But in light of the myth of Osiris, it is fair to read Milton's golden imagery in a more relativist sense. In the long run truth is what men will believe if they are not coerced; it is nothing more than the consensus of unprejudiced minds. It is Isis' search that matters, then, not the hoped-for discovery of a magical entity which will reward the searchers. Liberty is an end, not a means.

It is easy to recognize this theme in the relativist judicial opinions of Justice Holmes—his *Abrams* and *Gitlow* dissents, especially. Holmes probably placed such a high premium on liberty precisely because he doubted the permanence of any value. In just the same way Mill replied to those who argued that persecution of heretics by Christians differed from persecution of Christians by pagans because Christianity was right. Mill stated that there was no idea so perfect that it could be of greater worth than the views generated by free discussion, or even the free view of a solitary man.

If one accepts this belief Mill's distinction between self-regarding and other-regarding acts takes on a firm theoretical grounding. The goals of society may be misleading and open to doubt, but the process of talking about them is not. It is not just that the whole world may be wrong and the apparent crank may be right; there is no definitive wrong or right, only the strivings of human fallibility. This instantly shifts the center of importance from society to the individual. It is not the release of energy for the supreme good of the commonwealth which concerns Mill, but the gain to every man in his efforts to find his own goods in life. Thus relativism is an intrinsic part of this libertarianism. It is not only a relativism of beliefs, a refusal to say that some ideology is so wicked that it must not be tolerated, but also a relativism of values. If the mass of people want to spend their time playing what may seem (to others) foolish games—say, watching football games or bowling, or just wasting time—there can be no grounds for some stern censorial voice to advise about a social imperative. Millian liberty is for the drunkard or poltroon as much as it is for the scholar or agitator. It is for this reason that Mill may have been so anxious about the press of public opinion. It has been suggested that it was typically nineteenth-century to be so concerned with gossiping neighbors rather than the coercive arm of the state; Sinclair Lewis and Ortega y Gasset suggest that the problem is not dead. Surely this is one of the gravest dangers of a world where everyone may soon have a chance to look at, and judge others by, the same television programs.

In regard to public opinion Mill broadened the idea of liberty beyond the zones to which we have limited them. Strictly speaking, one has no right to freedom from the remarks of other people; efforts to make them silent would indeed be an invasion of their freedom. Furthermore, the opinion of the community is a necessary bulwark for liberty in our sense; it is partly because a man must face the censure of others for a mean act that it is no business of the state to punish meanness. Theory or not, moreover, people will talk, even in the blackest tyranny. There can also be no blinking the fact that the mass force of this talk will, at the least, inhibit behavior, more so with the timid, less with the unconcerned. Mill to some extent confused the issue of freedom from coercion with the price one pays for certain goods in society—in this case, the good of absence of social censure, or conversely, the good of social approbation. Considered thusly the question arises, is this price too high in our society?

Although Mill included an extrinsic issue, it is significant that that one involved a conservative judgment. Mill, to some extent borrowing from de Tocqueville, feared the pressure of a democratic society, one in which the concerted voice of a homogeneous population might crush all dissenters and level all of life to a common plane. This has become almost a commonplace of the right in the years since; it has always been implicit in aristocratic thinking, but Mill succeeded in liberating it from the class connection which it has often had and in making it a central part of the broader concern for individual development and autonomy. Mill was of course quite concerned with the plight of the poor—he is considered a sort of quasi-pioneer of socialism —but he imported into his book on liberty not a plea for the right of the poor to take the property of the rich, but the need of the few to be secure from the talk of the many, which comes close to being antithetically opposite.

This conservatism is a very different thing from the conservatism of custom, from the tradition of liberties with which we dealt earlier. Mill wrote in terms of rational determinations and did not stoop to use the patterns of past ages as a support. However, these patterns do have a connection with the conservative values Mill treasured. He was concerned that the juggernaut of public opinion would keep free discussion from reaching its potential, that it would substitute for the play of individual opinion a general, probably unthinking, mass opinion. In many ways this is the difficulty which faces the various customary liberties. The freedom of the press, for example, consists of a number of specific rights which rely frequently on the acceptance of individual difference, even peculiarity. The right to comment unfavorably about political figures often seems—especially in times of stress—to be an invitation to insolence or an incitement to disobedience. The zeal of reporters often conflicts with the interests of individual privacy or social decency, just as the claims of journalists to report on affairs of state will often seem dangerous intrusions. The scope of press freedom, of the privileges of the press, has been carefully developed and extended, often against the substantial and valuable rights of other elements of society. In the landmark *Bridges* case the United States Supreme Court declared its preference for this right over the right of the judiciary to be free of perhaps perverse criticism. In many other cases (such as the recent New York *Times* and *Hill* cases) the question of press freedom has been resolved in favor of the fourth estate. At every step a basically conservative right, available most easily to those with money, must be chipped out of an unfriendly or conflicting environment, so that a small group can exercise an often unpopular role. It is hard to say that the right of the reporters to be present at a trial is, in Berlin's sense, liberty, but it bears a much closer relationship than the right to an income sufficient to buy a newspaper each day. We have seen from experience that the struggle for equality will tend to augment the power of the state to the eventual detriment of liberty. Mill sought to extend the idea of liberty in the opposite direction, by accentuating the individualist, even aristocratic values of individual difference. Mill's concern may have been inconsistent with our framework of liberty, but his underlying regard for individuals against the mass is a fine part of the broader case for liberty as a conservative value.

It is therefore not so surprising that liberty has found so welcome a place in the conservative pantheon. When liberals were primarily individualists, when their chief enemy was the power of the state or the church, it was natural that they thought of liberty as a liberal cause. To the extent that they have once again come around to these tasks they become more libertarian —this has been a frequent lesson of our time, the message imprinted on a whole generation by the betrayal of hopes in Muscovite virtue. For the rediscovery of liberty is often accompanied by a re-evaluation of human hopes, a renewed respect for the lone thinker or the nonconformist. Hayek is right in pointing out that to be free is often in conflict with the desire to be equal or to be affluent. The bohemian community is usually rife with radical manifestos, but there would be less room for their vagaries in a mild socialist state than in an intolerant capitalist one— compare the United States of the 1890's and New Zealand today.

Probably much of the left does love the general idea of liberty, the concept of proud free men rejoicing in their freedom, but in fact it usually, like Plato, confuses this freedom with all the other goods. One must have a high regard for human nature to be sure that the varying acts of individualism will result in the other goods, and when the outcome is not so favorable it is liberty, negative liberty, that goes, even while the positive liberty is being proclaimed. There is a close relation between this dichotomy and that between individual reason and mass reason. In both these cases the attributes of individual thought or initiative are transferred, blown up so to speak, to a social group. In the process the idealization is enlarged, the range of potential is widened, and the actual quality is squeezed out. It is very fine to talk about the freedom which the minimum wage provides, but the direct result is the prohibition against paying or receiving less than a given amount for working. It is not accidental that liberals will often tend to see liberty as a means, rather than as an end, because it often seems a small thing when viewed without rhetoric. But it is the latter view which has deepened the meaning of liberty even as it has discouraged its fair-weather friends. So it is not surprising that liberty as a working proposition has become a goal of moderate conservatives throughout the world, as Gainza Paz and Learned Hand have shown.

Liberty may be valuable to conservatives, but this does not

answer the much more vital question of whether it is valuable to society—a question which has been asked very often on the right as well as on the left. Liberty is a high-sounding word; civil liberty, which is a reasonable designation for the particular liberty we have synthesized, is even more sonorous in its gravity and reasonableness. But if liberty means that Communists can try to persuade the people to revolt or vote out the established order, if it means that racist agitators can preach hate, if it even means freedom for brothels and permissiveness for drunks or narcotic addicts, why should anyone, certainly anyone of the center, be in favor of it? Many of the arguments given are of the "means" rather than the "ends" variety, and so often have embarrassing lacunae. It is said that liberty is a means for the spread of free and more vigorous expression, a prerequisite for culture. Elizabethan England was not libertarian in any of the senses here proposed—for freedom from Spain is clearly one of Berlin's positive liberties—and no one would claim that the Russia of Nicholas I was a hotbed of free thought. Augustan Rome was less libertarian than the Rome of Cicero or of Scipio the Younger; China under the Sung dynasty was certainly not very free. Each of these times was noted for great cultural activity and excitement, whereas the zestful freedom of late-nineteenth-century America produced a culture which later generations compete in apologizing for. It is gratifying to note the exceptions—Periclean Athens, seventeenth-century Holland—and to score the culture-killing blight which the Counter Reformation or Hitler and Stalin created. But the exceptions to this good equation are too numerous, and for that matter there is always a great intellectual to oppose even the best case—the Michelangelos and Shostakovitches will usually be around to adorn the case for constrained art. Forster put it well when he wrote, in his wartime defense of freedom given on the BBC, "I do not want to exaggerate the claims of freedom. It does not guarantee the production of masterpieces, and masterpieces have been produced under conditions far from free—the *Aeneid,* for instance, or the plays of Racine. Freedom is only a favorable step."

This is also true of economics. The British example of the mid-nineteenth century augured well for the alliance of liberty and economic progress, but the later history of Germany, Russia, and Japan have cast doubt on this relationship. Slavery may be a strong deterrent to economic advance, but this is by no means sure. Historically, slavery or at least systems of forced labor may have contributed to forced-draft economic programs. It is at least arguable that the Soviet industrial growth of the 1930's was largely made possible by the use of coerced labor in the millions. Persecution of skilled minorities, such as that of the Jews and Moors in sixteenth-century Spain and of the Huguenots in France after 1685, may well have held back these countries economically, but on the other hand the facile assumptions in this regard are no longer accepted without argument. Spain in the late seventeenth and France in the mid-eighteenth century were, despite all their problems, powerful and rich nations.

It must also be admitted that liberty will not ensure happiness. The paradox of the troubled mind, cast into a sea of turmoil by the opportunity for choice and the need for security or certainty, can be traced into the literature of the ancient Near East. Dostoevski's great parable of the Grand Inquisitor has phrased the question in its classic form, to be explicated by innumerable twentieth-century psychologists and political thinkers. Mill dealt with this in *On Liberty*, and concluded that it was better to search unhappily for wisdom than be contented and stupid. In so stating he did not intend to admit that freedom necessarily causes unhappiness; on the contrary, it is because of a mental illness that the sufferer recedes from the world of choice, abandoning freedom because of internal problems rather than being overcome by the terrors of liberty. The Freudians class all psychological problems as being in this category; to Freud freedom itself was to a large extent an illusion. But even if the plight of Socrates was a delusion or a vain struggle, to Mill it was worth the effort; the retreat from liberty was an abdication of the human potential.

In the end it comes down to this. Even if there is no direct road from liberty to any other good, liberty is a glorification of the inner human drive emanating from the reasoning faculty in man. When Milton complained that the parliamentary censors would keep the English nation in infancy, he touched on the core of the problem; one treats children with kindness, often with exceptional compassion, but they are denied the supreme testimonial of human value, the right to make all their own mistakes. One of the tactics of Chinese indoctrination of prisoners has been to reduce men to the status of infants by keeping them from using even their hands, thus breaking down their inmost dignity —much of the Nazi cruelty had the same purpose. Perhaps the enslavement of the Negro had a similar result. These questions of civil liberty do not involve the basic issues of torture and brutality, but this similarity is very important: In both cases, human dignity requires an autonomy, a sense of direction which is based at least in part on the potentialities of human reason. This civil liberty which we are considering is constricted by all the limitations mentioned above, but that is all the more reason why it is vital in its sphere. It is liberty from the clearly coercive power of forces directed against these individual rights which make up the adult dignity of men. For example, prohibitions on freedom of travel say to a man "The determinations of some men in positions of power bind you to remain in one land, or to give up going to another; you must consent to move about as the rules dictate." In time of war this is, like so much else, accepted; at any other time it is an infringement of a basic part of free choice, a symbol of adult freedom. "Self-regarding" is almost a pun; a man can regard himself highly only if he is treated as knowing what is best for himself.

This is the reason why the arguments of anti-libertarians often miss the point. Advocates of censorship will urge higher moral standards and foes of advertising will declaim against the debasing influence of vulgarity or unrelenting persuasion. In so doing they will assume that they know what is best, of course, and this is the usual example of absolutist philosophy serving as an enemy of liberty. They will also assume that morality or good form or proper consumer choice is an overriding independent good, a goal for society. But, as in the advertisement, getting there is half the fun, and more than half the value; in many matters, it is debatable whether there is any merit to a system that sets moral standards apart from the decisions of those who are to live under them. Laws against even the most virulent pornography can hardly be said to be advancing morality; they may remove what may seem unjustifiable incitements to lust, but they do not make anyone more upright or improve the tone of social conduct—they may lead to the opposite, by encouraging hypocrisy. Civil liberty is not perfect liberty, as we have presumed all along, and we may make an exception to our rules by banning, say, public billboards showing a couple copulating. This prohibition may be defended as a discouragement to an appeal to emotions so raw that it approaches the area of other-regarding acts; a dangerous doctrine, but customarily understandable at the outer fringes of normal behavior. But there is no denying that this prohibition will not be a moral act, but only a proper one; since morality implies a concept of private decency, this concept grows out of free action and not coercion.

It is, as this example shows, difficult to make hard and fast rules that have any chance of being accepted; simon-pure Millian liberty is as utopian as anything thought of by Fourier or Marx. The great merit of Holmes' clear and present danger test was that it tied the question of governmental restraint to an older legal rule which was closely related to the relationship of other-regarding acts, even if the connection may be stretched or weakened at times. No test will give a definitive answer for all circumstances. But if the exceptions to liberty are looked on with suspicion, and the ideas of Mill are considered the fundamental guide, the more uncertain implications of Holmes' or Learned Hand's flexible rules may be avoided; at a point it is necessary to set an inflexible line. At some point the weighing of values must cease, and once it is determined that the virtues of liberty are pre-eminent it is vital, in the sphere of everyday politics, to conclude the philosophical weighing of values with a positive decision. For instance, the argument against free speech is not contemptible. Free speech in the streets and halls of a great city is not a theoretical exercise in public thought; it is an active and, especially in exciting times, an often virulent display of invective and incitement to drastic change. The banquets of Paris in 1847–48 were frightening to the Orleanist government not because that government had a doctrinaire disregard for liberty—just the contrary—but because these meetings had a dangerous potential for violence or at the least a seething repudiation of law and order. It is common for modern historians to treat Guizot's suppression as a species of illiberal rigor, but it so often depends whose ox is being gored. The modern equivalents are the mass meetings of the extremist groups in Western nations. Would Germany have been better off without the Nazi and Communist rallies of 1931 and 1932, without the aura of success shed by such convocations as the notorious Bad Harzfeld assembly? Racism, from all sides, casts shadows today which are disturbing even to the most fervent libertarians; should Nazis and Black Muslims harangue without limit?

But if one accepts the ideal of civil liberty it is imperative to grant it even to those one hates, and even (this is often the harder task) in difficult times. If the line drawn is that of speech versus action, it is important to decide first exactly where such a line lies, in practical terms. Action is not confined to the physical moment of violence; it is fair to go a little farther back, and include such speech as may reasonably set off the violence, and is intended or could be construed to intend this violence. This is a difficult point—the United States Supreme Court wrestled with this in the *Feiner* case, and reached a perhaps anti-libertarian result—and is open to various opinions. But if one holds to four criteria at least the differences of opinion will be limited. In the first place, there is no right to limit speech because it may offend others—just because the audience may be violent or ill-mannered the speaker should not be curtailed. Disagreeable remarks are not for that reason forbidden; the existence of unruly crowds should mean curbing of the crowds, not the speaker. Secondly, the novelty or unpleasantness of an idea has no relevance to its right to be heard. The clear and present danger doctrine means, in this context, that speech can be checked when it verges on action, but there is no relationship between the wildness of an idea and its potential to make a crowd a mob—just the opposite, as a rule, for a truly radical suggestion will usually attract very few supporters. The speaker who preaches militant atheism or free love may outrage his listeners; today an appeal to a master race or a totalitarian state may be headier stuff, but simply because it is so distasteful is no grounds for suppression. The gravest problems arise when the speaker is clearly advocating the breaking of the law. These circumstances are often troublesome, but for that reason it is important to maintain the Holmesian principle that the exhortation to lawbreaking must be closely related in time and place with the opportunity to follow the advice for the speech to be actionable. This clearly rules out foolish laws against abstract protests, such as burning draft cards, which have no connection with the prevalence of order. Lastly, the fact that the speaker, despite his innocuousness, is a member of a world group which strives for domination by a powerful international organization is no reason to deprive a member from giving a speech. Each meeting must be judged on its own terms.

These criteria presuppose a dedication to the principle of free speech, even if the results are unpalatable. But they do more; they suggest arguments for the justification of the free-speech idea. The case against free speech relies on a vision of a bad society. Communities rent with bitter discord because of unpopular speeches, cities subjected to the proposal of the most disagreeable ideas, stated by men who may be connected with dangerous movements or who are hateful cranks whose discourse would not be tolerated for a moment in one's home (depending on whose home is involved, of course)—these are unpleasant pictures. What they have in common is a contrary vision of a smoothly-ordered, right-thinking state of affairs as a model. No rough edges, no agitations which might upset or disturb the ordering of society. It is ironic that these timidities are so often espoused by alleged believers in a virile or dynamic state—the right uses the former, the left the latter adjective, with equal gusto and imprecision—but who are afraid of a little rough criticism. The liberty to speak is a substitute for action, and it sometimes requires strong language to replace stronger action. There is a danger the one will lead to another, but this danger points up the advantages of an active population. A dead level of conformity would perhaps remove some of these dangers, but the result would be a static and unthinking state of affairs. This is clearer in the streets than in the books; it is just because a freedom of speech which excludes atheists, Communists, racists, or other exciting agitators is so empty that one finds that their rights are so valuable. The lower circle, the natural defenders of liberty, are as a rule reasonable, calm men, so that the state of freedom which seems natural to them is bland. But that blandness, if carried to the point of tacitly or openly restricting the arena to other bland men, will enthrone dullness and an etiolate spirit. It is not that extremists have the truth—this essay would be a mockery if that were the case—but that it is just the poles of thought, the excitement of dissent and disagreement, the whole *angst* of existence, that is the greatest argument for a vital conservative society. In the balance between order and excitement, order may be primary in that—especially to one who doubts human perfection—it is the precondition of contentment. But that makes it all the more important to introduce the disorder of thought, the testimonial to man's searching and to the common aspirations of all men. And since man is not perfectible, there is no sure answer to how these yearnings should be expressed; since there is no sure solution, it is the task of everyone to look for his own, to provide to the general good by searching out his own values and proclaiming them. Liberty is the greatest aspect of individualism, the exercise of thought in the multitudinous working-out of the infinite varieties of human action. The above-mentioned rules are therefore guides not only to a libertarian system, but to the heart of a diverse society, where each man is measured by the result of his own ideas.

This, too, is paradoxical; liberty is an end in itself, but it is justified on social or sociological terms. This paradox is implicit in these considerations of individualism; the merit of an individualist philosophy must be judged by its social consequences. In this case—and of course civil liberty is the core of modern individualism—these consequences are some of the essentials of civilized living. In discussing the relationships between the fundamental rights of immunity from torture and genocide, and the basic procedural rights, we suggested that they formed the core of civilization, the qualities of security from barbaric treatment which provided the fundamentals of decency. The liberty here at issue is not so basic, but it is similar. The little varieties of conduct, the opportunities for each man to differ from his neighbor or from the prevailing mode, are not incidental to the good life, but important aspects of it. One need only imagine a situation where one's least moves, the clothes one wore, the food one ate, and all the petty and vital actions of daily life were under the control of another. Civil liberty is valuable in large part because it preserves the preconditions of this diversity and variety, providing no guarantee of diversity (Mill's public opinion may prevent that) but the essential scope for its development, and its formal endorsement. Freedom from state power or other direct coercions will not ensure that no one or no group will crush the free play of variety and choice, but it is a necessary step; civil liberty is essential, if only in that it secures to each man that confidence in his individual status that makes the other values possible. This is the point at which liberty becomes a part of civilized living, for where the self-regarding decisions become matters of command and obedience a key part of manhood is lost.

This implies a respect for the value of human decisions which connotes some confidence in humanity—if not in human reason, at least in some quality of manhood which forms a vital part of social living. This is in some ways the liberalism in liberal conservatism, a heritage of the eighteenth- and nineteenth-century Whig and free-market thought which, to some degree in reaction to collectivism in general and totalitarian collectivism in particular, has become a feature of much of modern conservatism.

But this must come down in the end to specific freedoms, to the liberties mentioned before. The value of the four rules for free speech are important, for example, because they are effective safeguards of the principle that each man's right to speak will be considered as an important right in itself, and not a privilege or a freedom good only when not needed. Thus it is just when an idea is quite unpopular that its advocacy provides the proof of the varied dimensions of a free society; the guarantee that the hecklers and not the speakers will be curtailed is a vital part of ensuring that liberty is more than a tolerated or fair-weather part of one's system of values. There are numerous examples of this. Freedom of movement is surely a central liberty, a part of manhood and an absolute essential in any society that considers human choice a good. In totalitarian states the absence of this liberty is often the best sign of the prison feature of their system; it is easy to understand that in a land where even state officials cannot travel freely all of one's activities are at the mercy of authority. But in the United States there are men who applaud "liberty" who also support laws or regulations which require government approval before receiving a passport. Too often the power of bureaucracy has been supported by the very enthusiasts for free enterprise. It is hopefully significant that in the last fifteen years the nations of Western Europe have moved more and more toward elimination of passports and visas and the mass of trivial requirements which were so laboriously developed after 1914, and the reasons for this development are especially noteworthy. Europeans have lived through the meanness—the deprivation of the human spirit—which these rules entailed, culminating in the terrible regime of Nazi controls, where all-day waits were the lot of most travelers, and movement became a dread ordeal. The dragnet of German police stood in wait for the hapless traveler whose purpose was not permissible; torture and traffic controls were complementary parts of a system which combined the despair of paperwork with the swift horror of limitless power. The Berlin Wall is rightly treated as a symbol for this reason, because it proclaims that if the state chooses to declare a whole nation a prison, or a subdivision thereof, all men must become prisoners, willy-nilly. The most awful part of this, for inhabitants of the free world, is how this point of view can exist and be accepted, if it is for black men, or for Communists, or for some other specific group. The United States can well emulate the freedom of movement in Western Europe today.

If liberty is precious, therefore, it must be worth the price of subordinating other values. The rules in respect to travel present one kind of hypocrisy most well, but there are many others. The laws on sexual behavior appeal to many who would object to laws which would invade their own private activities. Free speech is often a watchword for minority groups until one brings up the subject of control of those who are spreading propaganda against the interests or nature of the group. At this point liberty turns into license, or so one would believe. But if these differences are supremely good one must be willing to put up with very disagreeable things; this is where it is especially important to consider liberty as an end in itself. It is often thought that liberty is excellent as a civilized value, but with the exercise of liberty dependent on that elegance. Thus it is necessary to defend the rights of a recognized opponent of the government, but not of some uncouth fanatic. Or, more subtly, speech may be defended, but not such a mean or demoralizing occupation as gambling. But it is often the case that it is just this attitude which renders these behaviors uncouth. Where all speech is protected —subject to ordinary limitations mentioned before—even the most bizarre forms become an acceptable part of the national spirit, as in Great Britain. Where gambling is licit the proprietors are not shady characters but often substantial citizens, and the whole atmosphere is not furtive and mean. It is not necessarily true that all actions are pure that are purely regarded, but the contrary is much to the point, and the constant badgering of the prohibited may make it what one fears, just as, in the more political sphere, the prohibition of the banquets in Paris of 1848 led to the revolution which was so feared. The working-out of a free society may well involve permitting the very nonconformities which are most shocking, and by so doing make them conform to the next generation's standards, and vice versa. Thus religious heterodoxy—deism, unitarianism, even atheism, became a part of the eighteenth-century richness after they so shocked and disturbed the seventeenth century. Sexual freedoms, in turn, have been incorporated into our present values; perhaps the nonconformities of gambling and (there is no point in hiding it) narcotics are next on the agenda. Since racial equality and the absence of class distinctions are now so highly regarded, it may be that the coming debate will center on the right to form invidious social or ethnic clubs. It is not fantastic to imagine a Labour government in Great Britain banning all non-state schools, or the practice of medicine outside the National Health Service, with the Tories upholding the cause of civil liberty.

The greatest threat to liberty usually comes in an area where there is no organized band of opinion or interest group willing to defend the trivial cases. It is a tribute to the United States Supreme Court that it recently came to the defense of narcotic addicts, whose only crime was an uncontrollable susceptibility to drugs. It seems strange that vagrancy laws might imperil the traditional values of property, but it is just the principle of freedom to labor where and when one wants that is involved in the defense of many battles over enterprise. It was natural for the British Conservatives to warn about the peacetime extension of Cripps' rules requiring workers to report to certain jobs—rules very sparingly enforced, be it said—but this is not so clear when questions of strikes in important industries arise. It is to Senator Taft's credit in this, as in so many areas, that he was firmly consistent and led the opposition to the emotional proposals of President Truman to draft railway strikers in 1946; conservatives must be especially cautious in limiting the role of the state in setting work regulations. In turn, advertising is a form of expression which often does not appeal to liberals, but the point of liberty is that it involves the right to even crude or tasteless or economically wasteful forms of self-regarding action. It is a commentary on many modern liberals that they do not see that the logic that holds that "incitement" is not inconsistent with free speech must apply this to commercial matters. But the inconsistencies of the left should be a lesson, not an encouragement, to the right.

So too conservatives should be eager to support the right to be immune from unreasonable search and seizure. This is not precisely a question of liberty in that it seldom involves physical restraint, but it is extremely close in that it affects one's immediate environs and living quarters—automobiles are now almost as much one's home as a house or apartment. The old conceit that one's house was one's castle symbolized the property consequence of this prohibition; a man's property is the extension of himself, and the freedom from searches is meaningful to the owner of the poorest hovel as much as to anyone else. The variety and richness of life requires protection, in most cases, of the bizarre or least protected group, which may or may not be the poorest; but in so protecting them the principal benefit accrues to those who most profit by the existence of variety and richness—the rich, as a matter of fact. The values of a lower-circle system depend on the appreciation of very un-lower-circle people, but the overall utility of these rights is of use to less peculiar folk who, nevertheless, make their own individual, if more normal, contribution to society. It is especially important now, in a world which seems ever more collectivist, for conservatives to perhaps go out of their way to champion the individual rights, the liberties which may help those they dislike. In that way the overall merits of diversity and individual choice will not seem class preferences or selfish advantages, but a true way of life, a genuine centering of the social purposes on individual freedom. There are limits to such Millian rigor, of course—no one expects a movement on the right to change the marriage institution into a simple contract, for instance. This is all the more reason why laws which abridge those areas of civil liberty which impinge on the issues of state power and bureaucratic regulation over private life—such as search and seizure, or laws governing private associations— should be scrutinized especially carefully. This is in one way a selfish sort of motivation, a use of liberty as a cloak for property or other conservative values, but the eighteenth century shows that impure motives may produce a purely excellent result.

This is backing into liberty. We have spoken of diversity and variety and the social benefits of individualist principles. But it is important to recall that liberty, especially in the narrow sense in which the term is here used, is an intensely personal right, a right to be let alone. In the twentieth century that is conservative in itself, for it is usually the forces of progress or the demoniac children of progressivism which press against that liberty. Whether these forces utilize one of the concepts of "positive" liberty or appeal to some other good, they are naturally ranged against that liberal conservatism that equates freedom with all the human vagaries, even if this does not fit into a theory of human betterment.

This does not mean that liberty requires nonconformity or odd behavior. The right to be let alone presupposes that the choices made will, usually, be quite ordinary. Most people do not wish to advocate revolution or dress like roughnecks, nor is it a condition of a libertarian society that there should be pressure on them to do so. Much of the fashion of nonconformity—in thought, dress, and style—is in itself highly conformist, although it is allegiance to a subgroup pattern. Liberty is in part the right to form groups and utilize them as an expression of one's beliefs; it is also the right to refuse to join groups, to be a group unto yourself or an enthusiastic follower of the national way. This is the greatest danger of pluralism. So much of the more rigorous pluralist philosophy—as it is found in Figgis and Laski, as well as in the corporatist ideas of the Fascists—implies that the group has replaced the individual as the lowest or most unique particle holding rights and privileges. But freedom, as defined here, is very personal, and it means above all the personal choice of conforming or not.

This may mean that if everyone wishes to be like his neighbor or like his sovereign, he certainly may. Everyone will necessarily value freedom differently; as Felix Oppenheim remarked, "If I know what I want most, my freedom to do what I want less is of little value to me." To a man whose overriding pleasure in life is carving old ships out of wood, a totalitarian society which leaves him free to do that without restraint is, to him, not injurious to liberty. If we say that carving ships is an unworthy or trivial occupation we are making the same superior value judgments which the critics of liberty make in a different way; all that can be said is that to that man carving is vital, and liberty is important to him if it is liberty to carve. Too often libertarians have thought of liberty as a matter only of speaking or writing; but man is largely a doer and not a talker. It is very often the right to act in a self-regarding way which, as it involves no ideology, is most suppressed. Why, for instance, should there be laws requiring adult motorcyclists to wear helmets, if the only sufferers from a failure to do so will be the cyclists themselves? This does not stir the spirit of intellectuals, nor contribute to progress. Perhaps liberty largely comes down to the preservation of the little peculiarities of life. There is little need to fear that a state of liberty will not adequately permit the spread of meaningful or multifold beliefs and practices. This too is conservative, for if one accepts the basic diversity of life and the variety of types of men and institutions it is hard to believe that there will ever be a time when all differences will cease of their own accord. This is especially so if, as it is hard to avoid, one accepts the importance of biological differences; unless chromosomes are thoroughly equalized there will be some distinctions which will inevitably come through to differences of belief. Of course the intensity of these differences will vary. It was not necessarily a blow to freedom that in some ages this diversity waned, as was probably the case in the 1950's or the 1660's. This may produce dullness, but that too is part of the variety of life; as long as these periods are a natural feature of the systole and diastole of social and political behavior they serve to freshen the impulses of revolt (as we now see) and not to deaden them. To some liberty will never be more than an unrealized opportunity, or even a threat, but that is no reason for depriving others of its blessings. We may end, as we began, with Milton, in this case a translation from Euripides:

> That is true liberty, when freeborn men
> Having to advise the public may speak free,
> Which he who can, and will, deserves high praise,
> Who neither can, nor will, may hold his peace;
> What can be juster in a state than this?

☆ X

Property and
the Free Market

In dealing with liberty we have interpreted it narrowly, as we have so considered the other basic values of a society. Procedural and substantive due process, as befits such legal terms, provide only so much in the way of protection or social utility. These values require broader support in the political system to maintain their function and to truly demonstrate their worth. It is just possible that the Soviet Union may evolve in the near future into a nation where these rights are tolerably well afforded, but if the broader aspects of individual values are not subserved and nurtured, the result may be tolerable, but very little more.

In a sense this involves the most debated issue of modern politics, perhaps of all politics. Should we look to the left of liberty, to equality, as the bulwark of liberty and the quality most designed to give it meaning and strength? Laski wrote that the nineteenth-century liberals worked for liberty as a tool for the securing of equality, but then substituted equality as a goal when they discovered that liberty did not automatically produce equality. This is a fair summary of the leftward view of liberty, the basic coupling of the revolutionary goals as common aims. Our circular view suggests that equality can slip over toward authority, and also that liberty can approach property or opportunity. The latter alliance, the move rightward, was the Whig formula as it was implicitly the premise of Mill, and is a corner-stone of free-market conservatism. It is, therefore, the heart of liberal conservatism.

The chief aspect of this alliance is, obviously, a defense of property rights. But before even beginning this task, it is important to throw out some property rights at the outset. Men might, logically, and have, historically, had property rights in the bodies of other men, or in the state, or in legal monopolies. But these kinds of property—and of course the word "property" is used as a right, not a thing; so many of the disputes over this point can be obviated by establishing this at the beginning—are not the kinds which a liberal conservative seeks to support. Property is a good only insofar as it is the right sort; an interest which arises out of the exercise of those individual opportunities consistent with human liberty. Slavery involves the elimination or serious restriction of another man's liberty, and therefore does not qualify; the directly coercive power of the state and the marginally coercive ones of a monopoly are also opposed to the goal of maximum freedom of choice. This is not a hard and fast distinction, as the prevalence of patent and copyright statutes attest. However, these are exceptions to the general proposition that the property rights worth supporting as valuable in the state as we see it are individualist, private, and founded on underlying principles of consent and choice.

This distinction was the setting for a famous case in the history of the United States. When the state of Massachusetts licensed a number of citizens to build a second bridge over the Charles River in the 1830's, the owners of the first bridge objected that this unlawfully interfered with their monopoly right which had, they maintained, been granted in their charter of incorporation. The Jacksonian majority of the Supreme Court disagreed with this view of the charter and overruled their plea; it was reasoned that the free opportunity to engage in business was a higher social value than the implied right of sole possession of a favorable situation. Here too, all these interests are relative —a man owning a choice corner lot, a technician or manager with unique accomplishments or skills are now considered by economists to hold a species of monopoly rights. In the last analysis, everyone has a little something that no one has and offers it for sale at a monopoly profit when he goes to work, but this is a function of choice, not a deprivation. At a certain point choice can defeat choice, as when a man sells himself into slavery; the dividing line comes where the choice is so self-defeating or the right is so exclusive that it transmutes the interest from an individualist right to a coercive power.

The literature on this test is vast, for it embodies much of the debate over social structure since 1776. The premise of Adam Smith and his successors was the categorization and defense of the better sort of property right, and this could take, as we have remarked before, left-of-center forms: the Jacksonians against the Federalists (as in the Charles River case), freedom of occupation against the guild and mercantilist systems of the past, above all, the campaign to extricate bourgeois property rights from any feudal taint—a line of thought which logically ended up at Henry George. By the nineteenth century this had crystallized to a large extent in a defense of contract as the ideally choice-impregnated, individualist legal tool for the establishment of the preferred kind of property right. This did not prelude the chance of monopoly or harsh dealing; in fact, much of nineteenth-century socio-economic thought seemed to envisage the economy as a great Parker Brothers game, in which equality of opportunity is afforded at the start, but sharp competition is the watchword thereafter. Contract has, as we have noted, proved too thin a reed for the cause of property; too savage in its rigor on one hand, and too dependent on the enforcement of the state to serve as an autonomously superior standard, on the other. This is not to say that contract has no place; the arguments against its importance have merely showed its limitations, not defeated its worth as a means for agreement to affect the condition of man within a society. But the emphasis of defenders of the idea of property as the result of individual competition and control have now centered their exposition on an idea which is both less state-affected and yet more flexible: the free market.

The current conception of the free market may be summarized

as follows: A perfect economy would function so that each man would bring his assets—his wealth, labor, knowledge, and any other salable goods that he might have—to market, to a great market consisting of the whole economy. At each moment that market would embrace a vast number of bargains and deals, all operating with incredible smoothness and without external control. The market in this sense would be an adjunct and a consequence of the substantive rule of law, for there would be no one ordering anyone, merely the plethora of decisions of buying and selling which make up a market. Everyone who thought rationally would maximize his well-being to the greatest extent, so that each man could allocate his resources so as to give himself the greatest total satisfaction; if on the other hand one chose irrationally or changed one's values, the fault would be his own. The more information which is available, the more rational decisions can be, but the market does not depend on knowledge. The commodity-futures markets often operate, for example, in conditions of thorough ignorance.

The beauties of the free-market idea are magnificent. If all goods were bought and sold on a truly free market there could be no corruption, for since everyone was trying to get the best price for his goods there could never be a margin to split with anyone else. There could never be exploitation, for no man could be shortchanged without his consent, at least his implicit consent. Price, the fulcrum of the machine, would always represent the meeting place of values, never a dictated settlement. To the extent that the market transmutes all arrangements into money terms, it tends toward the neutralization of more dangerous emotions or demands. Money is color-blind, and oblivious to social standing or family motivations. These other factors count in the market place, of course, just as all motives count, but the market will act to curb their importance. Thus if a man is prejudiced against Negroes, he limits his range of jobs or workers by carrying out this prejudice, and thus will tend to have to take less or pay more. If I run a store and wish to associate only with college graduates of superior breeding (by my way of thinking) I may do so, but the price of this decision in the market place must be higher labor costs and fewer sales. The same would be true if my tastes ran to hoboes—I might hire them for less, but I would pay more for a given sort of man that I would if my range were broader. This is true in any situation; Brecht, in his *Galileo*, satirizes Venice as affording liberty as a cheap way of attracting geniuses, which is another way of saying that the more free one's market is, the cheaper the costs will tend to be.

Perhaps even more importantly, the free market will provide a range of choices and opportunities which will make the liberty advocated in the previous chapter significant. One may be at liberty to buy any clothes one wants, but if there is no place to obtain them it is a valueless freedom. The free market is the best way to make sure that anything that can be made will be sold, and for the most realistic price. It may be that the only man who can produce, say, a fine kind of hat will still sell them only to his friends, which is his right. But the existence of a market system where he can discover that he might obtain far more money by selling them to anyone will always be a strong force in urging him to do just that, especially if he is married. It may be, however, that the goods which he most prizes are not money or money equivalents, but the more intangible riches of prestige or fame. In that case it is possible that the course of limited selling may be a very rational maximization of his resources. The market may not seem to work, from the customers' point of view, but that is because they are offering the wrong assets. There is a fine story about the nineteenth-century Chicago traction magnate, Charles Yerkes. It is said that when he lost his position in Chicago he decided to go to London, and realized that his opportunities depended on the good will of one man, an incorruptible person of importance who was an aficionado of astronomy. So Yerkes nobly contributed an observatory to the people of Chicago, reasoning (allegedly correctly) that in the market relevant to him that would be paying the best price for the good desired. The old maxim that every man has his price means that there is a market for any good; the freer the market the less peculiar, in almost all cases, the price. Moreover, one can choose not to choose. There are alternatives (like the ballot in the 1964 election in Illinois) too ponderous to be troubled with. In the free market one can, in fact must, disperse with some choices.

In this market world there is no room for guilt or duty, obligation or deference, except insofar as one consents to entering into arrangements which involve these qualities. Contract, therefore, becomes a tool of the market rather than an end in itself. If I agree to buy a car from you, there is no servitude on either side, only a responsibility to do what I think right or expedient. If I break the contract I may be said to be opting for damages or the inconvenience of specific performance; the market, like Holmes, will not put me in jail or send me to hell. The market may decide my credit is ruined, however; that is the economic parallel to immorality. Just as Mill's public opinion may be a tyrant, so may the commercial public opinion be very stern, but in the latter case there is always the opposing consideration that money may be made in dealing even with the worst of men. The free market has no one morality, as Shaw pointed out in *Major Barbara*. Undershaft looked on capitalism as a great institution, in that it meant that money was the key to everything; he would sell munitions to anyone, if he could get paid for it. His daughter, the major, saw the advantage just the other way—the merit was that in a free system she need sell only to those she wanted, without reporting to any superior.

The buyer has this option as well. If I think that a store is run by a prejudiced or politically undesirable man I can boycott it, and if there are enough like-minded folk this will hurt the store's business. This in turn will very likely cause the store to reduce its prices, presenting other buyers with a bargain and me with a dilemma. The market is neutral, so that the non-money motivations, rational or irrational, which the shoppers and sellers bring to it are melted down in the pot; if they are weak they will tend to disappear; if they are strong, they will make their appropriate mark. The older view of an economic man is therefore not important for the working of the system, nor is it vital that trust and reliability be assumed, as is true if one postulates contract as the key factor. Naturally it helps any market if one can do business on the word of another, and the most effective and freest markets, such as the exchanges and the money markets, depend on the flexibility which this tradition of honor imparts. But in grocery stores nothing is left to trust, yet the market works very well nonetheless. Some markets operate in transactions to be consummated over time, and are thus contractual in nature, and some involve bargains made and executed on the spot. Over the course of a month almost anyone makes numerous decisions in the economic markets of a capitalist country. Mises has reasoned that this shows the greater democratic choice afforded by free-market capitalism than by political democracy, in terms of voter choice. Naturally there will be buyer's and seller's markets, with the increases or diminutions of buyer/voter choice, but then one-party domination has been noted in even the freest political system. In the broadest range there is always a great choice, for if, say, houses grow too expensive one can always spend more money on appliances—in fact that is an illustration of one of the facets of twentieth-century buying patterns in the West. Finally, the free market by its purity is an incitement to excellence, a goad to the competitive instinct in man to do better than his neighbor. What he excels in may be dross, but in the strict sense it is excellence. This market place is not necessarily a commercial one; Reisman has reminisced about the competitive excitement of the *Harvard Law Review*, whose ranks were sifted by the most thoroughly demanding and merit-rewarding tests and whose staff in turn competed for prestige and influence by sheer brainpower. Just as the scholar glows in the thought of distinction won in the academic milieu, so the trader in a free market may glory in his prowess in bargaining; in both cases the pleasure comes from the sense of excellence disclosed in a competitive situation. So too the adversary system encourages this attitude among lawyers and, in similar ways, among athletes. Of course all lawyers and athletes are not equally capable, for freedom is not synonymous with equality.

All of this presumes that the market is free. A rigged market will not produce the desired results, for it will not impersonally balance off supply and demand nor will it provide a neutral proving ground for excellence. The term "free" presents the usual problems; is a market free when there is absolutely no restraint, or when it permits the maximum of uncoerced dealings? In 1829 the New York Stock Exchange required the man who engineered a corner to permit short contracts to be settled on reasonable terms, which Clews thought, in the early years of this century, to be an outlandish way of running a free market; now any other course would seem outlandish, and immoral besides. Once again, one must say that perfect freedom is the absence of restraint, but that just as murder is not condoned, so forestalling and monopoly control is out of bounds in the market environment. The rules of the market prohibiting other-regarding acts are designed to permit each participant the maximum choice within the scope of his abilities and resources. In the market context price rigging is equivalent to direct coercion, a disruption of the system of general liberty, which requires external control. This control can be exercised by agreement or internal regulation, just as arbitration or group government can settle the difficulties of a more political nature, but as in the latter case, the comprehensiveness of government has increasingly caused the decisions to be made in that quarter. The most notable examples of this are the antitrust laws.

The history of these laws presents, as in a microcosm (although not so micro any more), the issues of the free market. What has seemed to be the most clear-cut case of economic coercion to some seems innocuous, or to others a necessary part of freedom. For example, what of the case where one firm achieves a predominant market position through merit—General Motors or IBM may be cited as possible instances—and then continues to gain because of its size and note? If a law review achieves great authority in this way it would not be seriously suggested that it be split up into smaller units, or that its brightest candidates be shunted to another journal. On the other hand, great size in the economic market place may overawe competitors so that real competition in price or service may become illusory, or practices (such as franchising) which are normal with comparable firms become dangerous when exercised by a mammoth. Brandeis suggested that no firm should control more than one-half of the market, but then again as the recent work of the United States Supreme Court testifies, it is important to determine what the relevant market is.

If, on the other hand, it is decided that great size is not unlawful, per se, we must decide what types of behavior present the greatest problem. A blatant conspiracy to fix prices is obviously a violation of the free-market idea, but from there on the cases become harder. What of prices which are administered —that is, set identically by independent forces, each following the other or automatically following a leader? Or, conversely, what sort of competition is too raw—severe price cutting in competitive areas perhaps made possible by higher prices in less competitive ones, or efforts to drive a competitor out of business by tie-in or long-term contractual schemes? As one proceeds further the principal dilemma of antitrust law, and of the whole free market, emerges: the idea requires competition, but some sorts of competition may lead to an elimination of the market system altogether. If General Motors succeeds in driving everyone from the automobile industry, it will set a monopoly price just by existing. The question then necessarily arises: What sort of competition should be curbed, and what sort encouraged? It is easy to understand why such a paradoxical set of rules as now exists in American antitrust law, now fostering, now blunting the competitive processes, seems to many (and not only to doctrinaire business supporters) a species of meddling foolishness. But paradox is often a sign of viability and not of confusion; since the free market, to be free, requires constraint, these paradoxes may lead to the most workable arrangements. To a great extent this depends on the criteria which are used.

The first step in deciding these criteria is fundamental: Is competition or control the primary goal of regulation? This, of course, was the famous issue of the 1912 election, in which the Democrats espoused the idea of the New Freedom, a policy aimed at maximizing competition and the place of the small businessman, and the Progressives upheld the New Nationalism, designed to place a firm control over the accepted power of the large corporations. This debate has continued in various forms ever since; for example, Berle and his followers are clearly Nationalists in their emphasis on moral and political rules to govern the otherwise uncontrollable power of the corporate managers. In the uncertain movement in Western Europe toward antitrust policy since 1945 this motif has been predominant, as in even Britain, where the Restrictive Practices Commission exists largely to judge the social value of monopolistic situations or acts, rather than their competitive effect. This corresponds to part of the philosophy of the Theodore Rooseveltian tradition; nor is it a new doctrine in Europe. On the European continent capitalism has always been a system tied to governmental authorities somewhat more closely than it has been in the Anglo-Saxon countries, so that the regulation of monopoly comes as no innovation. Germany is a prize specimen; the growth of large-scale industrial and commercial enterprises in the late nineteenth century tended to make them a new branch of the state, so that Krupp became a sort of landgrave (this of course was before Hitler honored the family with a *lex* of its own) and even Rathenau achieved a sort of imperial position. This imperial control was a friendly control, but its friendship was rather Berlean—a sort of oligopoly mentality, whether the beneficiaries liked it or not. Roberts, a cogent student of Wilhelmian Germany, commented in 1913 that when the potash cartel broke up in 1909 the Reichstag passed a compulsory syndicate law "in the interests of the nation." The business of monopoly works both ways, as when the Italian steel industry asked the Fascist government for a cartel law in the early 1930's, but backed away when it appeared that this would bring along a massive degree of state control. The NRA, much of whose theory and practice derived from Berle, was an example whereby price-fixing entailed a compensatory wage-fixing—in the atmosphere of the time this seemed a very good bargain to many businessmen. The suggestions about state determination of administered prices involves this same kind of reasoning. If it is assumed that the large corporations must inevitably set prices at their whim, or largely so, and that there is nothing that other businessmen or consumers can do about it, there is a strong case for permitting the government to have a say on these prices. This has created a furor in the United States, often offending the very groups who advocate greater influence over wage rates; conversely, the friends of labor do not always see where price-fixing is likely to lead. The specific steps toward a favorable form of control are usually delightful, and steps toward curbing someone else are almost equally so—the rub comes later, but frequently not much later. Hutchinson suggested that there was a direct line from the high tariff on steel imposed by the Tory government in 1932 in Britain and the Labour nationalization sixteen years later. The American steel companies in their current concern over Japanese competition may well be making the same mistake.

The issue seems open and shut when the other fellow is being favored. In practice there is always a powerful reason for the government aid. Who would in this day propose a law to especially subsidize millionaire landed interests on a scale that Cobden or Ricardo would have denounced? But the farm-support programs, upheld by liberals, have come to do this, and the combination, in America, of rejecting both Benson's free-market policy and Brannan's in many respects complementary subsidy program means that the compromise is largely an outdoor relief program for rich farmers. "Cartel" is a dirty word today, but it has been advocated as a substitute for monopoly designed to preserve the small businessman. Cartels are a popular idea among many people, especially among the very group that has been the symbol of anti-trust, the petty entrepreneur, and when no one is looking "fair-trade" and "anti-dumping" subterfuges tend to get put into law to make them not just possible but unbeatable. The now-blossoming international commodity agreements appeal to many who would be the first to shudder if the pacts were called by other, ruder names. The gravest problem with the New Nationalist system is that, in the guise of accepting the implications of a post-competitive world, it frequently makes sure that it will be post-competitive. It is as when an heir proposes that he must learn to use his father's wealth, and strangles his father to make the point.

However, it is not enough to reject this to find a workable antitrust system. The paradoxes of competition become more troublesome if one accepts the value of the system, for then these riddles of competition devouring itself grow in importance. But much of the problem does come from an uncertainty of intent. It makes a difference what value one treasures most highly. If the criteria is maximum production or lower prices there will always be a slight bias toward the control answer, because it may be that in some cases an efficient or well-disposed monopoly may be superior at securing these. It is the same here as it was when we considered the idea of liberty itself; if the goal is outside liberty then it is all too easy to lose one's original objective as it becomes an unsuccessful means and not an end. This is also true of a more insidious factor in antitrust policy, the concept of competition as a tool in preserving small business. In the 1880's this may have been the principal inducement for the passage of the Sherman Act, and it has been a potent factor ever since, as the cartel illustrations suggest. There is a fine line between protecting the small businessman from the overwhelming competition of the mighty—overwhelming because of the advantages deriving from superior economic power—and protecting the less efficient from the skill of their more capable competitors. This distinction is the crucial one in an antitrust policy based on the free market, for it distinguishes restraints designed to make the market system work and those designed for another, often contradictory, purpose. As in other cases, the arguments for customary arrangements should give way in the final analysis to the values of individual reason. Much of the economic problems of inter-war France and contemporary Britain come from a romantic aversion to this conclusion.

In American practice this can be illustrated in a number of ways. The Robinson-Patman Act, for instance, can be divided into different categories. The rule that price discrimination may be justified only as a derivation of cost difference or competitive forces is in the free-market tradition, and uses the right standards. It should serve to forbid the sort of competition which is akin to forestalling or predatory use of size—underselling in one market because of the higher prices in another, or the use of market size to gain special advantage. At the same time it serves as an answer to those who want laws setting prices so that the in-efficient can survive—the fair-trade argument—and by so doing it is especially important as a tool in defending the free market. On the other hand this standard in practice can be very confusing and even anti-competitive, as has often been alleged. Brewster has suggested that it often defies economic rationalization, and that the act bespeaks a form of economic "equal protection" rather than the "due process" of competition. It may be that is partly a semantic disagreement; the test is the effect of these laws on pricing policy and competitive behavior, so that Brewster's conclusion can be defended only if using the act to encourage competition is, in fact, a failure. One can see this puzzle in allied areas. Tied sales are bad, but what if this prohibition leads to taking over the retailer *in toto*? After the electric price-fixing ring was exposed, the government feared that General Electric would react by cutting prices destructively, and sought to forbid this through the use of the consent decree. This seems highly inconsistent, for if the electrical-equipment makers had sinned by not competing, it seemed perverse to restrain their new-found zeal to cut prices. It would make a great deal of difference how much and in what way prices were cut. Cutting prices to some customers or in some areas would be a clear use of economic power which, in some cases, might result in an absence of competition. Cutting transformer prices to the bone while raising bulb prices would be a harder question. At this point some have advocated laws forbidding sales below cost. This involves problems of proof even more difficult than the non-discriminatory terms of the Robinson-Patman Act; it further enters into the area of forbidding a non-predatory competitive device. It does make a difference, it is true, what the size and scope of the company is—if General Motors so wished it could sell a certain screw in the after-market for nothing without noticing the cost, whereas this might drive the competition out of business. Where a company sells many products the various treatment of small items might be analogized to discriminatory treatment of geographic areas, as the use of power to warp the normal course of competition. The law of dumping in tariff negotiations might provide a guide to such treatment, but it is also a perilous guide. It is important to remember that a free market is a market and not a church; very often unfairly low prices of one's competitor are any prices lower than one's own.

So too, there are merits in laws designed to ensure that consumers have adequate information as to quantity and cost, but there is a danger that these regulations may force business-men into a limited range of services by eliminating new forms of packaging (literally and figuratively). It would be convenient to possess a formula which would disclose when increased con-trol ceases to make the market more free and begins to squeeze out its vitality, but each case must be tried on its merits.

The gravest problems come with size as a factor of its own, size per se, as the phrase has come to be. The easiest way to approach this is where the size has grown artificially. Lippmann pointed out thirty years ago that the United States Steel Com-pany did not grow, but was contrived. There should be a stronger policy against mergers or combinations than there is against the natural exercise of market power. This was implicit in the phrasing of the Sherman Act, and it seems to be the policy of the present United States Supreme Court and of much of Con-tinental anti-monopoly thinking. It is obviously no necessary result of the market if all the companies in a field are brought together artificially into one big entity; as Lippmann observed, on this Marx and Judge Gary were at one. But of course most mergers are not so blatant, and the gradations of market dom-inance, and its scope, are infinitely debatable. As part of this judgment the prevalence of privileges (such as patents or exceptional franchises) and special circumstances (such as inter-locking ownership or control) are very relevant. At the end of the matter there is the question with which we began, that of a monopoly, or more commonly, an oligopoly which has naturally come about. There is some merit to unwinding a too-constricted market, but it is a mistake to assume that, because the govern-ment is urging competition, a forced splintering of corporate giants will work to that end. The Japanese example shows that a fostering of free-market practices is often more important than a summary breaking-up of big concerns. Best of all, the encouragement of natural competitive forces, as has occurred in recent years in America in the aluminum and business-forms industries and in West Germany in the automobile industry, is the best way for the state to prod competition. Adelman Alchian has shown how the market has solved many of these problems itself; this does not prove the folly of laws, but it is a very important reminder.

The more one tries to describe standards for government action—and it is important and significant that this action be prosecuted through the courts, with their traditions of *stare decisis* and "neutral" considerations—the more complex the analysis becomes. What starts out as a support for the impersonal workings of the market seems to become a very personal intervention by the state into the workings of the business community, the very antithesis of the rule of law. For this reason Hayek has turned away from anti-trust, despite its affinities to his viewpoint, and has put his trust in the automatic workings of the market. But in so doing Hayek has, like so many of the free-market conservatives, taken the free market out of politics and made it into an absolute economic good. It is a vital part of the traditionalist Whig view to keep the political aspect of economics apparent. The rule of law, as has been noted, has varying interpretations with different priorities. There are distinct advantages for liberal conservatism in the use of relativist concepts in this area. Since courts do make law to some extent it is not enough to say that because an area of law lends itself to fine distinctions which reduce the likelihood of certainty courts should stay out of the field. If the basic philosophy is comparatively clear—and despite all the doubts it has become a winning doctrine of worldwide application—it becomes a part of the market, just as the legal provisions against burning one's competitor's warehouse is a part of the market system.

In turn, this philosophy, which is at the bottom one pivoting on the idea that all competition is to be encouraged until it becomes clearly a manifestation of unequal power or direct interference with one's adversaries, is, like the similar one of free speech, an exercise in relativism. The prices that emerge from it are ethically neutral or instable—it is inherently impossible to talk of a just price in a free market as meaning anything else than what people will exchange goods or services for. It is the job of antitrust laws to enhance this relativism by discouraging efforts to import a spurious stability into prices (for this is the usual aim of price-fixing, and not the attainment of some vast monopoly profit, which would only enrage everyone) and thus to make sure that the greater impersonality of market forces is furthered at the cost of some specific intervention. In the area of allegedly administered prices this means that instances of possible collusion should be scrutinized in a way that may seem to lead to constant government intervention, but if the standard is whether identical prices come from dominant leadership, or from a free-market determination, the proper course may be maintained even if in the process it may seem that the government is reviewing prices and intervening against companies at the whim of the chief antitrust officer. But is this not often true in criminal law?

It might even be said that it is in just those areas where the safeguards of procedural due process have been most highly developed—as in capital cases—that the discretion of the prosecution is most broad. This is so because this discretion is another protection for the accused in that it leaves the state free to measure its use of the machinery of criminal law. So too the antitrust laws have profited by the importation of flexible elements—the rule of reason (which was always implicit; no one has ever seriously proposed that an ordinary one-year covenant not to compete is a restraint) and the use of nolo contendere pleas, for example.

Moreover, if one views the idea of the rule of law as a concept of the fulfillment of reasonable expectations, one might conclude that these measures governing the workings of the free market are fine exponents of that rule. The limitations on stock-market corners, for example, ensure that activities on the exchanges will be immune from the incalculable results of manipulation. The purpose of laws prohibiting one company or a syndicate from monopolizing a raw material and prohibiting its sale to competing groups is to limit the hazards of procurement to price movements based on the normal circumstances of supply and demand. There can be spontaneous corners (as, say, the Northern Pacific corner of 1901) and sudden catastrophic price rises, but at least these arise out of economic situations and can be prepared against on that basis. The free market, like the freedom of civil liberties, is a value based on reasoning, deriving its point from the scope it affords reason—the individual, ateleological reason of the single man. To some extent antitrust laws are like laws against breaking up peaceable meetings, a state-imposed *sine qua non* for free discussion or free trade. They are limitations on doing what one wants, and in that literal sense, anti-libertarian; but they have value if, and only if, they increase the effective liberty, the negative liberty of those who abide by the rules. No Mill has come along to distinguish the self-regarding and the other-regarding part of market behavior, but its line must fall somewhere in this area of activities which preclude or permit the market to thrive. Finally, there is a direct connection between antitrust laws and liberty, for to the extent that these laws increase competition they discourage those private monopolies which could be considered, in terms of the previous chapter, coercive restraints on liberty.

It is understandable that a political-theory treatment of the free market must spend much time on anti-monopoly legislation, but it is unfortunate. This legislation is worth-while, from a free-market point of view, because it enhances those characteristics which the market itself possesses, but it is the market which is the jewel, and the laws are but settings. As we have remarked, the benefits are not primarily economic. It is usually the case that a free market will be the smoothest way of maximizing output and improving the wealth of a society, sometimes dramatically so, as in West Germany in 1948. But the fruits of a free market may be as strange or disappointing as the desires of the people and the nature of the economic organization. It may be that while the United States surpassed the world in the production of motorboats and high-horsepower automobiles the

Soviet Union was making meaningful strides in space exploration which put the West to shame. It may be that the money spent on Grade-C movies in the free world is spent on chess or physical fitness in the Communist countries. It may be that China will even more wisely, from the point of view of survival, forget about the chess. Once again, the defects of these comments are the fixed quality given to wisdom. Since there can be no answer, in a relativist world, to the question of what must be good, the next best, rather one might say the very best system is one where each man's values have their own result, where one can shape the economy by one's spending or saving. Advertising may seem a costly or jejune way of channeling this opportunity, but to object to it is to object to freedom of choice. If one accepts the idea that a man can be forced to buy one must hold a very low view of human nature—either a conception of the consumer as an easily swayed fool or as a hopelessly weak vessel, capable of being hypnotized by subliminal perception or appealed to by unconscionable hoaxes. But of course most of the opponents of advertising are progressives. They must therefore concentrate their opposition on the principle that the insidious bombardment of pressures to buy weaken the fiber of even intelligent people. If only, so the argument sometimes goes, the money and effort spent on publicizing some soap or cosmetic identical with all others were spent on fine art! It is ironical that the expositors of fine art have given up the very concept of "fineness"; Malraux has suggested that any sincere art is as valid as any other. Perhaps the advertisements for soap are not sincere, in the Malrauxian or in the popular sense, but who is to judge the world for sincerity? The last chapter of the irony is the use of the very artifacts of the soap advertisements in pop art as found objects.

The free market, since it is impersonal, has no use for sincerity. As with civil liberty, one must beware of trying to have things both ways—of gaining the independence and freedom of the market while counting on that freedom to produce just what one wants. Upper-circle thinkers are habitually sure that the people must have some overriding good and that it must be managed so that they get it—the radicals claim that people really want their goods (or would, were it not for exploitation, ignorance, or misgovernment); the reactionaries are more likely to say that the people ought to have their values, like them or not. When one comes down to fundamentals there is no arguing, but, as with the other issues of choice, we can consider what sort of world these values produce. The free market is not inseparable from a politically libertarian society; Mussolini seduced the Italian bourgeoisie by expanding the free market while he eradicated civil liberties in the 1920's. There is a chance that the Soviet Union may evolve into a society which may afford a fairly wide degree of liberty to its people while still failing to provide much of a free market. For a Communist system can, after all, provide only a limited-market system, since the workings of the market are bound to interfere with that smooth orderliness which absolute government control requires. We may see more and more examples of the tedium and ennui of Russian life, hidden in earlier years by the much vaster horrors of Stalinist tyranny. Once the graver miseries were reduced the significance of communism as an economic rather than a political system has come to light. It is not an accident that observers have concurred in their picture of a society which can produce sputniks but not durable apartment houses, which can achieve constant records in electrical production but has not managed as yet to produce many electric washing machines or refrigerators. Television sets have been produced in volume, for it is to the benefit of the regime to communicate their ideas to the people, but automobiles are almost as scarce as in 1945, for it is not advantageous to the regime for the masses to enjoy the mobility cars would afford. There is a small similarity between a concentration camp and an economy in which the seller is always right, for in both cases one must spend one's time in coping with the problems of procurement (or struggling against immovable regulations) rather than exercising the scope of choice; here too, scarcity produces a childlike dependence. One may eschew the market, but as long as it is there one may avail oneself of its opportunities when one wants. The free market, like other free institutions, is a chance rather than a guarantee, and this chance may produce disagreeable turns. There are seller's markets in a free economy as well as buyer's markets, and this is fortunate, as an antidote to the problems (such as unemployment) of a too-consumer-oriented world. The changes and readjustments of the market are not merely unavoidable evils, although they can become evils quite readily; they are also, up to a point, part of the climatic changes in the economic season which prevent one group or class from becoming too secure or important.

For in the last analysis the pleasures of the market are subjective. The sense of diversity and richness of a market enhance the breadth of life, and that breadth is an integral part of the conservative social system. Before the eighteenth century there was an intellectual preference for a sort of order which abhorred the vagaries of the market, and equated good government with proper prices and guaranteed sales (and taxes). The normal reaction of the governing classes of Byzantium or Ptolemaic Egypt or Tokugawa Japan to economic disturbances was to establish "order," that is, set allocations of production and fixed prices. In times of chaos a free market is always a risk, and an antisocial one; in wartime price control often becomes universally accepted. The Whig ideology treats this as the rare case; to others war is the norm. To some people now, as to many in a status-oriented society, price cutting is not the sort of thing a gentleman does, and certainly bargain-hunting is not for aristocrats. Most of the criticism of the commercial way of life before 1750, and perhaps well after that (as Hayek has suggested) was from an aristocratic and not a proletarian premise, and in many cases the twentieth-century critics on the left have, as in the matter of advertising and "mass culture," adopted the arguments of the aristocratic right.

This has been pointed out by many free-market conservatives, who often have deduced from this that the modern progressives are exponents of a "new Toryism." This is defensible only if one assumes that these critics are seeking to establish a new status-group of intellectual superiors, a possible description of the Bloomsbury influence but, in general, not a supportable claim. Rather, the older sense that the economy is too dangerous a thing to be left to its own devices, that law and order require a financial as well as a physical policeman, has come to fit into the ideology of the left. Most modern radicals fear the economy just as the reactionaries do, and—which is not surprising, considering the nature of the circle—for quite similar reasons. This paradox, like many others, can be rationally explained. In theory the extreme left, with its high opinion of human nature, should be pleased with a system of free choice, provided that it was allied to a program of equality and social mobility. The anarchist vision—shared by Marxists as the condition of the messianic age, when the state would wither away—pictured the freest market imaginable, when no tradition tempered the utmost choice imaginable, and all bargains were struck by equal parties. To make perfection truly perfect, to be sure, there would be such affluence—the Condorcetian dream, expanded by the utopian socialists and Saint-Simonians and by Marx—that there need be no market, and all would share in their just deserts, naturally. Even so, tastes would still differ, and there might be trades among various men or groups—perhaps, as Bellamy thought, syndicates which might establish cooperatives—and thus a free market. Many Marxist theorists have studied the workings of the market under socialist societies; Liberman has become famous as the exponent of this school. As is well known, many young Soviet economists have in recent years tried to develop the potentialities of market analysis and process to the Communist economic order.

But they have had very little success. There is a security in a fixed system which is built in. As long as demand is greater than supply—in the ex-ante sense, of course—one need not worry much about sales and therefore (insofar as the problem is redundancy of labor, and not materials or capital) there cannot be much unemployment. As the left is faced with one of the limitations of humanity, of human capacity in this case, it must always turn away from one of the potentialities of human action, and the upper-circle left tends to turn away from choice, from the individualist values, toward the authoritarian principles of a fixed society. *The Economist* once remarked that modern economies offered three goods: stable prices, low unemployment, and high wages, but like the godmother of a nursery tale, would permit only two at a time. Fiscal conservatism, the "conventional wisdom" so derided by Galbraith, usually picks stable prices as the fundamental value, and expects that competition will hold wages down to a level consistent with low unemployment; if not, it accepts the unemployment as a necessary evil. Liberals frequently opt for high wages, and are willing to let prices rise. This will not always be an easy process; under the New Deal either timidity about price increases (*pace* Keynes) or the natural reactions of a cowed business class in a mixed economy (*pace* Schumpeter) resulted in continued high unemployment. Hitler's greatest triumph, on the other hand, was his reduction of unemployment, which was his cornerstone. Real wages of employed workers, which rose sharply in the United States from 1933 to 1939, probably fell during those years in Germany; in both countries the price level was rising, but not rapidly. The Nazi answer, so consistently a reflex of order and a status-bound society, is the Soviet answer; as long as consumer goods are ladled out cautiously and inadequately and incomes are held down, so then there can be no danger of unemployment, while prices will not rise so swiftly as to destroy the value of economic relationships—the last being, one might say, the French or Brazilian choice. In concrete terms, this is a key to the problem of the radical on attaining power. While in opposition, or at least before he takes over all of society, he often talks of high wages and the eradication of unemployment, trusting that the rich will pay, often through the effects of inflation. But inflation debauches not merely the capitalists, but everyone—often the capitalist last, in an entrepreneurial system. So the radicals end up by being reactionary in their attitude to labor, quite literally, for they repeal pro-labor legislation, as Castro has quickly done in Cuba, and break strikes, as even Gomulka has consistently done in Poland. It is true that this holding-down of wages is usually done for the purpose of providing funds for capital development, and in this respect communism has often been compared to the ethos of an expanding capitalism, pressing down wages (as in post-Napoleonic Britain or post-Civil War America), but this misses the point. There was no consistent policy of withholding goods from the lower classes in those periods—as a matter of fact, the standard of living rose in many of these very years— and the market tended to balance out any swings toward excessive accumulation of capital by lowering the market value of capital. In short, Marx has been proved wrong in his central economic argument, the impoverishment of the proletariat under capitalism. But this condition is much more feasible under communism, just because it will lose its claim to virtue—the absence of unemployment and freedom from cyclical ups and downs— if it lets loose the market and permits wide consumer spending, with its appeal to the desires of the moment. It is no coincidence that Yugoslavia, where liberalization has outdistanced the Russian model, is the land now troubled with unemployment. To the extent that a Communist economy truly develops toward a free market, as Yugoslavia seems to be doing, the paradoxes of policy thus inevitably take on characteristics of capitalist societies. This is true even when personal private property is held down. In the long run, this may well require the revival of individual economic incentives. The righteous Maoists, like the White Queen in *Through the Looking-Glass,* are already in a rage over this diabolical process. The upper circle turns puritanical when it is faced with man, warts and all, and often concludes that mankind is like the description of a Graham Sutherland painting, warts and nothing else. The glamor of the free market then seems not only dangerous but even wicked, the extreme radical passes into a reactionary, and Mao resembles Hitler. From the other side of the circle the extreme reactionary finds that in a system of order businessmen are inconvenient, and that nationalism implies socialism (which occurred to many people, among whom one might almost include Theodore Roosevelt, long before Hitler). There are no merchants in a well-run army, and an officer is not promoted on the basis of his ability to discern the potential tastes of his soldiers.

The free market, perhaps even more than the civil liberties, is the antithesis of this military outlook. One might imagine an effective army of free-speaking men—for instance, the New Model

Army of the 1640's—or even a democratic army, but an army where profit or economic choice is the key value seems a bunch of plunderers. The essence of a market place is wit and freedom; the free market is the open society par excellence because one need not accept any dogma, one need not even, as if we have seen, be sincere. Plato was solicitous of the rich, but as a proper class in a Greek city-state (not in his perfect one), not as a bunch of peddlers or traders, very likely *metics* or emancipated helots at that. The market by its spirit breeds cosmopolitanism and intermixture of peoples and people; New Zealand may be more righteous but Hong Kong is the place where the refugees have been admitted and found jobs. To find jobs is a step toward Holmes' jobbist society, where every man does his work and lets the social order derive from that; fanaticism and bitterness are not a feature of a land of salesmen. De Mandeville would have admired Holmes and his philosophy; Lippmann, with all his respect for the jurist, has often (in his youth and in his old age, at least) scorned the mere job-minded routinist or narrow businessman.

Lippmann's disdain for the routinist is a more exciting philosophy than Holmes' credo of the man who sticks to his work, but excitement is not a safe commodity. In our time we have been forcefully reminded of Dr. Johnson's dictum that a man is never more innocently engaged than when he is involved in business. The terror of mass coercion and the unfeelingness of mass bureaucracy have pointed out the blessings of a market system. The liberal individualists of the eighteenth and early nineteenth centuries conceived of a money economy as a liberating force as against the status-bound systems of the past, and were derided for their naiveté or past-mindedness by their successors on the left; but within a short time experience has shown how many illiberal measures can thrive in a society where the softening and equalizing force of the market is absent.

☆ XI

The Case
for Inequality

Thus the glories of the free market have not, as many thought, vanished in the First World War or the Great Depression, but have survived to be proclaimed by a significant band of enthusiasts. The Chicago school, with its cosmopolitan mixture of Viennese wisdom and North American prudence, has seriously contributed to recent thought in ways parallel to the successes of the market in the least likely places. We have marked the victory of the "social-market" system in Germany, the homeland of the collectivist vision. At times the supporters of free-market conservatism have seemed to be members not only of a socio-economic group but also of a religious community, a band of believers. The ardent political followers have sometimes, ironically enough considering the individualistic nature of the free-market belief, qualified as Hofferian "true believers" or even, as with Ayn Rand, caricatures of individualist theory. This is comparable to the experience of Marxism, but with the important difference that instead of a lawgiver or prophet, free enterprise has only a doctrine, so that each believer can kindle his spirit at a self-made fire. Perhaps a closer, and at present more relevant comparison is with the Malrauxian religion of art. In both cases the believer seeks a man-made yet, somehow, cosmically related system of order; proportioned in each case in some mysterious way to the needs of all mankind and the intensely subjective requirements of the personal soul. The religion of art has truly developed since the triumphs of relativism have rendered all efforts valid, for what has been lost in the dethronement of the faith of superior art—the ideals of the pre-Raphaelites or the classicists—has been much more than made up for in the glorification of the concept of creation, not beauty or genius, but the rhythm of recreating the divine handiwork. In similar ways the acceptance of the varieties of tastes and needs has led to a broadening of the market idea, so that all values can be weighed on a scale of choices; the process of choosing has become the nub of life.

The scope of this now-perceived market is impressive. Competition exists not only as to price but also as to quality, and a truly accurate supply/demand schedule would include the varying costs and incentives of qualitative considerations. The motivations behind even the most abstruse or unusual set of demands can fall within the area of market impulses, especially inasmuch as mathematical theory has been accompanied by the marvelous techniques of computer technology. In fact, this greater awareness of the finer qualifications of thought has paralleled the increased sophistication of the arts. Stigler has observed that one fault of traditional market economics was its disregard of the effect that one man's taste may have on the demand of another; with the refinement of theory the nineteenth-century explanation of why diamonds are more costly than water has now been supplanted by the twentieth-century answer to the question of why some luxury goods sell more readily at a higher than a lower price. The grossness of trade now provides answers to the most abstruse of philosophical inquiries.

The very capacity of the market to take new circumstances, even extremely restrictive laws or situations, into account has been brought forward as a striking feature of economics. If goods are rationed, there will arise a market for ration stamps. If this is prohibited, there will be a clandestine market which will intrude individual rationality at some point into the system. The market is like a colony of ants; blockage of one pass will force the army to go in another direction, but the force of supply and demand will always exert its pressure. A generation of speeches in favor of the idyll of factories amidst the countryside were hardly noticeable, but the little matter of lower wages and taxes has changed the landscape of our society. In all this the market, like the ants, is thoroughly amoral. The Wildean cynic who knows the price of everything and the value of nothing is enshrined in the setting of the market.

This was, to be sure, the dread of moralists for ages, and especially in the Gilded Age of Victorian individualism. But we have seen how little money has to do with this. In recent years the importance of money has diminished substantially, and the less tangible but extremely important non-monetary factors have increased in weight. On the surface the impact of higher income and estate taxes has had much to do with this, as has the deadening effect of inflation, which tends to erode the meaning of money as a value. But in a larger sense the golden nineteenth-century security in the worth of wealth can now be seen as a sociological preference of a fairly brief era, a taste of that time. Socialism and, more important, social consciousness have inhibited the grandeur of affluence and the rewards of fortune, so that multimillionaires are timid and the rich secretive. In retrospect the flourishing of great wealth in the years from 1870 to 1930 was part of a historical phase, comparable perhaps to the aggrandizement of wealth in the early Roman Imperial period. To the inhabitants of Newport or the West End of London the sanctity of money and its unequal distribution seemed eternal, but the age when the rich had automobiles and the poor lacked bathtubs was very short indeed.

The ensuing age might have seen the despoiling of the rich and the end of the institutions of affluence. This happened in Russia, of course, after a time of surpassing inequality in the early twentieth century. But in the West the upshot has been technological advance for everyone and the income tax as a surrogate for revolution.

This has been a curious vindication of Aristotle's suggestion that private property and common use was the best economic system. The evolution of the modern tax system seems a peculiar answer to the pressures of modern demands, but in some ways it is in the great lower-center tradition of compromise between the pressures of equality and the dislocations of opportunity. Inasmuch as the trees do not grow to the skies, the unequal accumulation of wealth had to come to an end, and taxation—on the Anglo-American lines at least—has been a comparatively painless way. Of course, this has been a pruning and not a cutting, for the heights of wealth in the West are almost everywhere greater than they were in 1914 or 1929. The ratios of inequality tend to be less, however, and the Edwardian armies of servants and extravagances have been replaced by more expensive mechanical tools and less apparent, if often more costly opulence. But above all, it has been replaced by newer forms of spending and use of wealth, suitable for a system of life where even the poorest enjoy much of the new bounty of wealth. The post-bourgeois society affords too many people, even large portions of the working class in North America, Western Europe, and Australia, substantial aspects of the life of wealth, and so the richer must have other pleasures. As Gilbert foresaw in *The Gondoliers,* when everyone is somebody, why, then no one is anybody—but then the somebodies always manage to circumvent this fate. The simple Japanese home of the tycoon often conceals a prodigious expenditure of money, and the palatial yacht has tended to give way to the even more expensive, but little known, airplane. Above all, the new tycoon spends his money or enjoys his wealth through a corporation, in the form of perquisites rather than money.

Pay in the form of plush offices, convenient and emollient surroundings, and other intangible or at least untaxable goods has been subjected to the analysis of the new market theorists, who have attempted to fit these rewards into the broader value systems of economic choice. For instance, it has been suggested that in regulated industries excessive profits can be appropriated by the managers in the form of perquisites, and in this context more leisure (or its current aristocratic form, an otiose lack of hurry) is a prime example of such a good. These hidden increments can be viewed in different ways; to the free-market conservative they arise out of monopoly position, and it is significant that they thrive in the area of government. The public servant is likely to have a lower salary than his private counterpart, but also more freedom from the need to work hard, more vacations and sick leaves, and (at the suitable level) more limousines and ceremonial privileges. The lone entrepreneur maximizes money and minimizes the gaudy or leisurely extras. Viewed from the left, these extra goods are proof that the recent egalitarian developments of capitalism have only shifted the form of wealth, and not really changed it.

But this very shift is highly interesting. One of the causes for the intellectual disavowal of the individualist contractual schemata of the nineteenth century was the way in which that pattern of thought seemed to encourage, or at least sanction, the most unabashed worship of monetary success. The most agile crook or devious vulgarian was the hero of the Gilded Age, it seemed, and where Commodore Vanderbilt (who pretty well fit those descriptions) sat, there was the head of the table. It was not only convinced liberals or disappointed reactionaries who lamented this, for it seemed to strike at the basis of all intellectual value, especially in the United States, where it was most predominant. The speeches of Holmes, a conservative who made a success and felt a great stake in this very society, were as concerned as those of Henry Adams or Gustavus Myers with this cult of the businessman. When Coolidge stated that the business of America was business, Frankfurter corrected him by asserting that the business of America was civilization; today it is Frankfurter and not Coolidge who is the intellectual guide of the conservatives.

So business has become civilized, and businessmen talk—as they were already talking in Sinclair Lewis' *Babbitt*—the greater messages of service and public responsibility. Increasingly this has meant a growing emphasis on philanthropy. This is now too important, if not perhaps too wonderful, to be left to the Rockefellers, for even the pettier millionaires now have their foundations. Nor is it only an American phenomenon; much of the good works in Portugal are performed by the Gulbenkian foundation, and soon all the capitalist world will be riddled with these noble orders. The capitalist system may not be rushing toward socialism à la Schumpeter, but gliding toward its destruction, or permutation into a non-profit system.

But we have seen noble orders before; the phenomenon is reminiscent of medieval Europe or pre-Tokugawa Japan. No one has claimed that the seventeenth-century Englishman of means was a paragon of beneficence, yet Jordan has illustrated the incredible development of charity at that time. Learned Hand remarked that giving money away is perhaps the most supreme exercise of control over money which can be considered, and it can be argued that this can be seen throughout history. After a certain point all the consumable goods can be bought and consumed; it is an old cliché that a man can wear only so many clothes and eat so much food. Much of the pleasure in food and clothes comes from their distinctiveness—there must be many to whom *pâté de foie gras* and mink are status symbols. A Cadillac or a marble bathroom have their utilitarian values, but it is a safe bet that not many consumers of these articles buy them on that account. The task of the analysts of the market, of that greater market of today's thinking, is to weigh all of these emulative values alongside the simpler monetary values of the nineteenth century, and derive a system accordingly.

The term "emulation" calls to mind the ideas of Veblen, and it may well seem that an inspection of the nuances of privilege or prestige will confirm the theory of the leisure class. Veblen suggested that the fruits of power were the customs and nuances of leisure, of privileged splendor. He concluded that this was the invariable result of a society built on aristocratic values rather than on the pure values of the workman's society. But this Rousseauian faith in a noble way of life which was destroyed in the Stone Age was and is the unconvincing part of Veblen's theory—especially after our experience of managerial societies. The instinct of workmanship never seems to triumph— the Russian new man came forth, but Stalin made sure that it was the Party, and not the soviets, that governed, and his successors are politicians or perhaps (as may have almost happened in 1957) military men. The Nazis had their Speers whom they glorified but kept firmly in line. On the other hand, it cannot be said that these technocrats are devoted to freedom or humanity. Hallgarten points out that it was the owner-managers who tended to be against Hitler, and the organization men among the leaders of pre-Nazi German industry who supported the Nazis in 1932. A hypothesis that skilled craftsmen hold a more humane, cooperative view of social order might seem strange to civil-rights advocates in the United States or to Australians opposed to racial standards. Lipset has shown how faith in a workingman's class as a liberal or radical act of faith is foolish; the editors of *Dissent* dissent from mass culture almost as thoroughly as Ortega did, and find almost as little hope in the future culture of the masses.

Bereft of his naive beneficent instincts, Veblen's picture of motivation is a compendium of conservative insights. The important things in life gain their worth from the status afforded them, and as wealth has accumulated in our time the niceties grow more complex. Veblen, writing in the last years of the nineteenth century, believed that the new tycoons were coming to behave as Mandarins or Bourbon aristocrats, but he was in this merely too conservative—just as he mistook clean-shaven faces as an innovation unlikely to succeed among the upper classes. The forms are unimportant—it used to be that riches rode on horseback while the poor walked, and the former patronized the latter from on high, like El Greco's St. Stephen. Now when all the people have cars walking may be more elegant, or at least riding in sports cars so near the ground as to be almost groveling. Before the elevator the rich lived near the ground, and the attic was for paupers or bohemians; now it is the penthouse that commands the premium rent. Parvenus were always the ones most profligate with money, while the true *ton* preferred quality to quantity. These gradations increase as the standard of living increases, until the role of money becomes quite obscure.

Perhaps it always was obscure, and only the nineteenth century or the age of Petronius mistook it. Holmes, as usual, put it trenchantly when he remarked in his famous Harvard Law School

Association speech that the prize of the general is not a bigger tent, but command. It was unthinkable to Aristotle that wealth might mean more than political authority, and it is really unthinkable to the men of importance today. This is not merely a restatement of the primacy of the political over the economic, but a suggestion that in the last analysis economics is a branch of politics. The Vanderbilts quickly put their money to use in achieving social position; or in other words, in buying a form of fame. In so doing they took another way of establishing a social primacy which their forebears would have managed by converting their wealth from trade into land. But what is fame but the external symbol of importance, of social superiority (in both the narrow and larger sense of the word)? There are Father Josephs who will take power without fame, but in the main the two are interrelated aspects of political significance; and certainly power and influence, in Beveridge's sense, are twin forms of political worth. Warner has charted American social standing through the use of six criteria of prestige, for which he has been criticized for excessive concern with subjective standards. But Warner has merely written down what anyone who listens to the gossip of well-to-do Americans hears daily, and this talk seldom deals with money as an end in itself, any more than the gossip of fourteenth-century Flanders or Georgian England did. Wealth is so disappointing in itself; Schumpeter has well remarked how ineffective the Fuggers and the Morgans were in really exercising power in their heyday. The Victorian age may have had, as we have noted, a remarkably grave respect for private property and an awe of the workings of the financial system, but even the Rothschilds usually failed. Cavour outsmarted them, the Russian government paid less and less attention to them as time went along, and it was a singular triumph for the English branch to achieve merely the elimination of anti-Jewish parliamentary restrictions—a triumph made possible only by the victories of Whig ideology. As for the Rothschilds in the twentieth century, it is hardly necessary to go into detail how their power has counted for so little. Where a plutocrat wishes to be truly powerful, he must change his position. Rhodes is the perfect example; but Rhodes converted his money into power by building, literally, an empire. Nelson Rockefeller and Marcus Crassus are and were perhaps less crass; money is surely an asset to one who seeks power, but as these examples indicate, no certain passport to success. When Theodore Roosevelt inaugurated the Northern Securities lawsuit, Morgan was hurt and angered, and Roosevelt later commented that Morgan seemed to think of him as an adversary, an economic rival. Morgan almost always defeated those rivals, but the political ones were much more difficult. The Marxist would say that this is the façade, and one might, for argument's sake, admit it. Even so, what comes out in the end is a non-monetary system of values and a separate elite. If the tools of power are political and the distinction of importance is political, it will not take ambitious men long to realize that there are other ways to the top besides making money, and they will take them.

This may or may not leave the men of wealth in a perilous position. Throughout most of history even the most successful tycoons were very distinctly inferior to the political leaders in status and power, and to the extent that they became men of importance they grew vulnerable to the whims or policies of the ruler. The examples of Coeur and Fouquet in France and Yodoya in Japan bear witness to the ease with which the richest were dispossessed. The idea of socialism, of the concerted effort of the government to reduce the peaks of wealth, may be new (although the comments of Plato and the measures of Wang Mang leave this much open to doubt) but the sporadic leveling of the richest man is very old. Under the Roman Empire the property of the rich had a way of disappearing into the hands of the imperial *fiscus,* which was formally the private property of the emperor but became more and more, as time went along, the basis of state wealth. Instead of the risk of confiscation at death, allayed perhaps by judicious bequests, we now have estate taxation.

This confusion of private and public, this rendering of the world of business into an adjunct of the world of politics, was just what the Whigs disliked. The previously-mentioned examples of concern for the distinction between private property and public authority was a hard-won accomplishment wrested from the principle that wealth was an inferior form of power, and must be considered as such. In a way, the development of feudalism was a similar victory; the theory that the men of the thirteenth century were early Whigs has relied in part on the fragmentation of power which that culture afforded. A feudal baron was not a provincial governor, and the avenues of status and power were sufficiently diffused to allow many chains of social or political command. But what the medieval world lacked was the sharp distinction between public and private; the Whig system centralized political power while it separated it from economic and social influence. The prize example was the Third French Republic, where the political, financial, and social leaders inhabited different milieus; the schemata of current New Haven, as drawn by Dahl, is not so dissimilar.

It cannot be said that this view is well accepted on the left. To many this smacks of an egregious, perhaps a devious naiveté. Money may not be the measure but, it is maintained, it will buy the scales in any case. The contemporary talk about the "establishment" and the "power structure," insofar as it is not trivial name-calling or a political phrase, emphasizes the control exercised by the very rich and their allies (or tools). And, after all, if the key things in life are power and fame, does not money buy these—at least in the Western world today? The continual decline of the older aristocratic traditions in Europe and Africa is taken to mean that, except for socialist or Communist lands, money is the chief standard. Perhaps it always was, *au fond;* Napoleon was merely being realistic when he prescribed that his aristocracy must retain sufficient wealth to uphold their position. When the Roman senators had to beg Tiberius for imperial pensions to maintain their status, the game was up for the Senate; when the sixteenth-century Japanese emperors were reduced to penury their power was nil. It is a common argument on the left, not reserved to Marxists, that much of the talk about the separation of private and public is misleading; under a strong capitalist system Morgan will govern; even under a weak one a Bismarck or De Gaulle will serve as a guardian and proponent of the business interests of his country.

This is the point where modern scholarship has pricked so many radical balloons. Power will settle matters of wealth rather than the other way around. Wherever one looks at the most complacently big-business—or allegedly so—governments, one finds the inferiority of the rich. That paradigm of the plutocrat, the Orleanist monarchy, was run by journalists and professors who at times, such as during the Spanish Marriage crises, ignored the advice of the Bourse. President McKinley may have been the creature of Mark Hanna and the ideal statesman of the *haute bourgeoisie,* but his war policy infuriated Carnegie and went against the opinion of the principal business leaders, as Pratt has shown, while the high tariff enacted by his party outraged the principles of the greatest intellectual defender of capitalism, William Sumner. The merchant and banker communities almost always have sought peace, and yet the great conflicts have always pushed aside their flimsy opposition. It may be that the Rothschilds prevented a European war in 1864, but if so, such power was very much the exception rather than the rule; usually the great triumphs of pacifism have been the result neither of millionaires nor of pacifists, but of calculating diplomats, such as Metternich. The power structure usually turns out to be a deceptive building, with the strangest people in charge, or nobody at all. Dahl has suggested that the influence of the chief business figures is greatly exaggerated in the United States today (and the influence of social leaders almost nil), and what is true here and now was probably at least as much so in the past. Too often there is a confusion between buying honor and achieving power; the period of James I in England, for instance, was marked by the purchase of so many positions of dignity by the moneyed class that the old aristocracy feared for their status, yet not even Tawney claims that the rich ruled England at that time.

But surely money is good for something; the status symbols of Warner are in the main purchasable symbols, like James' baronetcies. The vital task is to put this into its proper perspective, and this is, like almost everything else, a political task. The gravest fault of the nineteenth century was to think that making money and owning property could be relegated to a sphere all its own. The ideal type of the prudent, thrifty man, working hard and saving his money, thereby increasing his possessions without the aid of the state, may have owed a little of its strength to the Calvinist or Methodist ethic, but it differed from those tenets by setting up an individualist system which could be shut off, like a section in a well-compartmentalized ship, from the political system. It was the dream of the bourgeoisie that the impositions of the state, or of any external system, could be eliminated, and that included even the demands of public opinion. This was all very well for a furtive, somewhat persecuted business class; it was expected that Huguenots or Jews would be concerned with money for its own sake, and hide it from the evil eye of the people and the state. But if the rich were the top class, this was another matter. The Quakers in Pennsylvania were unable to retain all the qualities they nurtured in lands of persecution. De Jouvenel has pointed out that the mass of people expect the rich to spend money on a grand scale, so as to permit them vicarious enjoyment and to establish a sense of grandeur at the social apex. To a great extent movie stars or singers do this today, and the thrifty rich are disliked as mean, in both senses of the word. The advocates of the free market often use the example of baseball players to defend large salaries; is this because the public can appreciate the spirit of sudden glory so much better than the (from a consistent market view) much more useful efforts of the commercial rich? From the point of view of economics, the peril of Victorian business-mindedness is too much saving, a problem which seemed so outlandish fifty years ago but now is well accepted just at a time when its crushing solution, inflation, may have rendered it a puny bogey. Wealth is one form of status, not the only one but important enough to be judged, willy-nilly, by sociological standards.

Most important of all, wealth becomes a danger when it supersedes other forms of status. It is likely that the so-called estrangement of the intellectual from the businessman, a matter of dispute at any rate, can be largely traced to one main sore point: the tendency of society to say at times—especially in the America of 1890, for instance—if you are so smart, why aren't you rich? The market fails as a political system when this results, for this means that the broad interchange of value orientations has broken down, or has been transformed like Croesus' furniture into lumps of gold. It is not surprising in those circumstances that the losers in the economic competition should demand a change in the rules, inasmuch as the game has become so paramount. If community leadership were determined by skill at golf, there would very shortly be a radical transformation of water hazards. This applies to the whole matter of worldly success, of course; a condition where rewards are evenly apportioned for success in one line must create a dangerous tension among the failures. Hayek remarks that value is a much better criterion for social success than merit, for if there were but the single yardstick of real worth, all the losers or deviants would have an unendurable life. Reisman points out that a society thoroughly based on merit might well be insupportable. Even in the Ming dynasty it was possible in some cases to enter the Chinese civil service without success in the examinations, although these tests—the great model for all meritocracies—did serve to stifle centuries of heterodoxy or originality. Socialists have long fumed that one talks of how much a man is worth, meaning how much money he can command. Yet there is something to be said for that, in that this is one form (it would be tragic were it the only one) of worth which does not depend on birth or compatibility with the accepted dogma. That, of course, is the reason that minorities so often become skilled moneymakers, and it is why a thoroughly cosmopolitan city or small country will so often be noted for extraordinary new shoots of creativity and an unquenchable zest for profits—seventeenth-century Amsterdam and twentieth-century New York, for example. There is always the danger that money will become too important, but this is not a grave threat today. The power of the state and the cult of art have combined in our times to present various avenues to importance, so that the exercise of financial power can be accepted today as it could not fifty or seventy-five years ago, without fear that this might, through arrogance and philistinism, stifle other value structures.

This is all the more so because the secretive virtues of the middle class have triumphed so. The defect of thrift has its virtue —lack of ostentation—and it is a very great virtue. The most disliked feature of inequality is the stigmata of distinction or the assumption of superiority. This is why the aspiring classes of colonial countries (and their social equivalents in the mother countries) are the most rebellious. The United States of 1880 or of 1968 was and is by no means egalitarian, but the comparative absence of hauteur is more important than the distribution of wealth. It is significant that only in the one area where economic distinctions interrelate with racial antagonism and traditions of caste inferiority does an element of bitterness exist. Britain gnaws over language/class differences after an epoch of social legislation, while the much greater disparities of wealth and tongues in Switzerland seem to arouse very little bitterness. The quiet millionaire may be less fun but better for the long pull than the brave spendthrift. Moreover, the development of the modern corporate form has created a class of absentee shareholders who make up a kind of aristocracy, suggesting that there may be a group of social leaders within the capitalist system who maintain the traditional distance from business, while at the same time the corporations and their chief executives occupy another distinctive role. Diversity provides the ferment which a simple awe of wealth might ruin, yet it is consistent with the existence of that wealth.

This has assumed the existence of various social and economic classes with differing material circumstances and prestige. This is the key issue of most left/right differences, of course, since equality is the badge of radicalism, and economic equality has been the most important issue of politics since at least 1848. How can one justify a system where one man has more than another, or even more, where the most hard-pressed or hard-working have less than others more luxuriously situated? And if there be some justification, how can one accept the present degree?

These sentiments have prevailed even among defenders of the free market. Adam Smith, it is now generally agreed, was an advocate of greater equality, and his successors as a rule were emotionally on the side of the angelic egalitarians. Marshall started his career as an economist with a desire to find an answer to poverty, and he always opposed the socialists on tactical rather than fundamental grounds. In a political democracy it is natural for conservatives to say that equality is a worthy goal, but that efforts to use the power of the state will do more harm than good. Before 1917 this often took the form of denying that socialism could possibly succeed; but in the last half-century we have witnessed the effective carrying out of revolutions which have wiped out the wealth of large classes, down to even petty proprietors whom in the nineteenth century no one would have dreamed would be vulnerable to confiscation. Moreover, the advances of technology have greatly increased the sum total of wealth, so that it seems that we need no longer always have the poor with us. The revolution of rising expectations, so we are told, compels us to quit hiding behind the old excuse that inequality is necessary for economic growth. The state will do the saving to provide money for expansion, and the world is rich enough to divide up its wealth and still not submerge all of culture below a minimum line of subsistence. In short, the old arguments that man was incapable of providing for equality without destroying all his other values is no longer true; man now seems very capable, and growing steadily more so.

The nineteenth-century arguments from capability always had an Achilles heel, for they presumed that there was only one goal (economic growth) and only one way to get there. But Lincoln Steffens could look into the future and see it work, meaning that he could see that there were other ways of arranging our capabilities. Russia has had economic growth, and it has permitted absolutely no capitalism whatsoever; to be sure there is one rub—the Soviet Union is not egalitarian. In the deepest sense the old cynical disbelief in equality was right, but one must look farther. Instead of feudal magnates or financial and industrial tycoons, there are Party leaders. The pictures of Khrushchev's villa show that the gap between top and bottom of the scale did not perish even under his "creeping socialism"; as for

Stalin, so many commentators, including the Yugoslavian socialist Djilas, have pointed out the remarkable income variants that this has become a stale subject. China does not appear to be so stratified as yet; this takes time (although Fainsod points out that the Smolensk Archives disclosed an amazingly rapid weakening of the Communist fiber much earlier than many had thought) and an attenuation of zeal. Nyére is finding it harder to enforce equality among the cadres than it was to expropriate the capitalists.

This is also perhaps a matter of capacity—the ability of human political systems to maintain a state of affairs which goes against the grain. That very metaphor suggests that it is perhaps more a matter of human goodness, of the spirit of man. Men are able to share among their immediate family, even perhaps among a looser family; very, very few can go much beyond that, and a great many can see no point in sharing with anyone else. Fromm postulates that a general love of humanity precedes and is more general than the individual love of a person or a few people; one is tempted to repeat the remark of the Duke of Wellington on being asked if his name were Smith, "if you believe that, you would believe anything." As Gordis, a biblical scholar, has remarked of a psalmist's speeches, these "might be a prayer or a pious hope; they were scarcely the result of empirical observation!" Confidence in equality presupposes a more elevated view of human nature than belief in liberty, for liberty only allows each man to go his way, but equality assumes that society can exist when all men go their way with the same fortune.

Nature, of course, starts men with glaring inequalities: distinctions of height, health, ability, and looks, which at times seem monstrous. But this is not conclusive, for man is able to balance these wrongs. Children born in the developed nations today have a vastly higher minimum of good health; they are likely to grow up stronger, hardier, and taller than any but a few could in past ages or other societies. Even appearance can be partly altered by artificial means. And if not, why should not the ugly people have compensatory advantages—a thought which must have stirred many of our twentieth-century autocrats, to judge from pictures. Yet there are too many ugly, and sick, and beaten men to whom no society has given the highest palm.

Medical science has indeed raised the well-being and life expectancy of the masses everywhere. Yet in some respects medical achievements have been an anti-egalitarian force, for as expensive cures have been developed diseases which once leveled rich and poor alike can be checked, but this process may require much time and expense to be used generally. Socialized medical services aim to eliminate these differences, but where any treatment is rare or exceptional this may accentuate them, for (as in the army) in cases where the market is outlawed absolute priorities must be determined, and the less fortunate must wait their turn. Even the clearest examples of progress do not produce an egalitarian system.

This does not imply that the overall minimum of public health and individual care has not been improved enormously in the West; it does suggest that that improvement renders the remaining disabilities and the new pains, and their social effect, often even more unpleasant because more noticeable. If physical stature is a desirable quality, it makes little difference if the minimum is raised; this may only tend to make the distinctions more deeply-felt, while the height distribution tends to remain basically unchanged even if the dimensions are different. The underlying truth behind the argument for inequality from nature is the constant presence of the bell-shaped curve marking the distribution of almost all quantities. Slichter suggested that this truth, easily acceptable when it refers to biological or ecological factors, explains the persistence of inequality in social and economic situations.

Pareto systematized this into a famous law, which he specified in regard to income but applied freely throughout the range of social conditions. In the 1920's Josiah Stamp, the English economist, discovered a remarkably even historical pattern of income distribution in Great Britain, and a consistent story elsewhere. Since then the depression, the Second World War, and the vicissitudes of inflation and labor-union pressure have intervened, and many students have concluded that Pareto has been repealed. Yet in the last decade there has been a tendency for the prewar patterns to reappear, for the curve to take on the older forms as if by inexorable force. In fact, it may be that the dislocations of the 1940's were largely a statistical error, the result of concealed earnings or faulty reckoning. The pendulum of income distribution is Galilean, and swings in a prescribed fashion even when it has been seized on the left by vigorous hands aiming to change the rhythm. As for the distribution of wealth, it has been even more stable over the years.

Why is this so? Under a pure free market—and of course no such thing has ever existed—one can hypothesize a natural distribution of talents which works itself out into a distribution of income. The rewards allocated to labor and capital will, under classical economic theory, shift to account for varying conditions but in the long run, and usually even in the short run, they will even out; land is a greater problem but the experience of the last 150 years has been that this too will fit into the pattern of the market without giving one group a permanent edge. If some important new variable occurs the relationships will change at once—as happened, say, when gold was discovered in California and Australia; but within a few years this will be assimilated, like the waves of the sea as their impact is spent on the sands. The Ricardians thought that this doomed the laboring class to a fixed wage, reasoning that Malthus' laws would see to it that the population growth would eat up the surplus; Marx carried this to the next step by formulating a law of diminishing wages. In fact, technological advance has steadily increased the real wages of the workers in capitalist lands; the iron law of wages applies only to the share of the income, and as the total grows that share, in absolute terms, grows *pari passu*. The restraint on that share is the availability of labor, but just so the availability of capital limits *its* share. As profits increase the opportunities for capital do also, and it appears (although this has been the subject of great controversy) that in the United States the proportion of corporate profits, after taxes, to other income and as a return on sales and investment has remained remarkably stable over the last thirty years, despite the numerous social changes. One year, even one decade may see great changes, but the balance is restored.

This flies in the face of one of the firmest beliefs of our time, a belief shared by both the friends and enemies of equality. Many who would readily accept the judgment that progress has been a mirage do accept the fact of increasing equality. But the closer one looks at the changes the less there is to see. For one thing, the present age is not more accessible to rapid social mobility. The opportunities available to poor boys in sixteenth- and seventeenth-century England, before and after the Civil War, must have been—if one accepts the evidence of Aubrey—at least as great as that today. Greater, perhaps, for the "old boy's network" was weaker in the twilight days of feudalism than it has been in our socialistic century, in socialistic Britain. It is now more important than ever before to have a college degree, here and abroad, and the chance for a person who has missed that degree by the age of twenty-five is poorer than ever. Perhaps a social revolution is now necessary to accomplish the swift change which the early modern period took for granted; the permanent revolution may be over, not begun. For every period like the second century B.C. in Rome, when mobility seems to have frozen, there are others like the fifth century in Greece, where there was little stability. The biblical complaint that the beggars rode while princes walked did not refer to a revolution, but merely to an unrecognized period of social unrest—even Allen would not have said that of our "big change."

We pride ourselves on our lack of hauteur, on the disappearance of monarchical grandeur or the mystique of aristocracy. Yet the President of the United States is not only more removed, physically and in terms of the size of his retinue, from the average citizen today than any of his predecessors were, but this remove rivals that of many of the Oriental despots. It has been said that Nehru would see anyone who came to visit him, but this was an anachronism even in his time. As house servants are allegedly disappearing, the apparatus of service is multiplying in official and corporate life, so that while the political and business leader of one hundred years ago might have written his own letters, even his sub-assistant has it done for him today.

To take another example, the gap between rich and poor has been subjected to more criticism, and to more remedial action, than any other problem of our time. Surely the poor are now more like the rich, surely the very idea of being poor has lost much of its poignancy in the advanced countries. Harrington has pointed out the flaws in the latter assumption, for if there are fewer at the bottom of the heap that very fact will make their plight more pitiful. It is not necessarily true that the best things of life are now almost available, more or less, to all; if the rich no longer have a monopoly on silk stockings, air conditioning now often is the mark of prosperity. The physical separation between the classes, which scarcely existed in medieval Venice or ancient Rome, has tended to increase in the modern age, until the suburb of the rich has become a standard of American life (supported in part by elitist zoning laws). In part, this is a result of the age of the common man, since an upper class which cannot lord it over the others may naturally seek to keep its distance. Santayana, in *The Last Puritan,* remarks of the shrewish Mrs. Alden that "the relation between masters and servants seemed to her profoundly inhuman, profoundly immoral—her moral idea was democracy, but a democracy of the elect—beyond the pale there could be nothing but outer darkness—an alien, heathen, unintelligible world, to be kept as remote as possible—luckily in America the immigrant working class lived apart in their own districts and tenements, like Jews in a ghetto. One need have no personal contact with them." This is more a distinction between centuries than between countries; even in modern Italy and Russia the villa or *dacha* is becoming the home of the elite, rather than their retreat. Aries marks "the great difference between the two societies, that of the seventeenth century and the twentieth century; the difference between a society in which people were carefully ranked but were mixed up in a common space, and a society which is egalitarian but in which the classes are kept apart in separate spaces." Special benches for aristocratic youngsters, such as those disclosed by Aries, shocks us, but it does not seem so odd that there should be separate schools. As one form of distinction is broken down another seems to come up; the intensities of race differentiation in the United States came in periods

(1830–60, 1890–1915) marked by strong egalitarian movements in white society; the victory of the Afrikaan class in South Africa is a perfect example of this.

One further consideration is in order. Many of the reform movements of the last two hundred years have been anti-egalitarian, in result if not (and sometimes deliberately) in theory. The effort to improve legal education in Georgian England had, as Lucas remarks, aristocratic overtones, as the elimination of apprenticeship training for the law in our time has limited the access of the poor. The civil-service movement was considered by many Jacksonians as a device to fill the offices of state with the well-born, a motive perhaps shared by the British Tories in their moves to upgrade the Indian civil service by tying the examinations to the courses at Oxford and Cambridge. These developments were no less inegalitarian for being both well meant or conducive to efficiency and good government; it is quite possible that intelligent men can put equality low in their scale of values for a good society. The immigration acts of the 1920's were undoubtedly some of the most effectively elitist laws ever passed, and the proponents included a large share of the most humane and well-regarded social thinkers of our recent past. Inequality, then, is not an expiring condition, but the result of either natural conditions or well-intentioned laws, or both. Even when the laws are enacted with the purpose of bringing about more equality, the result may be just the contrary. The legacy of the homestead laws, if one would believe many progressive critics, was much more to open up the West to a band of wealthy corporations than it was to ensure a farm for every willing worker, just as the free-incorporation laws have helped the Rockefellers and Mellons more than they have the filling-station operators. The Napoleonic tax reforms stood in the way of an income tax in late-nineteenth-century France when less revolutionary lands, such as Germany and Britain, had designed systems of taxation which were much more egalitarian. With time even the most searing changes will produce new systems, but also new forms of inequality.

A set of high, egalitarian taxes or a strong system of leftward controls acts to a great extent like a gold rush; it very much alters the status quo for the moment, but somehow the ratios return after a while, like the ants in our metaphor. For example, in the developed capitalist nations the use of taxation to reduce income inequalities became a major tool of left-of-center governments after 1930. This was not surprising nor was it new—the demand for this was made not only by Marx but by Wendell Phillips, and as early as 1894 Harcourt startled the British bourgeoisie by declaring that "we are all socialists" on proposing a tax increase which we would now consider trifling. The democratic socialists were debarred by their principles and the political realities from confiscating property outright, so that nationalization had limited value for egalitarian purposes without a tax system which would cut into the proceeds. During the 1930's and 1940's there was much talk of the rapid demise of great wealth; the new tax structures, with sharply ascending schedules culminating in more than 90 per cent levies, combined with even more crushing estate taxes would, in a few generations or sooner, cut everyone down to size. But the result has been very different. The normal development in Europe and America has been this:

1. In order to permit the system to work, exceptions have multiplied. The depletion allowance for oil income, the tax-free status of municipal bonds, and the special provisions for timber, iron ore, and livestock revenue are examples from American tax law; the exceptional status of foreign real estate (until recently) and the weakness of the gift-tax provisions in Britain are analagous. The corporate form has been the principal avenue of this special treatment, the best road of escape from the tax burden. Through the use of more-than-adequate depreciation allowances (significantly especially generous in Sweden, where the tax laws have long been very egalitarian) there has undoubtedly been a substantial postponement of tax liability, which can be prolonged as long as investment is sustained or increased. The corporate managers gain through taking as much as possible of their income in the form of expense accounts—once again most notable where the surtax rates are most steep. Above all, the cumulative growth of corporations is to the largest extent possible internally financed,

so that the lower corporate-tax rate is paid on the profits and the shares held by individuals are then sold at lower capital-gains rates or without any tax at all. All these and many more are often characterized by critics as "loopholes," another magic word which sometimes is intended to terminate discussion. One man's loophole is another man's simple equity; from the social point of view the key fact is that they make a private property system work by reducing the otherwise killing burden of taxes. The conservative argument that high taxes must stifle enterprise has not been substantiated on the whole just because, in these important ways, the effective tax rate has been much less than the apparent rate. This seems strange to many critics, for these tax laws are devised by representatives of the electorate, most of whom even in Texas are not beneficiaries of such largesse or special privilege (as this seems so often). But it always turns out that there is more to each exception than its bare bones, and uprooting is like hacking at tree roots; as often as not, a subcommittee bent on extirpation will create more exceptions than it destroys. As the laws grow more complex the needs for exceptions increase, and these needs lead to more provisions; once again, the simplifiers invariably write longer and longer statutes. It is a mark of the new breadth of conservative-liberal thinking in our time, and the real influence of conservatism, that the Kennedy administration recognized that a frontal attack on this required a lower rate-structure before all else. There are two choices in each case; to greatly reduce the seeming progressiveness of the tax structure, or to allow it to become increasingly riddled with exceptions.

This does not enter into the rightness of the progressive principle. As Hayek has observed, much of the psychological bases of the case for progressive taxation have been outmoded by the current mistrust of arguments of mass utility. Hayek, as a believer in natural law, does not mark what this signifies; it is a part of the relativist consensus of our thought that leads us to decide that there is no accounting for tastes, so that one man's marginal utility need not be even similar to another's. Two scholars sympathetic to the idea of progressive taxation, Blum and Kalvin, were compelled in their seminal work to admit that the case in its favor was "uneasy" and logically unsatisfactory. There is a close connection between this realization and the increased sophistication of attitudes toward wealth; as one views the opportunities of great wealth, or even comparatively small increments, as being vastly varied and highly psychological, the older assumptions about the rich man needing his seventh shirt less than the poor man requires his second seem very foolish. The rich man may want to exercise power, and this may be psychologically more compelling than seventy shirts. Furthermore, the power may, or in a different sense, must, be seized by someone, so that if it is not bought in place of shirts it may be grabbed by someone else who is substituting it for another good—in many cases invisible goods which may affect the social order more directly, like labor peace or honest government. Everything has its price, and everything has a value; so many of the leftist arguments against the use of money by the rich are similar to the rightist arguments about use by the state. It is not therefore surprising that in a capitalist system the choices for using money will tend to return, like a diverted stream, to the points of maximum flow. One might almost say that, as in Hayekian terms value is superior to merit as a tool, so value provides the real measure of superior utility, and the tax laws will be bent to afford these greater urges the needed scope. Of course it is not so simple as that; the money flows toward the new exceptions and builds around them, changing the economy of course, but also reworking the tax structure to fit the external demands.

2. But the high tax rates were not merely exercises of socialistic fiscal planning. Far from it; they were largely brought about because of the concomitant need for money on the part of the state, sometimes to pay for welfare measures, such as pension or subsidy programs, but very often to pay for wars. These costs remain and grow. Their beginnings are often—especially in the case of welfare expenditures—billed as subventions from the rich to the poor. At times this is deliberately a form of political insurance, in Joseph Chamberlain's phrase, for the well-off. But we have seen that, by and large, the rich do not get soaked, and even if they did they simply do not, as a myriad of statisticians have

demonstrated, have enough income to finance these costs. So the mass of people are taxed for their own welfare, or for the benefit of the military. This surely requires little explication today, after the base tax rate, which brings in the great majority of all direct tax revenues almost everywhere, has become obvious to even the poorest citizen. But what does come as a surprise is how politicians, very often aggressively liberal ones at that, can advocate as part of a welfare system a levy to be paid largely by the working class to benefit a more affluent group. Nathan Straus, the New Deal reformer, advocated in the late 1940's a program in New York for the construction of housing for middle-income families, the cost of which was to be paid from the new taxes on vending machines, admissions to amusements, patent medicines, tobacco other than cigarettes, and rents. By and large this tax would either have fallen regressively (in the case of medicine and tobacco, probably very much so) or would have been a barrier against improvement in the standard of living of the very poor. The gain would have been enjoyed by a group quite able to look after itself. This seems surprising to us: it was familiar to the Whig tax reformers of the eighteenth and nineteenth centuries, who were fighting high indirect taxes levied to pay for the sinecures and pensions of placemen. An even more well-grooved feature of taxation is the military requirement which grows on itself, so that the left and the right connect their ideological pipes to its flow. A crisis arises, and taxes are raised. The crisis subsides, and the left proposes diverting the revenue to a worthy cause ("Think what we could do with those billions spent on arms toward feeding and housing the miserable!"). The right rejoins that military needs must never be subordinated. The right cannot deprecate the miserable and their need, which would be callous, and the left is inclined to support the military program, if it must, rather than be guilty of lack of patriotism; it also wants the money to be around for a future time, when it can win its way. Meanwhile, it is very likely the working-class man who is doing most of the paying.

Of course high taxes do bear upon people of wealth, in some cases quite stringently, and there is some real progression in the tax laws. But the press of the circumstances spelled out above hold a limit, given the bounds of a viable capitalist economy, on this progression. Therefore new levies tend to come out of the pockets of lower-income brackets. Often this is made very explicit, to the credit of the honesty of the explicators. When further medical benefits were proposed in Sweden in 1959 as part of the consolidation of the extensive Swedish socialist medical program, it was specifically admitted that there was no expectation of obtaining the money from the rich; the funds were raised by taxes falling on the less affluent. It is the payroll taxes, often used to finance the pension, medical, and unemployment payment programs, which have risen most in the last decade and which always go up. We have noted how this has become a nightmare in Chile; Italy and France are not so far behind. Often this is in the form of a tax on employers, but of all taxes this is the most easily shifted, either backward on wages or forward onto the consumers. It is not impossible that the working-class attitude toward taxes may return to the medieval hatred; at the very least it is foolish to believe that everyone will be delighted in a bureaucratic control of income, merely because the bureaucrats and their superiors are democratically responsible.

Above all, this displeasure is likely to fall on the wealthy people or institutions who gain most. The likeliest targets of popular anger may well be the corporations gaining by government contracts or enjoying what may seem unjustifiable tax advantages when everyone is paying taxes. The value of corruption to the interested parties naturally increases in this bureaucratic environment, and at the same time the political dangers multiply. It is vital that capitalism not become mistaken for a sort of parasitic system in which success depends on whom you know or how much you pay. The gravest dangers do not come from the ordinary sort of bribery and favoritism, for those are old and unremarkable vices. It is the symbiosis of politics and business, the nurturing of uncompetitive industries whose future rests on the determination of governmental decisions which may discredit the capitalist system. Eisenhower warned, in his memorable farewell address, against the industrial-military complex which might lead to just this sort of condition. It is not only business which can come to rely on these favors; whole regions can become clients of a military or space project, or beneficiaries of a subsidy program; once the politico-economic roots are imbedded, the expenditures may go on forever, supporting a segment of the population without regard to their economic value or need. The highest ideals of liberalism often end up as arguments for these situations; that is the best reason for their success. In the United States one can enumerate many of these: urban renewal programs which often serve to benefit a powerful corporation or association (and often help to keep racial integration from developing), rural-electrification subsidies which benefit large companies, small-business loans whose criteria are political and whose beneficiaries are rich. All of these programs originated in campaigns against inequality; more inequality is often the result. Moreover, this kind of inequality fosters an atmosphere of favoritism and dependence, those very qualities which capitalism should and historically did minimize.

3. The final consequence is therefore quite frequently new patterns of unequal income and status, but patterns developed through governmental or other institutional constraint, and not by the market. This can be noted in semi-developed economies which have struck a pragmatic compromise between socialism, capitalism, and a sort of bastard patriarchal society. The Latin-American dictatorships have been most susceptible to this condition, as the new *jefe* and his crew tended to become ex officio members of the aristocracy and patrons of the rising entrepreneurs (if the entrepreneur does not want a patron, he will not likely be rising very long). This is unfortunately not confined to dictatorships: one of Mexico's greatest problems has been these pernicious ties between a revolutionary party and its plutocratic friends and members. This is, in a broader sense, the vice of the developing economy; the German and American tariff histories and the Japanese economic-political relationships have manifested a great deal of these relationships. In a way, one can look at mercantilism as an earlier form of this system, but with an important distinction. Mercantilist theory and usually practice was

an extension of the political theory and form of the state, an extension of political order and decision-making into economics, and it customarily reflected the right-wing concerns of the monarchs or the attitudes of the richest and most important groups. The quasi-capitalism with which we deal begins at least ostensibly as a part of proposals aimed at changing the economy through the state. Often these proposals derive from and more often use the impulses of liberal or even radical ideas. At times the state is not even a factor; it is ironic how much of the new class system is the result of the pressures of unions, especially unions of skilled workers, who seek and at times succeed in freezing some gradation. This has been most noted in the construction industry, where highly paid craftsmen, by keeping their wages high through monopoly tactics, often price housing out of the reach of poorer groups. This is similar to the guild behavior of the medieval and early modern period, but instead of being a part of an established authoritarian order, it now usually poses as a constituent element of social democracy, or at least of a democratically-oriented society. In comparatively poor economies these patterns often seem as strange as a great, twisted tropical tree; in richer lands they blend into the governmental and commercial forest as part of the arboreal landscape. And in the end, it is not easy to distinguish one form of inequality or fortune from another; to some economists and sociologists, and not all of them Marxists, privilege is so omnipresent that everything reeks of it.

At the worst, one thing leads to another in a vicious circle of favoritism and privilege. Yet it is not fair to draw too sharp a vignette; there is, even from a conservative viewpoint, some truth to the picture of capitalism as necessarily involving these inequalities. There is no such thing as a pure free market, and the impingements of government and institutional forces must always be taken into account. As we have noted, much of these inequalities arise, at least in their genesis, from a rough sort of compromise between the thrust of idealism and the exigencies of the economic system. These latter needs are often as vital to the public order as any of the considerations of the market; candidates to public office who are suspected of wishing to abolish social-insurance programs either disavow such reports, or they tend to do very, very badly. Beyond that, all of government involves non-market factors, and to that degree they imply an encouragement of these forms of inequality. Unless one has a supreme respect for human nature the need for police must be accepted, yet it is in that department that the most primitive, perhaps primordial forms of corruption come forth. The nineteenth-century distinction between "honest" and "dishonest" graft seems hackneyed today, like its partner the sexual double standard, but it is by no means dead. Honest graft corresponds, in a muddy way, to custom, to systems of habitual performance admittedly of a lower grade than honest trade; these systems do bridge the gap of the rigors of the market and loosen the joints of the stern benevolence of the state. Often, in the heyday of Victorian individualism, the forces of good government thought that corruption was a bitter excrescence, perhaps even a sign of racial inferiority. Our broader historical view sees that corruption is often a sign of social ferment, as in post-Civil War America, or a substitute for the passions of a more terrible age, as in Georgian England. It is not true that totalitarian regimes are pure; the Fascist dictatorships were notoriously corrupt. However, in these regimes, and in many other highly authoritarian systems, it is the pure who are most awful. Himmler was undoubtedly more austere than Goering, and presumably Eichmann than either; a man who cannot be bribed may be uncontrollably wicked, and so may a society. Charles II of England did not wish to go on his travels again, and he delighted in a toleration of shady conduct and religious freedom—not the worst combination, by any means. The great fault of Louis XIV was not the sums spent on Versailles, which may have been well worth it in the long run, but the invasion of the Palatinate and the revocation of the Edict of Nantes, which brought consequences far more undesirable over time.

The venial sins tend to be assuaged by time; and absolutely fervent free-market conservatism may end up with the worst of both worlds—a general unpopularity and a too-rigid system of economics—unless it understands that politics is more than a page of Marshallian diagrams. The imposed inequalities of a state-controlled capitalism are not the desiderata of our society, but their removal must be coordinated with a program designed to change their causes, or the result may be worse.

To a radical this will surely seem like an admission of the corrupt nature of conservative thought. If corruption is simply evil there is but one thing to do with it—uproot it, if it takes Robespierrian efforts or not. As for the needs of society which cause inequality, this must seem a wretched bit of nonsense to one with a radically high confidence in humanity. Of course radicals of all types will admit capitalism dies hard, but as Laski has warned us, the rich will stop at nothing to prevent their fall, and this includes the establishment of corrupt regimes—a sure sign of monopoly capitalism, for that matter. The difficulties of making capitalism work despite governmental intervention can be eliminated if you eliminate capitalism; the state will take care of investment and the tendencies of profit will not seek other outlets; they will be totally suppressed.

Until 1917 this could be derided as hopelessly impractical, but a very large part of the world now operates on this principle, and it is all too possible that much of the Southern Hemisphere may be converted to it. Nowhere has communism proved to be a complete failure, and it is undeniable that the industrial output of the Soviet Union has grown with remarkable speed since the Russian Revolution. Nor is it enough to say that these societies result in a great deprivation of liberty, for that is not the question. If the prime desideratum is equality, then it is no use to warn people that they will lose their freedom; many do not care (although few will admit that; freedom comes next to a sense of humor as every man's birthright) and others will subordinate it to equality as the chief goal.

The flaw in this we have noted; there is thorough inequality in Communist societies as well as in capitalist ones. The most important truth—and that word is used advisedly—which has been slow to be admitted is that a system in which the state owns all the means of production and distribution, or the great majority, need not be egalitarian. By and large, the experience of history is to the contrary. One of the most thoroughly state-controlled and ordered political-economic systems of the ancient world was Ptolemaic Egypt, a society which derived its efficient centralism from three millennia of Egyptian experience and the most modern skills of Greek intellectuals and soldiers. Colin Clark suggests that the highly developed royal monopoly system of the Ptolemies contributed to the low real income of the masses. During the later years of the Roman Empire, while the legal and social distinctions between *honestiores* and *humiliores* was widening and when the imperial dignity was shifting from an office to a sanctity, the scope of government monopolies and imperial power grew. Frequently during periods of stress various Chinese dynasties would nationalize the salt industry; the motive, it is generally agreed, was profit for the state and not advancement for the workers. So too, the railroads were brought under state ownership in the Hohenzollern Empire for reasons of national policy and not because the Junkers were Tory socialists; the Mexican railways were nationalized by the arch-conservative Cientificos for the same reason.

Economic freedom often seems, as in the late nineteenth century, an excuse for big business or a refuge of business apologists. But the current effort of American corporations to use the law to prevent ex-employees from using trade secrets or from competing in areas of special expertise is a current reminder that economic mobility and opportunity very often favor the little man. Maximum wages long predated minimum waves, just as mercantilism now often seems Keynesianism upside down. The long historical question is, of course, what is right side up? In the twenty-first century the Adam Smiths may be liberal again; in Russia that may come much sooner.

In the ideally hierarchical society the state would own all the economic factors so as to prevent the arising of any new forms of wealth or status; one cannot picture rich, independent shipowners in Plato's Republic. This of course is but one more example of the meeting of the extreme right and left—and as in so many cases, it is the idealism of the left that succumbs, as a rule, to the hard-boiled concepts of the right. Nor is this new. The

Catholic Church has always contained elements of a rigid authoritarianism and a messianic radicalism, but it is the qualities of order which have prevailed, even as the vows of poverty have been maintained. The Jesuits have been as proverbial for their reactionary élan as much (if not more) as for their absolute equality. In 1279 the Franciscans were deprived of all their property to enforce their vows of poverty, but in 1322 Pope John XXII restored the property; as Schlatter commented, "the Pope maintained that there was little ethical difference between owning and enjoying the use of property; he accused the friars of eating more butter and eggs after the Pope took over their property than before."

More butter and eggs; Djilas described the same thing, but with less poetry. The great disturbances of our time are far bloodier than papal decrees, and there are different friars, but the tales of Stalinist feasts in the misery of wartime point the moral. The Russian penal system remains so disproportionately bloody in respect to the economic crimes of incipient capitalism as a reminder of the proper methods of advancement, not to ensure equality. And this is all the more true of the subtler forms of inequality which are the most significant; the first steps of the French and the Russian (and it is a safe wager to add, the Chinese) revolutionaries toward a restoration of status came with degrees and dignities. Honors are simpler than money, and a proper form of proletarian reward, but then if everyone receives some medal it becomes like a high-school awards day; the real dignities come to be recognized soon enough, and they always mean power and affluence as well as a bright token.

Aristotle pictured exactly this tension when he warned of treating equals unequally, or unequals equally. "Since clearly the greatest transgressions spring from a desire for superfluities" the gravest need in a society is to award these superfluities to the most deserving. It is the superfluities—the fame, the manifold dignities of social intercourse—which must be unequal, and from this much of Aristotle's conservative theory derived. The Communists have set out to make sure that equals—all men—were treated equally, to each according to his need. The struggle for superfluities is the catalyst for altering this, and as we have seen, in short order. In a broader sense this is the story of power, that highest good of all. The ideologies of the left accept the use of unlimited, concentrated power because they trust that men will share it equally, but the result is that, very quickly, this power is used fiercely by the leaders. If, as Holmes remarks, the great prize is command, then in short order the Lenins will achieve a position of unequal importance far beyond anything a capitalist can possess. One need but compare him to Rhodes to see the point; the latter struggled against odds, despite the remarkable quality of his personality as well as his wealth, to achieve a flimsy power which the vagaries of Dr. Jameson almost annihilated; Lenin by 1920 held an absolute command over a vast population. Of course he did not translate this into an army of servants or a majestic retinue—he chose not to, leaving that to his successors. Once vast inequalities of power are established there can be little check on other, lesser distinctions. On a mundane level these qualities of importance are easy to spot—almost all of the newly independent nations can demonstrate their quasi-socialist officials converting power into elegance, like political alchemists. Mrs. Edusei's bed was a notorious example; the limousines of the diplomats are much commoner. What if the state owns all the automobiles, if I can use them when I want, and have a chauffeur thrown in to boot; there is almost always more butter and eggs when the public foots the bills. The reply of the beneficiaries is to the point; in a world where men's importance often comes from these things, where riding in the back seat of limousines is the way to reach the UN Building, this is a necessity for the new, poor nations. It is too easy to laugh at African *amour-propre;* it is often just our own sense of status, rawly put.

The argument for inequality as a fact of life is not a cynical one; it is a consequence of diversity. There are exceptions, of course; it is a hallmark of liberal conservatism not to reject the thought of human goodness in a torrent of misanthropy. Equality will work best in a small, homogeneous environment where the desire for status is most restrained by the same qualities which preserve unity in a family setting. The community of sharing which has produced, within severe limits, a communal society in the Israeli *kibbutzim* has not developed on the Russian or Chinese collective or state farms. As long as the scope is small, the participation at least partly voluntary, and the choice of leaving is available, the necessary elements for an egalitarian society are present. Yet one must note that, as with the communal settlements which proliferated in the United States before the Civil War, the main thrust of the economy and the goal of the intelligent young men is elsewhere; the future of Israel is clearly not in the area of collective farms. The brightest young New Zealanders go to Britain, and the clever Englishmen come, to the horror of the nation, to America. When taxed for social ingratitude and abysmal lack of patriotism, the emigrants reply that the pay and status are better elsewhere. Sweden is not going down the drain of alcoholism and sexual riot, but there is a nervous malaise which does seem to encourage discontent; perhaps the interest in sex in Sweden and in gambling in New Zealand are similar examples of a need for diversion from the uniformity of a classless society.

This is not intended to deprecate the nobility of those who reject the prospect of one man enjoying more than another; these virtuous souls are perhaps the most admirable men one can find. But their opinion is not the general belief of mankind. The great majority seek more status, and an amplification of the trivia of distinctions which life has to offer. The struggle of the skilled automobile workers for more inequality shows that the potency of this urge, and the willingness to proclaim it openly, has not been deadened by the century of the common man. The desire for equality is due much more to envy than to a disinterested love of equality, and the sign of a prosperous society—and it is a bulwark of conservatism today that this is so frequent—is the concern about the "superfluities," the concern of unequals about the menace or potential of equality. In public discussion this is almost always a matter of interest—about someone else. The other man who is keeping up with, or surging ahead of the Joneses; the ridiculous snobbery of the underling toward those under him. But a strong case can be made that this contest for the little superiorities is the choicest part of all of our lives. Plutarch's charming story of Cato's declaration that it was the luxuries which were essential is relevant to all of us—it is in fact the trump card of Madison Avenue and the despair of idealists from Isaiah to Stafford Cripps.

In the popular mind these men and their like are crabbed spoil-sports, and that is a shrewd observation. Spengler inquired "what is luxury but culture in its most exacting form?"; the treatment of the ballet by the Bolsheviks shows that this is not a uniquely aristocratic feeling. The argument that inherited wealth and the confident enjoyment of riches is essential for the propagation of culture is not airtight. These qualities have often produced the qualities of cultured living, perhaps one might say the hothouse climate of elegant thought. Henry James or Marcel Proust would have been at a disadvantage, to put it mildly, in Costa Rica or New Zealand. But there are of course other avenues to culture. The wealth of Maecenas was not the result of generations of breeding, but it made possible the flowering of genius of less wealthy men. Often it is the parvenu, like Albert Barnes, whose feelings of inferiority will push him to the most valuable acts of patronage or support. Today it is often the state or the great foundations that are most active. However, as de Jouvenel points out, it is still a question of a privileged class of artists or thinkers being given funds to live an unusual life. Money can preserve culture, and its spending must lead to a class environment; but one can perhaps conclude that it requires elegance and the more aristocratic virtues to provide part of the proper background for new reaches of culture. By aristocratic we do not imply the fox-hunting and hard-drinking world of sportsmen, but the greater, usually *haute bourgeois* one of refinement or earnest seeking after wisdom.

It is one of the prime virtues of the free-market system that it tends to provide for something of all these qualities. The constant flux of individuals and social groups provides a steady amount of social movement without the perils of unrest. It is not necessary that the rich must all be lovers of music or that every third-generation man of means contribute to the spread or origin of fine art. There will be some groups or ethnic sub-groups with special interest in various forms of life or culture, and the more diversity the more interaction of these various currents. Friedman has remarked how these "independent foci of power," nurtured by capitalist inequality, are breeders of both political and economic nonconformity. From the struggles of the Nonconformists in the mid-eighteenth century to the battles over academic freedom in the 1950's the role of the rich supporter of liberty has been vital. In fact, it was an American millionaire, Samuel Fels, who helped out the Russian Marxists when they ran out of money at their 1907 London congress. This merely carried on the tradition of bourgeois support which might be said to have originated with Engels himself. The French socialist party would have disappeared had it not been nurtured by men of means; Blum was both a man of the post-impressionist culture and a very successful lawyer, a perfect example of refined wealth.

The market itself, of course, is only the trading mechanism, the conductor. The great fault of the radio and television market has been its inflexibility, its incapacity to appeal to small and differentiated groups. This is not so much a reflection on its developers as on the condition of its structure; perhaps the development of the broader wavelengths will solve much of this rigidity. In the case of these industries, of course, the market is not free; but that is not the whole story. If everyone had precisely the same tastes, or if 98 per cent had the same tastes, the mechanism of a free market would not provide a diverse set of opportunities. But the structure of a free market will tend to establish these distinctions through encouragement of mobility, through encouragement of distinction and difference, and through inheritance.

No discussion of equality or capitalism can avoid the subject of inheritance, for it is the institutional peculiarity of the market system. Of course there is an inconsistency in saying that inequality is the result of human differences, and in providing that one man's skill is passed on to his heir. To some extent heredity will ensure that the son will resemble the father, but one can argue from that the fairness in making the son accomplish his own tasks. And therefore the liberal atmosphere of the free market, the early-nineteenth-century climate, accepted Jefferson's dictum that the earth is for the living, and rejected the idea that the dead had rights; inheritance of wealth cannot be justified in rigorously liberal terms as a claim of either the father or the son. It must be justified on more conservative grounds, on arguments deriving from traditional beliefs.

The argument from culture, as we have noted, is not conclusive. There is no guarantee that the scion of wealth will be more art-loving than his fellows; there is equally no certainty that he will ardently support the causes of nonconformity or diversity. It is just as with the arguments for liberty; one cannot rest a secure case on historic necessities. But what one can say is that inheritance, like liberty, makes these values of diversity possible in a way which its absence would not. Generations of wealth do tend to the inculcation of the qualities of cultural appreciation, other things being equal.

The audiences of culture are enriched by the generation of riches, perhaps at times to the point of decadence. This is not a question of genius or of patronage but one of social conditions, the development of those layers of inbred assurance which produce (as in France of the 1780"s) snobbery and splendor. Society is the richer for some of this—not too much, but at least a leavening. The matter of political novelty involves similar values, for we would not want a world of Corliss Lamonts, yet their total absence would be alarming. The Paris of Diderot and Cagliostro was much to be preferred to that of Robespierre and Babeuf.

Once again, it may be said that a state might make sure of all of these things, just as the British government provides the Leader of the Opposition with funds. So too, it is argued that the role of the capitalist class in transmitting wealth, and thus preserving the stock of invested capital, can now be performed by the state. But where there are independent sources of financial and cultural capital which can provide different answers, even if the central authority wants one product, one brand of thought, there is no need to rely on the dubious merits of state-created vitality. But if a man cannot leave his wealth to others, he is not so likely to work at amassing it. Furthermore the great stores of capital must be nurtured over generations, so that if private parties cannot do so, the state must. Wittfogel postulates the origin of the Oriental despotisms as being caused by these needs —centralized power builds on the vacuum which the absence of established private power affords. In the last analysis, the dreaded mass society, the uniform paralysis of the spirit coerced by bureaucratic rigor and deadened by the gloomiest dullness, the Gehenna of our modern art, is the easy result of a society without inheritance. And of course the family, the element of private tradition and individuation, is closely tied up with the idea of continuity through the ages; one of the greatest problems of the time is the weakening of the family with the diminution of this quality. Even if family life is stronger than ever, it will only be the life of the small family cell, existing on its own emotions and closely tied emotionally. There is a lacuna in the broader family spirit, the sense of an institutional loyalty which might add a greater color to man's spirit and to all of life. The great Whig families of England had their faults, but the corporate loyalties and traditional élan have done much to provide that sense of individualism which transcended the family, and their standards have often provided the guides for the mass ethos of the welfare state. It is possible to emulate the Chinese without all of their fixations; both they and the British worked out classic compromises between inheritance and opportunity to provide both these lower-circle values a chance to interact, and this may be the great challenge of our cosmopolitan society.

There can be, therefore, too much merit, just as there can be too much equality and too much aristocracy. The value of the market is that it will tend, not necessarily perfectly but in a rough way, to check excesses of itself, or provide comparatively easy ways to check them. This does not exclude the role of the state, however. Estate taxes are a much fairer way of discouraging dynasties of wealth than erratic confiscations or political seizures, and they have the merit, like the antitrust laws, of periodically clearing the air, of discouraging the over-acquisitive or the too-thrifty *rentiers*. The task is to set a mean which will do these things without checking the spirit of private ownership unduly;

the current systems in America and Western Europe are not failures, although they certainly might be improved in order to discourage the establishment of lengthy trusts. But above all, it must be the goal of the laws to encourage and not to discourage the continuation and development of private clusters of wealth and influence, to improve and not to supplement the market.

To be sure, even this much may be granted as the boon of the state, and then withdrawn after the governmental power is consolidated. Often in periods of great dynastic vigor rulers will draw property unto themselves, but leave the possessors and their heirs in untroubled control. The statism of the later Roman Empire was foreshadowed by the imperial policy of Augustus, but when he confiscated the temple lands of Seknebtunis in Egypt he granted permanent leases to the priests of the temple; the harsher tactics came later, but Augustus had prepared the way. So also the Communists commenced their cultural program by encouraging the most diffuse forms of activity, just so long as they were properly licensed. Stalin and Zhdanov came very quickly, so quickly that Pasternak lived through all the variations of the cycle, even down to climactic fierceness of the Khrush-chevian expansion in a time of softness. Once the power is securely lodged softness may seem more iron than the harshest buffeting of an individualist society.

This is not to say that the state has no role. The value of the state as a patron, as a provider of sinecures, has proved itself also. When Burke thundered against the prospect of placemen defending their unneeded positions Gibbon was forced to blush, but Burke quickly came to see the merit of traditional places, with a vengeance. As long as the state is one among many springs of authority or patronage it may even enrich the area of diversity so long as its competition is not unfairly powerful. The TVA argument of the measuring rod is consistent with the ideas of traditional conservatism, in our sense, and it has the special value of reminding both the public and private sectors of the interests of the other, and perhaps of cross-fertilizing them. It becomes dangerous when the intrusions of the state become a one-way street, when governmental competition can win but is kept from losing, and when even the oldest, least desired forms of state activity are politically sacrosanct. Perhaps a political deal might be struck, that government activity be encouraged in diverse new areas of the arts and the economy—state theaters and power projects, even steel mills and movies—if there could be a thorough examination of the older state functions, extending even to the mails and the social-insurance programs. Perhaps nothing would be changed, either way, but the very exercise would be invigorating. Nor is this so wild; there have been examples of denationalizing, such as the British return of the steel mills to private ownership and Mussolini's denationalization of insurance (the best thing the Fascists ever did; it is to be hoped that a democratic government might go to work on some of the lop-sided legacies of Fascist bureaucratic ownership). Mixed forms, such as the Histadrut in Israel or the mutual-insurance companies in the United States, have the advantage of being susceptible to change in this way. The greatest obstacle is the doctrinaire faith in the state still held by even conservative liberals, but this too may pass, especially if more McCarthys will demonstrate that state power can be a two-way street even in a free society. It is ironic to remember that as recently as the 1820's, a small time in the long view, one of the most liberal American politicians, Thomas Hart Benton, was an outstanding advocate of the withdrawal of the federal government from private enterprises of various sorts. Since then the leftist faith in government has expanded, but perhaps not wisely.

It comes back again to the question of human goodness and ability. It seemed an easy thing before 1914, to many on the left, to convert the state into a great instrument for the accomplishment of all the elevating tasks which the uneven work of the family and private enterprise was not doing well enough, or not at all. Despite the discouragements of the last half-century, this is still a widespread belief. But the gravamen of the conservative view is that human capacity is not so great, that these qualities of individual liberty, of diversity, and of power divergencies are rare and precious. It is not hard for the state to make sure that sufficient capital goes into investment for heavy industry; India may have difficulties here, but the Communists can show them how to manage it, so long as they use the simpler form of coercion and do not overplay their hand in a fury of mismanagement, as the Chinese did. The state can ensure that opera is heard often and in variety, as the West German governments, federal and provincial, have done so well. But opera does not guarantee cultural vitality, as we have seen, and the great investments of the Soviet Union have left the country a land of Spartans, as Grunewald has put it, with Athenian tastes. The massive state usually has the choice between giving people just what they want, which means the majority brand pure and simple, or deciding what they ought to want and giving them that. But the finer qualities may well be finer in both senses; precious and hard to discern without care. As Berenson remarked, "*au fond,* the genuine passion for culture is such a rare thing that it ought to be encouraged." The suavities of life are rare and require the careful nurturing that a diffuse, non-centralized system can best provide; just as an army cannot sit on bayonets, so a bureaucracy cannot well feed geniuses. The conservative sense of the preciousness of quality very much needs encouragement in our mass technological age, and this is just what can least be programmed.

At first blush the market might seem a poor tool to use in encouraging quality. When the Russians decide that some perhaps esoteric game or practice should be encouraged, resources are diverted from other uses so that it gets superb encouragement. In so doing they have learned to make use of market mechanisms to a great degree—that is, they do not command men to be chess players, or rely on intensive educational programs; they also provide the successful players with bigger apartments, more medals, and money. To that extent the market has proved to be the means of achieving desired results, but of course that cannot be considered a free market. The free market may choose the tawdriest and least precious qualities—cars with fins, yo-yos, and assorted examples to shock the Lewis Mumfords of the age.

But high quality and supremely fine works of art do not come when they are called; the self-conscious production of geniuses is always a failure. We live in a time of social mobility and mass education, so that it may be hoped that another Beethoven should appear; the only thing one can count on, however, is that the music of a contemporary Beethoven would sound nothing like that of the original. Genius, and a milieu fit for its advances, cannot be predicted. The more avenues of opportunity the more chances there may be that works of the highest quality will be produced or, more commercially, that the standards of excellence will be enhanced. If there were some accepted canon of distinction it would be different; one could look back with nostalgia to the court of Louis XIV or Lorenzo the Magnificent if one could be confident that their culture was absolutely better than our own. But since the best that can be stated, in keeping with modern thought, is that these periods show extraordinary vitality along certain lines, it is necessary to keep open new chances for such vitality. This does not mean that excellence should not be nurtured; much of the effort to do so, by encouraging intelligent schoolchildren or by refining the caliber of the civil service, reflects the effect of the trend toward conservatism at its best— free from the irrationalism of the upper circle as well as the egalitarianism of the left. And it is significant and proper that much of the propulsion in these directions comes from comparatively small units of influence—from private schools or research institutes or (as so often in the past) autonomous, inner-directed groups of thinkers—which thrive in a milieu of economic diversity.

There was unquestionably a philistinism in the nineteenth century which equated the choice of the market with a somewhat vulgar interpretation of the Benthamite idea of the greatest good of the greatest number. This problem, as we have noted, is ever-present in an individualist system. The liberal-conservative answer to this danger—and as perils go, it is rather mild; the modern philistines have never done more serious damage than their purported ancestors in Gaza—is the combination of the free market with the qualities of traditional conservatism. Nef has pointed to the superior instincts of the late Middle Ages and the eighteenth century as times when craftsmanship and moral restraint discouraged the excesses of mass production and war. It is not necessary to accept all of his ideas to see the special uses of environment which encourage limitations and seek form and precision rather than dynamic control. But this does not come by fiat; the development of these instincts usually comes hand in hand with the growth of individualist societies and private centers of power and influence. Nef shows how the aggrandizement of the state (or earlier, the king) put workmen to the tasks of increasing the tools of war and put soldiers in a frame of mind in which victory was paramount. It is not a coincidence that the Franco-Prussian War was noted for both the revulsion of the court ladies at the prospect of bombing civilians in Paris and the effort of the French to attract investors by raising the rate of interest rather than by printing money. As Polanyi has suggested, the whole free-market system is, viewed in one way, a convention itself, and when men are most punctilious about even such stylized customs as the gold standard it is not surprising to see them wage war with the most due respect for conventional rules. With all its enterprising crudity, the Victorian age did uphold and honor much of the seicento elegance. We have become more used to finding brilliance in the oddest places—perhaps this is the hallmark of the twentieth century—and the free market, with its vast outpouring of new ideas, gimmicks and all, has the longest-run chance of encouraging the best.

☆ *XII*

The Market
and the World

That judgment presupposes the varied contours of society; quite frankly, this means that there will be a wealthy class of one sort or another, capable of engaging in eccentricities or in outraging the majority. But while misery is as great in the world as it still remains, this seems heartless—doubly so, with the capacity of our technology. The liberal might reply to this defense of inequality with the comment that success in leveling the heights may never be complete, but that uplifting the needy must take priority. This will surely be the chief issue of the last third of the century, for with one world the vast differences between the poor of Bengal and the residents of Grosse Pointe surpass almost any range of inequality seen before; all the leveling successes of the last fifty years of progress now seem to have been partial triumphs in a small cause. Of course in the past the standards of living in different continents were not compared, and the life of the Hottentot was not even thought comparable; misery was quaint if it was distant in time and culture. In a short space of time that is almost dead; Henry Wallace has won after all. The debates in the United Nations, the arguments of Prebisch, the pressures of international diplomacy will increasingly push us to thinking of the welfare concepts on a world-wide scale, and there is no value in blinking this.

There are three things which should be considered in this regard.

1. It has become a cliché of the right, but no less true for all that, that the great improvement in the standard of living in the West has come from increases in productivity, not from social or political pressures. The efforts of labor unions to increase the income of workers have tended to reallocate the wages of different groups of workers; it is much less likely, as Morton pointed out, that it has truly elevated real wages. This works both ways; it is also to be doubted that the so-called "wage-push" cause of inflation has superseded the "demand-pull" cause as a reason for inflation. The overall monetary and investment situation will set limits to the effect and possibility of wage increases; too rapid a rise will much more likely produce unemployment, as in the United States in the 1930's.

When labor is in great demand, wages will often rise without the unions' doing anything; if anything, the role of union contracts may slow up the normal press. In the Common Market countries today it is quite possible that wages would rise faster in a totally individualist system than they do in the severely institutionalized milieu of plans and unions. During the forced-draft monetary expansion of the Second World War, when hourly wages rose 60 per cent in five years in the United States, the union rates lagged behind non-union rates. During the years 1897–1913, when unions were increasing in strength throughout the world and governments began once more influencing labor rates directly, real wages nevertheless rose much less than in the preceding or succeeding years in most of the major countries. Unions seem remarkably ineffective on a national scale; even sovereign states can rearrange the money rates sharply but seem comparatively ineffective in bringing about great improvement in the share of labor, or of any other sector.

What really improves the return to labor, if not the share, is the increase of the total pie by investment. Perhaps at times, as in the early years of the century, this may be very slow; at other times, as in the United States in the 1940's or in Sweden in 1910, this rise in real wages may be startingly fast. But over the last century the purchasing power of everybody, and most noticeably the ordinary workingman, has risen more than in many hundreds of years before. And yet recently we have heard the complaints about poverty once again, even in the United States. Part of this is comparative, for as Tawney admitted, even if wages were doubled there would still be the same grievance against the better-off. After a time of complacent prosperity it is understandable, perhaps healthy, that some soul-searching should take place. Mid-Victorian England was uncommonly pleased at the strides made in the standard of living, strides which seemed to place her society on a new high level of decency and progress. Then the critics came along and pointed out what had not improved enough, so that the readers of most histories would think that Booth and Rowntree and the others had discovered a miserable island of poverty and unconcern. The *Times* surely exuded a pompous smugness over the years, but it was a smugness engendered by the confidence that the poor were much better off than in the sixteenth century or in Sicily, and the *Times* was right, just as *Time* is right in its similar statements today.

Each generation must start out with new variations on the old problems; it is right that new concerns should trouble us. When a small minority went to college they made up an envied or respected minority; now when 30 per cent to 50 per cent go the others are seriously inconvenienced in advancing; a college degree seems to be changing from a badge of distinction to a necessity for any good job. An automobile in America in 1906 was very much what Wilson then called it, a rich man's toy; now even the poorest in the United States may find everyday living very hard (perhaps impossible in Los Angeles) without one. Harrington has warned of the plight of the "Other America," below the working-class level. Many members of this class, it must be added, are constituents of what the Marxists handily dismiss as the "*lumpen* proletariat." It seems that no amount of material progress will eliminate the down-and-out sector of society, the tramps and drunkards who drift downward to the starvation level. In a wider sense, each society seems to have a place for the failures, the people who gravitate in and out of the poorest jobs and barely share the consumer goods available in their time. It is understandable that in periods of prosperity these will be most apparent; when times are bad the plight of much broader groups come to the fore, and in poor economies the bottom sector is lost. But when the surge of social advance is powerful idealism will turn in these directions. Slavery became a moral issue in the ancient world in times of improvement and wealth; when conditions were harsh or when the social tensions grew the poor citizen and his advocates were too concerned with their own plight to be troubled by the slaves. In the 1890's the United States came perhaps closer to social revolution than at any other time, but there was no concern left for the immigrant from the Balkans, and the status of the Negro measurably declined. We now have the luxury, so to speak, of righting those wrongs; when the time comes to concentrate on the dope addict or the Samoan we will be fortunate indeed. But it is not cynicism to add that there will always be someone on the bottom, and that that bottom may seem cruelest in the aftermath of the most impressive gains in general well-being. And of course we will always have the poor with us if we keep raising the definition of what poverty is.

2. But there can be no doubt whatsoever that the average Indian or Ethiopian is poor indeed. Since we now live in a common world the gains in real wages in the Northern Hemisphere west of the Urals and in Japan reflect even more strongly on the torpor, or even real decline, in the living standards of the other sections. This is definitely not a reflection on the free-market system, for that system has not existed since 1914. Under classical economic theory, a disparity of real wages in different markets must soon be eliminated. If wages are higher in one area than in another, people will move from the latter to the former, while capital will go in the opposite direction, until there is a rough balance. This is not automatic or perfect, as there is some natural friction in respect to the movement of labor and, to a lesser degree, of capital. Nevertheless, labor and capital will move; the shifts in population and production between Rhode Island and Alabama, and between Yorkshire and Sussex, are proofs of this. Mississippi and Calabria may be problem areas, but with a little

encouragement factories will move in to take advantage of the cheaper labor, and with even less encouragement the workers will stream out.

But this does not apply to the whole world, and that is half the trouble of our time. In the nineteenth century Europe poured out its surplus population into the Americas, and even China was tapped for a small army of emigrants. The difference in living standards between the Galicia of the 1890's, (not to mention Saxony of the 1850's) and its contemporary New York, was less than the gulf between New York and Bombay today. Transportation was, by and large, no less expensive then than air steerage would be today; the case of Puerto Rico shows what might happen, if it could. It cannot because laws have been passed and more subtle pressures erected everywhere. True, there is nothing to keep Turks from coming to West Germany, except that if heavy unemployment developed and the Turks remained in numbers, laws would quickly be passed, as they have been in Britain, to prevent this from continuing. As for capital, it moves most readily in those areas which are comparable; from Switzerland to Italy, from the United States to Germany, but because of fears and political pressures it does not rush into the underdeveloped lands. What could happen is clear here, too; Mexico presents a land where wages are comparatively low and the economy is comparatively free and very receptive to foreign money; the inflow of funds has proved embarrassing to the critics of capitalism in their equation of private investment with neocolonialism. But these concerns, and the plethora of restrictions on the sale of goods made by cheap labor—it is probable that there are more barriers to the sale of textiles produced in low-wage nations now than before Gatt existed—strongly militate against a redistribution of investment.

All this must be considered when the subject of aid from the rich to the poor countries is discussed. To many these programs seem to have merit only as programs designed for specific aims— the enhancement of national prestige, or the prevention of communism (or probably capitalism, as seen from Moscow). The Marshall Plan was a temporary program and its great success was largely due to that very fact; much of the aid is now being repaid by countries whose recovery has been thorough and who now—and this is a very happy event—can often patronize their erstwhile benefactor. But the aid programs undertaken since 1950 are so often different—it looks as if there may be an "aid-India club" for the rest of the century—that to many conservatives it seems as if we have installed a global dole. In fact, the prospect seems truly much worse—that an international welfare state is coming; already the price-support programs of the rich lands, a very dubious success at best, are the ideal of the Prebisches, but on a world scale.

But before this is derided as a miserable step toward world socialism, we must remember that the machinery of the free market has been kept from working, especially in the labor market. As the barriers on labor mobility are superimposed on the new consciousness of a world community it is almost inevitable that some form of subsidy or support is evolving to bridge the gap. If we will not have one system of leveling—and the market works out as an unequal but steady leveler, as we have seen, reducing caste and color and origin to a common denominator—we must get another. As with the issue of liberty, it is the task of moderate conservatives to point out that the ideas of freedom and opportunity are not synonyms for a weak government or a contented upper class, but have validity which cuts many ways and may hurt as well as help the status quo.

Unfortunately, the role of custom here stands in the way of a free-market system. It seems monstrous to the descendants, often the recent descendants, of immigrants that millions of Orientals should pour into the United States. In a way, this is part of the revulsion against the individualism of the eighteenth and nineteenth centuries. To primitive tribesmen property was not, by and large, an individual thing, but an attribute of group domain, and the quarrels of tribes involved the control of land. But the Whig idea rejected tribal ownership of land as a central fact; the crucial question was *dominium,* the private ownership, not *imperium,* the public sovereignty. But today, alongside of the breakdown of the distinction between public and private, the importance of public ownership is once again vital. The citizens of the United States own the country, in a sense beyond the separate ownership of the land by individuals, and they have decided to ration closely this dignity. The greatest battle over equality will be fought in the coming years over the consequences of this aspect of nationalism.

3. As a corollary to the previously stated factors, it is evident that the poorer citizens of the rich countries have the most to gain by these conditions of geographic and spatial inequalities. The rich of America and Western Europe comprise the world's wealthiest groups, but not by so startling a margin. The Rockefellers may be richer than the Oppenheimers, and Henry Ford may outdistance Count Matarrazo (before if not after taxes) but not by so very much. The *haute bourgeoisie* are more numerous and more moneyed in the rich than in the poor countries, but the latter are, in their milieu, probably much more impressive; what the latter lack in yachts they make up in servants. Where the gap is widest is near the bottom, at the level of unskilled work. The advantage of labor monopoly power within the capitalist economies is exaggerated, as we have noted, but where this monopoly really exists is in the international areas. In the long run the importation of laborers from lower-wage areas will push the established working class into higher income and social zones, but the short run often does bring unemployment or sticky wage situations.

Politically, the result is to reward parochialism and a form of self-directed concern. For example, in recent years there has been a liberal drive to restrict the competition of Mexican wetbacks with domestic farm laborers. This has been justified as necessary to protect the living standards of the latter and as a protest against the poor conditions of the former. But the Mexicans would not struggle to enter the United States if there were not powerful material advantages in so doing. In the years before 1924 the AFL was a leading advocate of restriction of immigration, just as were the early Labour members of Parliament. If it were a matter of pure love of equality these men would have devoted all their efforts to improving the lot of all the immigrants, but instead they often insisted that unlimited immigration hurt both the native worker and the newcomer. This was, and is, nonsense; if the latter were not much better off he would not go through the difficult experience of moving. Furthermore, the point of the migration is the higher standard of living in the receiving country, so all lovers of equality should be overjoyed at the maximum amount of movement. To this the left replies that equality by population transfers helps the rich of the advanced country, whereas moving capital through government aid is better because it helps the poor of the poor lands directly, while raising the money by taxing the rich or at least well-off.

Once again, this can be described as an over-simplification. As we have noted, it is misleading to say that the revenues raised in the rich countries come from the rich. However, if you class the whole population, or at least the majority of the citizens of these countries as comparatively rich, it is fair to say that it is the world's more affluent who are paying, directly. But of course there are catches; if the aid is "tied," it comes in forms which provide subsidies to certain groups, employer and employee, in the giving country. In that case the real aid is from one sector of that economy to another; perhaps from the bondholders to the electrical-equipment producers. If the money is raised through indirect taxation, this may cause a drop in the demand for raw materials, the brunt of which is often, as we have been so frequently reminded, felt by the underdeveloped countries. Or the aid program may salve the conscience of the legislators of the rich country so that they see nothing wrong in setting high tariffs or restrictive quotas on just those goods, such as textiles, which present the greatest promise for poor economies.

If we then turn to these poor lands, the issue is also clouded. Of course there are many cases where the money ends up in the pockets of men who have no need of support, men whose after-tax incomes would be impressive anywhere. And it may encourage the corruption which often proves more demoralizing to the sense of accomplishment than the most degrading poverty. All this is part of the built-in risk; but beyond that foreign aid may become a crutch which may tend to discourage effort (as the Alliance for Progress may become if it loses its spark) or an encouragement to foolish efforts which tend toward inflation and perhaps accentuate inequality (as Shemoy has alleged is the case in India). It is just as with the taxes proposed by Straus— a system whereby the state takes a major role in reallocating wealth may be planned, but it does not follow that it is necessarily egalitarian. In fact, the greatest improvements in living standards in the poorer countries in recent years have taken place in Mexico and Hong Kong, with very little foreign aid.

However, as long as we do not have an international free market—and with all the splendid strides made by the European Common Market and other such ententes this seems a very long way off—aid will have to fill some of the gap. The distinctions between the rich and the poor countries seem to have become so ingrown that Disraeli's two Englands appear a monolithic society by comparison. The welfare systems have certainly contributed; the benefits granted to the unemployed in Britain and France, much less Australia or the United States, would impoverish the economies of most of the world. This means that the employed in the richer countries have a tangible vested interest, like the Roman citizen of the Republic, in excluding the outsiders from these goods. It was these very considerations that evidently most led to the antipathy of the British Labour Party toward entering the Common Market; if Italy seemed too disrupting one might imagine the reaction toward, say, Malaya. This has been traced, in part, to the nationalist tradition in even British radicalism, and it is instructive to read of the early nineteenth-century radicals and others who so scorned Wilberforce and his pietist friends. Their criticism that Wilberforce thought more of the distant Africans than the poor in the Midlands has been often quoted with approval, and so it is not unnatural that the successors of Carlyle, that perfect example of Victorian upper-circle thinking, are more concerned with the extensions of the welfare state at home than the much more meager equivalents abroad. If this is true in Britain, how much more is it so elsewhere!

In fairness it must be added that the right has often adopted these attitudes as its own. It was the chief argument of high-tariff advocates in nineteenth-century America that our exalted standard of living required a high wall of duties, for what was good for Carnegie was good for his workers. Politically, it is a great strength for the cause of conservatism in the developed lands, and this is palpably true in Russia, that the mass of the people have so much to conserve. As such it is a great vindication of the policy of Bismarck, but as things always work out, each victory sets the stage for the next battle. It is all too easy for even liberal conservatives to forget their free-market principles.

As the issue of international equality grows sharper, there will be numerous chances to determine how these problems will be tackled. The conservative position will not, certainly, be simple or clear, but there will be ample opportunities to define it. If the values of liberty and opportunity are placed in the forefront there will be numerous cries that such individualism is hopelessly out of date and an affront to the needs of the miserable poor of the Southern Hemisphere. On the one hand the policies of fostering one world economy, without the high barriers which are still growing, will seem very harsh and radical to the interests of the protected. At the same time the poorer countries will scoff at this program as much too faint-hearted. The development of the world consensus, of the framework of law, must conflict with other interests, just as each national movement has so disrupted the more local interests. The radical left which thinks that world government must bring and will be made easier by world economic change of drastic proportions, may urge a program to reach these goods. But the Sino-Soviet split shows that even Communists, perhaps especially Communists, can be torn apart by the older concerns; the Rumanians have demonstrated that the new Marxist planning can add stronger burdens to international fusion than to those it suppresses. The path of Cobden, reinforced by the cosmopolitanism of the eighteenth-century tradition, is preferable if it serves to shroud the still-vibrant ethnic animosities of our time.

But this is too much of an understatement. The greatest potential of the free market is the creation of a community, just as the Common Market seems to be doing in Western Europe, so that the many systems can be integrated without injuring the diversity of different cultures and the freedom which comes from various systems.

The responsibility of the rich north to the poor south has become accepted by New Yorkers and Milanesi; perhaps the whole Northern Hemisphere must now take up this burden. Before worrying too much about the eternal weight of this albatross it is valuable to recall how rich Sicily was in the sixth century B.C. and once again in the twelfth century A.D. An increase of mobility might solve many of our problems without the aid of our eager Tugwells and Baloghs.

In our global society of the future it will be especially important to press the advantages of the free-market system. It may be polemically easy to call this a crusade for world liberty. Negative liberty is consistent with economic liberty, in the Hayekian sense, but it is only a small part of it. For example, if a government were to pass a law making it illegal to smoke cigarettes because of the health hazard, this would involve a real question of liberty. Since smoking is (cigarette fumes aside) a self-regarding act, such a law would be a deprivation of civil liberty. But it would not be the same sort of deprivation for the cigarette manufacturer. If the law made smoking a crime, he would be free to produce, except that the purchasers would be restrained by criminal sanctions. If, on the other and more likely hand, manufacturing were the crime, the smokers might be technically at liberty to indulge themselves, but in practice they would be much restrained by the cutoff in supply. The manufacturer in this case is the one restrained, but his right is not so self-regarding; it does make a difference whether one chooses to ruin one's own health, or sells a commodity likely to ruin someone else's. In other words, we have four conditions arising out of two kinds of law, all of which clearly involve governmental coercion, but only one of which necessarily involves civil liberty. The case of the forbidden manufacturer is a matter of liberty in the Berlinean sense, but it sometimes may be compared to the laws against murder. In both cases the restraint does reduce the freedom to act, but it can be argued that that freedom interferes with that of another, or with an equally important right of another (life or health). In the case of the indirectly-affected parties, all one can say is that the interests involved fall into the category of positive liberties, that they are not liberties at all but disturbed opportunities.

But it is very important in a civilized society that many of these opportunities be preserved. Since conservatism chooses to ally liberty with its compatriot qualities to the right it is important to choose what sort of positive liberties it wishes to encourage. Much of the confusion of modern politics comes from calling these rights "liberty," for a cause seems unworthy which equates a deliverance from tax burdens with the immunity from a prison sentence. All the same, the former may, in its time and place, be more important than the latter; it may be that the indirect coercion of the smoker may be more harmful than the direct ban on the manufacturer. If we call these encroachments on choice, these interferences with the market some other name, say invasions of opportunity, we are not denigrating their importance, but pinpointing their place in the area of coercion.

The tax laws are obvious examples of this invasion. All taxes are unpleasant insofar as they exceed what would be freely granted by the citizen as a good-will offering. In a sense they deprive us of the freedom to use our money as we want. This is especially so in the use of direct general taxes, such as those on income. But the liberals do have a strong point in their argument that there is a difference between forbidding a man to do something himself, and taking away a part of his property. It is a distinction which lies at the basis of government, for these possessions derive at least in part from the existence of government, from the quiet enjoyment granted by the existence of the state. But even if, as some of the more ardent conservatives insist, property is a natural right, since all states levy taxes it is forlorn to talk of a man's freedom from taxes, for such a freedom is inconsistent with civilized life; to call a right which must inevitably be compromised "liberty" is to debase the very spirit of the word.

But once away from this dilemma we do not lose our concern. It makes a great deal of difference if taxes take 50 per cent or 10 per cent of the GNP, or if tax rates cut deeply into the marginal income of the taxpayers. My income may not be so much a part of me as my legs, but the one reinforces the potential of the other. There is no need to reiterate the old conservative tenet that property is the condition of liberty; as we have noted, there are many modern examples to uphold this claim. If the state takes 50 per cent of the national income this means that half of the income stream has been commandeered by an agency which is superior to, and in opposition to, the mechanism of the free market. Moreover, the government cannot keep this 50 per cent; it must do something with it. If it collects the taxes in gold and buries the gold, it is deflating the economy and giving a hidden subsidy to the fixed-income recipients. If it allocates the money in subsidy it is recirculating the proceeds into the market, but the market then becomes an appendage of the state. In Sweden and Italy today the government grants financial aid to those connected with movies which it deems of exceptional quality. This means that the taxpayer's money, which might go to support Producer X, is taken by the state and used to help Producer Y. The taxpayer can still support X with his other after-tax moneys, to a greater degree if the taxes are low, to a lesser degree if they are high. Producer X can still seek to attract these revenues. But alongside of the free market, the market of choice limited by the configurations of income distribution, there is a market for official favor. Perhaps that is the more informed market, perhaps the distributor of government money has a higher certified taste than the average moviegoer—and in terms of accepted canons of sophistication this will usually be the case, especially in a refined land like Sweden. But individual choice, the dross of life surrounding freedom, has been circumscribed by the force of government.

This is always going on—all armies are raised on this principle. But it involves a constant indirect invasion of opportunity.

Perhaps it would be a good thing if every such invasion were always subject to renewed surveillance. Why are private schools inferior to public ones, for instance? This is not merely a matter of socialism or government competition. If the state operated schools so that they were self-supporting the complete anti-statist would still have reason to complain. But this is different from the actual case where the schooling is sold below cost—in fact, for nothing. In the first case all one can complain of is that the government is engaged in a field where it has no business, and where the very fact of its competition might be unfair. In the second case the complaint is that the subsidization of one product must discourage the other. Public schools are like preferred films; their merit must lie in a non-free-market choice by a public official that what the market chooses is not what is best.

The usual progressive reason for this judgment is the complaint that the market rewards and enhances inequality. In a way, this is a situation in which two sorts of positive liberty, two schemes of opportunity are fighting with each other. These need not be inconsistent. If the state were to use the tax money, or better yet printed money, to give a set sum to each person, or each poor person, there could be no diminution of choice, merely a reassortment. This has seemed tempting to some free-market libertarians, such as Friedman, who accept the weight of the egalitarian urge but wish to blunt its welfare-state proclivity. Carried to extremes, of course, this would destroy private property, and make the potentials of choice entirely a demand-oriented function. The conservative side of the market, the supply side, operates to balance the forces of demand with a machinery which will reward the efficient producers. In other words, part of what makes the ideology of the free market a conservative cause is its reliance on the limiting as well as the broadening aspects of choice, its role as a governor. When the conservative talks of the fusion of human and property rights, as is his wont, he means that liberty takes some of its meaning from the restrictions that come from the discipline of property. We have noted that the trespass laws restrain free speech, but that without them some other sort of restraint, directly coercive in all probability, would be necessary. The market entails, in our sense, the need to make a profit or go out of business, so that it is not enough to feed money into the system; one must have a choice-oriented way of pushing it out as well.

This leads us to the case of the forbidden manufacturer. Here again, no society permits the free sale of any commodity which can find a willing buyer—machine guns or heroin. But this does not mean that liberty has no relevance, or newspapers would have no protection and booksellers no freedom. The distinction between acting oneself and persuading another to act is a small one, and it is not important whether the motives of the seller are mercenary or not. There is a distinction between words and print, and food and drink, but it is one of comparative degree—adults can almost always judge the danger. When it comes to machine guns liberty may have to give way to social needs, just as shouting fire in theaters may be too explosive. Some restrictions which seem essential at one time may on reflection or after controversy prove unwise. Probably the laws against marijuana come under this heading. In other words, the old analogy between the market place of ideas and goods is sound, but it is a complex store with many wares and varying rules, and a diverse set of prices. Above all, it is important to keep the place running, even if this means concentrating on matters far removed from free trade in the narrow sense.

From the right to talk, to the right to argue, to the right to publish, on to the right to sell, and finally to the right to sell in a market whose customers have not been pre-empted and whose producers have not been overburdened, is not a unity, but a continuum. This is the stuff of much of everyday political debate. The plight of Subscription TV in California, the viability of private journalism in Ceylon, the rights of independent televisors in Britain, and the potential of small entrepreneurs in Syria are facets of this issue. When the state acts to curtail the operations of private enterprise it is better that something of the private sector be retained rather than that a total socialism shall prevail, but often this compromise may subvert the structure of the private sector as thoroughly as a Marxist sweep. Between the right to liberty, in the strictest Berlinean sense, and the right to compensation for deprivation of property, the high islands of lower-circle substantive rights, are the valleys which nurture them. If the valleys are flooded the peaks will soon be in danger.

Certainly this is a matter of degree, like everything else. Since there are no aspects of the market which are not affected by governmental action it is necessary to balance the advantages of that action in each case. It is possible that liberty is not the best guideline in all cases; it may be preferable in some circumstances for the state to ban a product than to attempt the same result by a variety of more subtle actions which might dig more deeply. The interest-equalization tax, for example, may turn out to be more of a burden on the free movement of capital than a fixed quota—for one thing, it may prove more permanent and more confusing. The absolute ban on smoking by minors is more acceptable than a prohibitive tax which would act as a general bar. These are exceptions to the general rule that indirect pressure is preferable to coercion, but the exception proves the rule that it is the broad diversity of the market, and not the manner of control, which matters most.

So too, even the maxims of encouraging choice must be reconciled with the necessities of the social system. Friedman's proposal that cash grants be substituted for social-welfare programs is a tempting one, but if the result would be that the neediest would remain needy it would be a failure, and an expensive one. If we accept, as a part of the price of establishing a customary minimum, that some welfare spending will be granted irrespective of the market, it is better to use social-insurance systems to spread the cost. In our concern, which should never be abandoned, for the vitality of the economic and intellectual market, it would be most unwise to forget that there is a political market as well.

Friedman's imaginative ideas pose problems which are becoming increasingly troublesome for conservatives. On the one hand, the conversion of the depressing and status-permeated world of welfare into the market system is a desirable change.

If the values of individual choice and maximum mobility are worth upholding, they are worth extending to even the poorest. It is thus gratifying to find veteran liberals like Charles Abrams espousing market principles, and the enthusiasm of the ADA for rent supplements is a true victory for the individualist ethos. But on the other hand this must involve the state in an indiscriminate assistance, and in a rich society the gravest needs tend to be concentrated among groups with special problems. The issue then arises whether to double up the assistance for the neediest, or to benefit rich and poor alike, with the necessary slighting of the very poor. A typical problem arises in public housing—the housing authority tries to standardize the level of rent and to eliminate the harsh atmosphere of investigation and charity, but as the income of some of the residents rises the absence of means tests results in a class of specially-favored, tax-supported tenants. Once again we are faced with a choice— either limitless public housing, subsidies for the well-off, or welfare controls. There must surely be a compromise between the last two in a developing welfare-market program. All in all, however, the movement toward expanding the free market should be encouraged.

But it is not enough to say that a free-market system will maximize individual opportunity and that it is not a necessary barrier to some of the goals of equality. Many progressives will concede this today, but they complain that the splendors of competition are imaginary, that the theories of the market apply to a totally theoretical world. The objections to utopianism or to visionary thinking, applied so often to the ideas of the left, are thus turned around on the free-market conservatives. For this reason Polanyi termed the Victorion world view as an exercise in this kind of utopianism.

But, all in all, there were remarkable accomplishments then, and there are today. The issue of monopoly and oligopoly is a real one, as has been noted, and competition is not automatic. Nevertheless, it is continually remarkable how the forces of competition will reappear and assert themselves. When Henry Ford had captured 60 per cent of the United States automobile market in the early 1920's, no one predicted that a decade later he would be struggling for second place against a comparatively new firm. Fifteen years later the shoe was on the other foot, but a thorough recovery took, again, but a decade. In the late 1950's critics attacked the American automobile manufacturers for their folly in enlarging the size of automobiles; but these companies proved to be sufficiently canny to seize most of the small-car market at the appropriate moment. The steel companies were belabored about their slowness in expanding after 1947, and sometimes charged with a lack of foresight and even patriotic commitment to the goals of American foreign policy; in the upshot it is clear that it was the planners who were off the mark (as Arthur Schlesinger, Jr., admitted in 1950). In 1945 and 1946 the businessmen and conservative economists were right about the course of the business cycle, and the liberal economists and their allies were wrong; the state of our economy would have been injured if the latter had been able to operate under a Gaullist "plan," or even if they had been in charge of fiscal and monetary planning, as the experience of Gunnar Myrdal—who combated depression when the problem was inflation—in Sweden attests. This is not to say that businessmen have superior vision, but that since their mistakes are tested by the market, their survival or success will depend on their accuracy. The existence of a stock market will serve as a daily grading system, whose marks may prove worse than embarrassing for the poor student.

Monopolies, and above all, cartels depend very frequently on the support of the state. The experience of losing ground, or failing, is painful to anyone, and it is usually in difficult times that schemes to control the market are launched. Half of the work of antitrust laws might be dispensed with if the state scrupulously set its face against all assistance to price-fixing— the merest truism, it would seem, but that is not so. In 1932 the air was replete with proposals of cartelization, of which the NRA was an example; the experience of pre-World War I Germany is a good specimen of this. But it is notable how often this breaks down, just as the NRA proved an impediment to recovery, and the Germans, disciplined as they were, found themselves constantly patching up these arrangements. So too the systems designed to hold wages up or keep them down usually collapse. The factories are moved south (so often wages are cheaper to the south; it almost seems to be a tropism) when wages are too high, and workers manage to obtain higher wages when they are not obtaining the market rate, as recent Dutch and German events have shown. It takes a strong state—such as the Russian—to effectively hold wages down; it takes a good dose of inflation, that is, deliberate expansion of the money supply or a powerful forced-draft increase of velocity, to force them upward. Years ago Alfred Marshall wrote that "when one person is willing to sell at a price which another is willing to pay [for it], the two manage to come together in spite of prohibitions of King or Parliament or the officials of a trust or trade union." The economic and social marvels of the nineteenth century were very much the manifestations of this truism—the population of the Americas, the spread of British money and ability throughout the world, the establishment of industrial societies in many hitherto backward lands (for one must remember that cartels did not launch German industry; Krupp and Siemens and Rathenau were as good entrepreneurs as their Anglo-Saxon opposite numbers). This is not dead. The wonders of the petrochemical industry, for example, have come as a result of a steady and demanding competition; because the contestants are all great corporations does not limit the ferocity and sharpness of the rivalry in the slightest. The Russians have confessed their failure in this area; it is highly significant that the Soviet system is least effective in new areas of innovation; it is quite capable of doing what the capitalists did twenty-five or fifty years earlier, and perhaps doing it more rapidly, but the new accomplishments are best achieved, it seems, under the freest market conditions.

In this there is nothing new; Nef has pointed out that "not a concentration of power, but an increase in the independence of economic enterprise within the state—favored by the peaceful condition of Great Britain from 1548 to 1640—accompanied the genesis of industrial civilization."

One of the most powerful arguments against the market is based on a denial of this very flexibility. We have assumed that the transition from the agreement of willing parties, Marshall's inevitable coming-together, to the most efficient economy will be reasonably smooth. This does imply that resources will flow, without interference, to the most remunerative factor and that the same is true of buyers. In short, it presupposes that the supply and demand factors are elastic, to use the economists' term. If, on the other hand, raising prices will increase the total return, it is natural to expect that bad business will produce price rises and not reductions. This is a key issue in the debate over interest rates, where it is argued that higher rates will not increase saving but may decrease it, as the requirements for which savings are made can be more quickly met. It is maintained that higher tax rates may increase incentive, as men will work harder to obtain a given net sum of money. These are liberal contentions; but they resemble the classic right-wing argument that wages should be kept low because any increase would cause workers to spend less time working. Adam Smith argued against the last contention as a reformer, whereas Keynes argued for the first in his innovating role. One might say that the belief in elasticity, the belief that if one gets more for one's efforts the result will be even more effort, and not less, is another feature of the Whig epoch. There are reasons for this correlation. Much of the case for elasticity is based on a faith in individual reason, in the prudent management of one's affairs. Of course there is nothing irrational about preferring leisure to money, or thinking that one may reasonably set a fixed goal of well-being and work toward it. These reasons are surely legitimate, but they are in a large sense economically regressive, since they imply that economic goods are necessary evils. If one will work harder for less one must have an overriding preference for something which is opposed to work. The broader scope of market theory has a place for these preferences as its predecessors, with their perhaps over-Calvinist ideas, did not, but it remains a theory which is understandably convenient for advocates of slavery or high taxes, to use our examples. In the last analysis, one must say that if people, in the mass and over time, think this way, it will subvert individual reason by placing a premium on collectivist forces, or will undermine economic development altogether—and the first is more likely than the second.

This is more clear when you examine the supply side of the equation. The principle of monopoly or oligopoly is often defended on the ground that the vagaries of price fluctuations can only be checked by a powerful force which can then profit by the inelasticity of demand. That, in a nutshell, is the rationale of the agricultural-commodity plans which the developed nations have experienced, and which some of the poorer lands now so desire. Private cartels in this area have proved to be failures, because the rewards to outside suppliers were sufficiently great to subvert the united front; only under a governmentally-imposed scheme can this be overcome. In the case of essential foodstuffs this may ensure a good return. The most radical part of Keynes' thinking was his insistence that the total welfare might be enhanced by this emphasis on social or group control, or on state fixing of low interest rates, to the detriment of the choice of individuals. Given a premise of inelasticity, this mass reason is eminently reasonable as a doctrine, but its working-out substitutes the decision of a few men for the consensus of the market.

For example, if the central bank pegs the rate of interest, the demand for credit is met by new infusions of money by the managers. This course is supported on the theory that higher rates would not attract higher saving, since that supply is inelastic, whereas the role of interest in demand is small, either because businessmen pay more attention to other factors or because small borrowers are stupid or shortsighted. It then becomes futile to raise rates so as to gain a new source of capital, and pointless to raise them to discourage borrowing. There can be no normal rate except what the bankers think right; reason is changed from an exercise of personal choice to a decision of authoritative social value.

This is exactly what is behind much of the thinking of Berle and his school. As to much of the economy they start with the anti-market premises we have just examined, ideas which date from the New Nationalism and above all the early 1930's. Since demand in their view is inelastic on many occasions, and supply is almost by their definition the plaything of oligopolists, the work of reason becomes a task of philosopher-kings. The corporate managers are unchecked both within and without their domain, so the argument runs, unless either the state or opinion, or both, can set a new standard of reason. This must be a code, a planned system; it is easy to see why Berle is popular with Jesuit thinkers. Of course this comes down to a matter of fact, of the actual nature of the modern business system; it is enough to refer once more to the increasing body of works explaining the vitality of the market in this as in other areas. But one may fairly go further; is not much of Berle's thinking a case of wish-fulfillment? It is most unlikely that Berle would be pleased with a return to proprietor-dominated firms, just as Keynes had no hankering for the pre-1914 gold standard whose demise he used as the springboard for his new economics. It is not an exaggeration to say that the anti-economic and even elitist viewpoints of both men caused a distrust of the quality of reason which we are defending; viewpoints which perhaps reflected a disapproval of the hurly-burly (if such a pun be permitted) of the market. Ellis has attributed this, in Keynes, to the influence of India; if we look to the market as a civilizing force, and not the opposite, it behooves us to strengthen the factors maximizing elasticity (such as antitrust measures or moves intended to increase flexibility) rather than work for the opposite on defeatist grounds.

As a matter of history, the case for elasticity is very strong. The experience of the international financial system in the 1950's and 1960's is a testimonial to the use of interest rates as a force in regulating demand and nurturing saving. The effectiveness of high interest rates domestically in the last few years has demonstrated the continued potency of the money market to affect the economy. The producers of cotton and butter can attest to the excellent workings of elasticity in their markets. The truth of Marshall's dictum has been proved over and over again in recent years, the examples of agriculture and banking are exceptional only in that these were areas most cited by the inelasticians. The marvelous accomplishments of the discount operators is a beautiful example of the difference price can make in highly-organized segments of the economy. But this is to be expected—the case against the effectiveness of the market relies much more on an innate distrust of individual reason than it does on a studious analysis of economic history. It is not enough to tell the construction unions that the market for homes is truly elastic if given a chance; they find it cozier, as a rule, to take the short view and hoard their jobs. Elasticity is like liberty in that it involves both a cynicism about human motives and a faith in reason; the critics of both usually will not wait for the by-products of free choice.

This applies equally in other economic areas. The issue of automation became an important left/right area of disagreement recently, and the terms of this dispute are similar to those of the elasticity argument. The left case runs (and of course this is a simplified abstract) as follows: The axioms of the market have become obsolete in a society in which the rate of techno-logical advance, thanks to successes of automation, has eliminated the factor of scarcity. With the proper sort of planning there need not be any unemployment or want, since a few men can do the work which required many before, and the resulting surplus can be shared equitably. But without planning this productivity will result in unemployment, an increase in poverty amidst the euphoria of plenty. The market is equipped to deal with allocat-ing scarce resources, and it is not surprising that it breaks down at the opposite task of distributing surpluses; that job is political and requires the sagacity of public intellect and the courage of non-business minds. But until this new condition is recognized things will go from bad to worse as the skills of automation ruin lives and even result in less, rather than much more total wealth and happiness.

Much of the problem, if we would believe Theobald and Bazelon, arises out of the unreality of the contemporary economic system, a pattern of values and rewards which has become isolated from the productive process, a "paper" world which has an internal consistency but which has become too artificial to cope with these revolutionary potentials of a scientific, non-paper, automated machinery. The job (so we are told) is to slice through these artificial barriers, using if one will the Galbraithian antidotes to the conventional wisdom; perhaps all of capitalism will disappear, or the great corporations will become, à la Berle, public-service entities, or (since you must deal with deluded souls gradually if you have decided that there are other ways to make omelets) at least the market must be thoroughly re-oriented through the exercise of political leadership. A few of the magic words have been left out of this précis, and also the passion which often derives from a puritanism which scorns the comforts of modern living. This passion derives ultimately from the fundamental leftist view that man is the measure and the hope of the world, and that systems are made for man, not man for the systems.

There is perhaps an admirable quality in this, and some pathos after the 1940's ordeal of Marxism—the conversion of radical hopes into glorification of the most massive institutions. However, much of the fervor proceeds from the premises, which are usually treated as certainly true and shamefully indicative of the failures of the capitalist system. But if one changes the premises much else is also changed. The current rate of increase in productivity throughout the West is high, but not so extraordinarily so as not to be comparable to other great periods, such as the late nineteenth century. Between 1920 and 1939 industrial productivity in the United States doubled, and in the middle of that period, in 1933, there was much talk that men could not be adequately employed in the light of modern processes. The technocrats of 1933 made the same assumptions that their descendants now make; in fact, Stuart Chase is once again making the same observations after a quarter-century in other vineyards. Yet there were not too many men for the available work in 1947, or in 1966. The rate of increase of productivity in the United States from 1953 to 1964, the heyday of automation, was much the same as that of 1920–39; perhaps the next decade may see a falling-off, not an acceleration (this was what happened in the 1940's). It is argued that 1947 was an exceptional year of postwar readjustment, and 1966 was a year of war. But in Western Europe there has been a frequent shortage of manpower since World War II. There have been many years of peace and full employment such as 1929 and 1955 in the history of the United States, and these times of prosperity have come after the precursors of Theobald assured us that mass unemployment was basic to capitalism. Of course, Marx was a pioneer in these wrong predictions; recent commentators have shown how many of the recent dramatic forecasts, Marxist and non-Marxist, have been based on incorrect assumptions or disgruntled wishful thinking. Is it not arresting to consider that the work week declined in the United States almost steadily from the mid-nineteenth century to 1934, but that it has not reached the low of that year since then? A few years ago there was discussion of the dangers of a society in which there was no one to do the small or unpleasant jobs (and of course this is commonly said now in Europe and Japan); perhaps in a few years this will once again be the more frequent complaint.

If, then, we reconsider the question as one pertaining to a phase of the business cycle, the matter looks very different. At some times the upswing of entrepreneurial innovation, in Schumpeter's terms, will press against the labor supply; at other times there will be a tired quality about the economy. The Soviet system has avoided this risk by avoiding the innovation, and by ensuring that there will be no sudden burst of production in a new consumer-based area they guarantee that there will be no later setback. The tempo of automation makes these throbs of economic activity and slowness explosive today, but perhaps much less so than twenty-five or one hundred years ago—for those times, as we have noted, had great experience of technological change. The seventh century, we can be sure, saw few such agitations, but no one has suggested that time as a model. The current efforts to smooth out the business cycle have a laudable result in the softness of many economic declines, but perhaps the price is a tendency for the economy to endure periods of slack, or less-than-full employment and moderate inactivity. And of course there is another real issue; to the radical any unemployment is wrong, but over employment creates exactly those states of slovenly quality and inattention to consumers which are the bane of a civilization. In the end the push for economic advance must lead to inflation or to a rationing of scarce goods (for it seems that somehow, even in the 1960's, goods can turn scarce, and intolerably so) with all the bureaucratic rules which this implies.

In other words, the state of limitless productivity is a mirage. Men's wants grow along with production, at a somewhat different rate but quite inexorably. The limitless quality of human desire, the circular quality of life, ensures this, and modern capitalist society is not backward in providing the forces of aspiration with a powerful support. In fact, many of the same critics of the lag in productive use are opponents of the advertising machinery which is set up to inspire demand. Advertising cannot guarantee demand, thank goodness, but it is a rough way of bringing new innovations into the economic process. It is ridiculous to fault these efforts at adjusting demand to supply if the chief problem of the society is insufficient demand. Galbraith is consistent in denying the point of ever expanding the desire for goods, and in espousing a program of sorting out current production more evenly by, in effect, encouraging unemployment. His world seems to consist of men who naturally love work so ardently that they must be almost seduced into forsaking it, and a society in which emulation can be diverted by appealing to the better nature of the people. Galbraith's community might reasonably be called a society of affluent professors, except that Mary McCarthy and Bernard Malamud, to name just two authors, have drawn a less lovable picture of even academe. To a conservative the pleasures of planned cooperation seem as unlikely as the horrors of the competitive system.

Without these premises the Galbraithian plea for an expansion of the role of the public sector seems unconvincing. Surely the massive growth of that sector since 1914 in every country should satisfy almost anyone who rejects totalitarian ideas, it would seem, yet Galbraith pleads that the private sector waxes fat at the expense of the amazingly poor public zone—the latter resembling the thirsty earth which receives so much water and yet turns dry so quickly. Much of this paradox is related to one of the problems of automation which the new technocrats fail to mention—its amazing strides are extremely uneven. Workers in petrochemical factories or in steel mills perform wonders today, but barbers and doctors—and teachers and civil servants—have hardly experienced any increase in their productivity. The result, and this is most true of local government, is that more money often does not buy any more services. But this is part of a general problem; many services become very expensive because they are left behind in the productivity race, so that either they become luxury products, like private tutorial, or they require an increased part of the economic pie, like college education.

In a market situation low-productivity industries will tend to lag behind as their products become more and more high-priced; even, as with housing, when they are necessities they will drop behind in the competition for surplus income. If the products are greatly desired this will alter the pattern of spending. As services (which often show little or no productivity gains) grow in importance as against goods the real rate of growth of the GNP slows. This is one reason why the specter of mass unemployment is often spurious, and this development is a cause of inflationary pressure in the most stable modern economies. Of course, as these costs rise in proportion to others consumers will do without or with less, as even the barbers have discovered. In a non-market situation this need not be so, and rightly; the case for government support of education is partly based on the broad social need for this service which must override the class or age bias of the market. But then the price must be paid; the productivity of teachers will fall in a period of great attention to education, as more demanding communities require smaller teacher-pupil ratios and more desired teachers exact greater time for scholarship or research as a part of their income. The argument for education is frequently shallow, because it assumes that only lovers of ignorance or dedicated misanthropes will dissent from the premises; it becomes more clear that there are pros and cons to this as to almost all social decisions. If government aid to higher education is greatly increased (and that is of course not inconsistent with the purest liberal-conservative ideology, as the role of Lord Robbins has indicated) this may, in gross terms, be in one sense a subsidy from the already arrived (who will be faced with either a new competition or the anger of an educated proletariat) and the increasingly depressed (for those who do not receive this education, always sure to be a substantial number, will be materially disadvantaged by the increased emphasis on degrees) to the *novi homines*. The mode of this subsidy will be a transfer of wealth from high-productivity to low-productivity areas.

If we choose to pay this price we must expect compensatory drops in other parts of the economy. But efficiency is not a god to be sacrificed to; if more learning and a great spread of information are desired why let narrow cost considerations prevail? Here again, the plurality of decision-makers will tend to spread the risk and ensure a range of answers.

The overall question of bureaucracy is not so different. Parkinson's laws, which once expressed seem to have been lurking like Newton's as a great truth all this time, are in one sense another variant of the provisions for low productivity in an age of high productivity. Too often the conservative in our time has flailed at bureaucracy as if it were some beast whose coming could be laid to the door of Franklin Roosevelt or diverse socialists. Anyone who has served in a peacetime army can attest to the broader truth of Parkinson's dicta, and an experienced critic of the General Electric Company has suggested similar conditions in that private quarter. In theory the various breakthroughs in modern technology, and especially the computer advances which affect office work, must change this, but anyone so concluding must ignore the longer history of the bureaucratic spirit. That spirit has historically come with wealth and power—Alsop suggests that Agamemnon amidst the tax records is the great surprise of the archaeological reconstruction of Homeric Greece—and its course in the heyday of Victorian England is another reminder of the permanence of bureaucracy. The army of American tax-collectors, and their attendant tax lawyers, is really not, as Blum has pointed out, such a vast horde. It might even be said that if the clerks in the public sector grow at the same rate as those in the private sector, this is as much as can be expected.

Nor is it so shocking that the clerks will keep growing. An advanced society naturally enjoys a large tertiary sector—the sector of services and immaterial workers. Schumpeter has remarked that the surplus value of Marx is another name for the sinews of progress and of cultural advancement; so one might say that the useless are just those luxuries, as Cato said, with which we cannot do without. In any such society there are ridiculous impostures and foolish waste, but that does not mean that a "paper" economy is wastepaper. Neither a publicity agent nor a painter produce something which is immediately useful; in a pinch any man would turn to a farmer or carpenter. Certainly there is a difference between the publicity agent and the painter; it will be said the comparison is odious. But, once again, the relativism of our system prevents this from being a crushing rejoinder; a painter may be good or bad depending on one's evaluation of art or perhaps depending on his own sincerity—who is to say this is untrue of the publicist? Art may be our new religion, but it is not immune thereby from the doubts and hesitancies with which we survey the older faiths. Everything comes down to a sense of accommodation or compromise for a complex social organism, and the bureaucrats and advertising men have their place as well as the other "useless" people. The Chinese now scorn the Russians for their luxury, as we scorned the Chinese two centuries ago; the Chinese then held the prize for sophistication (and established forms which have never been equaled) as we do now. The men of passion, the true believers have always scorned the circumlocutions and fictions of effete societies; after our cataclysms we can see that bureaucracy is better than terror, that artificiality is better than crisis, and that the opulent archaisms of the Abbasids and the Habsburgs had merit when one sees what followed them.

Worst of all, to be sure, is terror and artificiality, the stark unreality of Kafka's world. The market has a built-in protection, with its philosophy that the customer is always right, against the sheer coldness of bureaucracy; Edmund Wilson and David Daiches, to quote two unlikely sources, have mentioned the steeliness of bureaucracy turned authoritarian.

When bureaucratic arrangements change from a superfluity to a necessity the context of society is changed—what is acceptable as one way of living becomes monstrous as a way of life. It is the distinction between the Habsburgs and the Nazis, and between Uruguay and Cuba—but the Uruguayans must be on their guard. The gravest danger of bureaucracy may be the sense of helplessness and irrationality which it spreads, so that (as may be true in Uruguay today) no rational action seems possible and a mass anomie sets in.

We have noted that corruption has its place; the great difference between a Tweed and a Huey Long was the lack of ability or brazenness in the former in doing away with the need to bribe or flatter the voters. A society or an economy in which life's rewards come down to the acquisition of claims written on little pieces of paper and spent by manipulating these into other immaterial forms, may be trivial or it may be a very great short cut to the simplification of the trivia and the supersession of the gross.

There is the danger that this may lead to a society where the least useful (this is of course never one's own function) is the most rewarded; an establishment of the more arcane Veblenian practices on a vast new scale. These might deter the maximum use of technology just when the potentials of the latter are so glorious. Certainly it is possible to imagine a society which sets the progress of industry (let us include consumer goods here; the Japanese today or the Americans in the 1860's may be better examples than the Russians) far above all else, and accomplishes miracles with all the constituent elements of the GNP. The question remains; *cui bono?*

☆ *XIII*

The Case
Against Progress

This is almost a heretical question today; who will be so brave as to state that rapidity of growth is not an absolute desideratum? We have marked above the claims of the capitalist system, admitted by Marx and Laski and Galbraith, to distinction in the game of economic growth. We have noted also the tendency of the free-market conservative to rely on this as a prime claim, despite the successes of the Russians. But after arguing the pros and cons, which are open to reasonable disagreements, the question still remains; what is so remarkable about economic growth in the first place, that we should all debate with such heat who is best at it?

One can take this on a narrow and on a broad plane. The narrow issue is familiar: at what price do we urge growth at the expense of the other economic goods—price stability, social adaptation, and the quality of goods and services? Fritz Machlup expressed these doubts in his testimony before the Joint Congressional Economic Committee in 1959, when he commented that "many of us say modestly that we want an 'adequate' rate of growth. But this does not commit us to anything. What most people mean is a dazzling growth rate, a record-breaking growth. Why does anyone want the fastest possible growth? . . . [the reasons] are least valid from an economic or from an ethical point of view . . . a desire to win an economic race as if it were a sports contest . . . I reject the 'maximum rate of growth' as a goal of economic policy unless it means something other than the fastest possible growth regardless of cost. I can accept it if it means the fastest possible long-term growth compatible with the institutions of a free society and consistent with the free choices of income recipients concerning their consumption and their savings and without confiscatory taxation.

"By confining my acceptance to 'long-term growth' I have also rejected the forcing-up of investment and employment by means of monetary inflation because such forcing-up is apt to be of relatively short duration and not conducive to a high rate of continuing growth."

It is hard to improve on Machlup's brief summation. It is possible to add one more point—growth is easiest to demonstrate in such "hard" statistics as steel production or in gross construction, but this may fulfill the wrong needs, or be a less-than-optimum satisfaction of the given desires. A successful market economy takes myriads of values into consideration, including the desire for leisure or the ebb and flow of particular needs. There are cycles in housing, there are fashions in clothing; to the growth enthusiast progress must go on without pause or transition. The final accomplishments of a free society, economically as well as politically, are usually in the long run—Keynes to the contrary notwithstanding. The forced draft may be unhealthy and truly self-defeating, as Brazil demonstrates; the comparison on the basis of annual statistics may glorify a Russia of the 1930's which gains economic laurels at the expense of almost all the values a free society prizes or a civilized society requires. Machlup was brave and wise to insist on what may seem "old-fogeyish" limitations; these caveats are more important than the principle they amend.

This is topically important in connection with the liberal argument for the non-coercive plan. Nossiter, for example, has proposed that the merits of the French plan and its Norwegian counterpart lie in the prod which they give to the economy without the dangers of coercion. These miniature versions of the Five-Year Plans of the Marxist states are proposed for guidance, not compulsion, and offenders may suffer nothing worse than a governmental cold shoulder. The stronger the state, the colder that shoulder must be—with the increase of state power even the slightest governmental hint becomes, increasingly, a command—but this is not the same as mandatory controls. The great merit of these plans, according to their advocates, is the encouragement they give to the natural urges of a dynamic economy. Nossiter admits that the Japanese plan has usually understated the rate of growth, but he claims that the plan has set a minimum which has served as a floor beneath the vigorous growth of the Japanese. Heaven help an economy which does not exceed the quotas, or an industry! The malefactors are denounced as slackers, or worse, the whole country must be charged with a new vibrancy—as Machlup put it, nothing less than an astounding rate will do, at least equaling the old records. This will almost invariably lead to inflationary problems and/or balance-of-payment difficulties, which will come like a ghastly hangover after the spree of forced growth. The Japanese have had the courage to use high interest rates to tackle these problems; the easiest (politically) way is to devalue; once started this can go on and on, as in Brazil. Growth becomes a fetish, and soon all faith in the currency is lost. But then the economy will often refuse to answer to the prods, as the normal cycles are pushed aside, as governmental expenditures are raised willy-nilly, and not only for counter-cyclical purposes, and as all the economic groups come to rely on more and more inflation as a spur. Once the process is well on the way, the efforts to stop the price rise tend to become increasingly ineffective. Great Britain is thus afflicted with stagnation, high interest rates, and a constant propensity toward inflation. The hardest thing to control is usually the budget deficit. When government expenditures exceed income, an inflationary tendency is created; at full employment this is inevitable. When prices then rise the unions naturally press for wage increases. But the rise in labor costs must increase the deficit, and so the game must go on until some fixed-income group has lost enough to satisfy the pressure. But today everyone is alert to this—pensioners get cost-of-living adjustments and even bondholders will demand flexible yields if they see what is happening. Closing the inflationary gap then becomes a nightmare; but this is so easy to imagine that it seems a dream that can afflict even the most secure economy.

What if we have one world economic system, obviating the formal balance-of-payment problems, and one currency which is thus constantly inflated in search of one vast, unending boom which must overcome all the complexities of world-wide confusions or stagnation? The price revolution of the sixteenth century, that time of bitter war and social misery, gives some indication of the result. Price and wage controls will be attempted before the worst happens, but this is likely to add more rigidities, penalizing the honest or the less economically or politically powerful without halting the process. And all along the voices of growth will keep repeating that more growth, more and more growth, is the answer, that each record must be broken or that the symptoms of tiredness which will multiply must be remedied in only one way, by more government spending or more encouragement to private spending, without halt or stint. Each new push meets more resistance, and so must be tempered with more coercive power. Perhaps, as in Dukas' whimsical melody, the sorcerer will return; he is not likely to be a believer in constitutional democracy.

On the narrow plane the discussion centers on the rate of growth; the issue on the broader plane is whether economic growth is valuable, per se. To many people this will seem a totally ridiculous or fruitless question, such as debating whether the earth should revolve around the sun. So much of the idea of progress seems dubious, as has been noted, and thus the weight of the expectations and activities of contemporary man centers on technological progress. Since at least 1800, perhaps one might say since the invention of the wheel, our lives have grown mechanized and our futures have become a factor of the state of technical knowledge. As Henry Adams predicted, this has tended to become a cumulative process, accelerating past the visions of earlier generations. We have become sufficiently attuned to this today so that the predictions of future technological conquests are not the daydreams of a few but the common discussion of the many, and the manner of spending the wealth which future times will bring us is no longer considered imprudent. It is as if we were on an escalator in a large department store, climbing at an increasing tempo, so that as we ran up the moving stairs we were already calculating what we will do several floors higher.

That too must seem an obviously good thing to many, perhaps most, people. What can be finer than the high standard of living now available to vast multitudes, hitherto reserved for a very few, or (in the case of new inventions) to no one? But one must then see what benefits these inventions have, in fact, brought. We have remarked on some of these problems, but more can be said. The automobile has served as probably the most revolutionary artifact of our time; it has thoroughly changed our way of living in less than three-quarters of a century. Is it absolutely certain that the automobile has been a blessing? In its favor it has very greatly increased mobility, permitting people to travel widely and move often, thereby increasing both economic mobility and the geographic unification of the world. It materially enhances the capacity of humanity, the sense of control over human resources. Moreover, it can be credited with saving lives by making possible the rapid arrival of doctors and the speedy transmission of the sick to hospitals or secure places.

On the other hand, the deaths caused by the automobile very probably outnumber the lives saved. Beyond this statistic, often cited, are those injured by automobile accidents, or affected traumatically. This would surely come out to a negative score, without even adding up the smoke and carbon-monoxide problems. Socially, the same might be said. The sprawling megalopolis is an invention of the automobile age; ancient Rome, so noted for its size, or the biblically-famed size of Babylon pall in comparison with their modern counterparts. The effects on sexual mores, on leisure habits, on status emulation, on standards of beauty (consider the fact that within another quarter-century the area for parking in every large city must be vastly expanded) have been widely discussed. Perhaps automobile traffic will be eliminated in the central area of all great cities in a short time—the gems of the past like Oxford and Florence consider it now, the turn of New York and Paris may be sooner than we would have expected a few years ago—thus bringing the pendulum of change full circle with great rapidity. Already the status implications of the wheeled vehicle grow pale; soon walking may be the means of movement for the bon ton. The phenomenon of driving hours to go to work or to the airport is common talk. One can fly from São Paulo to Lima, the work of crossing a great continent ribbed with a mighty mountain range, in half a day—it will be less when supersonic planes come into use—but it takes almost as long to reach the distant São Paulo airport from the city. It is not just that progress does not bring happiness; on a simple material level the wonders of speed seem to create problems which grow more vexing as we advance.

The marvels of transportation technology are equaled in the field of communications. The telephone, the radio and television are even more wonderful than the automobile or the airplane; even Leonardo did not imagine conversing between London and Naples. The faults of television have been canvassed enough so that it is not heretical to suggest that that invention has serious demerits, that its non-appearance might not have been a great misfortune for mankind. In addition to the sins of vulgarity, television and radio are the most popular of the modern inventions among the totalitarian leaders because of their overwhelming collectivist potential. On the other hand, the telephone has the opposite qualities; it emphasizes the capacity of the individual to expand his powers rather than the power of the large institutions to capture his attention. The police complain that the telephone has shifted the advantage to the criminal through its use as a means of instant, hidden communication; no one has proposed that television has given the individual any new skill in coping with authority. These are perhaps the most important things to look for; modern technology is not a datum, a uniform mass of improvement, but a cornucopia with many different implications, with diverse effects. A choice in favor of individualism suggests a choice for the telephone and the automobile, rather than television and rapid transit, as the better developments of modern science.

But, as in every other case, that is not sufficient. In the case of the automobile the affects on urban life have been noted, so that at least a complement of mass transit appears now as a necessary antidote. The telephone, golden as it appears as a symbol of the enlargement of the human personality, possesses less splendid attributes as well. The police's answer to its privacy is to tap the wires, a solution thought of by others as well. And of course the privacy of the telephone is only comparative; to one who really cherishes his seclusion or choice of companions it can be an intolerable instrument of intrusion. Brandeis, who so often carried individualism to extreme positions, very rarely would even use the thing. He fortunately died before discussion of a combination of television and telephone arose; now we are told that in the future every person will carry such a device on his wrist, so that no one will ever be permitted a second of privacy.

It has frequently been said that privacy is, in general, a victim of science. This may or may not be true—we should be slow to forget that the intrusions of policemen and neighbors are as old as history, and that wire-tapping is still, in the West, less prevalent than intercepting letters was a few centuries ago. The important point is that it is valuable to judge each new development and see whether it improves the tenor of life as each of us sees it. From the viewpoint here expressed, some judgments can be made easily. The atomic bomb was certainly a dreadful misfortune, no matter how many isotopes come out of it. The development of ever more efficient electronic equipment may be helpful in improving the reproduction of the human voice, and further disseminate music and literature, but its cost in the devising of listening devices and hidden amplifiers is almost surely too great. A world where we can hear many more things, but in turn can be always overheard, will be a poorer world.

Electricity itself, perhaps the greatest discovery of all science, has its dark sides, but it has made possible so many inventions which have lightened the burden of detail work and spread understanding that it can reasonably be placed in the plus category. Other improvements, such as the use of immensely powerful self-reinforcing tools such as computers, have merit or demerit primarily as a by-product of their final results; that is, their proximate effect is to increase production, and the uses of that production then become the issue. The principle inventions, in other words, have vital impact in themselves on life, the others have changed our living by altering the amount of labor (or sometimes material) required to produce goods or services. In that case we must ask ourselves the final question—in our world of large possibilities has the thrust been misplaced?

This illustrates the dilemma of scientific progress. Atomic energy has great possibilities for good, in medical research and cheap power, as well as the now paramount possibility for bad. The wonders of modern airplane travel would have been perfected much more slowly if it had not been for the military needs —needs which came about because of the demand for means of delivering explosives which could wipe out whole cities, killing men, women, and children indiscriminately. Scientific progress seems to be most progressive, as Nef and Mumford complained, in its capacity for devising means of killing. The recurring objection that the ability to use the scientific and technological gains has not kept pace with them is now an accepted part of our culture. Or perhaps of our two cultures, for this is part of the basis of Snow's criticism—the scientific culture ever advancing, but leaving behind the practitioners and the value of the literary culture. We do not reject the scientific culture even when it is very disturbing. We do not destroy all airplanes because of their dangerous uses, nor do we ban or discourage the automobile (which could be done more easily, since there is no fear of being at a loss in international affairs) because of the manifest number of deaths it causes. On the contrary, these new inventions are very greatly encouraged, even when we know that lives are lost every month on their account, and that they may lead to many more lives being lost. Even atomic power is sacred; if all the nations came to agreement on weapons control, is it likely that effective steps would be taken to eradicate all uses of atomic energy? And yet, considering the risk that widespread knowledge of the techniques of thermonuclear fusion may make life on earth truly problematical, is this not a form of madness?

As to that we can say that the answer seems too clear for much discussion. All the scientific marvels of our age, no matter how dangerous in potential, are now universally desired. Of course many of them are desired for their social importance, and not intrinsically; many people yearn for swimming pools who could not care less whether they ever dive into one. But that is, as we have noted, a part and in fact a desirable part, of a diverse society. The merit of the market is that it will sift and constantly re-evaluate a new process or gadget. If men really wanted a shorter work week we would have it now, if television had made motion pictures obsolete or movies had eliminated the need for the legitimate theater, the latter would die. There is always a second or often a twenty-second chance in a working free market. This buoyancy may well be the great merit of modern technology, rather than the accomplishments of heavy industry. The senses of new things, of constant opportunity, of physical excitement superimposed on the intellectual ferment of original thought, are far more worthwhile than the glorious fact that men can travel a hundred times as fast now as in 1768. It is as with the antitrust laws; the value is in the becoming rather than the being; the opportunity and the diversity rather than the completed state of progress. We see that in the arts this implies no progress whatsoever, and perhaps the same is true in technical matters, from a social point of view. We might say that there was no natural merit in the rise in productivity in American industry from 1920 to 1939; the value came from the stimulation this gave to economic, and above all to social life. In fact this meant that the poor man could refrigerate his food, which made life more pleasant, but it also came along with highway snarls, and a great depression. It takes even more credulity to maintain that culture and material progress are necessarily allied; there are so many examples to the contrary from the Stone Age to our own that the suggestion that there is a negative correlation must be considered seriously.

But we have said, for at least 150 years, that the costs are worth the price—the unions who demur do not, as a rule, bargain for lower wages and declining productivity but usually, as in the case of John L. Lewis, finally choose the opposite. A liberal conservative should be sufficiently moderate to accept the decision of the people as to this choice, even though the forms may often seem tawdry or not worth the price—as long as the price is understood. But some changes are usually not the result of the market, and the price tag is not always apparent. The push for supersonic airplanes is a case in point. The private companies quickly determined that it would be a poor investment for them, and it now remains a question for the various governments. The prestige of the state involves a vaster sense of dignity than private parties can muster, and a correspondingly larger outlay of money. If a company or an individual designs a new product, let us say a new automobile, it must take a chance on public acceptance, which in itself interposes those qualities of habit and custom which are the accompaniment of a stable society. But the state can throw this restraint to the wind. The atomic bomb could never have succeeded commercially, which does not prove it good or bad but is a reminder that the revolutionary changes come from something more than everyday choice, that much of "progress" is not inevitable, but contrived or pushed.

In the last analysis it is necessary to reaffirm the priority of liberty and property, the basic lower-center values, over material progress. This, of course, should not be a new argument or an unfamiliar one to liberals. The slogan that only a man with food in his belly can appreciate freedom seems radical in the plays of Brecht, but it is but a restatement of the message of Dostoevski's Grand Inquisitor. He promised bread instead of freedom; the South African nationalists do the same, in their boasts that the black people of half a continent go toward the Union, not away, in search of the higher wages paid there. The liberal reply that freedom and bread go together may or may not be so; the liberal rejoinder that bread must come first implies that if it does not, everything else must wait. There is some validity to this if you are really talking about starving people but most, perhaps all, of the argument is about men with varying degrees of well-being in search for more. To subordinate everything to that search may well mean that the whole cause of political aspirations will be chained to the wagon of material progress.

Neither industrialism or centralization is an inevitable datum. Rather, it is up to us to decide how large a dose of both we care to have, and this must require constant decisions. As we are faced with the consequences of our technical progress, choices are inevitable—they are either made by default or by methods which are chosen by accident. For example, the issue of traffic control, which is becoming a major question of social order and therefore of politics, involves several nice questions of economic and social priority. The automobile, by its nature, is a more individualist instrument than the train or bus. It offers a far greater degree of flexible opportunity, its widespread use and victory over its collectivist competitors is a token of the preference of our alleged "mass man" for individually-controlled instruments. But the automobile has proved expensive; the maximum of personal choice it offers is, economically, wasteful. The suggestions of the advocates of rapid-transit systems make sense in many instances. As long as the bus or rail systems do not become monopolies in transporting people in a given area, they are highly desirable. There is no reason for the automobile to be greatly subsidized by cheap roads, if that is the case. Part of the cost may be a social cost, the stifling crowding of our highways or the construction of vast highway systems which may usurp great areas, uprooting large numbers of people and disrupting urban life. But then the proliferation of rail lines may be equally perilous—the malodorous "els" were precursors of the monorail.

In a situation in which social costs are the key question and the market does not operate, it is especially important to decide what costs one wishes to pay, and what these costs are. Progress in transportation is often dubious, yet it is ridiculous to think that we can abolish the inventions of the last two hundred years. But it is not ridiculous to weigh the merits of fostering more rapid movement against the losses in stability and land values (including aesthetic ones) which new programs will entail. In so weighing the costs another matter must be considered—are the economic or social advantages of collectivist transport more important than the public preference—rooted in a valuable protest against mass pressures—for individualist services? Two caveats come in here: first, this is a question which cannot be answered in any categorical fashion; it is an economic/social decision which is like the exercise of economic choice, variable in intensity and liable to change with the changing facts. Secondly, the state has a very essential function, but it is precisely because that function is important that we must guard against the state monopolizing all power, or (more subtly) treating the issue as a bureaucratic matter rather than as a resolution of social and personal needs. The market is valuable even in these areas because it operates on the axis of that spirit, and any substitute for it must relate to these perhaps "foolish" demands. If people truly prefer driving their own cars we will make a grave mistake to press for monorails as a form of higher virtue. The collectivist liberal often talks as if a technical, and collective, course is the only progressive and therefore right way. We may choose an individualist way, or we may reject progress. If the price of progress does finally come too high even the most pragmatic conservative must draw the line, even at the expense of our most beloved toys.

XIV

The Price
of Stability

What is true of traffic is, *a fortiori,* valid in the larger political matters of our time. The free-market conservative has very often used progress as a reason for refusing to consider the difficult demands of the left; material improvement would take care of the dissatisfactions and anxieties of the unhappy, so nothing must be allowed to disrupt the social forces which produce this progress. Camus, as we have noted, complained of this sacrifice of the present to the future, a sacrifice which requires faith in the glories of the next generation while denying any choice to the present. The move of the Soviet regime over the pole of the upper circle, from radical to reactionary, can be traced to the time that the Stalinist admonition that everything must be subordinated to future wealth became omnipresent in Russia. But if we admit that progress is ambiguous and that efficiency has its drawbacks, then this argument will not carry the same weight.

Three examples from current political debates will demonstrate this point. The argument over automation and labor efficiency customarily places the labor unions in the role of traditionalists and the businessmen as apostles of change. It is deceptively easy for the free-market conservative, especially the American conservative, to say that progress is all-important, that he stands for the right side, and that this, moreover, shows that the business position is liberal and the unions wickedly conservative. The efficiency enthusiast advocates the long view, and argues that the personal difficulties of the present must be subordinated to the greater view. If this greater view is simply more and more material goods, this is a borrowing of the cult of the future perfectibility of man used as a justification for today's hard-boiled behavior. If we want to preserve our society from constant change perhaps the conservative impulses of labor make some sense. The rapid elimination of large professions or active trades will often create hardship, and just the sort of hardship which militates against the inculcation of stable values, of the complex gradations which seem so important.

These gradations, as we have noted, are the stuff which infuses the free market with vitality; if technology were to pulverize society into a level grade it would be a serious disservice. Yet the market has its own way of encouraging this system of gradations, and Luddite stubbornness would obviously make a market system unworkable. For the sake of the free choice and mobility of the market, barriers to technical improvement must be prevented, but that does not mean that within this framework numerous compromises, depending on the circumstances, are not in order. To be specific, Lewis was right in arranging for the elimination of many coal-mining jobs because the work was and is dangerous and disagreeable, and the social cost was therefore smaller than is true in the railroad industry. In the latter example, there is a case for a much slower process toward job elimination. If an industry becomes especially efficient it owes an obligation to its workers to ease the process of change; if external forces are the cause, society (in other words, the government) has a similar obligation. On the other hand, if labor and management agree on some factor or condition slowing change or compensating for it, this must mean that labor should accept the cost of this in wages or other benefits.

It seems to many that the market, if given its way, will sweep away everything that stands in the path of lower costs. This is true only if you interpret these costs in an unsophisticated fashion. If workers prefer to take their rewards in the form of shorter hours production will decline, and perhaps unit costs will rise. This may take the form of union agreements, which are after all a form of market determination in the labor context, or it may come about through the natural workings of employee preference. The market may sometimes be a juggernaut of progress, but it can often be very dilatory; the archaism of New and old England would be crushed in a Soviet system.

Capital also costs money, and there are many innovations which are technically feasible but which are economically too costly. Here is where the left is splendidly progressive, denouncing à la Veblen the sabotage of progress by the absentee owners of money. The Soviets, true to form, abolished interest altogether, and in their way they were quite right; what could be more basic to capitalism than interest, the return of a premium on the lending of barren money? The Ricardian return of income to the owners of capital is all interest (plus or minus arbitrary and economically unimportant windfall items), and interest plus rent equals surplus value in Marx's teaching. Grossman has shown how this refusal to accept the validity of interest as a cost led the Russians to push industrial expansion to points which were technically sound but economically foolish, and were therefore, in economic terms, wasteful. There are innumerable capital improvements around if, as the apostles of the overfull automated society proclaim, scarcity has been abolished. If we could all borrow money indefinitely without cost, what would not be within our reach?

The conservative believers in progress, and even such cynics as Schumpeter and his cohorts, argued that this role of interest was justified only because of the gains capital produced. The productivity theory of interest holds that since an expenditure of capital on fixed assets will increase the capacity to produce, interest is the charge for that increase. If the economy is stagnant, interest will go to zero, in this view. Since capitalism is inconsistent with a stationary economy, according to Schumpeter, growth is both a virtue of the system and a necessity; one can presume from there that private property (but not inequality, which

Schumpeter rightly considered a very different matter) is tied up with a continual press of rising wealth and increasing investment.

The greatest difficulty with this theory of interest is that it fits history badly. Periods like that of the third and fourth centuries or the fourteenth century were marked by economic retrogression lasting many years, but there is no indication that the rate of interest went to zero, much less that other more subtle forms of return on capital disappeared. In fact the strict rate of interest—the return on money lent—has declined in real, Fisherian terms in boom times. That is, the net return to the lender after taking into consideration the buying power of his money has often been less than zero in periods of inflation and rapid growth, and this has sometimes been true for long periods, as in the sixteenth century. During the Middle Ages interest rates were often quite high in periods of stagnation; men borrowed money to spend, and not to invest. This seems like a typically medieval thing to do, until we remember that the fantastic growth of consumer credit has reintroduced this on a vast scale today. The thrifty spirit of the Whig age (which certainly can be exaggerated, when one thinks of the gambling in the eighteenth and the banquets in the nineteenth century) seems quite past; men borrow money now, as in the past, because they prefer to enjoy goods now than in the future. The time theory of interest is based on this proclivity, and eschews the principle of progress in favor of an old-fashioned explanation of human insouciance.

If mankind is divided into natural savers and spenders, and if the latter are naturally more numerous and importunate, it is understandable that as long as there are any goods which require capital and/or labor to perfect, a price will be paid for these goods by the spenders. This price stands in the way of growth in the sense that it is money diverted from rewarding and encouraging greater accumulation of goods which can produce more goods. As with advertising, or horse racing, or the teaching of dead languages, moneylending becomes a feature of an indolent, or at least a particular society, and is quite consistent with a free market. There can be no doubt that Veblen and his disciples who so thunder against our "paper" economy and its silly pursuits are right in one thing—we could produce many more physical goods if we put all our might to do so. In Russia heavy industry does not have to bid against buyers of automobiles for capital. If we produced clothing or pianos the way we manufactured armaments during the Second World War, every man would have very much to wear, or hear. No marketing problem then intervened between the assembly line and the user, everyone who could possibly work had a job, and the statistics of industrial production showed a magnificent rate of growth. The drop in production immediately after the war in the United States was impressively bad. The free market and the maximum rate of economic growth are not Siamese twins.

A free-market economy can reward the strangest factors and the least likely people; it can also work hardship in its rigor. The settlement of some of these hardships has become a part of the market, insofar as the web of private pensions, union contracts, and philanthropic programs which covers the Western world have altered but also enriched the free economy of our time. Since the reason of the market is not an absolute standard but a distillation of myriads of changing reasons, this is not an abridgement of the rationality of the free market, but an extension. These reasons may include material progress but they will encompass much more—and rightly so. A big business, for instance, stands to gain by labor stability and attractiveness (which may well have been the reason for Ford's famous five-dollar day of 1914); the corporation may gain in good will or the owners and officers may gain internal satisfaction; and of course it avoids strikes or other bitterness. As conditions are now evolving these market responses are becoming part of the given situation, the custom which underpins the choices of the economic world.

This will continue, to be sure, and newer customs will intermingle with the old ones until the number and variety of employee fringe-awards stagger the imagination. Some of these will seem foolish; as more and more people live past sixty it seems strange that early retirement schemes increase, yet this form of enjoying prosperity is as natural as increasing the number of automobiles, and often less deadly. The great affluence of our time presents the market, thus considered broadly, with more choices, more varieties of development than before. In this multiplying sea of new institutions and subsidies the state will have its place (that much is sure) and as long as that place is to guarantee a floor it need not be uncongenial. The role of the state in making good the requirements of those who fall below the customary minima or outside the framework of private programs becomes more clear as these programs increase and the minima rise. As long as all of this serves to supplement and add scope to the play of the market it cannot be faulted on the ground that it slows up progress; moreover, the market will become more popular and more acceptable insofar as the toughest cases are provided for by supplementary assistance.

On the other hand, this is acceptable only as a supplement to the market. The permanent support of a class (which may be quite well off itself) is as objectionable as the forced-draft fomenting of change for progress' sake. The spectacle of rich men taking time off from denunciations of socialism to ask for or demand governmental subsidies or encouragement for private price-setting schemes is disgraceful. Moreover, the average man in the street in the United States and Sweden and perhaps even Italy is a rich man in relation to the rest of the world, and insofar as he becomes accustomed to special treatment he will come to regret it. But it is not necessary for this reason to reject the involved patterns of the welfare states which have contributed to the satisfactions of shared wealth and have encouraged new markets (as with the insurance industry) without destroying the old.

A second argument for moderation can be deduced from the fiscal and monetary institutions of our mixed society. In a pure market economy the workings of Say's laws would inevitably bring supply and demand into perfect equilibrium—not without periods of hardship for some, and drastic shocks to others. But such a pure market would require structural changes; bankruptcy laws might have to be restricted, union wage contracts would have to be substantially limited, perhaps even the limited liability rights of corporations would have to be eliminated or modified. The free movement of labor and capital throughout the world is a necessary *sine qua non* in this interrelated age, and perhaps even the existence of diverse monetary and legal systems would be insuperable obstacles to a world market system à la Say. Above all, if the state is to have no role one must make sure that military expenditures, the sanctioned prerogative of the state, must be absolutely held within very narrow bounds or somehow adjusted to the market.

Much of this is desirable, some of it worth working toward, but none of it is likely today or has been in this millennia. As long as we have an economy with traditional customs and institutions and as long as we are experimenting with new ones in our reactions to technological change and medical accomplishments, the question must be tackled as to how these governmental powers which are now worked into our system (and a good part of this we have traced to those very individualist Benthamites, it must be remembered) can be managed so as to enhance the freedom of the market and to keep growth from becoming either an overwhelming monster or a dangerous mirage. This is where Keynes came in.

Wright has detailed the conservative implications of Keynes, so there is no need to press these here. One point is worth repeating: when one inspects the theory the key role of wages is evident; depressions come because costs, and especially wage costs, cannot be reduced sufficiently within a quick enough period of time. If wages could be cut sufficiently rapidly, Keynes admitted, the profit opportunities would increase to the point where private investment would be adequate to charge the recovery. But this was impossible, Keynes reasoned, because of a natural dislike of lower wages fortified by the power of the trade unions. It is possible to argue from Keynesian premises that the key to depressions is an economy flexible enough, and a social system stern enough, to check those forces which stand in the way of quick wage reduction in bad times. The liberals who argue for higher wages in such times are obviously worse than foolish; perhaps only Marxists—in power, that is—will do.

It is not only a hesitation on the part of conservatives to resemble Stalin that accounts for a reluctance to play this role. The analysis may be eminently sound, but the application would not be worth the price in social stability. Keynes argued this, declaring that it would be impossible to effect such a reduction. He used examples from situations such as inter-war England which were not conclusive; it is better to say that the overall health of a society, the operation of a system which commands the loyalty of all citizens, will require that the market work as a broad system, envisaging numerous bargains rather than the sharp cut of economic forces alone. The Marxist state can push down wages because it has destroyed the bourgeoisie, and the new ruling class is firmly in control and beyond attack; if we accept the give and take of constitutional democracy perhaps the price we must pay is the friction of our economy, depressions and all.

This becomes more clear when we analyze the other frictions which Keynes specifies as a drag on recovery. He suggested that interest rates do not drop adequately because at some point people will choose to hoard rather than to lend money at derisible rates. This is known as liquidity preference by Keynesians, and the justification for the rate of interest at the level at which holders will prefer not to lend may be called the liquidity theory of interest—interest as a price paid for not hoarding. In many respects this theory of interest bears a resemblance to the time theory; in both cases there is a hypothesis that men will prefer to use money to fulfill prudential desires or to satisfy short-term pleasures rather than to serve the goddess of Progress. What Keynes proposed makes a good deal of sense: it may be true that classical theory would require that in bad times the rate of return on money should fall to zero, but the owners of money have good reasons to hold back their wealth as a safeguard against the problems and risks of economic disorder, rather than to lend it for almost nothing. This reluctance is, as Keynes stated, a twin to the reluctance of workers to accept sharply lower wages. In both cases the friction is damaging to economic flexibility and progress, and if pressed far can upset the economic equilibrium, but if one looks upon these as natural forces within the market system, working to preserve customary situations, they become understandable and even necessary. More, they become part of the prudence of an established system, which can be ignored at the risk of destroying the expectations which hold that system together. They are allied to the anti-bigness theme of antitrust laws and the omnipresent sense of class alignment; they structure a society and give a sense of reward within the market system, so that the noble reason has an alloyed base. In the world of politics, the statesman who refuses to accept this is swept aside like Bruening and Hoover; and in the meantime he finds himself approving forms of aid to banks and estates because everything cannot be let loose at once. Hoover himself told how scornful he felt of Mellon's conclusion that the economy would just have to go through the wringer—it is not recorded what Mellon thought of proposals to eliminate the tariff, *in toto*, to facilitate that process. It has sometimes amazed students how complete the Keynesian revolution has been; but it should seem strange how long it took to accept the theory which came with the universal practice of even the most capitalistic societies. That revolution, as we have often been reminded, led not to the Finland Station but to Bretton Woods; it was, as Cros styled it, "a revision of liberalism . . . which indicates liberal conclusions, never a general conclusion."

Nevertheless, if we are to incorporate Keynes into a moderate conservative political theory there is a lot of pruning to do. Part of this must be done with the original, more with the work of the Keynesians, more catholic in their zeal than the Pope. The chief objection, from the conservative point of view, to Keynes' teachings is his underlying disdain for the processes of business adjustment. Keynes accepted the fact that investment, his key to economic strength or weakness, was a lever which had been wielded with great effectiveness by the business community during the nineteenth century. He argued that investment by the state held the same potency that business investment had, and with some exceptions the thesis is reasonable. But Keynes, like most leftists, went farther; he suggested (at times, and always with skillful caveats) that in our time the élan or the moral worth of business investment had so diminished that there was more danger in reducing the power of the state than there could be in discouraging business confidence. It therefore followed that unemployment must always be answered by more government intervention and investment, that the "secular" issue, as Hansen later described it, was one of perpetual failure by private enterprise to generate sufficient investment. The counter-cyclical requirements—which are conservative in their emphasis on balance and degree—thus became subordinated to the liberal demands for a constant emphasis on state activity and prodding.

To be fair to Keynes, the writings of his last years shows that he understood the broader conservative implications of his thought. It is not only that he accepted the role of deflationary advocate in 1939 and afterwards, but also, as Harrod clearly shows, that in his last years he argued for the cosmopolitan tools of the market system as part of the needs of a world in which supply, not demand, was inadequate. In other words, he showed that Keynesian economics surmounted the political base of its genesis, and that in some times it could stress the conservative goal of maximizing transactions (production) rather than the liberal goal of multiplying the supply of money. In all this he confirmed the separation of Keynesian fiscal and monetary thought from the sense of inter-war despair and egalitarian earnestness.

As we look back over the events since the publication of Keynes' magnum opus in 1935, two facts prove very interesting. First, the depression-based assumption that economic decline would be the overwhelming problem has been quite inaccurate. If deficits are suitable in time of unemployment and falling prices, and surpluses in periods of inflation and high demand, we have seen more of the latter than the former. The gloom of 1938 (repeated in part by our worriers over automation today) was premature, at the least; but the fears of those who predict the depreciation of all currencies have been much more capably substantiated. Secondly, the fears of Keynes seem, like many of those of Freud, limited by the timidities of Victorian propriety. Keynes feared that states would fear to take needed moves because of their devotion to sound money; but it has proved, as seems to be a general rule in democracies, that unsound money will prove to be easier for a demagogue or a restless public.

In other words, the necessary amendments to classic economic theory made by the Keynesians must be considered in the balanced view of a broad conservatism. It is foolish to talk of a balanced budget as if the state were a petty bourgeois housekeeper; the better analogy is with a public utility, anxious to borrow to develop new wealth. It is unwise to talk of debt as an absolute, rather than as a ratio, proportionate to income and to production. In saying this conservative thought is not compromising; it is accepting the value of just that sophisticated reasoning which is needed in rejecting the absolutes of egalitarianism and social tinkering. Just as Marshall said that it was a constitution with which he was dealing, so we can speak of a market and not a peddler's stall. But if we are to be sophisticated we must take into consideration the capacity, and incapacity, of human nature, and the implications of governmental regulation. Since we have repeatedly observed the spectacle of vast increases in the public debt caused by military expenditures, it is not enough to say that in time of peace the debt has grown no more than the national income. A public utility will leave itself room for sudden growth of debt and will reduce that debt, proportionately, if it grows too large. It will not press to the limit of its resources as a general rule, and it will not rely on the devaluation of money as a crutch for its financing. It is one thing to say that if the GNP grows by 50 per cent, the debt may grow equally without ill effects. But if 25 per cent of that growth derives from inflation, we are saying something else—we are saying that the debt was supported by the GNP through the medium of price rises. This happened retrospectively in the United States after World War II—the debt increases from 1941 to 1945 fueled the price rises through the early 1950's, so that the debt reduction, in relation to GNP, came partly as a result of inflation, and reinstated the pre-1942 balance. In short, if we wish to balance debt and income, government spending and private investment, there are many ways, and the way of bigger government spending is perhaps inevitably keyed (as Clark suggested) to an inflationary solution.

Nor, to a sophisticated student, is the Keynesian balance as easy as it appears in the textbooks. Myrdal's famous mistake has been mentioned. It is important to observe Dow's findings that the German equilibrium since 1950 has been achieved in spite of rather than because of state economic acts, for these attempts to balance were invariably exercised at times when they worked pro, rather than counter, cyclically. The causes were structural (the delays in execution) and political (the attractions of money-spending schemes when saving was in order); the solutions were the same—the vast capacity for private saving which overcame the errant impulses of the government. The current problems of the United States amply demonstrate that it is much easier to talk of the deflationary potential of Keynesian thought than it is to put these ideas in practice.

But, it is argued, when the need is for less saving and not more, and the government fails to act, there is then no virtue in the private sector which can counterbalance this fatal propriety (as Keynes saw it) of capitalism. It is no condemnation of capitalism to say that it fosters, in time of healthy stability, a bias toward saving. As De Jouvenel asserts, the bourgeois spirit is private and thrifty in its basic makeup. The merchant class has always nursed a sense of virtuous solidity, the ethos of the ant as against the grasshoppers above and below in the social scale. This is one of the attractions which capitalism has for minority groups, for it is highly comforting to a man who feels that society and the majority are gross or malevolent to know that he has a reserve of money, attained by careful saving and inner control, to secure him against the power of his detractors. But perhaps capitalism as a way of life converts this individualism into a social system, and when the power of capitalism becomes institutionalized there is a tendency toward saving for its own sake. If the economy is growing rapidly this is desirable; but if not, there is a need for the spending forces to counterbalance this thrift. The exuberance of spenders is not so petty a force as some would have it—we can see this in the wonders of consumer debt—but there are many times when the government should also throw its free-spending inclinations into the scale. This is another example of the previously considered idea that if government is limited and disciplined, it can at the same time be allowed, even encouraged, to become a counterpoise to the otherwise overwhelming bourgeois values.

Obviously, from a conservative point of view, it will be better to provide for these deficits through lower taxes shifting purchasing power to the citizens than through higher expenditures increasing the role of the state. This is a clear-cut matter of individualism versus collectivism, and this issue is easily spotted as a key left/right distinction in today's politics. But a more subtle matter of taxation involves many of these issues. There has been an increasing tendency, in most of the Western countries, to channel tax reductions toward corporations. Thus depreciation allowances have been amplified and expense accounts have been permitted to become a major source of semi-income. It often seems, as the British example demonstrates, that the politicians of the left are angrier at dividends—the rewarding of the rich, it can be alleged—than profits, which can be accepted as a motive power for investment. In other words, the case for business is based on the need for financing growth, so that the collectivist tendencies of the corporate system are enhanced. In the United States we have experienced, in the years 1962–64, simultaneous increase of depreciation allowances and an elimination of the dividend credit. Above all, the gap between the corporate tax rate and the personal tax rate in the higher brackets (which has been reduced, to be sure, in many nations, and quite considerably in the United States—one step in the right direction) has greatly encouraged, far more than any other, Berlean, reason, the tendency toward corporate reinvestment.

If we cut down this blind faith, this tropism toward growth, the inexorable sacrifice of individualist values can be checked. If the prime merit of our social planning is the enhancement of individual diversity and heterogeneity, we should tax distributed profits less than undistributed ones, and channel the rewards of monetary policy toward benefiting the individual. Keynesian monetary and fiscal policy provides us with tools to refine such an intention more than the blunter tools of classical policy. In such a condition we would encourage the flexible use of governmental and quasi-governmental (e.g., central bank) power to encourage the maximum development of individual choice. For example, variable tax schedules have not really been tried as they might. To be sure, this does mean that the fiscal controllers will exercise a great deal of power, but it is significant that power will adhere to the canons of classical economic theory—it will operate through market influences and operate by influencing prices. Keynesian economic control is in competition throughout much of the world with the theories of direct control, of allocation of resources by rationing or regulation and the determination of priorities by political means. This is no mean virtue, for it places Keynesian policy within the framework of the market system. If that policy is then used to the advantage of the very qualities which are the reasons for and the causal forces behind the free-market system, we must say that the conservative idea of Keynesian thought is not just, as Schumpeter rather waspishly thought, a *jeu d'esprit*, but a real gain for the liberal conservative, government-spending programs and all. And, final irony of all, this is perhaps only fitting, for the Keynes who made a fortune speculating in the stock market and devoted much of it to the exquisite fostering of often unpopular forms of high art was a brilliant exponent of the very qualities to which we have referred. In the constant effort of the conservative rationalist to bridge the gap between the ideas of individual reason and the monolithic attractions of mass reason, the philosophy and the example of Keynes are two ways to reach a *modus vivendi*—no, more, a pattern of limited state action which can utilize the influence of the state to improve individual values. Viewed thusly, it is well worth accepting a few liberal values, some rather distasteful, as part of the bargain.

This good which we choose over its proverbial enemy, the best, can be noted especially in our final example. The growth of great private institutions has created forms of quasi-coercion which bedevil the individualist and encourage state power. We have noted the admonitions of liberals to reform our political views to take into account the "political" power of corporations —to increase the coercive power of the state in order to check or regulate new sources of allegedly uncontrolled power. The same issue arises with regard to labor unions. The matter of the closed shop and the union shop is also a case where private organizations have developed, within a narrow range, a degree of authority which limits the individual. But what, for instance, is a union shop? It is a given company or factory where all employees must join the union of the majority to hold their job. This is coercive per se, one might say, but it differs from governmental coercion in several crucial respects. No one has to work in a given job nor does anyone have a right to a job—this is obvious conservative doctrine—and a man who holds a job cannot dictate the terms of his employment. In the situations where union shops prevail the union, which represents at least in theory the majority of the workers, makes an agreement with the management that a part of the wages will go to union dues; if the wages were lower the worker would end up with the same income. The difference in payment is the result of bargaining which is consistent with free economy—collective bargaining to be sure, but not the result of a command.

It will be said that this is unrealistic, that it leaves out key matters which color the picture. What if the union requires adherence to internal rules—punishments for nonattendance at meetings or for strikebreaking, requirements of political contributions, et cetera? At this point we may say that the coercive situation becomes enhanced—a union which "fines" its members, like a ball club which "fines" its players, can be said to be exercising a form of governmental power, and control by the state pursuant to its monopoly on coercion becomes advisable. This control is valid even if the members join without constraint, but *a fortiori* if there is a union shop. The agency shop, which requires payment of dues but not membership, is a good answer to the objection that membership implies a too-severe tie. However, the mere requirement of membership is not a kind of attempt at sovereignty. The reason derives not from a demand that everyone must subordinate his will to the union idea—which would be dangerously collectivist—but arises from the sense that the non-member is a "free rider." If we are correct that the union role in raising wages has been exaggerated this may be often a foolish concern, but this difference of opinion—and in individual cases of course the facts may vary greatly; some unions have surely pushed wages up sharply in given situations—is what a free society leaves to the decisions of private groups and individuals.

In other words, in a complex society where there are many levels between the state and the individual, theory must work to balance these interests and not stake all on a state-enforced individualism. The primary issue of coercion and liberty arises out of the power to compel—the state's power to compel from the outside and the union's, and management's, right to compel from the inside. When the two conflict it is wise to remember which compulsion is most potent over the long run. The large fines inflicted by some unions are highly objectionable, but it is not fair to think of all of the labor movement, or even the closed-shop craft sector of it, as riddled with this. Political levies are also objectionable, and the United States Supreme Court has recently moved toward (and will perhaps move farther) holding such levies to be a form of quasi-governmental deprivation of due process when exacted by a union enjoying a union shop. Significantly, the same issue arose, and more starkly, with regard to an "education" program by a lawyers' association which every registered attorney was compelled to join—it is not a matter of unions alone. The British have always recognized the delicacy of these matters, and the left and right have argued only whether a member would have to agree to contribute, or volunteer not to contribute—"contracting in," or "contracting out," as they say—and not over the basic principle.

But these exercises of state control are perilous, and especially so to conservatives concerned with the separation of the public and private zones. It is especially striking to see rightists talk of the right to work, the Blancist slogan, and to argue for governmental control over contracts of employment. One sees the same thing in regard to the agitation for control over industry-wide bargaining. In 1946 and 1947 there was a considerable clamor among the anti-Wagner Act forces in this country for a ban on this dangerous weapon; now it appears that many industrialists complain that the unions refuse to bargain industry-wide, but seek to pick off the companies one by one. Therefore we now hear demands that nationwide unions be eliminated, or that at least the Sherman Act be applied to unions. The advocates of these positions by no means wish to dismember nationwide corporations, nor are they noted for their zeal in commending the Sherman Act in any other area.

This hypocrisy is matched, as ever, by the reverse spirit on the left. This is not accidental, for many of the radicals and reactionaries seek statist solutions for the benefit of their interest groups while talking a good moderate message. The result of the collectivist solution applied to one side is, very frequently, more collectivism on the other. The rules governing union behavior, like the antitrust laws, are complex, at times contradictory regulations aimed at preventing group abuses, and this is rightfully a major individualist task. It is not essential that each law deal exactly the same with one side as with the other. The antitrust laws are not immediately applicable to union conditions because the sale of labor is different, to a degree and only partially, from the sale of other commodities—this has always been accepted. On the other hand there are arguments for ensuring majority rule in unions, especially those which enforce union shops, which are pernicious in the money-scaled electorate of the corporation. The advantages given to corporations may rightly imply certain forms of state control, just as the Wagner Act and similar legislation or judicial rulings may suggest other—not identical—curbs on unions. The Berleans and the right-to-work groups deny that they seek to destroy the institutions they wish to control, but it must be recognized that at the point where all the activities of an organization become dependent on state authority the lifeblood of the institution becomes nothing more than an official lubricant. This will encourage the institution to influence the government, in turn, so that neither is truly independent. The unions in Batista's Cuba were powerful, not economically but as part of the political apparatus; the Histadrut in Israel is either the boss of, or the tool of, the government, but hardly an independent force. We know what happened to the free unions of Cuba—the unions of Weimar Germany which were independent, but like the Histadrut, politically affixed, also perished quickly when the political nexus turned sour. The example from the corporation side of the river is equally murky. The examples of too much reliance on the state are too numerous to require reiteration.

As with taxation, these issues, which seem so simple from the far left or right, are actually very complicated. For example, Friedman suggests that all occupational licensing is anti-libertarian and wrong, even that of doctors. This is a bold example of logical free-market thought, and its consistent devotion to free-market ideals deserves more serious attention than it will get. The doctors are a conservative lot, just as the most fervent apostles of zoning are often the rich people who hate the thought of middle-income people living near them. Residential zoning requirements and licensing occupations are good examples of how this collectivism can protect the interests of many people who are not very downtrodden. But the Friedmanian solution may be, empirically, very disappointing to those who equate the free market with progress or true freedom, in a philosophical sense. Friedman suggests that the good doctors certify each other, as a non-coercive form of control; this might humiliate and drive out the less-favored doctors. The total absence of certification might very likely be an invitation to a throng of quacks. So, too, the absence of zoning would not ensure social mixture; the non-enforcement of racial covenants has not brought about racially-mixed housing patterns. As the state retreats public opinion may advance, perhaps substituting a non-appealable and private tyranny. Subordinating the public goals to the multiplicity of private values maximizes liberty but does not grant the individual a mystical freedom, and it is not a panacea.

Often the individualist must balance many virtues, as in the matter of privacy. On the one hand, we have the basic desirability of human privacy. The experience of modern China, with informers by the millions and regulations for every act (down to killing flies), shows that the atmosphere of 1984 was not so wild a fear. In some ways privacy is anterior to liberty; it has been said that the right not to act is more basic than the right to act—without internal self-sufficiency and the physical distance to maintain this, the exercise of human reason may become, for all but the most self-contained or introverted, a fictitious freedom. This is another of Berlin's positive liberties, perhaps not liberty at all but it is closer to it than equality, because it affords scope for the individual to develop his separateness. Therefore one must say that if industrial progress means less and less privacy, either through the increase of the power of state interference with private lives or through the invention of new tools with which our neighbor, or any stranger, can pry into our existence, it may be a mistake to have the progress.

But, as with everything, there is the other hand. It is not enough to subordinate progress to privacy; there are other values, all of which must be considered. If we set as our goal the aggrandizement of privacy we must interfere with other rights, and often with other people's liberty. The issue of free press versus fair trial is relevant; the sanctity of the judicial process, a species of privacy, is often invaded by the efforts of the mass media to publicize even the most personal details. The laws against defamation are among the historic tools of defense against the inroads of overanxious journalists. Justice Black has held that all of these laws are violations of the Bill of Rights, a view with some logical if no historical basis. Since 1890 the law of defamation has been supplemented in the United States by an inchoate body of law deriving in large part from the concepts of the right of privacy advocated by Brandeis and Warren. No one has yet called Brandeis' handiwork unconstitutional, yet it may serve to discourage a large area of activity, such as the unauthorized publishing of pictures or interviews or the engaging in verbal harassment, which used to be thought of as part of one's freedom.

Moreover, if privacy is a highly prized good, is it not inconsistent to be concerned about the great area of governmental secrecy? Yet it is often the very same people who have so staunchly fought for the preservation of the Fifth Amendment as a defense of private judgment and a safeguard against inquisitions who also denounce the spread of rules restricting public access to state documents or reports. It is not merely that these people, conveniently for our purposes usually liberals, are exposed hypocrites, although some probably are; the problem must reach anyone who attempts to sort out a scale of values when the various goods conflict. It is certainly possible, for instance, to be in favor of some degree of privileged non-disclosure as a safeguard for confidences made within the executive branch of the government, while still opposing the broader ideas of restriction of information—the value of privacy of communication, in this case a sort of public privacy, gives way at some point to the value of the free flow of information. Moreover, secrecy in government is in some ways the antithesis of privacy in private affairs—the manifestation of the superior power of the state to control its subjects while still being above control itself. As Shils puts it, "secrecy is privacy made compulsory." Once again, the public/private dichotomy is a vital part of the conservative heritage, and the position of conservative liberals such as Shils is parallel to, and a support of, the conservative effort to maintain diverse but basically complementary individualist principles. The power of coercion in the state makes it a prime threat to individual privacy, especially when the state will not permit its own exercise of power to be scrutinized. It is significant that the Soviet Union is a land where even the most personal aspects of family life are flagrantly open—the housing shortage has been a suspicious convenience all these years—yet, as various observers have pointed out, telephone books are impossible to obtain and road maps are almost nonexistent. It should be the other way around—free information in regard to things which apply to public affairs, and a right of privacy in regard to the personal or the self-regarding matters. And that is why the executive right not to disclose can be supported while government regulations should be publicized to the maximum degree—the state too has its rights, its inner needs, and the best system will provide not a denigration of either public or private, but a close working relationship where important and a fair role for both. If we must choose, the private sector will come first; however, not as a sole claimant but as the perhaps most desirable part of a total synthesis. The gravest fault of free-market conservatism, its legacy from the radical past, has been to ignore this balance in search of the individual values; just because the pendulum has swung so far toward the collective one should not tilt it backward with too much zeal.

The great issues of public versus private often disclose these problems. The current controversy over the applicability of the Bill of Rights to private parties is very relevant. The advocates of broad application say, in effect, that although the Fifth and Fourteenth amendments to the United States Constitution apply only to the actions of governmental bodies, to "state action" as the lawyers phrase it, one must construe that term very broadly. Any action by the judicial branch, they assert, even the enforcement of a contract or a will or the settlement of a property claim or a trespass action, is action by the state. Or even further, some have advocated that any business or activity which is licensed by the state or under some form of state control presents a case of state action. Our analysis earlier is obviously in disagreement with that position, for this interpretation of state action makes all forms of state activity one, so that the existence of the government destroys the autonomy of private action. The gradations of public and private would be eliminated, or at least gravely weakened by a system of thought which categorized everything beyond the totally personal an aspect of social action susceptible to governmental control. This would indeed undo the great work of the Whig spirit, the eighteenth-century victory of the private/public separation.

But in fairness to these advocates one must recognize the problems which they are trying to solve. There is no clear-cut line between the two sectors—tort law, for example, represents a borderline between the zone of state control and private agreement—so one must find a vague sort of line which will answer the specific circumstances in this area. Social problems do not terminate at the border of state action, at the limits of the public sector. The problem of racial discrimination, for instance, obviously is not confined to the conventional areas of governmental activity. In this area the original wrong was pre-eminently a matter of coercive restraint, but the results of that restraint have affected even the most innocent aspects of social conduct. It is possible to argue that the intense awareness of race which has been inherited from slavery has so corrupted the market system that special rules are needed. These rules may be found in the Bill of Rights, and in so doing it may seem that a fine set of libertarian restraints is expanding its scope.

But that is a very superficial judgment. It is just when the problems are acute that it is most important to be aware of the fundamental criteria. It is one thing to pass laws to deal with problems of social relationships—such as those of racial discrimination in public accommodations. In so doing there must be a conflict with the rights of private property but it has been customary, and it is a good custom, for businesses to be subject to a variety of restraints in connection with their sales arrangements. A hotel does have an obligation to the public deriving from its historic role as a resting place and secure hostel and from its continuing role as a facility of civilized living. It would be a mistake, however, to confuse this obligation with an identity with the institutions of government. If, in the contemporary American context, hotels are governed by the Bill of Rights in the same way that post offices are, then the hotel is not merely controlled by the police power of the state, but becomes an adjunct of the state. The guaranties of freedom of speech and association which apply to post offices might prove unwieldy in hotels, just as the exquisitely designed, almost rococo distinctions which have developed in the area of religious establishment would be ghastly in all the fields in which the public interest has a place. Justice Black has pointed out that a fervent dedication to the cause of elimination of governmental activity in the areas of speech and press (such as the libel laws) presupposes an equal concern about limiting the areas of the government. If every man has a constitutional right to speak in the parks, a broad interpretation of the word "park" must endanger the principle or destroy all privacy.

This can be seen clearly in other areas. The conception of the quasi-state action thesis in American constitutional law has been traced to those cases which held that private corporations or groups which, in effect, operated cities or political parties became what they controlled—a kind of biological adaptation in political theory. With a company town this makes a good deal of sense, but from this Berle, and even more his followers, has sought to extend the principle to all companies affected with a public interest—i.e., every corporation. Formulas which dealt with the borderline cases of private action and held sovereign implications have tended to become rationales for a theory which equates the corporation with the state. Of course these are very often tight questions—perhaps AT&T is something of a sovereign in its exercise of power over the use of telephones. But if we proceed from that to treat it as a branch of the government, subject to the Bill of Rights as any bureau would be, we must then go—and this has already taken place in the thesis of some of the partisans of the extension of the Bill of Rights—to the local gas station or the village store. What starts out as an edifying expansion of individual rights becomes an elimination of the very distinction which nurtured these rights. In some respects the total victory of the concept of omnipresent state action is more disturbing than a thorough socialism would be; under socialism all of private enterprise might become government property, but under the formulas of constitutionalism the very choice between public and private is forfeited, as a matter of fundamental law. In this one material respect there lies a comparison with communism; the opportunity for flexibility and choice, for reversing the tendency of state power, is relinquished under a system which takes all of society as an entity judged by one set of rules.

These issues are implicit in the current rage for "participative democracy." As we have noted, democracy succeeds insofar as it allies the committed concern of the public and the authority of the state. But when this is imported into the private sector it well may flatten all of the autonomous and diverse arrangements into the uniformity of the mass society. Co-determination in industry carries the potential (although this has not yet come about in Germany) of rendering the market inoperable and the unions ineffectual or both. So, too, the demands for "student power" may destroy the traditions and the special qualities of university life in the process of democratization. The dangers of this can be seen in the history of higher education in Latin America. Greater collective power usually results in less individual choice, both within and among the colleges. The block meetings of the Chinese cities are the *ne plus ultra* of participation; it is not surprising then that when all contribute no one has any real say. The voter may end up as a subject or, as in the modern state, a national. The French Revolution would thus be re-enacted throughout society. There is a vein of feeling in the protest against alienation which must concern everyone who upholds the value of the individual. It would be a better world if most employees could be independent contractors. This, however, is a different matter than the universal rule of democracy. The reliance of the participator must be in the complex free market of the new neo-classicists. Even then, we cannot expect that the exercise of power will be uniformly passed around like social-security numbers.

The great movement of the seventeenth and eighteenth centuries toward the Whig system was not, despite a common modern conception, a naive crusade. Locke and Montesquieu were not ignorant of the claims of unitary philosophies intent on a single brand of social virtue; they were very cognizant indeed of the history of the Church. Much of the value of that firm public/private dichotomy, which now so often seems quaintly archaic, was seen at that time as a vital inhibition of the centralizing powers. The men of the late sixteenth century, such as Ponet, who argued for the separation of property and governing rights were not ignorant of the harshness of individuals, but they saw that danger to liberty was much less than the danger of state power, for what the prince can give he can take away, more easily if the opposition to his rule has been eradicated. Ewart Lewis has remarked that "it was the obstinacy of property that blocked the way of early modern absolutism, and in the fury of civil war befriended parliamentary government, civil liberties, and the rule of law." Huey Long was, as prewar southern politicians went, very enlightened on the race issue, and his subjugation of the private organizations in Louisiana might well have produced a better climate of racial equality. But it would have destroyed the chance for the NAACP, or any other private organization, to work effectively toward its own ends.

It is better to preserve the multiform net of private organizations, of free institutions and even intolerant cliques, than to force all of society into one mold. To be sure, this will mean that some improper conditions will grow, that some of the free societies will be arrogant or mean. Gibbon recounts how Julius Atticus, on finding a treasure, felt it necessary (men had been executed for failure to do this) to offer it to the Emperor Nerva. The latter, being a good emperor, spurned the gift, whereupon Julius Atticus, still fearful, insisted that he himself might not use it well. Then abuse it, Nerva responded; the message has validity today.

Nero, definitely not a good emperor, wished all Rome had but a single neck. Even the best society governed by one common set of fundamental laws would, in a very real sense, have one neck. If children were protected from their parents by writs of habeas corpus there might be fewer paternal tyrants, but there would also be many more policemen and less chance for family loyalty. It has always been the job of conservatism, and perhaps especially liberal conservatism, to attempt to look beyond the most attractive desires of an age into the broader desiderata of the society and to find these values in the widest possible range of ideas. Today it sometimes seems to liberals that private organizations are less noble than the spirit of legal justice, but if we substitute the NAACP for the White Citizens Council we can see the other side. The United States Supreme Court has composed some very fine essays on the rights of free association, and the logic of these opinions applies to corporations. Too often at this point champions of the NAACP often change sides. The same issues are at stake here, for the considerations of the worth of non-governmental organizations are as much at stake in the one case as in the other. Once again we come back to the argument which peppers the case for liberty or property or any form of individualist social behavior; the general rule is so much more important than the specific issue that it is a grave mistake to be confined to the needs of the moment. The great corporation is undoubtedly powerful in its way, as guilds and grandees have been before, but power, as Manning has well remarked, is a tricky thing, different as one views it from different stances. The key element of power, the coercive authority and the immunity from market restraints, distinguishes the weakest state from the most powerful corporation. If the corporation possesses these powers it then does become quasi-governmental, but then one must determine to what extent it has stepped over the line—i.e., it is a matter of how it has changed its role, not how powerful its position is. A telephone company cannot levy taxes, draft workers, or compel anyone to use its equipment, but to the extent that it has an official monopoly on all telephones it does, to that extent, partake of a state. That quality is so limited that it is gross exaggeration to say that it is a government; the most one might say is that if, in Berle's example, it refused to provide telephones to Negroes it would perhaps be depriving them, without hope of redress, of part of the fundamental exercises of civilized life today. Here too, we are formal—it is not AT&T qua big corporation, but qua monopoly licensor of telephones that partakes of sovereignty, and then only to just that degree which is appropriate.

Galbraith would comment, in objection to the above analysis, that we are confusing the meaning of "private" as non-governmental with "private" as pertaining to individual privacy. There is a distinction, but the key point is that this difference is less important than the difference between the fundamental one of private (non-coercive, fundamentally contractual) and public (coercive, based at the bottom on force). This is not to say that the family and General Motors are indistinguishable, but that the values of one are remotely those of the other. If they diverge too much the gap should be narrowed, not widened.

In other words, the quality of the "private" is at one time

precious and amorphous, the synthesis of the struggle for individualism and at the same time a variable in the political equation. The antitrust question bears this out; a body of legislation is required to ensure the viability of an economic arrangement which has as its reason for being the preservation of private institutions. The forms of our time have grown vastly complex and sophisticated, so that it sometimes seems that the only solution to baroque confusion must be to cut the Gordian knots of interrelations and mixed systems. To some critics the private and public sectors should be severely separate; but on the contrary this might either cause a revulsion against anarchy or might produce a parody of individualism in which real sovereignty, and a harsh form at that, was being exercised by phantom rulers. In a social circumstance, which of course is what politics is all about, private implies public as the other part of the picture. Aristotle, in presenting an answer to Plato's Republic, insisted on the public commitment of the citizen, for it was just because the citizen could be public-spirited (whereas the worker or slave could not) that he was able to defend and enrich his private life; Pericles' views were in this quite similar. It is significant that we are experiencing two seemingly opposite developments today. On the one hand we have the political pull toward the enhancement of the public sector, the triumph of the state over the individual and the political over the social or the economic. But on the other hand there has been a noticeable tendency for people to grow less public-spirited, more wrapped up in family life, in television or bowling or even making money. The individualism which de Tocqueville admired, the political independence of the free man, is giving way to the individualism which he feared, the individualism of non-participation and seclusion. This meshes with the observation of Aries that privacy has grown—the privacy of the small circle, which does not limit the state but flees from its contexts, is the modern fashion. One thinks of the parallel, again, with the third and fourth centuries' proliferation of cults amidst the tightening imperialism of the political order. (These years are superb specimens for the conservative, as Rostovtseff so ably showed.) As politics becomes more important the average man, paradoxically, becomes less political in his zest to avoid that whole realm. In West Germany the complaint is made that the voters are apathetic, unconcerned with the decisions of the state which are so extremely vital to their well-being and future. Is it a coincidence that this attitude follows the time of the Nazis when everything private was subordinated to the demands of public purpose? The breakdown of the public/private dichotomy will lead to a bipolarization, either across the society or at various times; the need for privacy will reassert itself, if only to weaken the foundations of the public system. To many authoritarians this division is welcome, perhaps necessary, but then in case of trouble even they, or especially they, will find that their social order has become a honeycomb of private orders—this may well be the central problem of a socially-evolving Russia today. But this public spirit comes, as Pericles (or Thucydides) said, from the inculcation of the private; as with Alice in the looking-glass, the best path often seems to lead in the opposite direction.

The way to discover the right path, it therefore follows, is not to choose a road with the most heart-warming signposts. For example, we have agreed that there may be too little public interest in politics. This does not mean that the more personal involvement in the public processes the better—the Nazi state had an extremely high degree of that participation, and the British have excelled the French in stability and liberty because of the brilliant Anglo-Saxon knack of treating politics just not seriously enough. There is a point in the view that North American university students are better off on panty raids (or were, before the Berkeley riot) than the South American students are in their riotous political demonstrations—Harvard has turned out to be a more reliable nursery of freedom than San Marcos. The North American apathy may be as deadly or it can permit as thorough a denigration of liberty as any Communist "student" in Peru would think of. And yet that apathy is a part of freedom; a nation of bowling teams may undermine the libertarian premises, but it is the task of libertarians to protect the right of the bowlers. It is often harder to espouse freedom for bowlers than for Fascists or Communists because this freedom is a freedom to the inactive, a defense of a *"piccolo rifiuto"* which must seem to the political devoid of social value. The value is in the right, the freedom to be different even in taste (so much harder to consider than opinion, and so often more vulnerable). A society built on this diversity may find, like the small tree in the forest, that it is not the monolithic groups than can survive the best.

But, then again, we ourselves may not survive. Change may truly show its final superiority by changing all of life, wiping out the last few layers of evolutionary development to bring home the lesson of hubris.

It is true that civilization has weathered severe pressures in our time. Much of the feeling behind appeasement in the 1930's, especially in Britain (and this is not absent today) was due to the belief that society would perish if another war came, but Britain survived and Germany seemed to shrug off, materially speaking, the bombings of the Allies until almost the end of the war. With Marshall Plan aid the British have quite recovered and the Germans have blossomed. Our technical skill may be a veneer, but it can be said that it is a tough one. Perhaps we are too fearful of our capabilities, and even of the natural ability of ordinary men to rebuild and revive. But let us beware of putting too much to the test, of playing this game of Russian roulette too often. As against the German example we might set that of Japan, withered almost to a state of economic catastrophe. And what if there had been no United States, or (much more important) no will or skilled group necessary for the task of resuscitation? It is a good guess that more civilizations have perished in this way than in any other—bereft of a guiding elite or of a sustaining faith, so that even if the material damage were small or (as with the Mayans) evidently almost non-existent, the élan could not be restored. We have remarked on Schumpeter's analysis of Marx's surplus value as the surplus necessary for civilized development; it is at least as important, perhaps, as the reserve against folly or disaster. We in the West are apt to look smugly at the blows recently struck at China's economy— perhaps of brutal intensity—when manic overexpansion was struck by the combination of bad weather, human recalcitrance, and the withdrawal of Russian aid. Who can say that much of this could not come to even the richest society in another time and manner? The gravest fault of Mao was his radical willingness to stake all (perhaps almost all is the better term) of the economy's forces on the Great Leap Forward. When everything is public one mistake may turn out to be fatal. The merits of diversity, privacy, and the undisciplined society are above all negative; the worst shocks cannot strike at the whole fabric so thoroughly when the strength is distributed throughout the garment. The hydraulic systems of which Wittfogel writes have proved very feeble in defeat, all too dependent, like thirteenth-century Mesopotamia, on their irrigation systems; the Dutch, with canals but with a libertarian spirit, thrived on their time of troubles. Challenge and response is in itself a tautology; what often provides the prerequisites for responding are separate sources of energy and the confidence to use them.

The great changes in our environment have made this more important. Fortunately more and more liberals have been persuaded by the perils of pollution and the threatened extinction of flora and fauna to recognize the fragility of all life and the dangers which change can pose to man and the world. In claiming that these changes have been overstated we do not mean to say that they make no difference, but that the difference is often a matter of more subtle feeling than is usually admitted. For example, Jaspers has remarked that the work of modern man in paving vast areas of the human surface has been an accomplishment equal to the invention of tools in the Stone Age. This has been an ambiguous development in human life, but its immediate results can easily be exaggerated. The yearnings of men for the country, the pace of thought and even (as our traffic jams show) of action are not so altered. It is the subtle shifts in attitude which may be more far-reaching. Jaspers asserts that "for the second time man has broken away from nature to do work which nature would never have done for herself, and which rivaled nature in creative power." But this results not in a despising of nature, but (as the rise of Thoreauan cults shows) a greater passion for the natural. Fairbanks comments that the love of nature, not as a normal part of life but as a special, superior quality to be consciously savored, came in China and customarily comes with the ascendancy of an urban society. Then and only then can nature be abstracted from the fields, hills, et cetera, which make up the daily round of the unsentimental countrymen. As we pave more we grow more anxious for the open spaces, for the idea of open spaces. The greatest problem of technology may not come from the difficulties of adjustment to the new, but from the paradoxical attachment to the old, feelings never really felt before. Even if progress is a juggernaut, it will not root out the natural impulses and make a wholly "new man." Toynbee, in fact, attributes much of our problems to this anachronistic nostalgia of the heart which he contrasts to the necessary rationalism of the head. This backward glance may, moreover, leave such longings and dissatisfactions that the spirit behind the new, no matter how efficient, may be hollow. This is recognized in Africa or Asia, where the impact of science on antique cultures is a cliché. It may be true everywhere. This is, to repeat, not because of the swiftness of our modern scientific age, sweeping all before it, but a result of the acceptance of the industrial ethos (the work now of many generations) and the consequent unhappiness with the thrust of some of this logic. If men are told that a paved world must be better than an unpaved one they will be disappointed; if they are reminded that it is very different they will build up visions of the unspoiled which will clash with the patterns of industrial life. It is not true that the machine has brought boredom to the life of the worker; this is true of some men and machines and not others, and a great deal of farming is hardly thrilling. But if the machine is relied on as a liberator that is a very different story indeed.

This is not to say that the life of work in the contemporary world is sordid or demoralizing. It is often the little individual matters, such as insufficient rest breaks or the lack of toilet doors or the scheduling of work hours without regard for personal convenience, which are most galling. The choice is not between mass production and an idyllic or miserable pre-industrial system, but between various standards of industrial life. It is apparent that men have not been driven to despair by life in a mechanized world, but despair can come if mechanization is treated as a single goal to which all others must bend the knee. Pavement is welcome almost everywhere, but if we think that we cannot have too much of a good thing and pave over all the private gardens and yards, the dissatisfaction and tension will be much greater than all the pleasure so far afforded.

In a bitter, excited evening of early August, 1914, Lord Grey commented that the lights of Europe were going out, and that they would not be relit for a generation. More than one generation has elapsed since then, and the progress in electrical illumination—the fluorescent bulb comes to mind—has been sizable. Villages whose inhabitants have retired at dusk for millennia now enjoy artificial light whenever they desire, so that one can say that Lord Grey was too concerned with the problems of his day. But perhaps he was not—the frequency with which his dictum is quoted leads one to think not. The brilliance of our electrical power is a vulnerable grandeur, susceptible to destruction in an instant by war or over years because of fear or caution. In 1914 we trusted that as the years came there would be more light and freer travel and more progress. We have more light now, as we had hoped, but we are unsure that a blackout may not come tomorrow, or perhaps the lights will be shining underground; travel is widespread but subject to instant restriction; progress is derided or despaired of amidst the fantastic triumphs of voltage. If we are to restore the pre-1914 confidence we must act on the same organs that caused, or at least transmitted the distrust; we must act politically to ensure the maintenance of economic, technical, or aesthetic balance. When the dying Goethe asked for more light he is now thought to have wanted the blinds pulled up, but this does not diminish the transcendental meaning of the request. When we want more light, it is not enough to mean only more power stations or more libraries; the power that can see to it that too much or too little of either does not imperil civilization is the state.

XV

The State

It is understandable in these matters to consider the individual as pitted against the state. Unfortunately, it is possible for anyone, with or without a uniform or badge, to torture a man. It is equally possible for kidnapers to abduct and for thugs to murder without the benefit of writs or court decrees. Even the sternest free-market conservative grants the state a monopoly on lawful coercion, a function in pre-empting the rightful areas of punishment and restraint and a task of preventing anyone from engaging in the totally forbidden forms of coercion. Furthermore, we have noted that a deprival of the use of the courts of the state is in itself a violation of procedural due process. This implies that the state will provide such courts, and that in so providing them it will grant open access on reasonable terms. This is not necessarily a monopoly power, and in a free society arbitration agreements and private compacts are welcome adjuncts to the state judicial machinery. This, however, does not reduce the need for the latter, for since only the state possesses (in theory) coercive power it is essential that the state provide courts to adjudicate private and semi-private disputes.

This is very elementary. It is very possible, though, in considering the limitations on state power and the rights of man, to ignore or undervalue the position of the state as a vital guarantor of liberty and security. Henry Adams may have claimed to have been a conservative anarchist (in truth he was nothing of the sort), but even von Mises scarcely would qualify for that description. In discussing the political scene as it exists the state has been the logical and traditional starting point from the time of Aristotle. We have begun more in the fashion of Plato, with the mind of the citizen rather than the form of the state, but as with Plato, this must lead up to the state. The circular disagreement in politics is the primary focus of the political situation, but it is very relevant to consider what the focus is on, what the argument is, in everyday terms, about. Almost invariably, from the biblical discussion on the ruler in the Book of Samuel to the latest ideological disagreement, it comes to a dispute over the kind of state to have, its power, and its organizational machinery. Even anarchists usually spend more time in arguing about what kind of state power not to have than in plotting the course of a stateless world. The greatest weakness of free-market thought has usually been its negative viewpoint, its failure to mention the needs as well as the faults of government from even a very individualist point of view.

The first step in analyzing the problem is the most worked-over one: How did the state originate? It would be fruitless to attempt here to review all the answers to this question—too many books have been written on that to require repetition. However, four suggestions are worth considering as a start at trying one's hand at the game, at least. The four might (and this of course must involve a vast over-simplification) be summarized as follows:

1. The contract theory.
2. The religious or mystical concept.
3. The theory of organic growth.
4. The force hypothesis.

To a large degree these overlap. For example, Hooker followed Aristotle in ascribing a quality of historic development to the state, but at the same time he maintained the traditional medieval philosophy of the religious nature of political systems. Bodin, who upheld the force theory, did admit to some ideas which partake more of the organic explanation. Part of this ambivalence derives from the dual nature of these theories—on one hand they are attempts to explain the fundamental reason for government, and on the other hand they often purport to be historical studies. There may be one explanation for the historical founding, but in a sense the state is refounded each moment, as some people are born and others die while the government manages to retain its lawful role. The current justification may differ from the first; thus the United States Constitution was a beautiful example of a conscious social contract, but its real nature may be (as Holmes believed) premised on considerations of power and thus on force. The stone which the builders rejected may turn out to be the chief cornerstone; in fact, the builders may have been using it all along, oblivious of their actual material.

In considering the American Constitution one does deal, however, with a remarkably artificial establishment of a new nation. The social-contract theory is different than the others in that it requires a much more deliberate, rational sequence of events. The remarkable theoretical success of the thesis of the social contract greatly changed political theory in its heyday, and has influenced the thought of the Anglo-American world perhaps most intensely. This theory was another, perhaps the most distinct, feature of the Whig current of thought which we have considered before. In this case the term "Whig" is unquestionably fair, for the idea reached its greatest influence as a propaganda instrument of the Whigs in the seventeenth and eighteenth centuries—Locke the great philosopher was here most obviously a blood brother of Locke the advocate for the Whig party. The progression of thought from Ponet to Jefferson, from the mid-sixteenth to the late eighteenth century, was one in which the specific programs of popular control were steadily widened into more fundamental conclusions about the inflexible rule that all "just power" derives "from the consent of the governed." The suggestion that all legitimate power comes from contract may be as old as the time of Athenian power (Popper traces it to Lycophron, a contemporary of Plato), but only with the advent of Whig ascendancy did social contract become so convincing that even reactionaries like Hobbes cast their ideas in its forms.

All this is long dead. Anyone so naive or antediluvian as to maintain today that the state originates in a public contract would be dismissed as hopelessly unrealistic. Aside from such rare cases as constitutional conventions—and even in the last two hundred years they have been rather uncommon—the element of consent is very one-sided. Plebescites are scarcely two-sided transactions, and in Africa and Asia even these have been largely omitted in favor of negotiated transfers of power between the old colonial powers and new, suddenly-evolved governing bodies. In a more basic sense, even when a fair election is held to determine the nature of the government as, say, in Uganda, such a vote is not a true social contract for there was a Uganda on the map and some sense of Ugandan nationhood long before 1963. Where such a sense has been least present, as in the Belgian Congo or in post-1919 Yugoslavia, the viability of the government remains in doubt even with changes in the form.

This suggests another difficulty—contracts are not successful over very long periods of time, and circumstances do alter cases. The Confederates of 1861 and the Norwegians in 1905 argued that one generation's handiwork must not bind all future generations; this was the opinion of Jefferson and, of course in a highly limited and theoretical form, of Locke. It was Burke who insisted on the chain of history, the duty of one generation to another, and Burke of course was the semi-Whig most responsible for beginning the attack on the social-contract theory. Yet we find that even, perhaps especially, the most ardent democrats cannot accept Jeffersonian doctrine here, for what starts as contract becomes an institution, rather like marriage. In the same way, the Jeffersonian belief in the limitation of powers has also fared badly. This too derived from the main current of Whig contract theory, for in its early years in the sixteenth century the idea of the contract arose in order to bind the rulers to the terms of power. But what limitation does the United States Constitution as now interpreted impose as compared to what was thought in 1789? What limitations have the Soviet constitutions imposed— and they are as much charters as any others, in form—or that of the French Fifth Republic?

Why should a contract imply limitations at all? Rousseau revolutionized the nature of the social contract in his famous book of that name by treating the contract as a grant of limitless power by the people to itself, now existing as a sovereign system. In so suggesting, Rousseau of course followed Hobbes' suggestion that the contract was a giving of almost absolute power rather than a reservation, but Rousseau's giving, because it is not merely a giving but a reassortment, is final and completely unchecked. The totalitarian use of Rousseauian terms has been much commented on; social contract has become in some places only a means to eliminating restraint. This too is of ancient lineage; the jurists of Imperial Rome deduced the supreme power of the emperors from the precise grant of the Senate and people. So we have come full circle; a theory designed to bring the state down to the dimension and control of the people has become unwieldy and unsuitable, and it has thus become a tool of those who would use it for the opposite result, from whence perhaps it came. But the results of this disillusionment are sad and thought-provoking.

It is hard to think of the state as the product of a contract, yet it is harder to see it in a different visage. Force is always present in the weighing of powers within any group of men, and as we have admitted that bad law is still law, it cannot be dismissed. In the last analysis everything does come down to a question of actual or potential strength, but in some ways it is the business of politics to avoid that analysis. Napoleon's celebrated maxim, that one can do anything with bayonets except sit on them, has been best confirmed by the behavior of the modern tyrants. The regimes which have most flagrantly seized power, and at times glorified brute strength, have come at one point or another to emulate Hobbes in discovering a contract to legitimate power (Hitler's plebiscites have set the fashion in the twentieth century, and he took them from Louis Napoleon, that ur-Fascist), or in finding a mystique of blood or class which ennobles the state. In strict Marxist thinking all forms of government are necessary results of economic patterns, determined by class considerations. In practice all Marxist regimes have relied on a complementary argument of social cohesion which is at least in part Aristotelian, and the moderate Marxists and the non-Marxist socialists have always stressed this even more.

With all this admiration for the state comes an equally dangerous worship of the state which is fundamentally opposed to the Whig premise. The mildest of radicals like Green and Lindsay looked upon the state as good per se; with that the entity of the state takes on a different form than any contract can produce. It is ironical to see how many somewhat innocent left-of-center idealists have awakened to find that if you get away from judging the state as you would another association, you may end up with a monster. Randolph Bourne presented the terrible picture of war as the health of the state; he did not sufficiently take into account the implications of the Roosevelt-Croly concern with the health of the state as the root of this evil. Edmund Wilson, after many years of supporting radical causes, came to realize that the monolithic state can produce many things at times, but that being monolithic is itself the greatest danger of all.

Accepting the facts that the state is a necessity in keeping order and in creating an entity capable of acting socially, and also accepting the fact that it may arise out of diverse settings and in differing ways, it is still important to say that it is a means, not an end. Even with all the magic and authority which we present in the governing process, the state must still answer to our purposes, to our lower-circle conservative intentions. The sovereign is not converted into a god by its authority. In 1891 Gray distinguished between the awesome power and the differing sources of the law; a similar distinction can be made between the potential and the desirable qualities of the state. Certainly, if we consider only power, a state can violate the minimum rights of due process, it can indulge in torture to maintain its control, and it can gain a certain right to do so by skillfully managed and over-managed plebiscites. No matter how deep-rooted the power or claims of the state are, a point will come when it loses its persuasive authority. The presumption in its favor can be rebutted. In less extreme cases we can agree that the state represents a consensus of the opinion of the people, but it is only one of the varying consensuses of society. There is no general will, only different individual wills composed in different ways.

No pluralist could fully agree with Kennedy's admonition to ask what you could do for your country, for this places the state on a separate pedestal. Some of the fervent anti-statist arguments of Figgis and Laski were excessive in their classification of the state as just one other association, but the comparison has much validity. To grow up in a country is to be the heir of that nation's heritage of experience, but that is a far cry from saying that it is incumbent on one to adore the state. What real difference would it make if North Dakota became a province of Canada, or Manitoba a part of the United States? More to the point, what advantage will it be for the people of Quebec to be "rulers in their own house"? It is amusing now to think of the many wars between Scotland and England, and then to consider how well, all things considering, the Union has been for both. The Maltese, or at least Dom Mintoff, wanted at one time to be a part of Great Britain and elect a Member of Parliament, and the Puerto Ricans have thrived under commonwealth status. The happiest tales are usually those featuring a peaceful evolution of sovereignty, and the opposite (perhaps the United States is an exception) are those which experienced violent assertions of native independence. What is true of peoples is much more so of individuals. *Ubi libertas, ibi patria* is the noblest creed. Perhaps to some people Themistocles and Alcibiades seem exceptionally mobile Athenians, but it is seldom considered how many millions of Europeans came to the New World for many reasons (usually economic) and found new loyalties quite quickly. Carl Schurz may have fled tyranny and the Sicilians may have left a bad society, but there were numerous Britons and Scandinavians who left their homelands just when these were among the most advanced nations in the world, or were rapidly becoming so. Recently much outcry has arisen in Great Britain on the loss of scientists to the United States, but why should it be a cause for sadness if a man wishes to live in one free society rather than another? People would deride a man who insisted that because one's grandparents had lived in a town, one must never leave it voluntarily.

These criticisms are much easier to take when one talks of a nation with few traditions, for so far the sense of being Gabonese does not militate against other loyalties. But even in the newest lands these nationalist feelings can run very high, as the Somalis have shown. Europe has seen the maximum miseries of these feelings, for almost every kilometer from Paris to Weisbaden has experienced the blood of ten generations of conflict, increasingly fought-over loyalties which were inconceivable in the ninth or fourteenth century, and which, hopefully, are becoming inconceivable again today. It is extremely disheartening to see the surge of bloody nationalism among new states in a time which has so shown the folly of such conduct. Wars over economics or religion or booty are comprehensible, even if so often avoidable with a little reason, but these wars over territory or pride are like the quarrels of ten-year-olds. The fault, as has been said so often, lies with the very idea of the state as a greater, more important corporate body to which one must give, not merely homage, but exclusive loyalty and even worship.

But the rights of the citizen cannot serve as a constant check on the activities of the government, or every state would be like the old Polish republic. Locke and Selden observed that the consent of the governed must be general, not specific; a man sentenced to be hanged cannot revoke his consent to be governed, for his living in the community conferred an irrevocable consent. Revolution is a very extreme measure, and secession must be a form of revolution, as the American Civil War demonstrated. The right to move is the ultimate individual right, and it is the totality of geographic power which a world government would possess by its very nature which is the strongest argument against its creation. But moving is a fairly extreme measure, and bound to be inconvenient and even miserable; the protection of the citizen against the government and the guarantee of the proper role of the state was the primary seventeenth-century answer. Going even further, the general acceptance of the idea that the state is a servant of the wishes, even the selfish urges, of the people who live within the borders of the country will usually insulate the governing officials from the virus of thinking of state power as a magic quality. In this respect the United States has been fortunate; the very word "state," with its power implications and untouchability, is reserved for provincial governing units. Cozzens, in *Guard of Honor*, contrasts the theorizing of a young intellectual, with his talk of "the state," with the incomprehension of his auditor, to whom states were lesser governing regions. German history is so bloody partly because this salutary ignorance, or provincialism, has been too much lacking since 1848 or 1871. If we look at the state as a convenience, we must of course accept the intellectual consequences. The private vices may be public virtues in the sense that the state subsists best if each citizen works for his own greater good, and subserves the larger good in that way rather than by heroic service.

This is open to fair objections even by those who share the lower-circle convictions. All the qualities of civic virtue, of public-spirited conduct, seem to be washed away along with the evils of virulent nationalism. Surely there is some common good; a general strike, or a concerted attempt to destroy the legal system, is not only bad in its results but injurious to the very system of ordered living. If we admit that the state has its necessary functions, and that there are some things that it must do or can do better than others, is it not dangerously injurious to condone or encourage a point of view that the state has value only so far as something is in it for me? This is the dilemma of much of liberal conservatism, torn between a conservative respect for order and the distrust of the massive state with its economic leveling and political absolutism. No matter how much one distrusts the appeal to the state as an arbiter of opinion— from Hitler's centralization to the vague but disturbing theses of the public interest—there still remains the value of the state as the final repository of social order and communal living. The general strike is one example; buying up scarce commodities in times of trouble would be another. It would certainly be an unreasonable imposition for the state to prohibit or severely restrict automobile-driving in a city, but this does not imply that traffic lights are wrong. Moreover, there is a stronger argument for observing the rules of the road than the simple fact that they have been ordained by the appropriate authority. It is not only illegal to go through a red light, it is also antisocial in that these rules make orderly living possible, and their wholehearted compliance does benefit everyone by bringing an accepted morality of behavior. This is what is meant, in a mundane way, by that elusive law that makes one free.

This is not so puzzling a difficulty. No Holmesian has said that because morality and law are separate, the existence of a law against murder implies the right of the citizen to try to evade the statute. To some extent law and the state are noble examples of social cooperation, and the fault of the free-market school has been to insist on the contrary too often. In our example, the system of courteous driving established by traffic lights and many of the driving rules are fine, in that they improve all conduct by imposing a code of good conduct. One need not thereby approve of every driving rule (say, a thirty-mile-per-hour speed limit where one would have ordered a forty-mile limit) although one must accept the power to enact it. The greatest worth of the state comes when it reinforces, by its majesty and importance, those values which would be weak or incompetent standing by themselves. Thus when a nation fights for a great libertarian cause, or against an oppressor, patriotism becomes a service to one's ideals as well as to one's homeland.

But what if one doubts that the cause is for liberty, and questions the identity of the oppressor? Civilized living requires that the state have great power but it cannot constrain the sense of devotion to which we have referred. If we return to the pluralist view of the state, we can find valuable parallels. Loyalty to a church, to a union, to many other institutions or non-sovereign groups can run as deep or deeper than loyalty to the state. These loyalties gain by the realization that they depend, varying on the fervor and self-interest of the person, on the use and quality of the institution. It has been remarked that fervent loyalty to a city would be thought quixotic, yet in some mild forms such patriotism is common and gives life to a social responsibility. The same is true of universities and philanthropic organizations, and in different ways of business and labor groups. If the test is devotion to a good cause and the collective capacity to forward these aims, it does not require the powers of a sovereign to inspire the requisite support. The history of the great reforming religions of the West proves that; organization plus belief works better when not mixed with the drosser material of bureaucratic regulation.

But these institutions cannot count on loyalty as an indefeasible birthright; the very Catholic Church has suffered savage diminutions of respect and loyalty. Even where a man has been trained to feel devotion, this admiration can be relied upon too far. There must be some things which, as Royce proclaimed, evoke unthinking loyalty, but they may be disrupted or they may conflict one with another. In other words, this is an area determined neither by pure calculation or absolute faith, but time and occasion dictate what sentiments will prevail. The state is no different, as Diocletian discovered; if it tries to defend its flank by creating a more evocative mystique it is only doing what religions or parties can do, and often do much better. Above all, there is no value in ascribing a special mystique or an organic essence to the state any more than to a club; if we see the value in a sense of awe let us be rational about it. The justifiable respect for the national ideal is not a value which can be profitably expanded into a limitless faith; worse crimes have been committed by men who have idolized the flag than by those who spit on it.

We may grant that with all the emphasis on individualism and the pluralist values, there is a place for the good of the whole community. In our example of the general strike, the labor group may have its own needs and interests, but the comfort and safety of the community, abstract as that term is, has some priority. There is certainly validity in this, but it is an elusive quality which needs much watching. Some general strikes are desirable (and the very use of words of good and evil involve tricky questions of relative value; there is no sure answer); one, for instance, countered the Kapp *Putsch*. Once we go beyond the acceptance of the state as a limited tool, to grant the state a presumption of rightness even against one's instincts or one's pocketbook, we are presuming that the common good has a greater value than expediency, assuming that the organic origins of the state outweigh the contractual.

Lindsay noted in 1914 that there were three justifications for the state: its power to coerce, its ethical role, and its comprehensiveness. The monopoly on coercive power is accepted, but it gives no greater aura to governmental action than the immediate needs indicate, and is no help when the basic premises are questioned. Surely only a state which proves itself as a fit governor, which succeeds in defending itself against the claims of objectors, can count on this as a right. In our case of the general strike, a uniform disapproval of the existing order would alter this monopoly, and perhaps very quickly; it is regrettable that there was no such strike to unseat Hitler as well as Kapp. The minimum prerequisites of civilization are binding on the state as well as on individuals, and confer no automatic respect for power.

This is where the ethical considerations arise, but here too we have seen that the conclusion begs the question. The state holds no irrevocable ethical quality, unless one assumes that the rule of authority has a value in itself; but that is the issue to be proved, not the premise. Our example of the traffic lights is relevant; the rule is basically a convenience, waived for ambulances and loosely enforced against the crafty. This convenience must not be dismissed lightly, but neither should it become a sacred totem. It is ironic that so many conservatives have, at various times in history, upheld the ethical quality of the state, for it presupposes a disinterestedness on the part of human nature which sits badly with a distrust of infallibility or pure nobility. Every time one points to some form of government or some ruler as the quintessence of the higher virtue, a sneaking suspicion comes through. Louis IX, when not sitting under his tree dispensing perfect justice, was persecuting Jews and Albigensians; Lincoln managed, perhaps understandably, to amass one of the poorest civil-liberties records of any American President.

The argument for comprehensiveness is the strongest case, as Lindsay himself suggested, and it fits in with the organic theory most readily. The state may be no better, or not as good as its members, and it may be called on to do things which would be classed as evil if done by an individual, but it alone can do the big things—it sets the traffic rules and the rules of community order. This is no abstract consideration today, as we see that if we rely on public order as a foundation of society we must depend on the power of the state to preserve that order. Moreover the demand for a world state must increase with the interdependence of nations and the close physical relationships between powers who possess vastly lethal weapons. If the world is a unity the nations are like groups within the society, and the combination of supersonic airplanes and hydrogen bombs makes the concerns of the world a common issue. In this situation we see the organic explanation of the state at its best—the world has by stages come together, so that the contractual consensus must follow, deriving its impetus from the basic needs of the human community. World government may be a "can't help," a result of forces greater than the thrusts of sudden power or transient debate.

In this partly-uncontrollable need for a governing system the test of statesmanship is to regulate the authority, to watch (in Juvenal's phrase) the watchman. So much of importance is political—this circle affects such a vast area of life; the crucial task is to see the political is not mistaken for the governmental, that all politics does not become a domain of the state in one way or another. Since so very much of life is political—the struggles for control of the large institutions and the trivial disputes of neighborhood groups as well as the more epic disagreements—it is all the more important that the role of the largest arena of politics does not so overwhelm all other units that nothing can be done without the state. As the world shrinks this becomes a doubly-threatening problem; a world with fewer and more powerful centers of coercive authority (for the current multiplication of states is probably a temporary circumstance) combined with a sophisticated regard for the political element through all of life leads to a stifling emphasis on the one road to power and authority. We see this in the Communist states, where everything comes to politics in its most obvious sense, where girl loves boy and boy loves tractor because the local Party organization has been instructed to arrange matters thusly; in China the first step can be omitted. In the non-Communist countries there are many zones of politics, but the threat is always present that the vast powers of the state may harness all the political urges in a common way, erasing the plurality of society. This is not new; it is a hallmark of Wittfogel's hydraulic societies, and can be observed in the civil-service world of Dostoevski's short stories.

The test of the viability of the moderate-conservative task is contained in this situation. The state, with its increasing powers, is very comprehensive, and that quality has become a watchword to the newer nations. It is a truism in Dar-es-Salaam and Rangoon, even if not necessarily true, that even if capitalism is not necessarily bad, the state must do many things that were previously left to private enterprise. This "must" so often disguises a "want-to" that it has become a disingenuous phrase—if a nation wants to expand greatly its steel capacity or to construct an airline, and asserts that private capital is not up to the task, the usual reason is that the effort is economically unprofitable, and the value of the investment is political. But these political values are present, and in a way they are the vital urges which the Benthamites and their contemporaries (including Marx and Engels) mistook for economic impulses. It is dangerous for the state to monopolize these impulses, but on the other hand this is the field in which the scope of governmental authority is predominant. For example, the prestige-enhancing capacity of the state surpasses, through the dignity of the government and its wealth, that of even the richest Maecenas or biggest corporation. The latter can sometimes compete in modern society—consider the Lever Building as against the United Nations Building—but the government is impossibly larger. Salaries may be higher at General Motors, but the crucial tasks of our society are in government, not in business, and the most brilliant men will tend toward the seat of power. If this is true in the United States it is surely much more so elsewhere, where the competition of the private sector is not so potent. The state is more comprehensive, and it is pointless to ignore that lure of state power in its multifarious forms today. Taming this monster thus becomes a matter of judgment and control, not merely restraint.

In reaching this conclusion we have considered the state from the aspect of human psychology. There is nothing magical about the state, and it is highly doubtful that we have so much advanced since the eighteenth century that the newer concepts of government are superior to the less powerful ones of the Enlightenment. Certainly by now it is no longer necessary to disprove the Marxist theory of economic determinism, inasmuch as everything that has happened since his death has demonstrated that the state of Marxist susceptibility is inversely related to economic development. It is not war or technological progress that has enhanced the vision of the state since 1914; if that were so, why was this not true after 1815, or 1648? It is a deliberate choice. In this respect the social-contract theory does make sense, for we are experiencing a kind of contractual choice going on, the repeated choice of the state to perform this or that task because this now seems the sensible course of action, even when the might of the state is greatly distrusted.

Contract can be, therefore, frequently a radical instrument. The emergence of the collective-bargaining contract in the sphere of private law has been paralleled by the growth of the state as a service instrumentality. Laski, in his pluralist days, commended Duguit for classing the state as an organization whose value was the service it could provide, competing against other groups offering similar services. At that time this was intended, by and large, as a denigration of the state and its uniqueness. But Laski changed that emphasis to one whereby the state became justified in great extensions of power because it could provide services no one else could. This does not make the governing principle less contractual, just as the substitution of collective for individual labor-bargaining has not made the contract feature of the arrangement less important. But it is a different sort of contract, not exactly Hobbesian, but far removed from that of Locke or Jefferson.

That mighty leviathan, the state, is made up, as in the famous cover to Hobbes' book, of multitudes of individual men, imprisoned or liberated by their beliefs and prejudices. Since the state is the center of politics it becomes especially vital to make the best of it, in both meanings of that phrase. We reject the concept of the state as the repository of all wisdom or power, but its positive place in the political scene is not to be equally dismissed. If we are to define that place, we must choose the values and qualities most likely to produce the sort of state we want. On a more practical level, we must decide just what sort of government we require and how we want it to operate. Even if we make use of other qualities and factors, the central emphasis should still be on reason and the rational allocation of social forces. Limitation of power is not enough; the greatest question is what to do with it.

Too often individualist thinkers have spent too much time on the limitations of the state and not enough on its composition, assuming mistakenly that if one restrains a dangerous force it can be ignored. The free-market tradition has tended to think of the state as an enemy, to be fought but not captured. When the state was captured, as a result, the outcome has been unhappy—the Brown Decade in the United States and the *fin-de-siècle* years in France demonstrated failures of the business minds to use government as well as they could limit it—and the revulsion has weakened the limits as well as the controls. The Whigs never made this mistake, as the United States Constitution demonstrates.

The Whig system of checks and internal realignments is not an outmoded eighteenth-century idea. The judicial and economic institutions of the Common Market have utilized the balance of authorities, with separate governing systems and constituencies yet with a common measure of purpose and overriding control, to good advantage. The success of multi-ethnic government in Lebanon contrasts with the spurious efforts at unity in Syria and Egypt. Constitutional government has succeeded beyond expectation in Japan largely because the jealous systems of restraint established in the past to equalize the powers of the noble clans can balance the wave of democratic impetus; for example, the election laws which so limited canvassing when elections were almost meaningless now provide needed restraints against the corruption and party-mania so common in newly-democratic lands. Mexico has developed a basically one-party state, but this has permitted the type of intra-party factionalism which is probably closer to the ideas of 1787 than the North American realities. Plumb has demonstrated a similar development in early-eighteenth-century England. Not every invention of our age is durable, but it is easier to look at the failures of the ingeniously-weighted electorates of the Central African multiracial states whose color animosities create problems overriding the subtleties of Whig devices, than it is to consider the promise of Yugoslavian and Malaysian systems or even the esoteric ingenuity of the West German two-court system or the complex devices of the Colombians.

The oldest of these devices is federalism, the chief cornerstone of the American experiment. How often in the 1930's liberals and radicals proclaimed the death of the federalist idea! Laski, who had thought it to be a bulwark of pluralist freedom earlier, wrote, so he thought, its death warrant by the late 1930's. Yet it is impressive how sturdy local and state governments are in this country. Much more impressive still has been the development of viable new federalist patterns in Australia and Canada, tending even toward a too-centrifugal tendency of power in Canada. In Italy today demands are made for a new system of disparate powers; in Russia a complete system of federal government has been established, needing only the breath of life to awaken it into a living system. There are very clear, modern reasons for this popularity. The federal system combines, as Americans have preached for years, those qualities of local autonomy and individual importance with the principle of national control and power.

This is definitely not another way of saying that federalism affords an opportunity to those who wish to dismantle the government. Federalism is not a scheme for an ineffective state, but a substitute. The idea of regional apartheid (leaving its dishonesty in South Africa to the side) presupposes a rigid separation, just as the Articles of Confederation or the United Nations assume a radical incomparability between the general weakness and the local power. The trick of federalism is to make the two or more levels complementary without stifling either party. The most successful, the Whig method of assuring this is to provide that interest groups, various social, economic, or ethnic groups will balance each other—not lump themselves in the different branches or states, but spread themselves through the system. When the left shifts from espousing localism to being pro-national, and vice versa, and the different regional groups change their positions from time to time, the durability of the system is enhanced and the processes of government are stimulated. This can be dangerous, as with the southern option for local power in American history and the Quebec agitation today, but the point is that no trend should be allowed to continue too far. The two-party system is of great use in preventing this, as is the multiplicity of power mechanisms, so that natural forms of opposition may arise. Above all, the diversity of the economy and the society feed back into the political arena so as to obstruct the unlimited movement of any or all groups to an absolute reliance on one of the poles of the federalist range; historically, this depends on the avoidance of those passionate attitudes, those nationalisms with or without a nation, which have most frequently broken down the equipoise of the Madisonian federal system.

Since the basic questions are circular, this hypothesis presumes that other preferences will not rigidly sort themselves out into a right/left disagreement. So often today it seems as if the left must support the central government, and the right the provincial government. But this is not a command of nature, but to a large degree a historical accident. Once again we too often become blinded by the disagreements of the moment to consider the longer situation. Jefferson was not peculiar or wrong-headed to oppose Hamiltonian centralization nor any less on the left by so doing, and when he followed in Hamilton's steps, the Quids assumed a position on the left and also on the local-government side of the issue. Their fathers were the Antifederalists who opposed the centralism of the Philadelphia convention, and their

sons and grandsons were the agrarians and Populists of the mid-
and late-nineteenth century. At one moment a John Taylor will
be radical, and the next his neighbor John Randolph will be a
reactionary, and both of them fervent anti-centralists, and so it
is today. The advocates in the United States of national divorce
laws or uniform commercial laws or controls over state taxation
are almost always to the right of center; the proponents of militant, national anti-Communist activities see no inconsistency in
decrying other powers of the central government. The contrary
is true, for the liberals who enjoy quoting Brandeis' apologia for
the value of local experimentation reserve it, as a rule, for causes
they approve.

In France this is a very old story. The heirs of Jacobin centralism were the first to uphold the communal privileges of Paris
and Lyons in 1848 or 1871; the *"mur des fédérés"* then marked
the death of radical federalism, to give way to the consolidated
visions of the Marxists. Yet today it is General De Gaulle who
is innovating in centralizing techniques, while the left espouses
local autonomy. In Italy it is actually the Communists who are
taking the lead in advocating the establishment of regional parliaments! In this case the agitation is patently hypocritical, but
it is often a matter of cycles—the liberals will urge greater central
control over and aid to education until the capacity of authoritarian central control becomes clear, and then will recoil at the
vision of an authoritarian master plan. Even in Russia the ebb
and flow of centralist ideas, the shifts of responsibility to and
from the provinces, is a minor theme in the Soviet system of
government; the same thing, to judge from Sloan's recollections,
has been true of General Motors.

This is also true of the attitude toward the various branches
of government. Today the executive is, especially in the Anglo-
Saxon nations, the favorite seat of power for the left. The cult of
leadership devised by the liberal theorists of government in the
United States today is a far cry from a call from *Führer-Prinzip*,
but a statement like that of Senator Clark's that "perhaps De
Gaulle has shown the way" in constitutional development is revealing. Clark's French equivalents have talked for generations

of the unique popular mission of the Chamber, yet in control of the government they too have advanced programs requiring increases in executive power. This, to be sure, may mark the telltale influence of modern collectivism on political processes, resulting in an inexorable tendency for left-wing preference for the power of the executive. But the same is often true of the right; it is wry to consider that Burnham is a principal supporter of the legislative branch, but his heroes in industry and his policies in foreign affairs tend in exactly the opposite direction.

To some extent there is a circular distinction in which the upper-circle people lean toward the authority and energy of the executive and the lower-circle tend toward the limitations and checks of the legislative or judiciary. Federalism, which implies a distribution of power and a recognition of local autonomy, would also appeal to lower-circle thinkers. But in making this parallel it is vital to keep two things in mind. First, it is clear that these institutional questions are much less important than the basic issues. Very few men will fight for local rights per se unless these rights are bound up in a cause or an emotion. Neither will a party or a group commit itself to a theoretical preference if this becomes inconvenient. The southern Democrats were urging an extension of the power of the federal government in order to apprehend fugitive slaves right up to the time when they declared for secession in the name of states' rights. The Bavarians were thoroughly imbued with the doctrine of local autonomy well along in the 1920's, behaving like Mississippians, while the Nazi party was gaining its initial support in Munich in its drive toward national consolidation. Federalism, as has been remarked, is a delicate balance, a state of poise, and implies sometimes more (as with the World Federalists today) and not less centralism. So too does a preference for one branch or another.

In the second place, the lower-circle emphasis on individualism and a limited governmental system does not necessarily imply a weak government. If one opts for a state with comparatively few powers and for a separation of those powers into diverse sections, it becomes more important (if one believes in the importance of the government) to make those powers as effective and well-coordinated as possible. It is significant that the upshot of the frictions and disloyalties of the Weimar period was a movement toward totalitarianism, an impatient search for authority; the dangers in American and Indian life today are often of the same type. Proportional representation, for example, may conform to the individualist canon of maximum consideration for each voter, but its resulting discouragement of party accountability and stable government have, as in France, been disruptive of limited government itself. It is a grave mistake for a conservative to treat the forms of government with the same measuring stick he uses for the power of government, for these forms are distinctly means to an end. No one has a right—certainly this should be conservative opinion—to a given share of governing power, because that power is not an integral part of individual freedom but a tool of social control. The one-man, one-vote idea, so foolishly and unhistorically read into the United States Constitution by the current liberal majority, was a war cry of the English Chartists, and betrays their simplicist view of politics. But the governing of even a small community is wrapped in the complexities of power and influence, which contradicts any claim that each voter truly controls his share of government. The public/private dichotomy works both ways; since the public is a separate domain, it must be permitted to run its own way, and not be confused with the liberties of the people. There is a close parallel between the status and income divisions in private life and the political equivalents in the public sector, but they operate differently, as businessmen in politics often discover to their sorrow. Too often conservatives, especially in America, have treated the public sector as either insignificant or as an arena where ideals could be displayed cheaply—the Sunday of social life, a moral realm where the good intentions of the private sector come into their rather saccharine reality; certainly not the vital world of Aristotelian politics. The liberals have, in their moral way, done the same thing and come to regret it; the simple levers of pure democracy, such as the initiative and the recall, have proved embarrassing to the left. It is also too tempting for the right to then acquire them, to say in opposition to liberal legislation (as the defenders of the House of Lords did in 1911) that conservatism requires a popular vote on a reform issue.

This is not to say that, for the sake of making government efficient, the party system or the electoral process must become the *raison d'être* of politics. The liberal-conservative preference for liberty in an ordered context must apply here also; in the case of party organization there is a clear indication of where its influence should rest. A constitutional state may have a hundred parties competing for rule, or even only one, but the most successful in our century have two. Two schools have developed in our times as to the nature of parties. These can be called, for convenience, the Schattschneider and the Agar schools. Schattschneider is a leader in the group of political thinkers in this country who have proposed that the two-party system be strengthened by intensifying central control over the party structure, by increasing the sense of party loyalty among the voters, and above all by having each party stand for a unified and consistent program. This will usually mean, of course, one party of the right and one of the left, and no nonsense about eccentric figures in the wrong party. The British system has been tending this way for two hundred years, and it comes very close to the ideal today.

Agar, on the other hand, has outlined the desirability of a two-party system in which each party contains disparate elements, grounded in large part part on local alliances and situations, and the value of compromise which such an alignment makes essential. The parties will tend, Agar suggests in his sketch of American history, to converge in the center, each bidding for the role of preserver of the broad social consensus and advocate of the most comprehensive viewpoint. There will be radical and reactionary elements—more of one in one party and the other in the other party—but these will customarily be kept from eliminating all intra-party opposition. In each party there will usually be politicians who seem utterly out of place in that team, but the absence of a censor or a synod will make consistency an impossible ideal—and a definitely undesirable one, in Agar's opinion.

There are many men who call themselves conservatives who

champion the Schattschneider thesis. But the tenets of moderate conservatism are closely linked with the Agar idea, the willingness to accept political compromise as a price, a very low price, for the limitations of social and economic demands, the discouragement of overriding passions, and the maintenance, in the last analysis, of union. The conservative idea of democracy itself should, as we have seen, be equated with the Agarian view of politics. The distinct-party advocates speak of the rational nature of a sharp party opposition, but this reason is, like the comparable mass reason in economics, one envisaged by a planner or a didactic philosopher. The reason of individual choice is built around the specific preferences and the small bargains of the voters and the politicians, reasons often, to be sure, deriving from customary situations. In Britain this individualism has contributed to making the Conservative Party, to the amazement of many, the majority party and in influencing that party toward Agarian compromises (Butler is of course the notable figure in this effort); much of the same sort of subterranean party-orientation works very well in Mexico. This sort of reason affords non-party organizations, pressure groups and lobbies (in the radical mind, even worse) a broad role in the governing process. Buchanan and Tullock have described how this role, far from being irrational, fulfills a quasi-economic, natural market function in the political realm. This market is very definitely not the economic market of the private sector nor the quasi-market of social gradations; it is political, but that does not make it less susceptible to the nuances of rational choice. In Agar's context the multiplicity of private groups is good—the more the better—so long as they operate in the context of rational influence and do not become rallying points of passionate allegiance. When that happens the forces of compromise and centrism tend to break down, and very often—totalitarian movements usually arise this way—these groups become parties themselves, but parties with a messianic purpose and a zeal to destroy their rivals (whom they usually will not even consider rivals, but as filthy corrupters totally incomparable to themselves). Political stability may be encouraged by suitable laws, such as the single-member district requirement. But the

Lebanese have shown that where antipathies run deep the institutional arrangements are not sufficient to ensure the survival of Agarian parties.

Compromise, moderation, and the encouragement of rational thinking thus paradoxically thrive when an undemanding, even sloppy-minded philosophy pervades. This has always been so. The potentialities for social disruption in a sharp two-party competition were noted by Plutarch, who remarked in his life of Pericles that "there was from the beginning a sort of concealed split, or seam, as it might be in a piece of iron, marking the different popular and aristocratical tendencies; but the open rivalry and contention of these two opponents [Cimon and Pericles] made the gash deep, and severed the city into the two parties of the people and the few." Thucydides, a moderate follower of Cimon who, however, thoroughly appreciated the genius of Pericles, wrote his great history to demonstrate the result of this gash; the same seam was to open in Rome four centuries later and is characteristic of the bitter periods of political history everywhere. It has become common for historians, à la Namier, to minimize the real singularity of parties in the past, to deprecate the radicalism of the *populares* or the right-wing quality of the *optimates*, but the contemporaries did not think so; Sulla sounds altogether like De Gaulle, but without a Malraux.

It is another aspect of the paradox of politics that some of these same symptoms can arise out of a plethora of parties. Here too there is no need for compromise within the party, and the inter-partisan compromises are too often shallow or turbulent; in the end the spirit of transformism breeds a dangerous air of public boredom or distrust. This has been a source of grave disappointment to many lower-circle theorists, especially perhaps to the free-market thinkers of the European continent. If competition in ideas and in goods is the life of the free society, should this not be equally so in politics, and should this not lead to an amplitude of parties? The jokes of the Italians or the Spaniards or the East European Jews, with more parties than there were people, grew out of the same spirit of individual liberty which produced such different results in the Anglo-Saxon world—and even today Italy and Israel cannot seem to devise political arrangements to fit into their much more impressive systems of social and industrial order. The Anglo-Saxon secret is a manifestation of the Whig idea; reason dovetails with custom, the institutions of convenient government structure the areas of choice so as to maximize choice in the long run. Just as the traditional conservatives have accepted the implications of the state's monopoly on legitimate coercion, so they have accepted the unique requirements of the quasi-governmental institutions and the needs of the political machinery, qua machinery. But within the parties internal competition supplements the party machinery —the direct primary has been one invention to serve this purpose just as the convention was before—and a place is set for even the least admired private supplements.

There is an old chestnut that the French turn off the central heating on March 22 because, after all, winter is then, by definition, over. The French have not been the worst offenders in this worship of a too-brittle reason, although it has sometimes seemed so. One must say that the Germans had the worst record in that their multi-party experience, once the restraints of custom were thrown over after 1918, led to a textbook horror of too-frequent election, obstinate irresponsibility, and rapid disintegration. The Germans have had their tradition of formal rationalism, of doctrinaire dogma, and it perhaps proved most fatal when it was mixed with a fear of the laxness, the improprieties of everyday politics. The individualized party encourages this, for it seems to assure its members—who very likely read its partisan newspapers and before 1930 or 1940 tended to live in its own little world—that the world must be shaped its way or the rest of society can go it alone. And the Schattschneiderian party tends to give the same message—a more realistic, potent message to be sure, but also a declaration of the primacy of politics and the superiority of the right brand of politics. The totalitarian party gives this message as a command and as a religious proclamation. As the small sect becomes a ruling party the intolerance grows (as we have seen with the Syrian Baathists) to become a menace to stability. The Agarian party, bumbling and unmethodical, is largely immune to this virus. At its most effective, like the American parties of the post-Civil War years, it can achieve a strong place in the popular mythology, like a baseball team. The comparison to sports has been made before, likening the Anglo-Saxon rivalries to a sports contest; the critical fact is perhaps the ability of the partisan to be fervent yet curiously uncommitted. Victory or a rather insignificant (intrinsically) set of trophies makes the best prizes. And if the rogues are betting on the sidelines, arguing about material things, this is no harm, as long as they do not manipulate the game nor infect the sporting spirit with too great a dose of economic consideration. Politics is of primary importance, but just because this is so it is advisable, indeed very rational, to segregate its fevers and structure its activities so as to encourage the formation of customs which will keep it civilized.

Yet, despite all this, the Agarian path to social virtue is not the only one, nor is the alternative chaos or tyranny. It would be worse than ridiculous to write off Britain as a viable constitutional state, and even France's latest Republic has not fulfilled the fears of more dedicated republicans. Just as it is foolish and self-defeating to identify one strand only of governmental machinery with conservatism or liberalism, so it is even more wrongheaded to insist that certain systems are essential for a stable and libertarian society. The British Labour Party is in theory a splendidly consistent apparatus, operating for distinct ends and opposed firmly to the ideas and ideals of half the country; in fact it has succeeded only when it has been willing to consider some of the views of this other half. Butskillism, the much-denounced "me-tooism" of the British, is a form of internal response to the needs of union, and its constant reordering of Labour policy through political processes has outraged the leftist militants. The moderation of the new Fabians has been one aspect of this, the ethos of compromise which Wilson has come to champion is an everyday example. The Italian parties are trying in their way to learn the same lesson, to substitute for the intransigence mixed with devious scheming which has too often characterized their past as a sort of policy trading. One can always boggle at particular results, but the willingness to accommodate on the majority of issues makes firm stands on the major issues more practicable; the experiences of Weimar show that it is too easy to cry wolf at the wrong time and be defenseless when the real crisis arises.

These accommodations take many forms. In the first place, the delineations of the moderate conservatives of one generation can be barriers to the aims of those of the next generation unless a willingness to adapt is present. From Dicey on, the late-Victorian conservatives warned of the dangers of administrative law, the perils of the growth of discretionary tribunals. This fear had many roots, such as the Puritan and Benthamite disapproval of an uncertain body of law, the concern for wholesale change of the standards of traditional legal principles, and the fear of popular disdain for order. The dislike of tribunals, unimpeded by the safeguards of law built up over the centuries and clothed with wide powers over private areas of society, was and is—as we see daily—not an idle fear. But these tribunals were not designed just to provide issues for demagogues; they arose as a rule to provide a new branch of the judiciary to deal with the newer areas of state power. The answer has been—and it has not been repeated often enough how salutary developments have been all over the free world in the last fifty years—to make them ancillary courts. This has often been a pure good, from the individualist viewpoint, when these tribunals have evolved into courts dealing with the otherwise unchecked power of the state. The French *conseil d'état* is the prime example of this, the grandfather of administrative agencies which has become the upholder of private rights in a land too subject to bureaucratic power, and a glowing example to other peoples. Were there no *conseil d'état*, there would be no recourse at all in many instances; the history of this court has been a net gain for the realm of law. The latest hope for increasing control over the state through semi- or purely judicial agencies is that great Swedish invention, the omsbudsman. This governmental official has as his role the reception of complaints by citizens that some action by a government official, although not necessarily illegal or actionable, was unfair or unnecessarily mean-spirited, or that it evidenced an overbearing attitude on the part of the state. It is significant that this has proved a popular system in democratic socialist countries such as Denmark and New Zealand, where the power of the government requires exceptional control.

The institution of the omsbudsman is unusual in that it entails the establishment of a government official, not a judicial officer, who nevertheless can act as a sort of independent upholder of individual rights or privileges, or at least as a safety valve. It is not a revolutionary notion—in Sweden it has existed for some time, and it can be traced back roughly to the Roman institution of the tribune. The position of public defender as a counter-weight to the public prosecutor, the informal police-review boards, and other such apparatuses, are other examples of this tendency to counterbalance uncontrolled state power. And, it should be remembered, in the more formal areas of judicial or quasi-judicial supervision, there has been a complementary trend toward converting agencies into courts. In the United States the Tax Court, which has evolved in name and manner from the earlier Board of Tax Appeals, has now been joined by numerous tax-appeal courts at the state-government level. The separation of the administrative and judicial arms of the National Labor Relations Board in 1947 was also part of this development, as is the steady emphasis on importing judicial principles into administrative matters.

It is vital to note, however, that this accommodation of the newer aspects of governmental machinery to the Whig concept of government involves theoretical risks and problems. When the paraphernalia of the state is expanded the balance between private and public, and between the various social interests, must shift. Simply because the newer institutions include machinery for controlling administrative discretion, or for limiting the non-judicial aspects of this "fourth branch," does not obviate the significance of this shift. To put it another way, Dicey and Lord Hewart may have been too pessimistic about the inevitability of the future of administrative law. The harshness and arbitrariness of bureaucratic power can be counteracted with the very tools of administrative law and organization until a new body of law can grow up and ripen into valuable individualist precedents. However, a grave danger may then arise: a trust in these new procedures or powers as a substitute for limitation of government or as a tool to restructure society. The idea of co-determination in industry involves the extension of administrative and quasi-judicial systems to the area of business. If the system of constitutional law is the highest good, it may be argued that in return for controlling bureaucrats, the new administrators or their systems be used to control everyone. This is a case where the traditional conservatism requires the leavening of the free-market ideas, where the values of diversity must take precedence over those of constitutionalism. There is an irony to this: the followers of Berle and the other advocates of a system of constitutional authority over both public and private sectors are following the path of the Victorian conservatives. In both cases the tools of governmental control were elevated into absolutes, and the idea of constitutionalism, which is of course a valued part of our heritage, was construed as a final good (in different contexts, of course). And in both cases the rationale for this constitutionalism was found in an absolutist, natural-law philosophy.

We have discussed earlier the problems involved in using the ideas of limited government, of the Bill of Rights for instance, as a broad guide applicable to all of society. Once we accept the thesis that the government, in its role of protector, must supervise an area of private activity, there is bound to be a net increase of state power, even if the immediate result is an enhancement of some individual right. Of course the whole judicial system is such an abridgement, as twelfth-century Englishmen realized, and no one would dismantle that: the crucial question is one of degree and manner. If the power of the state is used to replace market controls with administrative ones, it may be much harder to avoid leaving everything to the government. The tools of control, with all their vaunted protections, may prove less effective than the outmoded (and it is so easy for progressive critics to find institutions outmoded) checks and balances of the past. Years ago Mosca considered this problem in a manner which now seems amazingly contemporary. He wrote that "the office of *defensor civitatis* was created by Valentinian I in the year 364. This 'public defender' was just an employee appointed expressly to shelter the urban plebs from the tyranny of high officials or of the rich who made common cause with the high officials. His particular function was to see to it that the complaints of the poor were admitted to trial in accordance with the law and that their appeals reached the foot of the throne. But in spite of the best of intentions on the part of the legislator, this effort of bureaucratic absolutism to correct and control itself can have had no appreciable effect."

The failure of the omsbudsman idea in the fourth century should not depress us, but it must be a reminder that the "effort of bureaucratic absolutism to correct and control itself" is not the very best way to uphold individualist principles. But that is not the same thing as saying that it is of no use at all or that some increase of governmental power may prove unavoidable.

There is always a difficult question as to the role of the conservative in considering progressive legislation. On the one hand, if his principles have meaning he must find many proposals undesirable, and no less so for having been suggested or passed years before. It is craven to uphold all the past changes as good —in retrospect—but to want to stop just now; merely because this has been a common attribute of conservatives from Cicero to Luce does not alter the self-defeating quality of this position. On the other hand the passage of time should resolve some questions; more, in a lower-circle system this must happen as the concomitant of constant tendency toward accommodation and compromise. In the very long run (as we see in Russia) the results of new institutions and laws will tend toward a new conservatism, and this should be welcomed and nurtured. The conflict between these two considerations has proved, as we all know, one of the most difficult issues of liberal conservatism.

This problem is easiest resolved on a totally theoretical level; as one travels right along the circle the arguments increase against modifying one's beliefs for expediency or accommodation's sake; and since by definition the really important matters must not be sacrificed, the purer the faith the firmer the resolve. Goldwater found this austerity much easier than Taft (who was a perfect example of the conservative who accepted the last change and sought to work, by compromise or partial acceptance, to alter its radical thrust), but less easy as a presidential candidate than as a senator. If, like the Bourbons, one is not willing to admit the permanence of any change one is likely to find oneself, as Henry V did, standing in the way of achieving anything. Once again, one must be somewhat relativist, for if you accept the idea that you will not budge on any important issue and if you call too many things important, there can be no future over the long run, as the Bourbons (and their opposite numbers everywhere) discovered. Part of the mechanism of the circle is its steady movement in respect to details, so that the natural movement of thought takes new forms within the old mold. For this reason old men are saying in every generation that they have not moved but the times have, rendering them reactionaries or conservatives in spite of themselves. Of course they are right, the times have changed, but to borrow the Horatian tag, either we change with them or we are changed. There is no crime to being so changed but there is a limit, more in some times and less in others, to the practicality of standing so pat.

Another way of considering the problem may help. In the dealings of the United States with the Soviet Union over West Berlin, we have said that we would not bend under force; then when no force is applied we let well enough alone. This has so far been successful, but it is a policy which contains many limitations. In fact, we say that we will not budge, yet when difficulties arise we seem to suggest that, in other conditions, we might. What the French in dealing with Germany said they would never consider, in 1924 and 1931, they permitted in 1936 and 1938. To say or do one thing in time of ease and another in time of stress is to condemn one to a situation where the most hateful opponent will secure the greatest gain. Thus the practice of conceding to an extreme opponent what one withheld from a moderate one will invariably reward the former; we see this in the context of racial riots today as we saw it in European politics a generation ago. So it is with many on the right—in easy times they are content and in troubled times they talk of compromises later, or proffer in the end more than they need have done earlier.

Modern history can show many examples of the latter conduct. The behavior of the Tories at the time of the agitation for electoral reform in 1867 was a classic case; for years comparatively modest proposals of suffrage extension were blocked by conservatives, yet when the demands mounted they gave in more and more until the Tories ended up by devising ever-more-generous franchise proposals in order, they hoped, to "dish the Whigs." In 1832 the right had fought tenaciously, but ended up by granting more than they would have had to yield in, say, 1822. In this century the Tories ignored all talk of reform of the House of Lords until the evil day came, at which time they began all of a sudden to talk of greatly novel schemes for membership or of a national referendum—much more radical proposals than even the Radicals had espoused in the 1890's. The converse is also true—a smaller concession early may be more successful than a large one later. Bismarck was a hero for many years in the social-insurance area to workers who demanded and received much more extensive schemes than he had provided, when the time came in Britain and the United States. Often, the longer the wait the more the conservative philosophy will be wrenched from its moorings, often with the help of those who previously would not even disturb the anchor. If a matter is very important, and there certainly are many such, consistent opposition is a duty. But if one can foresee the need to compromise later perhaps it would be wise to do so earlier, perhaps by suggesting a suitably moderate proposal while this will seem an advance (as, for example, the Committee for Economic Development has done) and not a concession to the inevitable (as the National Association for Manufacturers so often seems to grudge). Of course, this may be tactically unwise; it may breed further and further compromises—an appearance of firmness may help in gaining better terms or it may discourage the opposition. But this viewpoint should not be confused with a philosophy of pure principle, nor should it be allowed to become the sole tactic of conservatism, lest cantankerousness seem the badge of the rightist tribe. There is a virtue in being on the offensive, of political *cran* which can make the difference between mere opposition and a spirited campaign. However, it is a liberal delusion that time must always favor the passage of leftward legislation. Often the press of change comes from the right. We have observed this in labor matters in this country for the past twenty years, and the shoe here is on the other foot—the liberals end up advocating or accepting what they earlier opposed. It is a worthy answer to the liberals who deride the "do-nothing" attitude of the conservatives; all new ideas are not stamped "progressive" by any means. This too can have tactical use, for when the liberals press for their objectives it is helpful for the conservatives to have theirs too, which can at least be bargained with.

But new plans or legislation, or a new or thoroughgoing system, is not good per se. The Fascists were useful at least in this; they demonstrated that the reactionaries could develop new orders and extensive programs, and even capture for themselves the very idea of élan. Where it is appropriate, absolute opposition to the new—whether it comes from right or left—is essential. And in those cases one should be consistent and oppose these ideas when they seem secure.

The willingness to compromise on the expendable matters does not eliminate the need to be adamant on the important ones. Just the opposite, it is easier to succeed in the great debates when one has not wasted one's furor on the details. Nothing is inevitable or past discussion; in 1810 the Bourbon restoration seemed as whimsical as a Jacobite restoration. To those who think the income tax is inimical to social order or equity, there is no reason to support it today to any greater extent than they or their grandfathers did in 1910. The concept of custom has two edges—what is tolerable may best be contained by incorporation within the political system; what is not must be fought so as to prevent this from happening. The suggestions of compromise, if carried to extremes, mean that nothing would be worth fighting for. There is a tendency in conservatism toward this, for if everything comes around in the end, if inequality and the circular realities must make themselves felt in the long run, why should one struggle against petty shifts? If Stalin was another Nicholas II and Khrushchev an Alexander I, what was the fuss about?

Besides the long run, as Keynes observed, there is the short run, beyond which we will all be dead. The Spanish Inquisition coarsened and brutalized the tone of political and religious life in much of Europe for perhaps two hundred years, and one need but consider all the things which happened and the people who came and went between the time of the birth of Torquemada and the death of Galileo. Perhaps the Russia of 1984 will be a country acceptable to libertarian canons, a resumed member of the humane family of nations—but what will have transpired, in malicious cruelty and abuse of power, in the meantime? Much of politics is a judgment between the long and the short run, between the overall requirements of social stability and the needs of the time. Traditionally, and rightly, conservatism was the custodian of the long run, and at its best it took much which rubbed the wrong way and refashioned it. But the natural-law component in conservatism always protested against this, to some extent, and the free-market strand has reinforced the sense that one must stand with the right even if in the long run it may make little difference.

It is futile to say that the ends cannot justify the means, for we proceed every day as if they did. But we must, at some point, say that these ends are too much—too much for this moment, too much for the gain, too much (in respect to torture) in any case, as if there were absolutes. For this very reason it is perilous to waste one's ammunition in firing at too many things, for when the crucial time comes there will be nothing left to shoot. Strategy must take over from tactics at a suitable time, and certainty from a too-pervading sense of doubt. It is too facile to say that is the very job of political theory; it is, but we cannot have a complete intellectual apparatus to give us the answer to each problem. This is precisely where the organizational side of political thought comes in, the essential role of political science, so to speak. A political system toward compromise in most areas, toward the perpetuation of lower-center practices, and suffused with an individualist spirit will (as Bagehot pointed out) obviate the need for the making of tough, intellectual choices. If it is understood that really radical (in the root sense) proposals are off limits, and if the sharpest differences can be composed, if in fact much of the verbal violence is a façade (even the work of the "Establishment" or of the "Sixty Families" designed to fool the masses, as it is said) then tactics can supersede strategy to a great extent. The conservative liberals now generally see that two can play at the strategic game, that even the shining toys of the Progressive movement, such as the referendum, can produce dangerous eddies of passionate fervor. This does not mean that a state should be, in Macaulay's language, all anchor, for then the passions will break out against it, as in France. The passions should be incorporated within it, perhaps in the internecine arcane of Agarian party politics or in the interplay of group lobbying. There must indeed be safety valves.

But there must also be the great institutions capable of keeping the valves from becoming volcanoes. In the United States the judicial system, capped by the Supreme Court, has fulfilled this role. There is always a danger that it may press its power too hard, as in 1857 and 1936 or perhaps today. It may do so in ways, as now, that at times seem inimical to conservatism; after all nine men appointed by the President can be a squad of liberals. In the long run, once again, the conservative nature of their role will come through (the Taney Court started out as Jacksonian leftists and ended as Buchananite reactionaries), and that role is well-worth defending even when it seems a thankless task. The symbol of the Constitution as a sacrosanct charter, yet adaptable for various purposes, serves as a reminder of the permanent nature of conservatism and the Court, even in spite of itself, must uphold this idea. In fact even the efforts of the Court to maintain a special place for so-called "human rights" tends to spill over into a defense of property, as the case of *Morey* v. *Doud* indicated. An activist Court will be one which strains the popular will, at one level or another, through a sieve of historical or philosophical restraint, and that restraint is a valuable principle. If the state as we envisage it is to be viable it must therefore rely greatly on the support of institutions and attitudes whose guiding principle is balance and compromise.

The argument for a strong distinction between the public and private sectors (with deference paid to the freedom of the latter), the concern for separation of powers and power within the public sector, and the attention paid to limitations on the political processes, just because politics is so important and pervasive, are all factors in this matter. Clemenceau's dictum about generals is so true, and the question remains—to whom do we leave war, or money? To say "the politicians" is not ridiculous, for politics is the overriding concern of the state, the principal collective effort in finding the good life, as Aristotle wrote. But if we so expand politics, we must broaden the field of politicians. The central bankers, the managers of the radio and television networks and the newspapers and magazines, and even the generals (especially today) are politicians in their mixed spheres, and the more of them to leave things to, and the greater competition in power, as well as goods and ideas, the better.

☆ *XVI*

Groups
and Classes

There is one aspect of this analysis which will trouble many conservatives. The bankers and the judges are experts in their field, and this is as it has been for centuries. In our generation the areas in which experts have come forward as being supremely qualified to manage things have multiplied, until it has sometimes seemed as if there would be no area of general skill left but only a patchwork quilt of minute and ever-dividing cells of arcane knowledge. The graduate schools multiply the numbers of areas, and the graduates feed back new distinctions into the society and to the schools, automating the march to specialization. Weaver has complained that the workers at Oak Ridge did not know what they were making; how much less justifiable are the administrators of hospitals and universities to whom the sum total of concern are the details of administration, and yet who seem increasingly in control of the institutions. In scholarship fields grow ever narrower, so that whole lives can be spent studying such a small section of a field that the rest becomes equally blurred, while no one can invade that little cranny without equal (and therefore impossible) study. And with this comes the frenzy for degrees, without which one cannot be a pharmaceutical administrator, or a librarian, or perhaps soon a general or chairman of the board of directors. As knowledge becomes minute the only way to tell the players is by the numbers, and this in turn prompts the germlike spread of bureaucratic rules and elaborate machinery. One victim of this must be, as it is often argued, the old-fashioned idea of excellence, of general capacity for knowledge and action, since this is ill suited to the dim precision of a specialization-centered world.

One trouble with this view is that things keep happening contrary to its forebodings. Churchill and Roosevelt, to be sure, were obvious misfits, as were Hitler and Mussolini in their way. Kennedy was a perfect non-specialist, and Stalin the organization man was succeeded by the genially old-fashioned Khrushchev, with the brilliant but quite universally skilled Mikoyan ever in the wings; De Gaulle is too easy an exception to need belaboring. Since at least Ortega we have been reminded of the coming age of the technocrats, sweeping all before them with their narrow brilliance, but we keep waiting. To be sure, there has been the brilliant Monnet, always straining to rise above the second level in world affairs, and today Kosygin and Harold Wilson in their several ways, represent this new man—not a very stunning case for the technocratic revolution. Even in the academic worlds there have been more on the lower than on the higher levels—our century, from Einstein to Toynbee, has been affected by the generalist quite as much as any age, whereas the writer of monographs, like his forebears, has had a much more minute effect.

Specialization, like its cousin industrialism, is only a bogey to those who refuse to break down its component parts. To the extent that this concentration on the parts is due to the increase through growing knowledge of the number of separate parts, we can only take the one with the other. The man who can synthesize these increasing areas will, on the other hand, become more admired and powerful. It is not a coincidence that in the field of historiography the Germans tended to move from that love of detail which made them notorious in the nineteenth century to an orgy of generalizing and philosophizing, so that Ranke and Pastor have been succeeded by Dilthey and (in his way) Spengler as the ideals; American historians, ever one to two generations behind the Germans, are now setting out diligently on this voyage. As the biological sciences have grown more diffuse the areas connecting them with other fields—physics and chemistry for example—have increased, so that the miniaturization of studies at one end lends itself to the widening at the other.

In politics this specialization has also had mixed effects and potentialities. Of course there are many more narrow areas and narrow specialties. This has been caused in part, of course, by the very growth of government; one hundred years ago the role of scientific advisor was not so special but there were none, or extremely few, and government was itself more specialized. As the state widens, and as the whole range of society is widened by the new specialties, there is a new breadth which takes in, by its very size, more little areas. But, with perhaps the exception of Salazar, the distance between expert control and real power has widened in turn. The various modern emphases on leadership, even the mild Neustadtian variety, treat the specialist as a detail man surely subordinate to the charismatic leader, and so it usually proves.

This has, in fact, tended to water down the traditional zones of expert guidance. In diplomatic affairs, for instance, the so-called old diplomacy relied on the independent discretion of professionals, both at home and in the field. The post-World War I radicals sought to bring this system into discredit, and to remove from the professionals the control over all but very petty issues. This movement, as Craig and Kennan have pointed out, did not lead to democratic rule, but to amateur control. And this amateurism (using the word without any pejorative intent) has not tended to increase popular control in any meaningful way, except insofar as increased publicity has changed the manner of diplomatic intercourse. Many of the same issues can be seen in the battles over the autonomy of the central banks; a victory for Wright Patman might well change only the seat of power.

Of course that exception is worth something—the change from an expert-dominated to a less-professional system will tend to break down secrecy—but at the same time it can tend to eliminate the necessary privacy, which in the case of diplomacy has been a vital part of successful policy. In other words, even within the

affairs of the state there is an important place for the private
virtues and for the values of non-public distinction. There is an
analogy here to the question of quasi-governmental agencies such
as central banks; in the continuum running from the center of
state power to the outer ranges of social affairs there are grounds
for vital gradations. In this case the continuum does not run
from public to private, but from policy formulation through implementation to the fine points of political activity; both gradations are essential to a limited government. Of course everything
contributes in some measure to the making of policy, and for that
reason the thoroughgoing totalitarian will see to it that the professional loyalties are rooted out ruthlessly. But to the lower-
circle thinker this makes plain the advantage which experts have,
over and above their natural skill; their custom-bound orientation
and their proclivity to seek for compromises bind them to the
values of moderation. This contains the dangers of bureaucracy
which have so concerned conservatives, but this is not chargeable
to specialization. The problem of excessive bureaucracy requires
answers dealing with the scope of government and the role of the
market, and not with the staff of the civil service. Parkinson's Law
can be combated by cutting down on the expenditures for administration, not by hoping that a new bunch will remove the
problem.

In terms of diplomacy this has been demonstrated in the last
fifty years. The Wilsonian promise of open covenants openly
arrived at has worked badly. On the one hand it has proved
unrealistic in that, as international affairs have grown murky
the role of secret treaties and devious scheming has grown, not
shrunk. But the invitation to publicity, which in itself is fine but
which serves so often as a counterfeit of information, has made
this secret diplomacy dirtier by clouding the visible area of the
iceberg. The frightening brutalities of November 1956 were as
dangerous and *sub rosa* as anything in the nineteenth century,
but at least in 1870 we were spared the mean coarseness of the
official correspondence of 1956 and 1957, which serves to poison
relations even now. How much better than the Wilsonian phrase
would be, as has been suggested, "open covenants, secretly ar-

rived at"—the vindication of central or democratic control of policy but the relegation of tactics and procedure to the diplomats. As the latter can stick more to doing their job and less to being seen doing it, as the use of official channels is emphasized and the place of *ad hoc* advisors or peripatetic foreign ministers is diminished, one can expect better and perhaps more democratic results. The latter paradox can be understood by drawing another analogy—if international affairs convert into world affairs the area of diplomacy may be transferred into that of ordinary politics. Legislators may replace ambassadors—a tricky move, as even the Common Market indicates—but not a revolutionary one in this sense. Legislatures at their best work exactly on the theory of open covenants secretly arrived at, and the secrecy of their chambers contains, for good or ill, those elements of compromise and pressure which comprise the Agarian political background. When we speak of giving experts their head a carte blanche is not intended—that is the idea of the Veblenians—but only that degree of tactical independence which will permit them to operate freely within the limits of a diverse and limit-conscious society. When Burke told the electors of Bristol that he would vote his own way, and they could judge him accordingly, as an elector and not as an agent, he pictured the legislator as a specialist in one sense—a man whose ability and thought warranted enough attention to entitle him to tactical discretion. Whereas a century or more ago the radicals rejected this as undemocratic, the modern radicals (one may consider the Schattschneiderians here) accept the idea of delegation, but merely substitute a party for a man, a fixed ideology for a variable system. If the opponent of the expert means to say that he dislikes expertise because it stands in the way of total unity of purpose—and that is why Von Ribbentrop was more useful than Von Neurath—he is objecting to the customary qualities of specialization, qualities which in the legislative arena or in military affairs tend toward increasing and not decreasing public control. If the objection is to the distance of the expert from public scrutiny, it must be asked when the public should have a say. Is there a necessary merit in public control, in the sense of relentless publicity at all levels of government? And in those areas where there is too much secrecy—and these certainly exist everywhere—is the fault too much specialization or too much power? Many experts, such as scientists, become easy whipping-boys when they are only trying to adapt their special skills to positions of mixed authority and administration.

This assumes that when it comes to policy we will not and need not leave the matter to experts. Since political theory is by definition a matter of opinion there can be no experts on policy per se, and so leaving the matter to experts is only another way of saying that a certain class, highly skilled in some field (diplomacy, or war, or physics) is handed the roles of authority in the state. This is, in essence, the Platonic solution, in his case awarding the prize to philosophers (properly trained). In other words, this question of expertise is a very old issue having little to do with any modern innovation in technology or ambience. To some Americans, for instance, the problems of the 1950's required special leadership, and that meant General MacArthur; to others also it may have required expertise, but they had in mind Linus Pauling. A reasoned case was made for both men, utterly contradictory of course, but equally starting from the premise that the special tasks of the time demanded men who knew exceptionally much about how to handle the details. Usually these men, when they occasionally come to power, turn over most matters to the habitual politicians whose expertise is the time-honored one of accommodating the circle to realities—the only specialization which may be considered truly viable in politics. MacArthur, to the dismay of his fans, ruled Japan like a left-wing New Dealer; it may be that Pauling would have ended up a quasi-Taft in the White House. Perhaps MacArthur was naive or perhaps things look different from one position than they do from another—an old joke at the expense of specialists—or there can be many other explanations. What is clear is that there was nothing inevitable about the specialized role of MacArthur in his job of proconsul, for the Japanese conservatives who have followed him have attempted to undo much of his work.

The worst that can be said of the expert, then, is not that he is an insidious danger to democracy or to the values of excellence or tradition. The most telling objection is that the idea of expertise, if carried beyond those narrow bounds in which it reinforces the conservative concepts of separation and balance, is a delusion. Conservatives are as apt as anyone else to make the mistake of overlooking this. The businessman in the United States has blundered in politics frequently because he has forgotten the distinctions between the two fields and mistaken his success in one as a sign of special skill in manipulating all social affairs. But then the warrior class in Prussia (and over the years in many other lands) has erred in the same way.

The rule of experts, therefore, is more often to err on the side of weakness than of strength. How often the solution of turning a problem over to a group of specialists is an excuse for inaction! The more rarefied the skills employed the less comes out. This seems to be a drawback of intelligence, but it is usually not a demerit for thought, but for an inapplicable sort of thinking. The decisions of the political circle require political ability and not erudition, so that when everything is left to the specialists they are being pushed out of their milieu. The most brilliant mathematician would probably be at a loss if he had to build a bridge, which is no reason to denigrate the debt owed mathematics by civil engineering. When mathematicians begin to argue their universal skills they frequently make fools of themselves; they do not often become dictators.

Seen without any preconceptions, experts outside of their precise zone of skill are merely members of a particular class. Popper and Chroust have claimed that Plato himself can be described in these terms, and that his philosopher-kings and lawgivers sound suspiciously like a new meeting of the reactionary Four Hundred equipped with distinguished academic endorsements. Traveling this path we come, as Laski came, to a class view of political organization, a consideration of politics in terms of power.

The very word "class" has a powerful emotional effect, like "race" or "exploitation," suggesting a specifically radical or reactionary world view. The colorless social scientists have sought to rescue the word, but have added a wearying marginalia of social detail. This detail does reflect a timeless reality, more discernible perhaps to novelists than to sociologists (as Marquand showed in *Point of No Return*). There are an abundance of classes, and they keep reappearing, as Djilas insisted, just when they are supposedly dead. This is not a phenomenon restricted to the tragedy of Marxism; the coming of an American aristocracy after 1865 and the emergence of a new Tudor aristocracy in sixteenth-century England are examples of the constant pattern of new classes forging ahead when the prospects might seem most dim.

This interpretation of class structure owes much more to Proust, however, than it does to Marx or Engels. In the Proustian panorama the world is divided into clearly-defined sets, but within each set there are innumerable shades, and the definitions, so precise at a distance, become extraordinarily hard to discern close up. There is seldom a lack of class consciousness, but it often takes forms which disappoint the Marxists—that is, the consciousness is of a class other than those so arbitrarily determined in *Das Kapital*. Hitler confounded the Communists and socialists by making a whole nation think in terms other than the traditional, so that the class conflicts were indeed heightened, but on Gobineauian lines. The upsurge of racial controversy is having a very similar effect today, to the dismay of the left and the concern of the right. The vigor of nationalism can be considered another variant of this, and there are many more examples.

In a way this is what Madison contemplated in his No. 10 essay; the plethora of classes reduces the dangers which he saw, and we have seen, arising from sharp dichotomies. It is ironic and instructive that Beard, when asked if he were a Marxist, replied that he was a Madisonian. His work on the economic background of the Constitution did develop some parts of the Madisonian idea, yet it can be said that MacDonald's refutation of Beard has carried this Madisonian analysis even farther, using the broad complexities which Madison envisaged to contradict Beard's narrower and more Marxist Madisonianism. It is part of our contemporary sophistication that we can identify and isolate more and more classes, perhaps even subgroups, which become viable social organisms under the refined magnifying glasses of our thinking. It would take only a small extension of this analysis to equate classes with the opinion groupings which populate the political circle. This would denature the idea of class too far, however; there is a value in considering the class as a group with cohesion other than identical or similar views on politics; if the latter only is meant, the use of the term is rendered so vague as to be not worth having. This is, at the bottom, the difference between those elements who make up the circle, the constituent parts of the political society, and the underlying groups from which they derive their ideas. The managerial class of the American Midwest and the landowning class of Iberia may both comprise an opinion group which is highly conservative, somewhat reactionary but manifestly veering away from the extremes of totalitarianism, but it would be ridiculous to say that they were both members of one class. For that matter the socialist working-class of Syria and Great Britain are, despite their similarity of theoretical goals and even their spurious Marxist "objective" identity, worlds apart in more than space. A class is something more homogeneous than all those with a common view of human nature; how much more is the work of much of recent political science. Class in the modern world is as elusive as in the salon of Mme. Verdurin, if on occasion it can be as striking as in the court of Justinian.

It may be objected that this does not distinguish properly between class and caste, or class and race. These delineations are valid and certainly have their uses, but if they are to be employed it is necessary to keep them in their place. There are important differences in the social order in cases where the dividing lines are rigidly hereditary, or based on economic criteria only, or are a result of occupational or purely voluntary alignments. But these distinctions go to the workings of the class (using the word broadly) system, not to its reality. The great folly of the left has habitually been the optimistic belief that if once the particular type of distinction which served to separate the classes of one time were destroyed, no new ones could be devised. Carnegie stubbornly insisted that the new America had achieved the classless society, to the great amusement or contempt of the Marxists. They have made exactly the same error.

In basic Marxism classes would quickly disappear once the economic basis for their existence vanished. But this has proved unconvincing even to dogmatic communists. In China today a theory of permanent revolution has evolved which presupposes a constant battle with the reviving forces of dead classes. But surely old classes cannot keep recurring in a classless society; the tension between the theory of the new society and the struggle against old sins must lead brash theoreticians in Peking to wonder whether the dialectic persists even in the Marxist millennium. Since the time of the early Christians radical movements have been chagrined by the intractability of human nature.

That, today, means the Marxists more than anyone else. The primacy of the political over the economic is a valid consideration here. Not that there are political classes, for that assumes that politics is a way of life rather than the center of all life, but that in the political aspect there are many subordinate realms, of which the economic is but one. It is, moreover, a part of the mass reason-thinking of the older left that men must cohere on an economic base which conforms to a Hegelian model. The tariff-loving, Republican, thoroughly proletarian workingman has perfectly fine economic reasons for his position; for that matter the $6,000-a-year man who is aiming for $8,000 a year has much more tangible economic interests than the archetypal worker struggling toward the Marxist state. The contemporary economic rejection of the idea of measurable utility has made the precisely-fashioned theories of economic motivation even less acceptable; if we cannot chart a man's objectively right market behavior, how much less can we determine his objectively right political affiliation.

This is the point at which the question of experts becomes relevant. The political primacy of a group of experts is another way of describing a system in which one class, deriving its cohesion from an identity of ideas or occupational position or economic self-interest (and these three interact to a very great degree, as C. P. Snow has illustrated), brings its point of view into the process of government. This is by no means an irrational alliance, for most occupations have conformities, or deformities if you will. It is not just that bankers will, even if they are not affluent, be a conservative bunch; chemists and engineers seem almost always to be to the right of mathematicians and physicists. Social workers, either because of their training or the attraction of the field to those who have a high idea of human nature, will invariably tend toward the left—they will be likely to think that their skills equip them especially to run society. There is nothing criminal with this idea, it is not the figment of tyrannical or over-ambitious minds; the fault comes in accepting its premise. If we decide that we want programs involving social work (and this is clearly a question to be answered first) it would seem self-defeating to follow this up by distrusting all the men who work at perfecting the skills useful in social work. The suspicion of businessmen directed at welfare bureaucrats doing their job is as mean as the complementary distrust of diplomats engaged in diplomacy, or of businessmen running businesses. But when any one of these crosses over the line between procedure and substance (and we all know it is a gossamer line, always crossed in small degrees) the matter changes to one of class interest.

Class, then, is another aspect of the Holmesian theory of degree, a manifestation of the division of labor in a concentrated form—as the medieval moralists always said. What is professional skill viewed from one end is domination by an interest group as seen from another. The separation of substance and procedure is as essential as it is difficult, especially as each new group is likely (the case of the nuclear physicists is now a classic one) to present the matter in a new light. And since there is inevitably power in society and the state, a given datum, and since no hero or saint can discover an altruism untainted by interest, it will be possessed by a class or by classes. In this Marx and Laski were definitely right. Even Arrow has admitted that welfare economics has failed to find a workable pattern of judgments which can establish a value system acceptable to everyone. The game theorists now call this an attribute of a zero-sum game; in other words, unlike trade, no one can win without someone losing, if only an intangible place in the order of importance. But the problem of the experts is a real one for this very reason; the dangers of bourgeois or military class-rule are old hat, but we have found in our generation that the spurious expertise of these new classes can be a tool for a disingenuous effort at class mastery which often takes society by surprise. Robert de Jouvenel's maxim that two deputies, one socialist and one capitalist, have more in common than two socialists, one a deputy and one not, is a wry joke on this very thing.

For the word "deputy" one can substitute the generic term "politician"; in a narrowly political world the ruling class is apt to be composed of politicians. As the rewards in power and perquisites accruing to the political chieftains have expanded, the road to politics has become more crowded, even as the talk of low governmental wages has persisted. The businessman-turned-civil servant has become a staple of government throughout the capitalist world—there are so many dollar-a-year men now that they worry about their salaries—and as a rule it is the governmental role which, as in the case of McNamara, yields the highest importance. The historic British example of public service as the supreme career of the aristocrat is something of a model, but there the office was a part of the patrimony of the class, accessible to be sure in varying degrees but withal a part of the aristocratic milieu. Now the political prizes define the aristocracy; this is most true in Russia or Tanzania, least so in Switzerland, but everywhere a distinctly separate area of power.

The success of the industrial managers has been compared to this and with good reason, for the bureaucratization of big business has politicized private enterprise, as we have noted, and has rewarded the new class of managers with less power, more money, and a comparable status to that of the political chiefs. Berle and Burnham in their separate ways have described the position of the managers, and in both cases they have wondered at or criticized the political nature of the managerial group. To some extent this is unrealistic, for in the nineteenth century the entrepreneur held (and still very much holds) political power. The great change of our time has been the conversion of the procedures of business and public-private relationships into political settings. Businessmen complain that they must spend much of their time dealing with the unions or coping with government regulations. Throughout history, however, this has been true, and it is debatable whether the discounters of today are more or less immersed in politics than the merchants of the staple were. This preoccupation requires a political orientation, a concern for power relationships rather than market judgment, which so often causes men of business—especially the old-fashioned sort—to bemoan the superiority of union leaders trained in political tactics and wholeheartedly devoted to these arts. But this frustration is not reserved to the business community; in Russia the industrial managers have evidently been engaged in the same unequal (or is it so unequal, in the long run?) struggle with the party workers. The greatest successes in industry are the men who can manage both worlds—Romney of American Motors and Beitz of Krupp were two outstanding examples. It is significant that Beitz reportedly achieved an exceptional rapport with many Communist leaders, another illustration of the French maxim.

This does not describe a hierarchy, but a welcome confusion of interacting levels of power converging on the political center. The confusion does not imply anarchy because the principal rewards and avenues are, even in the most mixed society, quite well marked. The interactions may derive from a bureaucratic world, but bureaucracy is the setting, and not the road to power; it is striking how unimportant the paraphernalia of organization is in the last analysis. Even Stalin and, in a very different fashion, Dollfuss ruled with Machiavellian strategems and (especially in the case of Stalin, of course) brutal authority on coming to power; the red tape has a way of defining the terms, but not of interfering with the key strokes. How frequently there can be endless debates over organization and chains of command, only to have everything quickly determined by a new man or a new group! This happened in France after 1799, and in the opposing direction in Germany after 1948. Power abhors a vacuum, and the hand that operates the vacuum sweeper will not be a light one.

There are serious objections to this categorization of a new ruling class or classes. In the first place, the positions of power are usually non-inheritable, so that each generation must produce its new class anew. When the Soviets are taxed with their anti-egalitarian course, they often reply that when Khrushchev retired he forfeited his magnificent *dacha* and presumably subsists on his appropriate pension like any other citizen. Khrushchev, be it noted, did not retire voluntarily. The need for a new struggle cuts both ways; if there is no cushion in private wealth or transmittable power, the urge to hold on to the positions of power will be most intensified. In Renaissance France these urges caused the Crown to make many state positions inheritable, so as to reduce the pressure of aristocratic power-politics. This invasion of the public sector by private values, far worse an affront than any Galbraith has mentioned, produced stagnation and venality, but its genesis was understandable. But the modern tendency to reduce the importance of inheritance, the post-Whig, in contrast to the pre-Whig inclination, has historical parallels as well. The Roman Empire, for instance, ran badly when the hereditary principle was applied, the Antonines thrived on a system of inheritance by appointment and adoption; when Marcus Aurelius permitted his son Commodus to succeed him the decline began. To the extent that this tension between effective leadership and an excess of ambition is decided by standards of efficiency and opportunity, as it generally is today, the members of the political elite will generally be chosen without consideration of genealogy, and the ruling class will be correspondingly amorphous. There will be more Henry Adamses than John Quincy Adamses, and even more scions of old families who fail to enter Harvard. It used to be argued that preference to sons of the rich or powerful in education was necessary in order to train the future leaders even at the cost of not training others who might have been leaders; now we try to see to it—corporations as well as government—that everyone is equal in the race.

Or so the theory goes. The prevalence of Harrimans and

Rockefellers, Macmillans and Hammarskjölds in our egalitarian age is nevertheless worth considering. Plato thought that heredity would largely determine the membership of his elite, despite the openness of careers to talent. Now the argument (unfortunately so often tied to disputes over our modern incubus, race) over what is early training and what is natural bent carries on this issue. The potency of the family instinct has reasserted itself after periods of revolutionary efficiency throughout history; much of the stuff of the cyclical pattern in the Near East involved the revival of family connections after the old families had been dispersed. As Mosca wrote, "All ruling classes tend to become hereditary in fact if not in law." This is of course a central part of the conservatizing force which overtakes revolutions, that force which has already blunted the zeal of the Soviet Union. But in class terms it is also the spread of cohesion and stability in its most thorough form. It is possible to consider a class solidarity so strong—such as that of the Jesuits—that no ties of blood are needed and no hostages to social peace are allowed, but it is dangerous to count on this. If the key elites must be reconstituted on merit, the powers that determine what is merit— and that can be as relative as anything else—will gain in importance. The elite may (as the Jesuits have been accused, as Plato's golden class surely would have been) become imbued with a separate morality, perhaps like the Albigensian pure or the Huxleyian smart, far above the common rule, but as hostile to the majority ethic as any hereditary system might provide. But in the end blood will tell, and unless celibacy is enforced heredity will come back through the side door.

The Whig reply to the threat of class domination had been to limit the power of any class (as the nineteenth-century Whigs did even to their aristocratic patrons) rather than to attempt to purify the elite. The prospect envisioned by Berle and Burnham assumed the "coming-to-power" of a new class, but the striking reality of modern experience has shown how oversimplified this view was. The example of Fascist Italy, the homeland of Pareto and Mosca, is a case in point. The variety of classes which tended to support fascism in its early years might be categorized as these: the new industrialist class which had come into being from nothing, with some aristocratic intermixture, only within the last fifty years, portions of the old landowning class, different strata of the middle class, especially that area of the lower middle-class which Hitler so well predicted would rally to his cause, large areas of the professional groups, and the bulk of those who thought of themselves as self-consciously young or especially patriotic. The older socio-economic rubrics proved inadequate to describe the new alignments because there were new ways of dividing the population—professional and age distinctions, for instance, which proved more important. These new classes were not merely opinion blocs, although in many cases they may have begun so, because they tended to solidify into interest groups with a stake—but not necessarily an economic one, of course—in their values.

Dahl has shown how in the city of New Haven these various ways of delineating groups can make more sense than the older, simpler divisions, and also how, even when you have parsed the matter thoroughly, there is no sure way of identifying either the elements of each class or its power. In this the American thinkers have always been more right than their feudal-conscious European counterparts. The complex pattern of the Jeffersonian political machine, that extraordinary alliance which won the election of 1800 and laid the foundation for the Democratic Party, was built on theoretical insights which now seem brilliant, as Agar testifies. One of the strongest arguments in support of this judgment is the state of contemporary Soviet society. There is not just a new class but a fine network of diverse classes, to replace the Czarist social structure. For example, the dichotomy between the political class, the party executives, on one side and the industrial elite, largely alumni of technical schools, on the other, has become marked. There is certainly a class of the young also, in the vague but meaningful sense that divisions of age are manifested by a difference of identification and social spirit. Much of the confusion of recent years may be attributed to the growth of new classes, so that the views of professional people or middle-management executives cannot be ignored.

And recent events show that the old classes—soldiers, peasants, Jews, Georgians, or poets—are as class-oriented in our sense as in 1917 or as in New Haven. Perhaps the Chinese, of all people, will eradicate the influence of blood on social alignments; the Russians have clearly failed the Platonic test.

There is a second objection to this class theory, the case against emphasis on power or political authority. Too often, to be sure, in political theory the assumption is made that power is an irresistible goal, yet power involves work and danger. To a great extent the highest pleasure of power, or of money, is the aura which is separate from the rigor, the fame or distinction which power conveys. But there are other ways of achieving fame. Galbraith has separated what he calls the contenders for the serious positions of importance in society—the businessmen and the politicians and the academics—from the possessors of frivolous fame, the idols of the entertainment or publicity worlds. These people seem utterly negligible in importance to political thinkers, and yet they are much more significant to a very large part of the population, perhaps a majority, than the proper subjects of awe. Anatole France has caught this in his wonderful short story, *The Procurator of Judea;* because Mary Magdalen is a footnote to the important message of her time, as it is generally seen now, is no indication that that is the way the Roman or Judean on the street felt in that time. The young person of our time, whoever that may be, is more likely to have looked to Marilyn Monroe for emulation or daydreams than to Eleanor Roosevelt or her husband.

To say that this is politically unimportant is to separate one part of social standing or class value-rating as being meaningless. The sociologists who have criticized Warner for his preoccupation with social rating have too much minimized the role which these comparisons have always played in life, and the splintering and heterogeneity of modern times has made the ambivalent or illogical attitudes of social awareness more important. Perhaps one might say that in 1100 there were few classes (although this may not be true either) and that class attitudes were simple and direct. But this is certainly not so now; public distinction is often the clearest form of reward which social elevation can bring. Parvenus have always operated on this theory, as Petronius showed, but now the nuances of a Brando or, to reach the reductio *ab absurdum*, the Beatles, in terms of fame and influence are much more refined.

Let us consider a small but very potent group, the radio and television commentators. To begin with, it may be true that many of them have reached their positions because of a smooth voice, rather than because of innate wisdom or incisive mental quickness. They may vanish from the public eye as quickly as they came into view. But while they are there, they possess many of the attributes of high importance. To be sure, their power may be limited in the sense that they can perhaps not even tell a network vice-president what to do; in another sense, they may tell millions of people what to do every day. Their influence, in Beveridge's sense, may not equal their audience, as H. V. Kaltenborn discovered. But their fame may outdistance both, fame which may center more on the appearance of the speaker than on his ideas, and will of course have no relationship to his ancestry, which will not be known, or his salary, which may not be known, or his ownership of status symbols, which will be known only if the publicity agents work hard enough. These men make up a definite group, a sub-class, in the sense that they have a shared economic situation vis-à-vis their employers, their public image derives from their job, and they hold a special place reserved in our age to men who do what they do. Of course, they seldom present a united front, although in the event of efforts made to reduce their influence or fame they easily could. Their jobs are not transmittable by inheritance, although to some extent the fame of the father can be passed on or at least used. In other words, their position can be analyzed in various ways; their role as entertainment idol, their position of sage, and their job of reporter all have separate socio-political implications.

In a more minute way this can be said of anyone operating in the different positions—skilled workmen, or member of a church, senior citizen, etc.—which may overlap one on the other.

And if fame is the spur, it is an error to overlook the possibility that that part of one's life which most appertains to fame will be the most highly regarded. Thus, if all well-known announcers earn large sums, they should tend toward the right in politics, by accepted standards of political orientation. But the contrary is often the case because the radio-TV "opinion public," if one may so call it, is by and large somewhat liberal, so that the claims of note impel in the leftward directions. Just as the rich man soon surpasses the narrowly financial rewards and seeks fame in material or immaterial forms, so politics can evolve into a struggle for fame, a search for publicity, as the uncharitable may have it.

But this does not lessen the reality of class differences. The entertainment world may be as randomly mobile as the purest disbeliever in inheritance might want, and its philosophy of economics or politics may be non-existent; nonetheless, it will make up a very distinct order, with very sharp standards of behavior (different, perhaps, but no less definite that that of the old Yankee or the gentry) and of inclination. The simplicists always want classes to have their niche on the political circle neatly marked and carefully observed, but things do not work out that way. And a good thing, too, for it is the discrepancies and mixed outlook of the various classes, as well as their number, which ensure that difference and dissent will not disappear. Within a few years an element may alter its political leanings because of new stimuli or economic changes. This can be observed by a de Tocqueville or, in more everyday terms but almost as skillfully, by a Lubell, and these changes may vanish or be altered in turn or may freeze into a historic pattern. If class equaled opinion-group the Marxists might be right; the hope which they cherish of a composition of all differences through the settlement of class distinctions might seem more feasible. But it is precisely because opinions vary so, and classes do themselves, and work on each other in such an uneven and unpredictable fashion, that these hopes are so unrealistic.

This does not mean that the antagonisms are unreal, however. The complex jigsaw puzzle of multiple interests may not be

Marxian, but it is at least in some part Machiavellian. Downs, and Buchanan and Tullock, have in their different ways pointed out how naive it is to assume, as so often the liberal has (and the liberal conservative at times as well) that somehow politics can purify the selfish or strong-spirited demands of conflicting groups, so that, à la Rousseau, a general will superior to the individual wills may appear. By splintering the picture of the class the self-willed ego has not been drained but rather enhanced, for no class can claim, just as no opinion can, a superior virtue, and no society can deny its class bases. Laski was most naive of all, for once having considered, with the vast erudition which he possessed, the extraordinary varieties of class interaction he came around to a faith in a system which would end the game and dispose easily of all the problems. His answer was to point to the threat of a selfish plutocracy, but he did not reckon on other classes being selfish, or new classes arising to replace the old. De Mandeville, with all his curiosities, had a better answer to the problem of selfishness.

In this the free-market conservatives are most realistic. The motive spirit of the market is of course self-interest, and no one expects altruism to be the guide to price in a free market. It is logical for them, therefore, to accept the fact of self-interest in politics and other areas of social action. The traditional conservative, on the other hand, most often veers away from free-market ideas at this point by rejecting the very idea of class or group antipathies or by seeking to sublimate them in a broader unity. This is often the source of the spongiest kind of conservative thinking, the Pollyannaish, we-have-no-differences sort of communal harmony which is the comfort of Babbitts and the derision of critics, the sort of ideology which tends to justify Mill's criticism of the conservatives as the stupid party. The greatest flaw is not the emphasis on social interdependence or the proposition that in a viable society everyone has a vital stake in order which surpasses his stake in revolution—these are very legitimate arguments. But to go from there and deny that there are differences, or to assume that one can lump together the various stakes into one fungible interest is unnecessary and foolish. The famous metaphor of Livy, in which the various classes of early Rome were likened to organs of the body, would have suffered if it had been presented as an argument for an elimination of the differences between head and foot.

Vive la différence! we might add; it is the radical who truly seeks to make sure that all classes will have a common and inseparable interest. The reactionary, such as Plato, who designs a system whereby the elite look after all vital interests, and the radical, such as Marx, who seeks to make all the population one such class, agree on the proposition, a key upper-circle idea, that group differences are wrong and subject to elimination. When a lower-circle thinker accepts this idea, even if in the form of a society dedicated to "justice" or "stability," he is often elevating the procedure of government into a potential tyrant. This is the worst use of the idea of the rule of law, the booby trap in natural-law ideology. Historically, it has involved a transfer of authority to a class allegedly superior in wisdom or judgment which could enforce the system of laws without fear or favor. A body of doctrine which refuses to recognize the realities of naked power cannot escape it, for the vacuum will be filled and all humans, as conservatives are the first to remember, are prone to weakness of one sort or another.

The modern candidate for the guardian of righteousness is most typically the intellectual. It may be said that the subject of the role, the position, and the nature of the intellectual has been the subject of more literature (and junk) than any other issue of political or social thought in this century. When the Russians began to consider the intelligentsia as a class—and this has been attributed to nothing more sacred than the nuances of the class nature of the eighteenth-century imperial program— they thought of a fairly cohesive group—odd, perhaps, in that old Russian manner of combining Western fragments with Eastern uncertainties—but not too hard to distinguish. Originally an intellectual was a bureaucrat, perhaps, like Radischev or Dostoevski, a deviant, but basically part of a stratified society. To many current observers, this is still true—much of the talk of the intellectuals tacitly assumes that they consist of, and are roughly the same as the academic community. This community comprises a class in almost any usage of that term—a body of men with common intellectual backgrounds, economic interests, and social ties. The academic world, thanks to the growing premium placed on higher education and the development of a system of specialized communication and international intelligence, has become more and more important in the last fifty years. But if by an "intellectual" we mean a "professor," we have simplified the problem at the cost of begging the question. This assumes a community of interest between the two cultures which not only Snow must doubt.

What of the artists, who as Barzun has pointed out are very different in their nature from thinkers, and what of the non-academic scientists? And what of intelligent men outside the ken—the body of professional men, for instance, and anyone else who cares to think of abstruse matters? The Russia of the 1870's included Tolstoi as well as Dostoevski, and Loris-Melikov and Pobedonostsev as well. In their various ways they all thought about the basic problems of political theory, and they all had answers at diverse levels and at very diverse places on the circle—yet to some only Dostoevski was an intellectual. In that case, what is the value of using the term? But if we try to include all those who have a place in the House of Intellect, the chance of a class consensus almost inevitably goes out the window.

In the United States this parochialism is generally, and fortunately, not very much pronounced outside of the murkier waters of new criticism journals. Stevenson, the splendor of the intelligentsia, passed few of the restrictive tests, and his popularity was a tribute to the respect for urbanity and breadth of thought as an integral part of the intellectual process. But in saying this we must consider three points. First, most definers of intellectualism are not talking about intelligence as a datum, smartness if you will. If tests were given it would be easy to conceive of Thomas Dewey outscoring Adlai Stevenson with facility, while William Buckley might cop many of the prizes. No one seriously is talking about the sort of intelligence which can allegedly be measured. Secondly, success in scholarly or similar fields is hardly the class standard, or Schlesinger should join forces with Malraux. The broadest wisdom may be inconsistent with the narrowing confines of contemporary academia, just as a man who would revolutionize mankind with a new philosophy in our time can be guaranteed not to be a certified teacher of philosophy. There is no automatic merit—or demerit—in being a professor. Finally, it follows that one cannot derive any political conclusions from the status of intellectuals.

The definition with which we are left is so wide as to include Lenin and Luther and perhaps even Hitler. In the end, therefore, the people who talk of intellectuals, if they do not mean a social class, come around to meaning those thinkers who think right. Put baldly, it sounds as unconvincing as it is. But it is seldom put so baldly. A typical argument may run thusly: The thinking element of the population may be divided into those who think about petty matters, Plato's baser sort, and those who think of the vital matters. But of the latter there are some who let emotions or prejudices cloud their views. Only those who use rational means of reaching fundamental truths can fairly be called true intellectuals—the word true is, as always, a very handy tool. Now this august bunch, by chance, invariably holds opinions identical with the expositor. Since the others are at times the irrational supporters of totalitarian ideas it is sometimes comforting to the lower-circle rationalist to espouse this idea. The flame of Whig ideas was kept bright through many years of modern French history by groups maintaining this view, serving as the inspiration of the anti-Boulangists and the pro-Dreyfusards, the consolation of the foes of the Action Française and the Vichy regime. When Maurras fashioned a subtle and powerful right-wing argument, the liberals said that the reason of the reactionaries was an appeal to unreason, which was often true and thus no reason at all, which is dangerous. Just as the libertarian suffers a dangerous erosion of his beliefs when he permits himself to deny liberties to others because they would refuse them to him, so the rationalist who insists that all reasoning must lead toward Reason condemns himself to a sterile philosophy of thought. That sterility was the bane of the Third

Republic and a warning to those who talk of intellectuality, for by defining terms so closely one way, the others are not mollified but emboldened to irrationalism.

This is true of that great exposition of the intellectual idea, Benda's *Treason of the Intellectuals*. It is disagreeable to criticize this great essay whose spirit typified so much of what is best in the heritage of the Englightenment and whose prophecies have cast so much light on the horrors of the years since 1926. To use the offhand term of political slang, Benda was for all the right things. But it is instructive to see where his absolutism took him, nevertheless, and to judge whether we want to follow. Benda looked to a class of thinkers, of intellectuals, the *clercs* in his untranslatable original, who must preserve the sense of natural justice, of probity and reason amidst a bad world. The role of the clerc, he argued, was to be separate from the state; even inexorably hostile—"the State, in the name of its practical interests, to defend which is its function, has a right—perhaps a duty—to punish them." But they must always stand above politics and for the right—a timeless function rooted in history, yet violated, Benda conceded, by Cicero and Dante. This intellectual class would perhaps always be a persecuted minority, but must always maintain perfect independence. Benda's intellectual order, therefore (and this is often forgotten) was to eschew power but to gain lasting influence, somewhat like the regular clergy in the Middle Ages who were the ancestors of the modern clerc. Benda did not say, but obviously thought that what the clercs maintained was a sacred faith in reason, much righter than the gross duties of the state and its servants. Yet he never could say exactly why, for he admitted that there were other brands of reasoning, and he did not say that reason was the only road to the good life. Benda's *tour de force* was won at a great cost, for it meant segregating and isolating the qualities of reason from most of political life.

Many who quote Benda would like to have his cake and eat theirs too; to appeal to the pristine purity of the clerc and use it to advantage in the rough world of affairs. In fact, the course which is often advocated—in *Dissent* or *Commentary*, for instance

—for the intellectual is precisely what Benda thought of as treason, the conscious preference for political controversy over scholarly rationality. This is usually joined with an assumption that the place of the intellectual is securely on the left. Benda's clerc rejected the Marxist as well as the Maurrasist vision—just as his adversary, Sorel, combined both—and had a low opinion of welfare as a prime goal of society. Benda would probably have agreed with Brogan in the latter's comparison of Romain Rolland and his confreres, who refused to believe the facts about the Soviet Union, with the anti-Dreyfusards. If the intellectual is on the left, there is no presumption that reason has put him there. It may be that the term has been drawn, as we have noted, so as to include only a certain community holding certain jobs. Or it may be that the climate of opinion at a given time, a fad in fact, has brought this about. In Weimar Germany, most of the academic world was on the right, and often far to the right. Hoffer suggests that a disdain for the mass of humanity has been typical of the thinker throughout most of history, and his case is stronger than the opposing one. No one has ventured to propose that the literati of Sung China would or should have comprised a force for radicalism.

To be sure, the professor or the painter can avoid some of the obvious work-centered self-interest of the laborer or businessman. It is true that the economist who advocates rapid growth or full employment may be supporting a program of inflation which may hurt him more than most. It is also true that the comfortable signers of left-wing manifestos are placing principles ahead of economic gain. Often this is a sign that other goals are being sought, that power or fame mean more than money. The Marxist intellectual who thinks of himself as one of the future leaders of a classless society may envisage a very substantial accretion of importance for himself, if not for his class. The same economist whose theories seem so finely disinterested may be devoting much of his efforts to scaling the academic ladder with ruthless zeal.

It is naive to think that because a man does not subordinate his political opinions to his immediate pocketbook interests, he

has achieved a clerical superiority. Political motivations are much
more complex. Yet Benda had a strong argument in his appeal
to the qualities of reason. It is not necessary to believe that that
reason embodies some form of truth to accept the value of men
who, upon reaching a general system of values, accept its implications even when they are personally inconvenient. This is what
Wechsler has been writing of in the area of judicial decisions
(which is a microcosm of the intellectual problem); neutrality,
in his sense, means just this ability to be consistent and fair-
minded up to the point of basic commitment. Rolland may have
chosen to admire Communist Russia for many reasons, including
the adulation which this elicited from the far left. It is pointless
to go into that very far; Freud, among others, has demolished
the simpler purities of believers in unclouded rational rectitude.
But having once adopted beliefs which were attached to certain
principles, it was shocking that Rolland refused to let arguments
aimed at those very beliefs sway him; his substitution of prejudice, in the literal sense of that word, for thought did mean
an abdication of the role of reason. There is no presumption
that a merchant, or a longshoreman like Hoffer, should be less
capable of exercising this neutrality, this reasoning stance, than
a professor. But if the professor has tenure, or the judge has a
fixed guarantee of his post during good behavior (in the legal
sense), he can more easily put aside the immediate concerns
of money. Beyond that, the training of the clerc, and here the
religious parallel is most telling, may fortify this tendency. But
we all know that there have been savagely intolerant or fanat-
ically narrow clerics, and there are equally unneutral clercs; the
virtue is not to be assumed but yet nurtured. It is a virtue which
is akin to the aristocratic qualities of detachment and *noblesse
oblige:* the *philosophes* flourished more under Louis XV than
their successors did under Waldeck-Rousseau. The rich man who
espouses liberal causes is a butt for jokes, but his impartiality
is (even if it arises from guilt, as may very well often be the case)
most above suspicion. Chaplin had less to gain from his opinions,
in a monetary or functional sense, than his critics; this did not
mean of course that he would, for this reason, have been a good

judge to follow. To others (to most, perhaps), reason confirms the lessons of class; Melville's Captain Vere was presumably no less sincere because his hard-won convictions paralleled the easy assumptions of his peer group. There is a place for both sorts in a society which cherishes many opinions; the merit which comes from believing against interest should not be exaggerated into perfection, for we know how complex interest is, but it should be honored—and the stratified society which makes it possible should be honored as well.

But, Benda to the contrary notwithstanding, these qualities must be judged within the world of politics if we are to discover their political significance. The businessman who talks of free enterprise but supports restrictive zoning and tariff laws is a traitor to the idea of private autonomy, but he is carrying out the short-range goals of his practical life. To be consistently within a reasoned position is nothing more than to hold a thought-out position on the circle (ranging over a lesser or greater area), but that circle brings no answers. The absolutist tradition in the law that counted on the judges to hand down an inevitably correct law—*jus dicere* and not *jus dare,* as Bacon put it—will not wash, and no amount of praise for the rule of law or of neutrality will bring it back. All too often the picture of the most detached, intellectually honest scholar is a reminder that there is a gap, a necessary gap, between righteousness and political sagacity. Benda admitted this, and made his clerc a habitual dissenter from the work of the state. There are many roles for the professor, and the artist (consider the wily Rubens, whom Trevor-Roper has described as a key figure of the Counter-Reformation drive for a closed society) as well, not all of them so high-minded. But then the same can be said for the businessman—even Mark Hanna displayed a breadth of imagination which was as fine in many ways, and much more sound, than that of Brooks Adams.

Buchanan and Tullock have distinguished between the behavior of the man who seeks his immediate self-interest, whom they style the maximizer, a sort of grubby La Rochefoucauld, perhaps, and the man who considers his own interests as part of the total good whom they call, for obvious reasons, the Kantian.

Kant's message, or the Golden Rule, will appeal to few men if it does not produce a better state of affairs for the upholder; this is as clear in the models of voting on highway projects as it is in the larger arenas. Plato derides Glaucon for saying that justice is the result of the decision of the many who are weak to have law to protect them from the few who are strong, but that is a fair defense and explanation of the social contract, as Hobbes and Locke showed. No one is so noble, or should be, that he can ignore his own interests altogether. What Wechsler calls principled judgments, what Benda perhaps refers to in his description of reason, is the quality of subordinating the grosser forms of interest to the wider ones, the capacity to take the long view.

It is folly to expect a class to be altruistic, and even greater folly to make this expectation a principle of a good society. From the conservative point of view, however, it is suitable to encourage and reward the establishment of longer-run ideas, so that the more altruistic rules (although never perfectly so) can flow from the nature of political processes. The apostles of the market are not wrong in emphasizing the gain-getting features of politics, but it is one test—and a very important one—of civilization whether the gain is interpreted broadly or narrowly, through layers of developed principles or roughly and directly. We so often see, as Brecht has bitterly commented, how in times of crisis everything comes down to feeding one's face; the efforts of statesmen should be to avoid these crises and to make the digestive process more edifying. There is no contradiction between believing that everyone is out for what he can get, and also holding that in a good society he will also try to get what he thinks is good for everyone.

☆ XVII

The Open Society

Unfortunately, there is no reason to believe that even the longest, noblest view will ensure the best in society or in ourselves. As denizens of the lower circle we cannot say, "Here is your great function, guaranteed to produce the good life for all men," once the liberal, for instance, talks of political efforts to ensure self-fulfillment, he runs the risk of assigning politics an impossible job. When Jefferson substituted the pursuit of happiness for Locke's property, his liberalism inspired a dubious concept; it is frightening to imagine what the Fifth and Fourteenth amendments would be like if they were couched in Jeffersonian rather than Lockeian terms. There is no magic wand, and the sum total of rights and opportunities present in the best society we can envisage do nothing more than grant, within the context of the time, the best of possibilities, distributed unevenly, which civilization has yet made possible. In some ways—materially, especially—these possibilities have expanded; in others there are severe doubts.

It is hard to know what to call this best society. In any such analysis as this, though, the term of Popper—the open society—comes to the fore. Popper contrasted the perfect systems—closed because of their very claims to perfection—of Plato and Hegel with the legacy of Pericles and Democritus, an open society. It is possible to paraphrase Popper (and alter him, to some extent) by considering four meanings of openness in this regard: 1) Open in that the precise structure of the state and the role of classes within society are not fixed, but subject to constant reinterpretation or abolition. 2) Open in that social mobility is guaranteed, and the chances for everyone are maintained even at the cost of some social disorder or loss of efficiency. 3) Open in that nothing is sacred, closed to the free discussion or irreverent treatment of free men. 4) Open in that nothing is considered absolute, and the diversity of standards and values is permitted the widest scope consistent with basic good order.

These are interrelated but not identical desiderata. We may say that all are not of equal magnitude of desirability. Number 2 implies economic criteria which may, if they lead to great governmental powers, conflict with no. 1; the "liberal" Marx whom Popper tries to disentangle from Hegel is a prophet of a very dubious open society. The "openness" which is most valuable is that play of freedom which permits free inquiry and the absence of taboos—no. 3 in essence, but with something of no. 1 and no. 4. It is not just liberty, although that is of course a key part of it, but the whole environment which surrounds the details of liberty with an encouraging milieu.

It is an integral part of the open society that it cannot be sketched or prescribed as a closed one can, for its virtue is in part its variability. How often it has seemed unsatisfactory that the foes of Fascist or Communist powers could not propose a clear alternative, but that is as it should be. This essay has been an effort to define one such society, but it would be unfair to deny that Aneurin Bevan or Gunnar Myrdal have not had a similar objective. One way to describe this would be to say that a closed society is its own standard; Sparta is the result and prize of the Spartan idea, but the open society exists for the enrichment of its citizens and the varied opportunities it may provide. The Spartan youth let the fox eat his stomach because it was good training, whereas the worth of training of the open society is judged by its utility in preparing men for usefulness in a more diverse world.

The abstraction of these principles can be seen better in precise cases; two have been pushed to our attention most urgently recently. Firstly, consider the Berlin Wall and the flight of refugees from East to West Germany. In a period of comparative peace, over fifteen years after the end of World War II, a state places brutal barriers to the movement of its population across the borders, and yet ordinary men risk their lives to surmount these barriers. What qualities in the open society are so tempting to those in the closed one? The answer of material goods is not persuasive, for if that were so humanity would be far more on the move. Many of those who flee have career opportunities in the East greater (in part because of the labor shortage caused by emigration) than they can hope for in the West. The reasons go to the heart of the qualities of the open society. Many young refugees complain that the mildest political or social heterodoxy, (such as interest in historical forms or traditions or "formalist" books) not only subjects them to criticism or punishment, but makes them forever suspect, a name in the ubiquitous dossiers. Everything that one does is judged against a fixed set of rules whose nature is not subject to debate or curtailment. There is a pervasive sense of doing and thinking "right"; a well-intended essay on even the most obscure subject may be termed in opposition to the "right approach," the currently approved Marxist-Leninist (but no longer Stalinist) line, and even if the line changes, the error may remain on the books as a now irrelevant but permanently scarring reminder of nonconformity, like long-past behavior in an Edith Wharton story. There is nowhere to turn—one road to advancement, one taskmaster to judge enthusiasm in athletics or parades or conversations, one seller who manages to provide too little of everything, so that hurry up and wait becomes an eternal requirement. There is the sense that even at best, as in the opera, variety and opportunity in a closed society like East Germany must still serve a purpose, must be integrated into an overall picture beyond dispute. Finally, there can be minute criticism or trivial humor, but there cannot, must not, be a thorough detachment, a disdain or laugh at everything, a helter-skelter incongruity. In that lack the abyss of the concentration camp is always present.

This can be seen in South Africa. Here there are few refugees but more bitter tensions, no wall but a self-imposed moat. The

sense that, since the rest of the world is wrong and engaged
in a conspiracy against the right everything must be channeled
in a desperate fight, can lead to paranoia in a society as well
as a person. The white South Africans either rebel against the
social foundations or, inexorably, huddle closer together, and
that close solidarity has produced the system of passes, of
prickly sensitivity and increasing social uniformity which must
freeze out dissent and wayward spirits. The Russians have encouraged television, so that this one consumer good is everywhere; the South African government fears it, so it is banned.
Both act without regard to the standards of the open society;
it is not material goods but the sense of freedom which is
significant. The tolerance of Cape Town and the cosmopolitanism
of Johannesburg grow more and more suspect and illicit, just as
the theater of East Berlin leads a half-life, and even Brecht died
under suspicion. South Africa has not reached the point where
white citizens must be approved to buy food without restraint,
but the irregular sentences and house arrests mark the coming
of conditions of imprisonment amidst normal life, of the Kafkaesque state.

East Germany is a Marxist state, so that its failures are
legitimate arguments for conservatism. South Africa is considered
the liberal bête noire—liberal is a nastier word in Pretoria than
in any other place in the world—but what the white South Africans are doing to themselves is a page from the conservative
book of errors. What is apartheid but the infliction, insofar as
it is meant seriously, of vast burdens on the burgeoning market?
And if not so meant, is it not a kind of quasi-slavery for statist
purposes? The mining magnates such as Oppenheimer are critical
of the Nationalist policies, whose proponents derive their strength
from the Populist spirit of the Boers. The Boers look back in
nostalgia to the independent virility of the days before 1899,
but sterness mixed with enforced discomfort, the Spartan answer,
when fused with a brutal policy toward the helots becomes the
authoritarian sharpness of the upper circle.

But what is there in the United States or Great Britain or
West Germany which is better than this, which brings people at

the risk of all their possessions or their life to try to become inhabitants? It is the opposite of what we have been considering— societies with innumerable poles of power, where one can thumb one's nose at the dossiers (which is why Joseph McCarthy, with his worship of the unforgetting secret record, was such a menace), where one can be bizarre, where one can construct one's utility schedules on peculiar lines, where one can strive to become important in a very private way by writing antisocial plays or by saving and investing money. In this sense, no. 2 definition of the open society may be the most conservative of all, for the free mobility of the capitalist system may be less tumultuous— no upturning of the old or benefits to the certified deserving— but more open, more accessible to random patterns or individual efforts.

The lover of openness will tend to follow Popper in choosing liberty over full employment. The free-market conservatives have brought to the conservative cause a zest for variety which ensures that at least the conservative will not forget that con- tinuity, the conservative watchword, must be tempered with the elements of change. This must create a tension in con- servatism but it is just this tension, the paradoxes of capitalism and democracy, of freedom and the preservation of order, which have troubled every belief. Surmounting the inconsistencies is the challenge and the opportunity of a doctrine that doubts humanity, yet strives to make human society most flexible.

This contradiction is not beyond re-examination, to be sure; it is not enough to say that a policy tends toward increasing openness in society. There are limits to the values of all four criteria; even no. 3 cannot be accepted at full value. A con- stant radical refusal to accept any beliefs as secure would lead to nihilism; in some ways it is the strength of a stable society that some matters are beyond discussion, so that others may be considered without rancor. In much the same way, the fixed contours of status and position make social mobility meaningful and peaceful; in a system in which each day one would have to defend or seize a spot in the sun, the competitive tensions would be unendurable. The moments of complete revolution are perhaps the most open times of history, but they are not our goal. In other words, the open society can either be a conservative system or a radical one, depending upon the degree to which these open qualities are pushed. South Africa may be a good example. Of course the incredible caste system which apartheid and its more baleful ideological predecessors have tried to inculcate are the opposite pole from an open system. And the collectivist program of national solidarity of the government, which involves intimidation of the press and a constant racial and intellectual check on everyone, is also directly opposed to the principles of the lower circle. But part of the quandary of critics of South Africa lies in the dangers of overturning all of these apparatuses; a wholesale destruction of all the institutions of South Africa would produce a pure open system, but it might lead to a new tyranny as in Egypt, or complete anarchy. The free-market idea has always sought to mediate this antithesis, establishing a rule of reason between absolute openness and the codes of control. Thus it would be no improvement to replace rules of the state saying which races could own land in different areas with an open melee in which no one had any claim to land. In a way the Communist experience bears out the fault of this extremism; the license of land-grabbing proclaimed in Russia in 1917 and at the beginning of each Marxist revolution gave way in all cases to the severe constraint of state ownership or control.

Openness is then no magic word guaranteed to bring the good life. If carried too far it will produce chaos, or its adversary the closed society. The conservative mistrust of solutions requires us to doubt even those which fit most well into the scheme of values which we hold most dear. There is no perfect schema, no great phrase—open, or good, or liberal—which can sum up all the values which must be developed. In the last analysis, the merit of liberal conservative principles relies on the curbing of all values—even liberty and free trade—so as to mesh the numerous desiderata into a social machine. Just as the market is a compromise between decree and complete permissiveness, so custom is a compromise between the market and the force of the coercive authorities. And custom is in itself a blend of old rules and new adaptations; the process is endless. To the rallying cry of the Marxists or the racists or any of the groups with positive answers to all issues, this makes a weak answer.

But so it must be. When the liberalism of the nineteenth century settled down, especially on the European continent, to fixed rules it froze its vital urges into dogmas. The vulnerability of the worthy French rationalist intellectuals to corrosive attacks and the fragility of their Republic arose out of the substitution of anticlericalism for the concern with religious freedom, and the development of bureaucratic precision in the place of social mobility. This was never as bad as was claimed; the École Normale Supérieure has never become the Platonic school of France, and the assault on the old clercs has produced a myriad of intellectual and artistic flowers more rich than all the glories of the schools. But this shows that there is more to openness, or civilization, than the approved forms; the fanatic reaction of Maurras and the anti-intellectualism of Picasso may have alarmed the upholders of reason and diversity, but they contributed to these very qualities by their excitement. French politics may have lagged behind its art just because the outside influences were too sterilized or were cast outside the pale; De Gaulle may be a good influence on constitutional government in spite of himself. The British superiority is not just in the English pragmatism, but also in the ease with which the secure British can experiment wildly, even philosophically (cf., the Fabians) without disrupting the system. Disraeli showed this in his opportunist but brilliant refashioning of the Tory doctrine, importing imperialism into public life without upsetting the political mores. The British and Italian liberal parties today are faced with the need and challenge to do much the same thing, and it is a misfortune that the Italian party, much more impeccably conservative, betrays not the freedom from cant which that should imply but the immersion in old ideas which seem so often inseparable from big pocketbooks. When a party or group may propose novel ideas without disturbing the underlying customs the viability of the state is attested to, but also the value of the party.

To an unfriendly critic this seems to be a defense of change and excitement, just so long as those ferments do not really come to anything. Changing the terminology a bit, we may accept this charge as true. The acclaim given to diversity and new ideas depends on the limits which must implicitly be placed on them; not the change, but the willingness to change is the merit. Just as freedom of speech can be extended most widely when incitements to riots are rare, so the underlying dissent in society, no. 1 of the meanings of the open society, can be nurtured when there is little likelihood that it will result in violence. Liberty means freedom for those who would destroy liberty, but if the latter are powerful, liberty itself becomes a perilous system. This is why conservatives can better defend these liberal values; their sense of limitation, if fused with confidence in the worth of choice, can provide the necessary combination.

This is true of the state itself. For the processes of government to work there must be a willingness to ignore the dictates of pure theory and pure interest. To that degree the openness of any working system must be a little theoretical; Great Britain is a perfect example. At every time of crisis some people, or some classes, will always ask what worth the social stability has for them. In turn others will say that any change negates their concept of the social contract. Thus in Mississippi today the blacks in small towns where they comprise a large majority may feel that nothing short of complete control is their due after years of inferiority. The white minority seems set on retaining their historic domination at all costs, reasoning that life would otherwise be intolerable. This is a clear Laskian situation, except that inevitable bias toward the majority which Laski held overlooks the nuances, even in Mississippi. Since there will always be classes and always dissatisfied men and women, there will always be temptations for some group to ignore the established processes. It may be the upper class, à la Laski, or the lower class or a middle class or anyone else. In the short run there is always a price which can be exacted by refusing to play the game "reasonably" (that is, according to the set rules)—unless the powers that be are extremely rigid. There is a pressing need for a philosophy with enough "give" to permit these pressures some leeway, but not so much as to subvert government. The Whig invention of the social contract is not acceptable today, but in essence we must have something like it and on a world scale. The worship of the state has proved fatal to civilization and not even efficient, for the battle of who shall run the state then replaces the question of whether the state is to be accepted. Open or closed, strong or weak, the social framework must be given enough intellectual support to withstand too much selfishness, even in a world where selfishness is accepted as the first fact of life. But the open society, because of its fluidity, most needs this support. Openness can suggest the maximum in fluidity, but it will work much better if it is allied to the long view. An open society will have room for maximizers, but if it is dominated by them it will be open to its own destruction.

The social contract was a fiction, but like all good fictions it summed up the "as ifs" which seemed most helpful to society. These fictions must persuade the unthinking, like the Platonic noble lie, but in the best of societies there will be few of these and more citizens who knowingly prize the condition which the fiction glorifies as the long-term basis for the good life. When a group resorts to unconstitutional means it is saying that it can get more this way than the normal way—in our desired society no group could believe that in the long run this would be worth-while. This is where the ideology of the market diverges from Neitzschean individualism. A system which moderates the selfish or determined urges of its believers so as to improve the long-term chances of enjoying wealth or power stands the best chance. There is nothing more to free-market or traditional-conservative thought than this at the end of the road, for no matter how much its supporters appeal to freedom or responsibility, these goods must pay. Political democracy has so paid, and that, and not the moral superiority of the majority, is its finest quality. Civil liberty pays in the same way; since even it is not an absolute one can only decide its limits by these principles.

These conditions must lead to specifics. In the short run the road to order and liberty is made up of individual strips of pavement, and these strips are important. It is just because there is no final answer that we must design our own scale of values and hold to these. In Mississippi it makes a difference whose order is maintained and if we accept a rejection of the processes of majority rule and equality under the law there we cannot expect to see it unchallenged elsewhere. The reactionary lovers of order turn out to be less than consistent in these cases, just as great moralists like Theodore Roosevelt can commit the most immoral acts, such as the Panama coup, without blinking an eye.

It would be fine if we had an automatic gauge to determine degrees of immorality. The radical critics of American society sometimes talk as if hypocrisy were sufficient grounds for revolt. The political order breaks down when the governors are treated like dishonest business partners. But of course sometimes they are just that; the justifications for the counter-revolutions of recent years ring true insofar as one accepts the impossibility of the pre-existing governments. Sukarno (and to a lesser extent Goulart) had broken the implicit social contract, but the very most one could say in Greece was that the Papandreous might have been conspiring to do so. This is a dangerous game—dangerous even in the Indonesian context. The experience of revolution, as we have so often seen, will not necessarily benefit the most deserving but often the most demanding; the law-abiding are often treated like the brothers of the prodigal son. Above all the better course of action must be profitable, so that it will not be able for a cabal which rejects this consensus (such as the White Citizens groups in Mississippi) to get away with murder either literally or figuratively.

The specific strips of pavement are not isolated acts, in other words, but significant acts, acts which embody the concepts of our thought in action. The Panama coup of 1903, for example, was not so extraordinary in itself; it was very short in duration and it probably had little effect on the daily life of the Panamanians. What was very important was its moral effect, both on inter-American relations and on the condition of Roosevelt's reputation and behavior. No matter how distasteful it may be to lovers of capitalism, the TVA has had a symbolic meaning more striking than all the remarkable efficiencies of the American Electric Power Company. In turn, the spectacular success of the Japanese economy since 1946 may or may not be a net good to the Japanese people, but its awesome accomplishment is a beacon to all Asians, even the most ascetic. Democracy itself is in a way the same sort of achievement, rich in symbolic meaning and in ceremonial implication. The same, as we have noted, can be said for the idea of material progress. Therefore, when we say that every system or idea must prove itself as being worth the price we must include, among the most salient benefits, that of appealing to the sense of fitness, of social elegance and grandeur. At this point theory and practice converge, for a body of ideas can take form in these symbolic acts in a way which is more meaningful, and certainly easier to understand, than in a philosophical system. Locke was reinforced by the Declaration of Independence; vastly more people have been thrilled or impressed by the latter than ever read any of the former's books, or even those of his pupils.

This is one of the main weapons of totalitarianism; the vast ceremonies of the Nazis were carefully designed to appeal to this sense. But there is just as much potential in the open society; the very spirit of openness, the very term itself, is a rallying-cry, a stimulation of the spirit of symbolic action. Today collectivism seems to be most suitable for this, but from 1775 to 1850 it was the individualist programs which possessed the excitement and there is no reason why this cannot be recaptured. But rather than leave these to the foes of reason, it is important to ally the mysteries to the logic of politics. As with religion, so here this involves a conversion of pure idea into an exciting program.

An Agenda
for Conservatism

This may seem an invitation to gimmickery and in a way it is. However much this is condemned, day-to-day politics are always a collection of bright slogans and appealing phrases. It may be that some voters may decide issues on the basis of pure interest or even precise consideration of the public good unclouded by broader implications. Such men are very rare indeed. The articles of professors giving their reasons for voting in a given way seldom confine their attention to the exact results of victory for their side—say, an 8.4 per cent increase in public funds available for schools, or a 7.5 per cent reduction in excise taxes, or the ejection of Communists from Central Africa. The same is true of businessmen; these eminently rational men all end up with visions of the good life tied to programs designed to do more than accomplish a given result. Nominalist critiques could deflate almost any program. For example, the Victorian moderates doted on free trade, but even the most drily analytical of that drily analytical bunch did not rely on a simple statement that elimination of custom duties would reduce consumer costs by x amount, increase the area of competition by y amount, and perhaps even result in a z improvement in public revenues. The men from Boston and Manchester ended up with glowing visions of the good society and appeals to social morality which were duly scoffed at and caricatured by the protectionists who waxed lyrical about the status of the protected workingman and the national interest. It is not just that man does not live by bread alone; he also does not live by gunboats alone, or in a textbook environment. Political thought is a way of bridging the gap between the immediate and the potential.

But the circle also shows that different men will bridge that gap in different ways. There is no guide to what is a moderate-conservative course of action. The example of Theodore Roosevelt and Panama may seem offensive to some who hold all the beliefs presented here but whose conception of symbolic action involves a different wedding of theory and practice. It would be naive to think that the relativism of political goods must apply only to theory. On the contrary, nothing is more common than the prospect of men starting from the same premise only to disagree over the vitally important details of political action. This is as it should be, for it bespeaks a consensus which affords the opportunity, and requires the excitement of disagreement on the results rather than the premises of theory. The "me-too" platforms of both right and left parties have been the source of much of the most constructive conservative action in recent years, charts for the consolidation and de-radicalization of much of the ferment of our times. In the course of so doing, naturally there has been enough room for controversy, often quite virulent disagreement. And reasonable men can argue sharply about distinctions which may seem petty to those who are detached. The policies of Acheson and Dulles were in essence not much different, but the divergence of style, of emphasis, and of (to some extent) symbolic meaning afforded a very large scope for acrimonious argument, and still does. The fact that each side developed what might seem a small difference into one marked by opposing ideas has proved, from a pragmatic point of view, very helpful to each party; the more heat aroused, the more the party distinctions have been accentuated. This is not to say that nothing real was involved, but it is to suggest that what is most real in politics is often the connection between the facts or the programs and the broader significance attached to them.

For this reason it cannot be enough for any conservative to

sit back and say that the status quo is sufficient. This is often hardest for the liberal conservative, who is content to accept the accomplishments of the last wave of reform or counter-reform. But this laziness, and it is often no more than that, is to abandon the world of political manifestos and day-by-day maneuvering. In recent years there has been a growth in the proclamation of moderate conservative programs in diverse areas tending to present not merely political suggestions for the moment but programs for the next decade. The following proposals are in that category; they are obviously not designed for immediate passage, and they may be disagreeable even to those who may agree with all that has come before. But that is natural and right and each person might well fill in this space with his or her own schemes. Considering all this, the following are suggestions for an unorthodox liberal conservative running for office in the United States or, to some extent, elsewhere in the free world:

1. The matter of taxes is obviously central to any governmental policy. A great effort at simplification is clearly called for yet each such effort leaves more complexities in its wake, like a tidal wave which covers the sand cleanly, only to deposit more debris than it washed away. The progressive rates have been, from all but a puritanical point of view, largely a failure or a half-success. Hayek has suggested limiting the highest rate of tax to the probable proportion of gross income taxed, which is intriguing but both complicated and socially too dis-leveling to be feasible. Long's proposal to reduce sharply the absolute rate on condition the taxpayer take no exemptions, is better; perhaps a mandatory exclusion of all exemptions (except perhaps interest) and a top rate of 35 per cent or 40 per cent on ordinary income might be a reasonable aim. Kaldor's proposal of a graduated spending tax was designed as a measure which would reach at wealth as against income, but it might be put to more conservative uses. In times when inflation is the chief problem it may serve as a good substitute for the income tax. Of course the sales tax is nothing but a spending tax and complete reliance on the latter would clearly be comparatively regressive, but it

should not be altogether avoided on that account. By and large, however, the income tax is more equitable; one tax piled on another would compound the burden. The next question which would then arise would be the capital-gains tax. But there are four aspects to capital gains which might be treated separately— if we have simplified the rest so drastically a little complexity here would not be too alarming. First, there is the gain from inflation, which should not be taxed at all for a gain in money which merely makes one even in purchasing power is no gain at all. This would require perhaps a cumbersome reliance on cost indices, but that is true of much else today and no insuperable objection. Second, there is the gain from reinvested corporate earnings, which comes out sooner or later in higher securities prices. This might well be taxed at ordinary income rates, but then in fairness double taxation of paid-out earnings should be largely or completely eliminated, as in some countries of Western Europe. Tax credits are an awkward and illogical way (for instance, there is no way to see how far the corporation has gained by raising prices, since the benefit to the taxpayer is not geared to the cost to the corporation); a rebate to the coporation for dividends paid out, covering at least half of the tax, would be fair as part of this package. Third, gain from land profits does involve, as Henry George pointed out, a special circumstance for the gain here is due to a form of unique monopoly situation caused by population pressure or social policy. With the ordinary rates low enough it might well be logical to apply them here, but distinctions between timberland, agricultural land and commercial real estate might well be in order. Of course the inflation index must be used here and in no. 2 to ensure equity. Lastly, there is the case of simple skill in speculation, not caused by anything but good guessing or economic-market skill. Logically, for every gainer here there must, over any period of time, be a loser, so that as long as losses are treated the same as gains— and the fear of manipulation has led to some injustice in treating them differently—there is no advantage to the state in taxing this gain at all. For reasons of puritanism, perhaps a difference between long- and short-term gains may be imposed here, with ordinary taxes for short (one year at most) and no taxes for long-term gains; but strictly speaking there is no reason for any tax at all. There may be cases not enumerated; gains from excessive depreciation should be treated in category no. 2, for instance, and any other cases should be put in one of these cubbyholes.

But this is applicable only to the tax structure in a state of repose; for static as against dynamic analysis. The concepts of Keynesian economics and the mechanisms of the neo-Keynesians can be profitably linked to this program to give it a flexibility in time. It is ironic how widely the proposals of the Committee for Economic Development were applauded fifteen or so years ago, and how little they have been followed by tax authorities of either right or left. The CED proposal was geared to a balanced budget—providing neither surplus nor deficit—at a point of employment perhaps a bit under full employment. This point is open to debate; on the one hand a secular trend of rising population and productivity may permit the even point to be put at full employment, increasing the level of probable deficits. On the other hand, the likelihood of recurring wars and major crises, causing sharp rises in the debt, may urge the setting at a low point. This could be re-examined every decade, also keeping in mind the overall dynamism of the economy—the period 1947–57 might have justified a more conservative deficit point than the decade 1957–67 appears to call for. But within the period there should be, war or similar crisis aside, a consistent following of the system; if the even point is set at 96 per cent of the working force it should never be changed because of political pressure. Even at the decennial time of examination it would be valuable to have a tradition of continuity, of non-political expertise such as that which prevails in the area of central banking, to discourage demagogic appeals for deficits.

On the other hand, if we have established a fairly firm, "neutral" system, the proposed powers of quarterly change in taxes which have been mentioned would make a lot of sense, even if it meant delegating customarily legislative powers to the executive. Tax changes are not only more speedily effective, but they also concentrate the anti-recession program in the area of enhancing the private sector, thus nullifying one of the chief dangers of leftist Keynesian economic thinking. As the years go by the result of these systems may be a trend in the supply of money which may be different from that at the start. This implies a judgment on the rate of inflation—or deflation (which should definitely not be a dirty word). The decennial review will have to consider this; but at other times this will be pre-eminently a matter for monetary policy. The Friedman proposals for a fixed increase in the annual money supply has considerable merit, but its rigidity, even connected to our flexible fiscal policy, is too restrictive. Here again a fixed guide—say 4 per cent a year— might be declared as a public policy, leaving it to the judgment of the central bankers to maneuver in the interests of monetary order and trade normality within this guideline. Of course all absolute limits on the debt must go, but the question of gold reserves in the banking system must be relegated to policy in international money management, which we will reach later.

This, in the context of the United States' tax laws, must be somewhat bold to be effective. It must mean an end to depletion allowances, to all depreciation allowances greater than amortized replacement cost, to special benefits to cooperatives and enterprises trying to look like cooperatives (such as savings and loan companies). The question of tax-exempt securities will be hard, but with the top tax-rate cut so the pressure on this front will abate, and their elimination (advocated, after all, by Andrew Mellon) must be considered. In the context of much of the less tax-trained nations, such as even Italy, this must be combined with a serious and perhaps at times rough policy of tax honesty. If this means compulsory stock and bond registers and the prohibition of bearer bonds and stocks, that must come. The more underdeveloped the country, the more pressure there will inevitably be for special features of the laws to be allowed to provide for more rapid economic growth. It is probably a good idea to say "no" to this under all circumstances; if aid is to be given, let it be in the form of an open subsidy, where everyone may see that it is a subsidy and where its artificiality may serve as a steady reminder that it should be temporary. It would be a good thing if any such subsidy were prominently posted in the capital, so that everyone could be aware of it.

This proposal has not entered into the matter of estate taxes, because they involve separate premises. One must accept these as primarily, perhaps almost entirely, worth having for purposes of enforcing equality, so that a different standard is in order. But that is not to say that a completely radical system must be adhered to here; there are degrees of equalizing, too. One way of reducing the crushing burden of these taxes, permitting a simpler, less loophole-studded system and yet still providing for some equalizing, might be to vary the tax in severity with the number of generations in which the money has remained in the family. A leading authority, Casner, has commented of American law that "if the tax-exempt trust arrangement becomes widespread the estate-tax law will become a kind of laughingstock." Now trust maneuvers put a premium on lengthy holding, but the opposite, as a matter of discouraging modern entailing while preserving individual initiative and private saving, would make more sense. Perhaps penalizing rather than rewarding trusts would be one way of so doing, perhaps taxing securities unsold after generations more rather than less heavily than newly-bought ones would be another. The complex or quaint ways of avoiding these taxes which are so common in Great Britain have come from too-high rates; both the rates and the avenues of escape should be cut down together, as with income taxes; but the rates need not be cut as much as the income-tax rates are, since the criterion of individual choice is clearly much less prevalent here. With the cut in maximum income-tax rates it would even be worth considering the proposal of the Carter Commission, in Canada, to tax bequests as ordinary income.

This cannot hope to cover everything; expense accounts and royalty income clearly also need going into, and there will always be new devices after the old. There will always be room for changes, and there will always be income taxes. The far left and the far right concur in the desire to eliminate the income tax, but neither Kosygin nor Hunt have reasonable alternatives except high sales taxes, and even the Russians cannot succeed in relying only on these. The income tax, as it has developed since 1914 in almost all the Western lands, provides the Hamiltonian service of reminding everyone of their stake in the state and their economic burden, and this is a valuable reminder. It gives a sense of responsibility, at best a feeling of participation in great affairs. If we do suffer from financial euphoria it would be better to eliminate almost all of the excise taxes, which are usually regressive anyway, rather than relieve many working people from the income tax altogether. A narrow progression, without tempting exemptions for the rich or disguised levies on the poor, is the goal and the best time to start in this direction (or in this country to continue on the way) is now.

2. Taxes are half of the equation; spending is the other half, and a tougher segment politically. But the automatic mathematically-oriented individualism of our tax policy can be applied here as well. We know that we will have a large bundle of welfare measures with us for as long as we can see; the next question is how to cull and control them. The best way will be to limit their purported benefits to a given standard of living. If agricultural subsidies are designed to raise the farming sector to a given level, we must support subsidies—not price-fixing schemes—with given objectives. Food-stamp (and housing-stamp) programs are preferable to direct state gifts or housing, as they shift the choice more to the consumer. If families reach these levels they are to be phased out of aid (many now supported should never be let on); others who obviously operate marginal farms must be gradually subsidized off the land, up to the point where a certain minima of farmers may seem, for social reasons, worth maintaining—and with a cold eye this will be a smaller number than the sentimentalists still talk of. The uprooted farmers may join the urban poor and should be treated accordingly. It is wise to have in mind specific wealth levels as targets, so that as income rises the welfare rolls do not also rise. Specifically, this means that the residents of public housing should pay somewhat more rent as their incomes rise and that the Galbraith principle of varying unemployment-compensation

might be instituted, but with much more of a bias toward cutting down the whole system in good times than he suggested. The pension system, too, should be designed with an eye to reducing the percentage of take over time, assuming rises in gross national product; in France and Italy this should be the first order of business but it has relevance almost everywhere. If a new social-insurance program is introduced on the theory that it will elimi-nate some old form of dole or direct subsidy, there must be a concomitant program introduced to phase out that old aid, and if this fails there should be an immediate drive made to root out the causes of that failure and to correct them. Insofar as this does not involve too great an invasion of individual privacy, all subsidy- or aid-recipients should be identified; a dividing line as to the amount received might be in order, but it should be set at no higher level than the average weekly industrial wage, so that anyone receiving as much as the normal wage from the state should be so labeled.

In the broader view, the counter-cyclical nature of public works has advantages, but this should be synchronized with the long-run needs of the government. If a road-building program is decided on over a ten-year period, the "normal" level should be set a little low, so as to give some room for anti-recession expansion without bloating the budget or the range of state activities. Similarly, every time full employment is reached for more than twelve months after a period of poor business, there should be a re-examination of all programs launched in bad times, with the intention of weeding out as many as possible of these avowedly temporary programs. If a program devised for other purposes, such as military preparedness, comes to serve economic ends, this must be carefully separated so that the in-sidious combination of varying purposes does not result in a constant rationale for a program which might be curtailed or ended if it had to be justified by one consistent purpose. To this end, it might be advisable to provide for a definite time limit for each new money-spending program, with a schedule of de-creasing expenditures in many cases. If there is no intention of reducing the spending over time, that should be pointed out and planned for from the outset; if in those cases long-term appropriations are called for, it is more and not less conservative to provide for them at once rather than have them become an inevitable feature of appropriations each year.

There will be some programs in this category, so it is absurd to talk of a governmental spending limitation without considering them. This is true of building needed highways, dams, schools, et cetera—the felt necessities of a mechanized and educated society. Some of the costs can be recaptured through charges designed to tax the beneficiaries as the market would. This should be encouraged to the extent that these costs are distinguishable and insofar as the users are able to pay their way.

But in many cases, such as schools, there will be no repayment at all. In these cases it is preferable to make the most out of the situation, and to capture the imaginations of our time and satisfy the ever-abiding search for grandeur with a mixture of political shrewdness and magnificence—Malraux has his lessons far removed from matters concerning Angkor or Vermeer. The exploration of space scarcely seems to conform to the rules of social utility, and its results may be worse than disappointing. But to the extent that it embodies a thrust of man's urge for exploration, it will be with us more and more. When the time comes, as it appears that it will (although very likely much later than the optimists believe), to send colonies to the moon or pathfinders to Mars, let us try to concentrate on a few missions and manage these with a lavish, even extravagant magnificence. If, for example, the point of having a man on the moon is prestige, it will be better to provide him with a glittering city replete with all the elegance the coming age will cherish; the petty calculations of gain or loss would be ridiculous, like a man who spends $1000 to go to Salzburg but then argues over the price of the seats at the opera. On this earth there is always a place for monuments and for symbolic magnificence. It is better to choose to erect fewer monuments, but to have these overpowering, than to be always agreeing—usually out of political weakness or uncertainty—on some little plans and to be always regretting these decisions. Versailles cost much more than its many German imitations but it has proved to have been a good investment, historically speaking, while the latter are as a rule subjects for derision or oblivion. These monuments, like the highways which are in part symbolic glories as well, will be built, but the men who do it may be Hitlers or Jiménezes. How much better that a government committed to individualist principles and the free market should show that, even in those areas which pertain to thoroughly statist action, the open society can outdo its adversaries! Pericles boasted of Athens not only for its freedom but for the splendor that that freedom produced; the Parthenon has rivaled the pyramids to this day, and there is no need to defer even here to the accomplishments of the hydraulic despotisms.

But part of that freedom is the opportunity, and the challenge, for the private sector to rival the public. The tradition of the United States has always been congenial to this competition. The seventeenth-century explorations by the English afforded chances for diverse groups—the Crown, great families such as the Penns, and (most successfully) companies of religious dissenters. Much of what the latter, Puritans as they were, accomplished was partly symbolic; the anxiety for higher education "in this wilderness" was directed at the prospect of becoming culturally déclassé. So too our modern corporations look to their image and to their place in a system marked by competition for power through cultural status. We should combine a willingness to spend on the part of the state with an exuberant *brio* on the side of a secure and wealthy private sector. Where the banks and soap companies compete with the cities to produce not only artifacts of beauty but new styles of achitectural grandeur there will be, surely *longueurs*, but also the chance for civic greatness.

The concentration of governmental effort, it should be kept in mind, will require distinct favoritism, for there can be only so many TVA's, and the Soviet Union has failed to recreate in its diverse power projects the intense glory of Dnepropetrovsk. But if there are many private foci, each concentrating their separate efforts, the local prides and the crystallization of diverse minds may amplify the chance for cultural successes. And failures, too, but in this area the gravest danger lies in mediocrity and wasted effort; if one bravura gesture succeeds while ten fail that one will be remembered—witness even the Eiffel Tower—but if all are demi-failures the whole period will be scorned. The state can help achieve the former by spending on one hand, and on encouraging others to spend on the other. For it is good for conservatives to remember that frugality is no merit per se—who would praise an electric company for building few plants?—but the wisest use of money consistent with freedom of choice and individual opportunity. As in *Through the Looking-Glass,* we may reach a more limited government by sometimes broadening the rhythm of state activity.

3. This has non-economic implications as well. A code of law as to matters concerning privacy is overdue. Some instruments of electronic listening or seeing should be banned outright, others should open the user to civil action by the overheard, and more of them should be subject to limitation as to the judicial admissibility of their evidence. This need not be a one-way street, for privacy is not a sacred cow; in the question of criminal trials the rights of the accused to enjoy protection from the press should be set against the rights of the press, and while the present British balance goes too far in that its mandatory curbs on reporting while a case is *sub judice* are over-harsh, it has valuable lessons to teach. But more guidance should be given the judiciary by the legislature before scandals or revulsion push the balance in defense of privacy in a fit of fervor or before the demands of publicity become all-dominant. If the telephone equipped with television becomes common, or the walkie-talkie sweeps the field, the rights of the dissenter must be protected. If we do have cities enclosed in great glass or plastic domes we had better secure individual thermostats from the start. If all sidewalks become movable the rights of each block or each family to have some control over the speed of its sector should be established from the first. There are many other suggestions in the technology of the coming time which will require firm individualist decisions from the outset, and it is a disservice to the rule of law to leave all of this to the ebb and flow of judicial

opinions. On the other hand, once the rules are prudently laid out, we should leave the details of enforcement to the courts, and we should encourage the establishment of guidelines to encourage individual efforts—e.g., separate geodesic domes—rather than submit to a monopoly of state action which must stifle the search for different answers. In other words, we must permit a variety of new devices but these inventions must never become the masters of society, leaving each man free to interfere with the conditions of all men so that the effective choice of everyone will be curbed.

This is the problem of the automobile age now, as it may become the problem of the air age if individual space travel is perfected. We cannot leave every man to his own devices, but by channeling the control into market forces (such as meters) or through the civil law (as with our jaywalking example) the potency of state power is diffused. But if it comes to the point where the automobile becomes a tyrant, where all traffic must be taken off commercially vital streets or where insurance bonds must be required of everyone, so be it. A standing commission to examine social costs, designed after the *ad hoc* Royal Commissions, might well be established with the regular task of determining what taxes and governmental limitations should be proposed. But let us watch that the members be individualists; no Robert Moseses should be encouraged! There is room for the aggressive planner but he can find his place on the other side, running the operations; the need to supersede the market at times should always be controlled by those with an abiding faith in the overall rightness of the market.

To that end the area of governmental restrictions should always be subjected to pruning. The market here referred to is that broader market of ideas, as well as trade, and there is plenty to do. In the context of our country the goal, not altogether suitable at once but always to be kept in mind, should be the repeal of the Smith Act, the McCarran Act of 1950, the Logan Act, and most of the local edicts forbidding self-regarding acts in the area of gambling, vagrancy, sexual misbehavior, and censorship. This is a good place to divide the libertarian sheep from the goats. But these are the obvious goals of a libertarian program; the potential of liberty is greater. We should work toward a complete abolition of passports, so that in time of peace anyone not under indictment could go without impediment to any place on the globe. Even during wartime the examples of eighteenth- and nineteenth-century freedom, which grew out of the limitations on warfare then extant, might well be emulated. And social mobility should be left open—which is not the same thing as encouraged—in the same way; all forms of licensing which smack of monopoly restrictions on free entry should be either eliminated or at least curtailed. This means that no closed shop should be permitted unless there was proof that entrance into the field was truly open. This should be extended to apply to doctors and lawyers as well as carpenters and river pilots. Friedman's suggestion of prohibiting all licensing is too radical, but the weight of governmental force should always lean toward encouraging private groups to set up their own standards and award their own (non-exclusive) certificates. In fact, the whole area of private opinion should be encouraged, and while Justice Black's dictum that libel laws are violations of free speech per se is too extreme, the law should presume the superiority of free comment over the value of immunity from defamation.

Since liberty is not an isolated value, we must see to it that it enjoys hospitable soil. The media of communication should be owned privately—the state should never own more than a minority interest in any medium and even that, considering the realities of government competition, is not wise—and the number of competing entities should be maximized. The technical potentials of UHF broadcasting may make possible a degree of competition in television which will solve many of our present problems —a reminder that technology need not always be an enemy of freedom. This should result in time in the demise of the Federal Communications Commission. One goal of the next fifty years might be the elimination of all the regulatory agencies, the children of the New Nationalism, and their replacement with perhaps a few courts like the Tax Court, where necessary, and by a perhaps larger antitrust division. This may not work, but the separation of judicial and administrative agencies à la the NLRB should be pressed, and the administrative remainders should be closely questioned as to their worth. In many cases the greatest critics of their abolition will be vested interests within the industries affected; these groups should be given their say but should be granted the least consideration. The same must apply in local circumstances as well—zoning is an obvious case for change.

Finally, all standards which classify people on the basis of status or predetermined identity should be scrutinized very closely, with the purpose of eradicating almost all of these conditions. Clearly the remnants of old racial laws or regulations should be repealed, and laws which penalize a man for membership in a group or party, even the Communist party, without regard to personal activity, must be questioned. In matters of race, progress has been gratifying to date; the real triumph will come when, throughout society, considerations of race will vanish, so that job quotas will be unthinkable and school districts will be determined without even talking of racial distribution. This must be accompanied by a like forgetfulness on the part of buyers and sellers (of houses especially, of course); not to be expected at once, but a condition which should be nurtured so that its coming (substantially, as perfect color-blindness is too sanguine a hope) might relieve the need for the multiplicity of laws now being passed or newly enforced. In all these matters the perfection of a free market where no prejudice or irrationality is large enough to mar a condition of the broadest individual choice, and where everyone is on his own, should be the goal; the power of the state should exist to complement that market and to alter its conditions as smoothly and as little as possible. All actions which are proposed for the benefit of the people despite themselves—conscription, the control of advertising, the selection of "proper" forms of education—should be eliminated, and if it is decided that one of these measures, such as conscription, is necessary for other reasons, we must always watch to be sure that the iron philanthropy of the state does not thrust its way in.

All this has been outlined with respect to the politics of the United States, but its application elsewhere is apparent. The comparatively petty controls of the Pilkingtons or the Malrauxs fall within the forbidden zone, for even Britain and France (especially Gaullist France) are prone to the dangerous combination of aristocratic virtue and welfare-state planning. The maximization of choice always sounds better as a goal than as a reason for specific acts, but these acts should be pursued even when they mean raising rents or withdrawing controls over land which (as in England) have produced both bureaucratic despotism and land shortages. In nations where powerful religious organizations coexist with constitutional governments, such as Italy and Israel, this juxtaposition will often be the chief problem. The Millian rule that the church should be free to say what it wants, prescribe its own rules, and attempt the most intensive persuasion, should be set off by the freedom of the other people from any coercive control by the church over their lives. The dietary and marriage laws in Israel are in the latter category; the right of rabbis and bishops in both lands to excoriate their adversaries is probably in the former, but the defamation laws, although construed very closely, should be the same for prelates as for journalists. A free church in a free state is a concept with two sides, as advocates of state aid to religious schools should remember. In the newer nations the problems of private autonomy may often become intermixed with the older questions of tribal or quasi-feudal arrangements, but in the diverse contexts of the various countries the rules suggested above are applicable here. Unpopular as this must be at the moment in most of these lands, the infusion of the capitalist spirit and the market way of life, with its impersonality and emphasis on free choice and automatic processes of change and economic selection, would be a great help in developing the right balance. The proliferation of import and export quotas, license and franchise rights, *et hoc genus omne,* can only serve to entrench a bastard plutocracy, discourage free enterprise, and result in a move toward a socialism which will almost surely suffer from the same sorts of corruption (as in Ghana) without the safety valve of a market economy. Even if capitalism as we think of it proves too strong a dose, the other forces of lower-circle society, autonomous institutions and independent (and freely chosen, as against tribally determined) groups should be encouraged as far as possible. Coser has put this well when he remarked that "one of the ways to achieve the development they so passionately desire without totally destroying the roots of national culture, is to build a pluralistic society, as against the model of centralization that is presented by the East; if we could show them that what is essential is to have a dispersed elite with roots in trade unions, in independent universities, in independent newspapers, etc." Perhaps some of the forms of independence may be novel, or antiquarian in origin (the interplay of tribal groups, political parties, and perhaps business or cultural organizations may produce some odd results, even more hybrid than the Histadrut). It may be that Ghana, after having been an unhappy pioneer in dirigisme, may become a showpiece of the way of diversity. There may be a resulting unevenness in development, but it will be better for the state to compensate or subsidize, within limits, the poorer areas than to hold everyone down to the level of the least enterprising.

In discussing these options we have ignored so far the impingement of alien big business or the influence of the great powers. In a free world these cannot be kept out, but neither should they be encouraged too much. The experience of Diaz's Mexico is an illustration of the perils of the latter leading to the former; in some cases, as in Venezuela, the potency of foreign capital is unavoidably an overwhelming factor which can so easily inhibit the balance of local capitalism. The moves of Creole Petroleum and the IBEC to encourage, through minority participation, local business should be followed everywhere, just as the political interests of the developed nations should be expressed indirectly. In the main "neo-colonialism" is a trick word, without any content other than dislike of rich outsiders, but we must remember that its message, styled differently, was the common coin of American politics until at least 1914, and was the solace of the Jacksonians and Populists. It worked out without much more than noise here, as it seems to be working out in Mexico and Brazil, because it provided the way for the development of powerful local interests and markets which could take over much of the foreigners' position. In the long run, given real neutrality on the part of the local and the foreign states, this will happen in almost all cases, for in economic terms the costs of doing business abroad, because of ignorance or social differences, will always be greater than home costs. The task must be to keep the scales even and to encourage the growth of the local forces which can develop into powerful groups. Puerto Rico is on the way, Australia up to the U.S.A. circa 1870, and Malaysia may, with good fortune, begin its journey. If, as a part of this process, nationalization with fair compensation takes place, this need not be a setback. Land reform, if it succeeds (Denmark is the prize example) in reducing social tension and in establishing an independent farming-class, is a worth-while undertaking even at the cost (if the notion can afford it) of some loss of efficiency. As long as this is an ongoing process in which new opportunities for capitalism, and for local culture, can coexist with the shedding of the heritage, economic and social, of the older world, a limited degree of nationalization can be a benefit to an underdeveloped land.

The world is truly one today, and the criteria of Ohio are not much different from those of Togo. It is by no means premature to begin speculating on what sort of world political and economic order we want; if conservatives see visions it will prove that it is not only visionaries who can dream the dreams of our century. In 1787 it was the conservatives who sought a larger national order, and as a matter of fact many of the circumstances are the same today. For example, an international code of property rights would fulfill a role much like that of the much-desired (and almost never used: such are the ironies of history) contract clause in the American Constitution. So, too, even the most crusty isolationists become concerned with the plight of Americans arrested abroad and subjected to foreign and sometimes unfair trials; since the gunboat age seems to have perished, surely an international code of law should be welcome as a guaranty against such incidents. If this means a world government, what sort of state should we support which would not become the despotic tyrant which so troubles many of us today?

A world state seems an inconsistent goal for an individualist credo, but this is not necessarily so. Size is not in itself a peril to freedom; surely it was fortunate that Louisiana was a part of the United States in 1935, as it is desirable that Mississippi be made more so today. The quarrels of the sovereign states breed the rankest forms of collectivism. Of course the threat of a collectivist world-state is not illusory, but neither are the pressures of international unification. Too many conservatives picture the disadvantages—the prospect of a single coercive power, the opportunities for global planners—and overlook the advantages—the potentials of a world system of law and commercial practice, the reductions of nationalist forces. This may be the arena for the most complex and rewarding work of balancing yet.

The best place to start in considering these problems is the tasks which we do not want a world state to assume, and the forms which we do not want a world government to have. If the cult of "one man, one vote" is pressed, the chances for a satisfactory system of voting will be slim indeed—and not only from the point of view of the United States. On the other hand, the present voting arrangement of the United Nations is obviously unsatisfactory. It is the latter which attracts the critical comment from conservatives today, but the former is much the more important one in the long view. The issue of separation of powers is almost equally important, for the separate development of the World Court and the other U.N. bodies will make far more difference in a fledgling world government than it does today. Even if we started entirely from scratch, the precedents and traditions of the World Court would surely fashion any successor institution. These precedents will follow a common-law pattern which is already set in the framework of the rule of law. This is especially important when we consider the groups and institutions who would be looking to other precedents, which would tend almost inevitably toward a world welfare-state.

Now that in itself is not a signal for wailing and gnashing of teeth. The present world imbalance of economic conditions is a grave anomaly, as we have noted, from any free-market point of view, and will surely be changed in some way or another. But the way of change will make all the difference. The richer nations cannot succeed in deciding for all times what changes they will permit, and it will be increasingly difficult for them to refuse to agree to closer ties because of their fears. The solution most often accepted is a world government to one with powers so limited that its only role will be to keep the peace. The prospect of a world state with a monopoly or commanding position in arms, responsible to an electorate composed of the population of the world as we find it, remaining impassive on economic and social questions is very hard to believe, and it will be harder and harder as time passes. But there are many sorts of welfare states, and at home the fears of the Liberty League have proved almost completely wrong. The principal purpose of a world welfare-state, from the point of view of the affluent societies, would be to dampen down the discontent of the remainder while the conditions were being improved. If the world state were bound by certain limitations—not all-encompassing so that the powers would be flagrantly tiny at the outset, yet valuable restraints in a pinch—the accompanying duties could be accepted all the more readily. This applies as well to the political arrangements. The following is one suggestion as to the form and powers of a world government which might fit this thesis:

1. There should be a world constitution setting forth rights and duties in a manner similar to our own, with judicial review by the World Court, whose judges should enjoy life tenure. This constitution should have entrenched clauses (not subject to amendment for many years), not that these mean so much over the years, as South Africa has demonstrated, but they are worthy guides. Weighted voting in at least one house, slanted toward one or more of the criteria of wealth, literacy, industrial production, or tax contributions (the last was an idea of the July Monarchy, but none the worse for that) should be required. A mandatory limit on income- and estate-tax levels for, say, fifty years should relieve the fears of sudden confiscatory taxation. Over the very long span, such a limitation would not be defensible

in the military sense, but policies once begun might develop into lasting precedents. The very procedures of taxing power, lodged in the legislative branch, should be entrenched, so that a world tyrant would push a trip-cord on embarking on special tax legislation. Finally, the separate existence of each nation should be guaranteed at least for fifty years; it is not always remembered that that is the one entrenched clause, in the context of senatorial representation, in the United States Constitution.

2. The world bill of rights should be divided into two sections, the greater applying only to the world government and the lesser and more basic part applying to all sovereign (in 1965 terms) nations. In this respect the theories of judicial conservatives in this country such as the late Justice Jackson on our Fourteenth Amendment would be written into the supreme law from the outset. The Fourteenth Amendment's very phrasing on life, liberty, and property should well be adopted; in any case, property must be included among the rights preserved against the world state. In addition to the customary right to fair compensation, the judge of which would be a court whose members enjoyed protected tenure, an additional clause should prevent the world state from establishing a monopoly of any commercial enterprise. Even the mails should be excluded so that if individuals, or more likely lesser sovereignties, wish to operate postal services they should have a right to do so. The place of Monaco or the Thurn and Taxis service (metaphorically speaking) must always be secure, for if the world state succeeds it is just these little old systems, even archaisms, which will be most precious. The greater enterprises will of course be included in this protection. This will not preclude international TVA's, but the scope of such programs will be restrained by this ban on official monopolies. This proviso should please the Soviets (witness their objection to the Baruch plan in 1946) as much as it would any capitalist.

The question of which branches of rights, which liberties should be secure from the actions of the world state should present an opportunity to establish a broad zone of individual rights from the outset. The First Amendment freedoms should be specifically broadened to secure an immunity from wiretapping or arrest (except *in flagrante delicto*) during the night. This would be a fine place to set forth explicitly some Millian formula protecting acts which have no direct effect on their parties— e.g., gambling—from interference. Such a clause will present difficulties of explication, but that should not discourage us in setting forth the ground rules for a developing world community. Of course there must be a ban on genocide, and it should be included as a part of a broader interdiction on any world-state activity which treats any person or persons specially because of their race or origin. All of these terms are applicable to another planet or satellite that the authority of the world state encompasses, so that a global colony on Mars would be entitled to no less of this law than a citizen of Philadelphia.

The permitted world-state monopoly on non-commercial matters will allow the necessary, almost literally vital control over nuclear arms. Such a power will always be a potential source of terror and a source of great tension, so that it must be subject to especially great controls. A mandatory limitation on the percentage of men and officers in the world army whose home is in any one area should be included. No more than a given percentage, say 30 per cent, of all nuclear weapons or chemical-biological ones should be allowed in any one place, and the legislative branch should be required to appoint a standing committee, with a permanent staff whose upkeep should be raised from the revenues of the world state and be a first charge on that revenue, to enforce this and other limitations. But no constitutional terms can ensure safety in this all-important zone; the best one can do is to make things as hard as possible for a tyrant or a madman. Perhaps a ban on any draft of scientists would also be in order, and a clause requiring the military budget to be posted each half-year like a bank statement, in some detail, so as to permit knowing people to watch for hidden expenditures on unusual weapons.

These suggestions have been directed to the power of the world state. The question of what restraints should be placed on the lesser states, the present sovereigns, will be a very hard one. In the United States there were very few until after 1865; in Switzerland there were almost none before 1874. The world state, to succeed as a free government, must resemble the early structure of these two examples. But even more to the point, its all-encompassing nature (so far, in our universe) will make the rights of the diverse local governments all the more important. A certain amount of compromise between the politicians of the nation-states and those who want restraints on various forms of present state action could be doubly valuable for the moderate conservative. Thus if genocide, physical torture, and deprivation of life or imprisonment for more than one year without a fair trial were paired with seizure of property without fair compensation as acts beyond the ken of all governments, we might achieve a minimum code of world freedom that would appeal to the broadest stratum of lower-circle opinion and be enforceable throughout the world courts. At the same time the principle of States' rights on other matters would be secured. Perhaps more would be added later, perhaps not—the trend toward centralization has not, as has been noted, been inexorable —but the framework for world decency would be established in a setting designed to permit differentiation among regions alongside of individual liberty.

3. This world state, then, need not be a source of constant anxiety for the conservative. This is even more clear when we consider what this government will do. First of all, it will have jurisdiction over the open spaces of the earth, now so much vaster than ever before. The rules of space will be set out so that the conflicts of the sea may be avoided, while the latter will be brought into line as well. In years to come this may seem such an elementary boon to the interests of world commerce and culture that it will seem incredible that anyone styling himself a conservative could have opposed it. No lesser sovereignty should be allowed to own a satellite or any space station, so that all the disputes over controls or privileges will be taken out of the inter-state area. When this condition is fused with the ban on world-state monopolies the maximum of private use, in security and under a uniform law, of the means

of transportation and communication will be assured. If it so develops, this may make possible a solar-system policy in which none of the rancors of nationalism will accompany the feats of exploration. And in keeping with this, the international waterways will come under world supervision.

Secondly, we must work toward one world currency. The current debates over a managed world currency portend great changes just as soon as a world financial crisis comes. The tentative expansion of the international monetary base at Rio de Janeiro will surely be followed by more grave alterations if the shoe really pinches; what will happen when the drawing rights are overdrawn? In that case we may see the more radical parts of the Keynesian or Triffinian monetary schemes adopted; how much better it would be to develop a new system at a time when a less frantic, expansionist attitude can be maintained. The world central bank should be a much more potent institution than the present World Bank, just as the World Court will gain in power. This, however, is not the same as conceiving of this bank as an unlimited source of money. Some rule like our old 25 per cent gold-backing requirement might be a prudent regulation. This, however, has the disadvantage of being tied to gold—finding a substitute or substitutes will be very difficult, but it is the seminal question of the coming era of world finance, and it must be solved. On the other hand the reserve figure should be treated as a sort of entrenched guarantee not subject to waiver or simple alteration. But of one thing we should not fool ourselves— the now-foreseeable supply of gold will not support the probable economic life of the world in the coming years without widespread devaluation or deflation, and the latter seems politically impossible. The longer we wait for something to happen the more dangerous contingencies may be possible. If the choice finally comes down to gold or the Brazilian printing presses the adherents of stability may not be able to recapitulate the victory of 1896.

Certainly a unified economic system would foster conservative economic values, just as the unity of our nation discourages schemes to alter the balance-of-payments problems in Maine or

Mississippi. Under one currency there would be no opportunity for one of the present states to ignore the lessons of economics by financial juggling. This would of course require a decision as to the basis of the world currency, but we could allow a twenty-year transition period to settle this. It is possible that that choice might be dangerously wild so that the currency would be subject to constant inflation. On the other hand, an initial determination at a time when the interests of the richer nations is listened to as at present (deferred to, a Prebischian might say) will be more sensible than one might picture later. Even some compromises would be worth the price of a definite world money-system, whose advantages for international trade would be immense. As is so often the case, the proposal which seems at first the most radical may well be the least. One restrained central bank might be much superior to the present club of frightened uncentralized bankers.

But, in the third place, this will put a strain on the weaker areas, which may then be led to very autarchic solutions. From the beginning the world state must have control over these political-economic areas, delicate as many of them are. Tariffs and import quotas must be phased out. This will most injure the undeveloped nations, so as a *quid pro quo* there must be a concomitant end to restrictions on immigration. Despite the complexities which this will involve, some formula linking progress in eliminating immigration laws with progress in abolishing tariffs should be designed. The final goal, which cannot be included in the constitution but which should be no less a target of statesmen, should be absolutely free movement of men and capital throughout the world, the achievement of the Cobdenian dream as part of a system of world order.

Fourth, as a price for this, some aspects of a world welfare-state, in a precise sense, will be in order. SUNFED is a logical and intended precursor of such a program, but for the sake of the image of the world state the thrust of global economic expenditures should be on projects of maximum visibility. Since the oceans will be world domains, this may prove a perfect place to begin large welfare programs, such as desalinization or hydroelectric projects. Logrolling will always be with us, but as a guiding rule we should start with a policy that world expenditures which are not expected to pay for themselves in money should be concentrated where the need is greatest. In the long run, mobility of labor and capital will reduce the absurd concern for geographical areas now existing; if Java is too poor there must be more capital (and this the Javans must make possible by permitting and attracting its creation and development) and/or fewer people (and this must mean more Javans in Australia and the United States). As these imbalances grow less the canons on welfare spending proposed for the present states should be imported into the world state.

Part of the business of welfare is of course the old-age-, unemployment-, and health-insurance systems which, strange as it may now seem, will be demanded on a world level, and even a global minimum wage. The world cannot afford anything on these lines which will not seem paltry, extraordinarily miserly today and perhaps for a very long time. But we should beware of the Cuban situation, where an over-protected urban working-class coincided with a neglected peasantry. A goal for 2020 or 2030, say, for an international old-age pension and a minimum wage is not so dangerous—perhaps it is the embodiment of caution—with the built-in safeguards of requirements that the pensions and wages be tied to proportions of the wage levels in Asia and Africa, and a condition that the establishment of these welfare systems develop *pari passu* with our goal of mobility of capital and labor. Social insurance is the goal, so as to develop the pattern of responsibility connected with a partial payment by the beneficiary toward his pension, but on a world scale the problems of poverty may preclude this. Perhaps only those earning above a minimum—an extremely low one, to be sure, by American standards—should be required to contribute. The nurturing of these plans might be the job of what are now the specialized agencies of the United Nations, but the authority of the regular organs of the world state must be assured. Taxes levied to pay for these programs must be part of the overall tax structure, limited by the constitution (Clark and Sohn's idea of a levy tied to a world GNP is a good one); or perhaps they should be a separate, but also strictly limited levy. If one part of the world suffers from unusual unemployment these taxes might be reduced for them specially or the minimum wage might be reduced, but only on request of the appropriate local authority or authorities, and perhaps this right should only be available to underdeveloped areas.

4. Fourth and last, certain powers of regulation now possessed in national areas by the states might well be extended to the world state. Our old friends, antitrust and security-regulation laws, are in this category. Since part of the advantage of world government from the conservative point of view will be the internationalizing of business and finance, the appropriate and market-enhancing powers of government should be internationalized as well. This is especially important because one of the gravest impediments to the success of capitalism today is the suspicion of many, including (perhaps especially) the leading groups, of the people of the poorer lands that free enterprise means economic hegemony by the elite of the States; such fears exist even in Paris. No degree of reasonable control can assuage what are in large part irrational concerns, nor can anti-monopoly laws ensure local ownership. But at least some of the problems of absentee ownership—and in a world of global enterprise there will be more absentee ownership than ever before—can be checked or prevented; above all, the idea of remoteness, of irresponsibility may be mitigated while the advantages of a fluid, world-wide financial system are gained. It will not be enough if the annual meetings of General Motors are held in Zurich as well as Detroit unless the Swiss shareholders are given all or more of the safeguards and (above all) opportunities now possessed by those in Michigan. A world-wide securities market will in itself provide the main opportunity, but a body of world-securities law, perhaps compulsory cumulative voting (or similar devices) and special forms of class actions, might be of almost equal importance. In these areas a little more power for a world state might mean in the long run a much greater chance for a diminution in the prospects of a truly centralized, all-powerful commonwealth.

In considering safeguards, it would be unfortunate if the experiment of ombudsman were not tried out in our new republic. The natural fear in the early days of a world state would be that power would be lodged in a government composed of aliens, residing perhaps many thousands of miles away and subject to the most remote controls. A staff, and with a limited world government this need be but a small staff, of men who would check injustices of even a weak government would from the outset establish a pattern of respect for individual rights and interests. Perhaps this office might also be entrusted with the job of considering boundary disputes between the lesser states. That will certainly be one of the ever-pressing troubles of the world community, for if war is ruled out as a means of changing boundaries a political source of friction will persist for which politics will have no answer. The courts will not be too easily suited to adjudicate these matters, for the rights and wrongs will so often involve matters of social emotion whose force and political nature might endanger the stability of the world judicial system. The ombudsman, as special arbitrator, might be a good choice to look into the situation, acting as a sort of tribune, but of course his recommendations could only be that; the legislature would have to be the final court.

We have avoided the question of the makeup of the legislature, which may well be the knottiest question of applied political theory in the next fifty years. Clark and Sohn proposed that the present principle of delegation by member states be abolished, which is an absolute prerequisite for a government as contrasted to a confederation, and that the representatives be chosen in the same fashion as that used in choosing representatives in the most numerous house of the legislature of the lesser state. But what if there are no legislatures, or if they are sham institutions? Without some theoretical framework the edifice must lose its fundamental nature; a world state in which one-third of the legislators were puppets of a totalitarian regime could not be trusted by the citizens of constitutional states; yet without some consistent rule there seems to be no alternative or only the alternative of a fixed standard which might usher in the absolute mass state which the conservative so fears. The solace of tradition is absent, for we must invent our own.

But the invention of traditions is precisely the task, the

chance, of conservatism; if the need is felt and the alternatives are perilous, the job of theory must be to suggest answers. In squaring this circle several considerations are important. We do not want to allow the imposition of a one-man, one-vote rule in the individual districts any more than among the several districts, nor will we preclude any system sanctioned by usage and conformable to a minimum constitutional standard. That standard may have to be slowly worked out, as in American constitutional jurisprudence, with a basic premise that some forms of discrimination (race, for instance) are irrational—i.e., not supportable by any accepted rational opinion of the time. This would not affect intra-national elections, and its enforcement might be managed through reduction in representation (as in the unenforced section of our Fourteenth Amendment) rather than through mandatory decrees. In considering what we mean by irrationality, the concept of a constitutional tradition must be imported into substantive law, but this concept should encompass any tradition consistent with limited government anywhere so that the Thai heritage may be as acceptable as the British. In this context our various categories of the rule of law are centrally important, for the minimum procedural definition may be used to define what systems of law conform to the constitutional pattern sufficiently. To be sure, the right to a fair trial does not ensure any voice in government, but a society which ensures the former will as a rule provide some meaningful (perhaps not satisfactory to everyone or even to us, but enough) representation. In other words, even the most lopsided or indirect representation will, in Burkean terms, be virtual if it is a part of a system which provides some sense of community protection and individual right to all the citizens. If we mean what we say about the open society and the virtues of a truly opportunity-oriented world capitalism, we should have solutions for the costs which will come with the benefits; perhaps even the costs may seem benefits to the Hamiltons of the future.

The best test of any theory is the way in which it will function when its magic words are turned into disagreeable conditions. The open society has a virtuous sound, but cosmopolitanism seems more suspect to many, especially on the right. Yet what is the idea of the cosmopolis but the open city writ large, the Periclean state broadened into a greater community. This should mean that culture, for example, should become international, as it has been tending since at least 1890. Intermarriage among peoples and races—and how can a society be called open unless there is a potent current in favor of marriage outside the clan?—should increase. If we admire Hong Kong today, the whole world should aim in that direction—of course it will not reach it tomorrow. Perhaps by 2000 students will study one year at Heidelberg, Ohio, and the next at the original on the Neckar. The arts need little new encouragement on this front except the elimination of the impediments of narrow-minded governments and the broadest degree of freedom of travel. But literature must face the puzzle of the anarchy of language; even the permissive Roman Empire had but two chief languages. A world society would, if it developed an élan, tend to the narrowing of common tongues to at most three or four, and this would require that these few be understood by anyone claiming any world culture. This would of course imply an abandonment of a vast amount of past culture, but translations would have to fill this gap. A merging of cultures is not necessarily radical; it might, à la Eliot, mean a suffusing of traditions into a stream of modernist absorption of the past. The men at Philadelphia quoted Livy while bringing forth a new nation, and this resulted in a society both different and—to the disgust of the radicals—very much the same as that of the past.

But in a world society this fusion presents the threat of obliteration of diversity on a terrible scale. To some it will seem crazy to establish an open society at the expense of the forces which produce openness. There is a danger that this new culture will be fearfully elitist, an accomplishment of a clique of Parisians or New Yorkers with everyone else left out. The perfect mobility may cause everything—cultural, economic, and political—to gravitate to the center as all Britain now seems to coagulate in London. But is this such a misfortune? If all the British wish to live, if not within the world of Bow Bells, within its conurbation, perhaps (assuming that they are shouldering all the social costs of their decision) that is just as things should be. The Brazilians and ourselves have perhaps moved away from this single-focused centralism within the last generation, but everywhere people are moving to the large cities. The cities have just those qualities—multiple opportunity for education and enjoyment, breadth of opportunity, and potential for privacy—which are some of the staples of our open society. The mecca of the great city has a universal appeal, and the pop culture of the great city follows it; in the future all the world will once again be America, perhaps a concentrated megalopolis. The greatest critics of the immense cities usually live in them or depend on them for their ambiance. The world cities of the future may be more or less noisy, or more or less impersonal and chaotic than the national centers of today; if we do move to a global society, one thing we can be sure of is that there will be a move on the part of people from the farms and villages to leap over national boundaries as they now leap over provincial ones, as they swept over oceans in the nineteenth century.

We have recently been reminded that people, not trees or land, constitute the elements of the body politic; the liberals who applaud this often do not see the inconsistency in their concern for "depressed areas" or backward regions. In a libertarian world—and the period from 1815 to 1914 came close to this—people, not governments, did the moving, and imbalances of wealth and income were reduced through the mechanisms of choice. What came out of these *völkwanderungs* was not exactly a cosmopolitanism nor a necessary nationalism, but something of both. This too is not unnatural; the Italians and Germans who came to the Western Hemisphere added a Central European flavor to a new society, while those who remained behind—often the most backward, almost all of the elite—tended to become more nationalistic. In a mobile world society we might see much the same thing, culturally speaking, with great new centers of mixed groups coexisting with more ardently local foci of traditional culture (New York and the Sewanee group in the United States in the 1930's presented a parallel situation). If the cosmopolitan culture proves more potent, is that not an example of the winds of doctrine awarding the prize to the most powerful truth?

The Hellenistic age was marked by a similar state of affairs. The creation of a civilization dominated by Greek art and ideas, far vaster than the previous area of Hellenic predominance, forced culture and thought into new channels. The pictorial and statuary forms of Asia were soon infused with modes of a quite different background; the very way of life, the use of leisure time and the attitude toward work and religion of every thinking person from the Indus to the Adriatic was changed. The result was a new emphasis on urban life, as Alexandria attests, a self-conscious sophistication which enraged the puritans and attracted the intellectual elites, and a great rush to reinterpret the past in forms acceptable to the present. We could almost be talking of the mid-twentieth century; in fact, the current attack on new critical introspection could have been lifted directly from third century B.C. Egypt, along with the emphasis on libraries and government regulations. In some ways this was a stultifying time, but in others a very fruitful one, and without its transition from the -polis to the cosmopolis the global society of Rome would have been impossible, or bitterly brutal.

But was not the price an acceptance of despotism; who, after all, ruled in Alexandria? We will not take a world government if it means a despotic empire, or a world fought over by the Epigoni of a Marxist crusade. That is what the last thirty years have been about, and we need be no whit less appreciative of the essentially important victories of that time to look to the next chapter rather than to the last. What is now important is to see what kind of world culture and world civilization can develop without despotism. If the checks on despotism require an inhibition of culture, this is a price to be paid—for there is always some price. If the price of a world state seems to be the destruction of all local cultures, this too would be too steep. But social change is more like an Oriental bazaar than Marshall Field; prices can and must be adjusted. If the world state possesses the characteristics suggested above we may yet enjoy the combination of political order and personal freedom. Perhaps we may get a

Weimar as well as an Alexandria out of the mixture; in any case we must get the sort of world which most conforms to the individualist premises. We will inevitably fail if we think of success as the crowning of all the programs of that cause with triumph. But if we think of the cosmopolitan age, on whose threshold we hope to be standing, as merely another episode in the continuum of life, so that chances for the maximization of individual talent and creativity, or perhaps only comfort, are just a bit better than those enjoyed at other times, we may be pleasantly surprised despite all the menaces of the bomb or of conformity.

Yet we know that the privacy and mobility offered the free man will bring more of the impersonal sense of alienation, of anomie, which now plagues us. The problem of identity in a computerized, vastly unfeeling world seems to trouble us more than ever before. In many respects it is the dark underside of liberty, and our model society, by maximizing civil liberty, may also maximize social loneliness. And the bigger the area—and the very increase of population enlarges the human area—the more difficult it must be for even the man of substance to see his own place in the center of things. It is easy to see that a world in which famine and the starker miseries of poverty are eliminated will see more of the problems of overpopulation among the affluent, "the crowding which adds to the feelings of claustrophobia and neurosis in a society where men often feel burdened by the works of men," as *The Economist* sagely put it. A unified world may very well intensify these feelings by removing the starker perils and accelerating the centripetal forces. In that case the political issues of 2020 may revolve around the control of family size and of city size. We see the contours of this dispute now, with the radicals and reactionaries arguing for genetic controls or systematic planning, while the middle forces seek to combine liberty and property with as few forms of social instrumentation as possible. If these latter qualities are emphasized in a world society, the critics of the extremes will join as always in decrying the mistake of anarchy. Perhaps some program of market-oriented control—the more effective levying of taxes to pay for the social costs of crowding and breeding are obvious examples—should be thought out now, and not restricted to the details of local automobile traffic. Since the trees do not grow to the sky here any more than in other matters, we can be sure that some force—disease, asceticism, nuclear war or something—will keep the world from becoming a crowded plaza of swarming humans. The more we can make this thinning a matter of choice the better the adjustment will be. The broader problems of individual responsibility require equal concern. We have seen how programs such as co-determination or guild socialism will grow in popularity unless market-oriented alternatives are suggested.

But electronically-monitored town meetings of the world or simultaneous global markets will not relieve men of the fear of freedom, nor will the specter of helplessness be easily assuaged in a great world of six billion people whose gigantic contours we can never fully master. This is both a challenge and a test of the conservative political philosophy. Even the highest values will present perplexing problems; even the most cherished freedoms may seem at times a burden. But once the option was made for liberty and its attendant virtues, we crossed that bridge; if it were proved that neurosis could be banished in a world where all orders were sent from top to bottom, while no man disobeyed, we would yet refuse. Just as we will not let the susceptibilities of youths guide our policy toward the printing of books, so we cannot let our fears for the mental stability of some, or the disorder of many, block our vistas of freedom. It is one thing to encourage more chances for participation, or the sense of participation, by more people, and a resultant system of gradation of power. And in the last analysis we know that power is there and that it cannot be spread evenly, so we hope to diffuse its sources and enrich its uses, looking not only to custom but to reason as well.

☆ XIX

The Spirit
of Politics

What then of the individual in this individualist theory? It is paradoxical that even a lover of personal freedom—consider Rousseau—must talk of social forces in a sketch of political philosophy. But it does all come back to the human being in the end, and to his nature. Since the fundamental questions come down to this nature, even the most technical discussion must bear on the qualities of the individual personality.

Conservatism has by and large taken the leftover clothes of liberalism and pressed them, but it wears them with a difference. All the potentials of capitalist constitutional democracy, all the marvels of the free market, will not change the weaknesses of man. The chances which are open to man in this age will not make him more capable of using them wisely, and this applies to liberty or opportunity as well as to equality or fraternity. The men whose rights we seek to protect are just as any of us—beings who we know are selfish and subject to evil urges. The monstrous crimes of our time have very often, but not always, been committed in the name of and through the means provided by totalitarian regimes. But the men who committed them and inspired them were men and, very often quite ordinary ones. How quickly the layers—perhaps it is only the façade—of civilization and decency can drop away, negating the careful efforts of all the political theorists. And when we are most brilliant we produce atom bombs.

At times all the world does seem a grim fantasy composed by Robinson Jeffers. In such a world what can the political thinker do? All thought seems ineffectual in the path of despair's fatal lava.

> Eagle and hawk with their great claws and hooked heads
> Tear life to pieces; vulture and raven wait for death to
> soften it;
> The poet cannot feed on this time of the world
> Until he has torn it to pieces, and himself also.

The conspiracy theories of the far right are not merely the products of diseased minds, but an understandable if wrong-headed reaction to a complex world which seems to go wrong, to a globe of three billion people inclined to doing evil. In a time which seems as godless as any in recorded history all the customary checks on human misbehavior are fragile, all discouragements to hubris vanished. For example, we have recently seen that the peoples of the Third World have often learned the lessons of hate rather than those of tolerance from the bitter history of the developed nations; the Chinese in Indonesia and the Ibos in Nigeria are suffering as the Jews of Europe did for the sins of energy and cosmopolitanism. Moreover, even the accomplishments of peace are suspect. The more sophisticated we become the more this acuteness leads to a general malaise, as if all the world (or the richer parts, at least) were afflicted like jaded aristocrats. Berenson predicted that the spread of wealth and comfort would bring a surfeit of contentment, a boredom; to escape this perhaps even a collective suicidal frenzy could arise. One can hear people say that the tension of the cold war is unendurable or unnatural; even thermonuclear war would be better than this waiting. Perhaps man can carry his genius only so far, so that the greater wisdom produces but greater vexation, and in the end he must escape from a society too complex for his nature—Adam once again eating the wrong fruit.

We are back to talking of premises, beyond which there are no arguments. Perhaps we will blow up our civilizations, perhaps even all cognitive life. There is nothing inevitable about it, unless it has been predetermined by a no-longer-patient God. But while we live, let us live with dignity and reason. No matter how wicked men are, it is the purpose of those who have suggestions to make concerning social order to diminish the worst results of that badness. At the very worst we can try to avoid the cycle of barbarism and deceit in a Hobbesian state of nature; we can seek to reward the social virtues with the fruits of order and liberty. Those on the far right too often throw out all the benefits of social cooperation in their distrust of achieving anything; because bad thoughts may corrupt, they assume a universal corruption from the start. At times their expectation of violence compels them to condone any form of official brutality, making worse what they discerned from the outset.

But there is no reason for us to assume the worst at all times. There is a case—not conclusive, to be sure—that in some ways men are improving. The sensibilities of our age, the apparatus of welfare, even the attention paid to immorality of various kinds, mark a path which is not all ignoble. No one who has looked at the drawings of Callot can think that sadism is unique in our day; the career of Francis Bacon is a reminder how at least some standards have been elevated. Maybe. But that "maybe" is a constant inducement to convert the possibilities of a better life into specific actions and systems. It may be that religion is incapable of holding the rapt attention of men of our age, although it would be foolhardy to assume that it must always be so. But if God exists it is strange to think that He will abandon mankind because of human doubts or uncertainties. Conversely, if Ingersoll was correct in maintaining that an honest god is the noblest work of man, there is no excuse for not pressing our honesty forward.

We have concluded that scientific progress is no guarantee or sign of progress in politics. Whatever progress we seek to gain there must be fought for in its own manner, on its own terrain, and within the limitations of the political circle. But if politics is no science it is something of an art. Despite the many differences between the various mores, the test of the statesman is his capacity to direct and improve the customs of his time and place.

There is a sort of museum without walls encompassing the politics of all ages, a spherical building in design, and within these imaginary precincts there abides the same devotion to the good and the beautiful which exists in Malraux's temple.

We do not want, however, that worship of the political art which will make of this museum a church. Rather, it is the subtler artistic qualities, the nuances of custom and of human relations which are most worth cultivating. The little but vital episodes of life which Bagehot and Wallas remarked on as the supremely important details of existence comprise the source of politics, and the never-ending effort to heighten these experiences, to improve the tone of social intercourse, will never end. The gesture of Roscoe Conkling welcoming his Negro colleague from Mississippi when the latter's fellow-senator refused to do so for reasons of bigotry may have been more truly important, more significant than the long-dead dishonesties of Conkling's public life; Warren Harding's compassion in letting Debs out of prison may seem more meaningful to the historian of the next century than all of his stupidities. On the other hand, the famous story of Lenin marking some names and passing the list to Dzerzhinsky, who thereupon executed men whom Lenin had not wanted to kill, is equally instructive. Lenin treated it as an unimportant mistake, a trivial *gaffe*, and by so doing he marked his own manner, his style of politics, more than anything else he did. Perhaps these are not exactly matters of morality. From one point of view Debs deserved to stay in Atlanta, and the Mensheviks were better off dead. But the inculcation of other standards is what politics—at its highest—should be about. Berenson put this well when he remarked that "I value activities more for what they do, for the physical and moral health of the individual, his group and community—than for the importance of the product, considerable, great even though that may be." We start with the individual in defining politics; so we should end with him. To understand man it is of course vital to consider him in the context of his time, under the light of history. But it is precisely because there is no escaping from the inexorable reality of historical experience that the worth of human dignity and the masterpieces of individual accomplishment are so fine. We know that time is a tyrant, but then it is "only through time that time is conquered," as Eliot reminded us.

The finest part of that conquest lies in the appreciation of human reason. The disappointments of mass reason, of the theories of perfectibility should not make us forget how grand the exercise of human intelligence can be. Perhaps the great dreams of political thought will never be more than dreams, but if the legacy of political thought is the recognition of the claims to dignity of one persecuted man it is not a loss. Brogan, in his great description of Colonel Picquart, tells of the magnitude of his decision to accept the results of his investigation of Dreyfus' guilt despite his preconceptions. From this fidelity to reason the ultimate vindication of Dreyfus, which has come to symbolize so much of the enduring nature of truth in our century, came forth. Custom and reason, in the macrocosm of politics as in the microcosm of the individual, serve to uphold the qualities which can transcend history; let us be glad and rejoice in them.

☆ *Index*

Date Due
